Moral Vision and Tradition

**STUDIES IN PHILOSOPHY
AND THE HISTORY OF PHILOSOPHY**

General Editor: Jude P. Dougherty

Studies in Philosophy
and the History of Philosophy   Volume 31

Moral Vision and Tradition

Essays in Chinese Ethics

A. S. Cua

THE CATHOLIC UNIVERSITY OF AMERICA PRESS
Washington, D.C.

The paper used in this publication meets the minimum requirements of American National Standards for Information Science—Permanence of Paper for Printed Library materials, ANSI Z39.48–1984.
∞

LIBRARY OF CONGRESS CATALOGING-IN-PUBLICATION DATA

Cua, A. S. (Antonio S.), 1932–
    Moral vision and tradition : essays in Chinese ethics / Antonio S. Cua.
        p.   cm. — (Studies in philosophy and the history of philosophy)
    Includes bibliographical references and index.
        1. Ethics, Chinese.   2. Philosophy, Confucian.   3. Philosophy, Chinese.
    I. Title.   II. Series.
    BJ117.C83   1997
    171—dc21
    96-53933
    ISBN 0-8132-0890-4

To my wife, Shoke-Hwee Khaw,
for her love, lifelong companionship,
encouragement, and sacrifice

Contents

Preface

The present volume deals with various problems that arise in a philosophical explication of the nature of Chinese ethical thought. The essays focus principally on what I consider to be salient features of Confucian ethics. For the most part, the approach is analytical, attending mainly to the conceptual and dialectical aspects of Confucian ethics. Most of the essays reflect three different sorts of concern. The nature and significance of the Chinese Confucian moral vision of *tao* is examined, from various perspectives, in Essays Two through Five and Essays Seven and Nine. Essay Two is a response to a contemporary philosophical conception of the mystery and transcendence of the world. The ancient classic *The Doctrine of the Mean (Chung Yung)*, is used as a text for discussing the Confucian vision or ideal of the Unity of Man and Nature (*t'ien-jen ho-i*). This essay proposes a nonmetaphysical interpretation of the Confucian vision without discounting the importance of the metaphysical interpretations advanced by both Chinese and Western philosophical writers. The interpretation is largely inspired by my early study of the works of Wang Yang-ming (1427–1529), which was subsequently developed in Essays Seven and Nine. Essay Nine in particular deals with Wang Yang-ming's vision, his stress on self-reliance as a precondition for the pursuit of *tao* or *jen*, and the role of *liang-chih*, akin to Joseph Butler's conception of conscience. The essay also supplements my *The Unity of Knowledge and Action: A Study of Wang Yang-ming's Moral Psychology* (1982).

Any attempt to deal with Confucian moral vision must also explore the insights of classical Taoism presented by Lao Tzu and Chuang Tzu. Essays Three and Five address this topic. What appear as Taoist paradoxes, such as "forgetting morality" and "opposites as complements," are, from the Confucian point of view, insightful ways of displaying the deep and "hidden" aspects of Confucian ethics. Essay Four takes up both the Confucian and the Taoist versions of the *tao*, their respective merits, the nature of responsive agency and the role of factual beliefs in discourse about the Confucian *tao*.

Essays One and Ten deal with the logical and rhetorical aspects of

Confucian ethics. These essays are a riposte to the view that the Chinese Confucians have no interest in argumentation and that their conception of discourse is largely persuasive, displaying little regard for the soundness of reasoning. Discussion of the desirable characteristics of the participants, standards of competence, definitional issues, and diagnosis of erroneous ethical beliefs may be found in my *Ethical Argumentation: A Study in Hsün Tzu's Moral Epistemology* (1985). Essay Eight presents a Confucian perspective on the role of exemplary or paradigmatic individuals in moral education. A fuller discussion of the relation between Confucian morality and paradigmatic individuals is given in my *Dimensions of Moral Creativity: Paradigms, Principles, and Ideals* (1978). Essay Eleven draws attention to the avoidance of self-deception in personal cultivation or self-education. Some misleading attributions of the "self" to Confucian ethics are considered. A proposal for the study of the reflexive locutions is suggested after an extensive analysis of the indispensable role of "sincerity of thought" in the Confucian classic *The Great Learning (Ta Hsüeh)*.

Essays Twelve, Thirteen, and Fourteen were written after my four 1993 Taipei Lectures delivered at National Chengchi University, National Taiwan University, and Fu Jen Catholic University. Shorter versions of Essays Twelve and Thirteen were presented in 1995 at the National Tsinghua University, Hsin Chu, Taiwan. These essays present a kind of progress report on my recent efforts to develop a systematic Confucian moral philosophy. Essay Twelve explicates the living Confucian ethical tradition implicit in Chu Hsi's conception of *tao-t'ung* or reconstitution of *tao*. After a discussion of tradition as an interpretive concept, I turn to Chu Hsi's conception and the way he struggles with the problem of change or modification of tradition. In Essay Thirteen I turn to the problem of interpreting the cardinal concepts of Confucian ethics as an ethics of virtue. Much of the effort is spent in shaping concepts such as *jen* (humanity), *i* (rightness), and *li* (ritual propriety) in the light of the Confucian ideal or vision of *tao*. As an ethics of virtue, however, Confucian ethics must also allow for principled interpretation of some of its basic concepts, especially in the interest of making reasoned discourse concerning intercultural conflict possible. In Essay Fourteen, I suggest five principles of adjudication as ground rules for intercultural discourse, presuming that argumentation is a cooperative endeavor aiming at a reasonable resolution of conflict. A fuller development of these principles and their practical applications in conflict resolution remains a challenging task for subsequent inquiry.

The essays appear in the chronological order in which they were written. Of the fourteen essays that make up this volume, ten of them

(Essays One through Nine and Essay Eleven) have been previously published. Essay Ten appears here for the first time. The last three essays incorporate materials revised from some of my recent publications. I am grateful to the editors and publishers of the journals and books for permission to reprint and/or incorporate previously published materials, and to the Chiang Ching-kuo Foundation for International Scholarly Exchange for a research grant for lecture and completion of the last three essays. For fuller details, see "Acknowledgments." In pursuing the project, I received valuable advice and encouragement from Dean Jude P. Dougherty, Professor Daniel Dahlstrom, and Professor Vincent Shen Tsing-sung. For preparing this work for publication, I am deeply grateful to Ms. Eunice Rice for her concern and patience in typing earlier versions of the manuscript. I also appreciate the helpful suggestions of the copy editor, Susan Needham, for improving the style of presentation.

Acknowledgments

Below is a list of periodicals and books in which the previously published essays appear:

"Reasonable Action and Confucian Argumentation," *Journal of Chinese Philosophy* 1 (1973); " Confucian Vision and Experience of the World," *Philosophy East and West* 25 (1975); "Forgetting Morality: Reflections on a Theme in *Chuang Tzu*," *Journal of Chinese Philosophy* 4 (1977); "Chinese Moral Vision, Responsive Agency, and Factual Beliefs," *Journal of Chinese Philosophy* 7 (1980); "Opposites as Complements: Reflections on the Significance of *Tao*," *Philosophy East and West* 31 (1981); "Morality and Human Nature," *Philosophy East and West* 32 (1982); "Harmony and the Neo-Confucian Sage," *Philosophical Inquiry: An International Quarterly* 5 (1983); "Competence, Concern, and the Role of Paradigmatic Individuals (Chün-tzu) in Moral Education," *Philosophy East and West* 42 (1992); "Between Commitment and Realization: Wang Yang-ming's Vision of the Universe as a Moral Community," *Philosophy East and West* 43 (1993); "A Confucian Perspective on Self-Deception," in *Self and Deception*, edited by Roger Ames and Wimal Dissanayake (Albany: State University of New York Press, 1996).

"The Possibility of a Confucian Theory of Rhetoric" was presented at the NEH Conference on Rhetoric: East and West, at the East-West Center, Honolulu, in June 1988. The last three essays incorporate, with extensive revision, the following papers: "The Idea of Confucian Tradition," *Review of Metaphysics* 45 (1992); "Hsün Tzu and the Unity of Virtues," *Journal of Chinese Philosophy* 14 (1987); "The Concept of *Li* in Confucian Moral Theory" in *Understanding Chinese Thought: The Philosophical Roots*, edited by Robert. E. Allinson (Hong Kong: Oxford University Press, 1989); and "Confucian Moral Philosophy," forthcoming in Routledge Encyclopedia of Philosophy; "Status of Principles in Confucian Ethics," *Journal of Chinese Philosophy* 16 (1989); and "Reasonable Challenges and Preconditions of Adjudication," in *Tradition and Modernity: East West Philosophical Perspectives*, edited by Eliot Deutsch (University of Hawaii Press, 1991).

Moral Vision and Tradition

Essay 1   Reasonable Action and Confucian Argumentation

This essay revolves around the theme of reasonableness and argumentation as having an important bearing on a contemporary understanding and assessment of Confucian ethics. By 'Confucian ethics' we mean the body of moral notions, precepts, and examples derived from the teachings of Confucius *(The Analects).*[1] Characteristically this relatively loose system of action-guides is taken by the committed agent as in some manner constitutive of a way of life, with the ideal of *jen* or human-heartedness as a dominant target of moral achievement. Our central aim is to offer an informal reconstruction of the role of Confucian notions in argumentation. Section I is devoted to a preliminary discussion of reasonable action and its relation to argumentation. Section II presents a map of various validity-factors in Confucian argumentation in terms of a schematic discussion of various sorts of appeals in discursive vindication. This section reflects my selective decision on the sorts of considerations to be emphasized. Throughout I assume the position of a reflective Confucian agent in search of a contemporary elucidation and evaluation of Confucian ethics.[2]

I

The stress on concrete rather than abstract values is a noteworthy feature of Confucian ethics and moral practice.[3] This normative atti-

1. In "Reflections on the Structure of Confucian Ethics," *Philosophy East and West* 21, no. 2 (1971): 125–40, I have attempted a conceptual reconstruction of Confucian ethics by way of a discussion of the relation among four principal notions (e.g, *jen, li, i* and *chün-tzu*). A revised version of this essay was incorporated in chap. 4 of *Dimensions of Moral Creativity: Paradigms, Principles, and Ideals* (University Park: Pennsylvania State University Press, 1978).

2. By "a reflective Confucian agent" we mean a committed Confucian agent who is interested in the significance and plausibility of Confucian ethics as a normative theory. See my "Reflections on Methodology in Chinese Philosophy," *International Philosophical Quarterly* 11, no. 2 (1971): 236–48.

3. For the conceptual structure of this normative attitude in the *Analects*, see my "Logic of Confucian Dialogues," in J. K. Ryan, ed., *Studies in Philosophy and the History of Philosophy*, vol. 4 (Washington, D.C.: The Catholic University of America Press, 1969), 18–33.

tude underlies the ascription of values to "a living being, a specific group or a particular object considered as a unique entity."[4] It has recently been remarked that Confucius's teaching on the five universally binding obligations—between ruler and ruled, father and son, husband and wife, older brother and younger brother, friend and friend— reflect the importance attached to personal relations among beings who constitute concrete values for one another.[5]

This is a just observation based on the distinction between concrete and abstract values. Theoretical focus on one rather than the other displays a divergence between two different conceptions of the nature of morality: the ethics of rules and principles and the ethics of personal relations. From the point of view of the epistemology of morals, the former regards moral notions and principles as having a cognitive status independent of particular situations and actual contexts of application. Justification in terms of moral principles or rules is seen to be an appraisive process contextually independent of the requirements of personal relation and the predicaments of individual moral agents. On this view, justification is tied to the abstract notions of objectivity, validity, and truth—notions that are often regarded as exemplifying a generic property of rationality of human beings in general.

On the other hand, an ethics that stresses the concrete value of personal relation is more concerned with the import of moral principles to the moral agent and to the particular situation he confronts. Objectivity of judgment and justification of moral conduct are founded more on the notion of reasonableness than on a rationality governed by the application of logical canons. In general, reasonableness is a characteristic attitude of moral agents toward the appropriate or fitting expression of emotions, desires, ideals, and aspirations in situational and cultural contexts of judgment and performance. In Confucian ethics, one seeks in vain for a self-consistent set of rules for moral judgments. The various sorts of appropriate behavior are not matters of a priori cognitive assessment, but matters of occasional and temporal determination in particular cases. There is, as classical Confucians often insist, the respect for *li* or ritual rules required of moral agents, but the *li* furnish only a focal reference for objectivity; they do not a priori determine the reasonable or right actions to be performed in all the situations that confront moral agents.[6]

4. Ch. Perelman and L. Olbrechts-Tyteca, *The New Rhetoric: A Treatise on Argumentation* (Notre Dame: University of Notre Dame Press, 1969), 77.
5. Ibid., 79.
6. *Li*, of course, cannot be understood apart from *jen* in Confucian ethics. The discussion that follows assumes this qualification. For more discussion, see Essay 13.

The stress on concrete values is tied to a conservative attitude toward change. This seeming defect is compensated by the Confucian notion of *chung yung* or central harmony. As Perelman and Olbrechts-Tyteca have noted:

Concrete values can always be harmonized; the very existence of concrete implies that it is possible, that it achieves a certain harmony. Abstract values, on the other hand, when carried to extremes, are irreconcilable: it is impossible to reconcile, in the abstract, such virtues as justice and love.[7]

In practice the Confucian insistence on the importance of *li* often leads to resistance to change. This phenomenon may be partly accounted for by the main function of *li*—the establishment of order and harmony. In view of this object of *li*, a reflective Confucian agent need not adopt a dogmatic attitude toward change. A respect for the ritual rules does not entail that ritual rules can resolve all moral problems and dilemmas. We should expect that a reflective Confucian agent would accept any sort of regulative procedures that are functionally equivalent to particular ritual rules, that is, the procedures that perform the same role in regulating human conduct. Implicit in this acceptance is a regard for the central aim of harmony and reconciliation of conflict between individual interests.[8]

The same remark applies to other Confucian notions. The Confucian stress on ritual rules is often connected with the notion of *chün-tzu* (superior man) as an exemplary guidance to conduct. A *chün-tzu* is a paradigmatic moral agent who embodies the Confucian virtues (inclusive of *li*) and maintains a neutral attitude toward judgment of conduct prior to actual performance.[9] A *chün-tzu* is an exemplary *reasonable* agent. For our present purpose we need to attend to two features of reasonableness in *chün-tzu:* respect for ritual rules (and for the uses of other moral notions) and respect for the nature of an occurrent situation. Reasonableness of actions, consequently, their acceptable justification, depends on actions that comport or harmonize with ritual

---

7. Perelman and Olbrechts-Tyteca, *The New Rhetoric*, 79.
8. See J. Grote, *A Treatise on Moral Ideals* (Cambridge: Deighton, Bell & Co., 1876); S. Toulmin, *The Place of Reason in Ethics* (Cambridge: Cambridge University Press, 1950), 137; K. Baier, *The Moral Point of View*, (Ithaca: Cornell University Press, 1958), 201; R. M. Hare, *Freedom and Reason* (Oxford: Clarendon Press, 1963), 157; and G. Warnock, *The Object of Morality* (London: Methuen, 1971), chap. II. Compare with *The Analects*, 1:3; *Hsün Tzu: Basic Works*, trans. B. Watson (New York: Columbia University Press, 1963), 89–111; *Chung Yung*, sec. 1.
9. A more detailed discussion of the plausibility of the notion of *chun-tzu* is given in my "The Concept of Paradigmatic Individuals in the Ethics of Confucius," *Inquiry* 14 (1971):41–55. A revised version of this essay was incorporated as chapter 4 of *Dimensions of Moral Creativity*.

rules or the demands of particular circumstances.[10] These two features cannot always be made consistent in advance of confrontation with particular situations, for ritual and other preestablished requirements may not provide definitive guidance in exigent cases that fall outside their scope of regulation. Further, the given ritual rules may conflict with what the situation demands as an appropriate action. A reflective Confucian agent may *rule* them out as irrelevant. Moreover, a respect for ritual rules and the normative force of moral notions in general need not be diminished on account of the novel situations in human life. The point is that they do not by themselves provide conclusive solutions to all human problems. Of course, in the normal setting of human intercourse, the preestablished ritual rules and other moral notions do provide clear guidance.

Although we cannot hope to offer a satisfactory epistemological principle for explicating the notion of reasonable action, we may attempt to understand this notion by way of explaining the following schema.[11]

Schema A: "X is the reasonable action to be performed in a situation S" is roughly equivalent to "X conforms to the time of S."

We introduce this notion of *time* of a situation as a convenient way of focusing upon the temporal character of action as appropriate to a particular situation.[12] A reasonable action is thus an *occasional* performance that befits the demand of an occurrent situation. "Reasonable" here is obviously a term of reflective judgment. The time of S is thus

10. In view of the classical emphasis on the pervasive significance of *li* in Confucius and Hsün Tzu, we have restricted our discussion to its application to normal situations. As we shall later discuss in Section II, other moral notions may be involved in normal cases that have a role to play in Confucian argumentation. For a more detailed discussion of the distinction between normal and exigent situations, see Section II of the essay cited in n. 9 and my "Relevance of Moral Rules and Creative Agency," *The New Scholasticism* 47 (1973); or *Dimensions of Moral Creativity,* chap. 5.

11. We are here suggesting "an experiment in ideal explication" for the Confucian notion of reasonableness. We claim no evidential support from the Confucian texts except what we regard as implicit in the notion of *chün-tzu* as a paradigmatic individual. The explication is not satisfactory from the epistemic point of view, since, as we have noted, the notion of reasonableness is a temporal, floating notion that is not governed by logical canons. See G. E. Anscombe, "Modern Moral Philosophy," in G. Wallace and A. D. M. Walker, eds., *Definition of Morality* (London: Methuen, 1970), 229–30; J. R. Lucas, "The Philosophy of Reasonable Man," *Philosophical Quarterly* 13 (1963), 105. More extensive discussion of the Confucian notion of reasonableness may be found in my later work, *The Unity of Knowledge and Action: A Study in Wang Yang-ming's Moral Psychology* (Honolulu: University Press of Hawaii, 1982), chap. 4.

12. This notion of time plays a key role in interpreting the hexagrams in *I Ching* (The Book of Changes). See R. Wilhelm, *I Ching* (New York: Bollingen, 1950), 1: 384–85.

open to two different sorts of judgment or interpretation by an individual agent. It may be regarded as a *normal* time understood in terms of a requirement of a ritual rule. In this case the situation *S* would be construed as an instance of the application of a ritual rule. In short, *S* is regarded as a normal situation that falls within the regulative orbit of preestablished *li*. Here is exemplified a respect for accepted conventions as having an immediate relevance to action. The time of *S*, on the other hand, may be regarded as an *abnormal* or novel one not determinable by *li*. In this case, the *S* would be construed as an *exigent* situation that calls for an appropriate action not predetermined by *li*. In this sort of situation, for the agent an apparently relevant *li* is an important consideration in deliberation, though he may *rule* it out as irrelevant to his own case. This ruling in an exigent situation is not a matter of creating exceptions to *li*, but a judgment or decision that is tied to the particular occurrent situation. In this way, the ruling in exigent situations is allowed to have an import apart from preestablished moral requirements. This is not to deny that the *li* possess a general normative import. To Confucians the *li* are an expression of a cultural lifestyle embued with an ideal of *jen*. The *li*, along with other Confucian notions, furnish a framework for the identification of the normative import of actions. However they do not provide descriptions for all possible situations in human life.

If our account of reasonable action is deemed clear, it does not offer an adequate answer to the question "How does an agent recognize or know the time of *S*?" In a normal situation, the agent can answer the question by citing an appropriate ritual rule. In an exigent situation, the question cannot be answered except perhaps by a sort of retrospective story of the factors that influenced the agent's judgment about the appropriate action for the situation. There is no need to appeal to intuition to settle any query. The agent can be challenged for his judgment and action that issues from it. To justify his ruling in exigent situations is in effect to *vindicate* himself, to clear away any suspicion or charge of a wrong or arbitrary action. To vindicate himself, the agent may point out that *his* action is what the exigent situation demands as an appropriate action, in the sense that an examination of the nature of the situation leaves him no choice between alternatives. The action is the only "permissible move" to make within the context of the situation. The agent can be mistaken about this, for it may be the case that his retrospective account of the features involved in deliberation is incomplete or that some irrelevant features of the situation were mistakenly considered and influenced his judgment. The process of vindication is a dialogic process, i.e., an open discourse that may well

involve a wide range of factors not readily captured in some predetermined set of criteria of relevance. The acceptability of a piece of vindication depends on the nature of the audience.

Before we turn to this theme, we must take note of the character of
ruling in exigent cases. A ruling is an occasional exercise of *i* (rightness,
righteousness) or judgment of the relevance of ritual rules in particular
situations.[13] By virtue of its tie to an occurrent situation, it cannot be
construed as an act of legislation for all like cases. The authority of the
ruling holds for the agent who makes it in relation to his *own* case. It
pretends to no declaration of universalizable principles. Nevertheless,
the rulings of some agents, when accepted by others, can function as
paradigms for future agents. The universality of the function of paradigmatic rulings is contingent upon acceptance by others. Instead of
issuing universal moral principles, Confucius's emphasis on the importance of *chün-tzu* as a guidance for agents is best construed as an
emphasis on the projective character of ruling.[14] This *projective* character can take two different forms. As an individual act of judgment it
projects its relevance onto the agent's own future experiences. In this
manner, a ruling can have an integrative function for an agent's own
way of life. A ruling, when vindicated and accepted in discourse, projects itself as a paradigm for other agent's conduct. However, this sort
of projection is basically an "experiment in relevance." By itself, a ruling cannot certify its own paradigmatic status. There is no general formula for doing what is reasonable or right in particular situations. The
Confucian agent may say, with Aristotle, that situations, particularly
the exigent ones, "do not come under the head of any art that can be
transmitted by precept, . . . the agent must consider on each different
occasion what the situation demands."[15]

We now turn to Confucian argumentation,[16] discourse in which an
agent responds to a challenge of the correctness of his rulings in exigent situations. We shall assume that the agent engages in this sort of
discourse, not for its own sake, but to vindicate himself in the face of
suspicion of a wrong or unreasonable performance. This is quite in
consonance with Confucius's remark that a *chün-tzu* "acts before he

13. Cf. Chung-ying Cheng, "*Yi* as a Universal Principle of Specific Application in
Confucian Morality," *Philosophy East and West* 22 (1972): 269–80.
14. Cf. L. Wittgenstein, *Zettel* (Oxford: Basil Blackwell, 1967), 290–94.
15. Aristotle, *Nicomachean Ethics*, trans. Martin Ostwald (Indianapolis: Bobbs-Merrill,
1962), 1104a.
16. Our discussion here makes use of Perelman and Olbrechts-Tyteca's work and
Carl Wellman's *Challenge and Response: Justification in Ethics* (Carbondale: Southern Illinois University Press, 1971).

speaks, and afterward speaks according to his actions."[17] The general aim of argumentation is to gain "the adherence of minds, and by this very fact, assumes the existence of an intellectual contact."[18] From the logical point of view, philosophers would quite naturally raise the question of assessment of the validity of reasons given in support of the speaker's vindication. The focus is on the validity of arguments as determined by rules of inference. Since Confucian ethics does not possess a set of inference rules, its discourse is best viewed in the light of various dimensions of assessment, deemed to have persuasive force with the audience. Unlike the philosophers, the Confucian agent in vindication is more likely to appeal to a particular audience, to a sense of "community of like minds"[19] who share a common attitude toward certain factors that play a role in dialogic vindication.

In this light, a piece of argumentation must be assessed as a speech-situation that occurs within a cultural matrix in which moral notions have a peculiar "logical force." A philosopher is bound to appeal to ideal agreement among a rational or universal audience.[20] A reasonable individual, on the other hand, would address himself only to a particular audience. Since the object is to answer a charge of unreasonable action, the agent need attend only to factors that are accepted by the audience as vindicating factors in argumentation. This is not to deny that the speaker's speech-acts can be legitimately assessed in deductive terms, but to focus on moral justification within the context of vindication of judgments and actions rather than on moral rules or principles that can be articulated in an epistemic set. Confucian thinkers do present arguments that can be formally explicated.[21] Our interest here centers on vindication in discourse rather than on the logical pattern of Confucian reasoning. Furthermore, in this essay, we are mainly interested in a map of various factors in Confucian argumentation rather than in offering a theory of Confucian argumentation.

In general we may regard vindication in discourse as a piece of argumentation that occurs in a practical context characterized by the presence of moral rules or notions. What is taken as a moral rule depends on the sort of activity deemed important by the participants who share a common way of life embedded in a culture and a *form of life*. The moral audience is a particular audience within a cultural setting.

17. *Analects*, 2:12. See also 4:22; 14:21; 14:29. See also *Hsün Tzu*, 149.
18. Perelman and Olbrechts-Tyteca, 14.
19. Wellman, 97.
20. Perelman and Olbrechts-Tyteca, 31.
21. See, for example, M. D. Resnik, "Logic and Methodology in the Writings of Mencius," *International Philosophical Quarterly* 7, no. 2 (1968): 212–30.

The acceptability of a proffered vindication depends in part upon the degree of assent to the moral practice. Characteristic reasonability thus lies in the degree of respect displayed in viewing the moral notions and rules as relevant considerations prior to the performance. In normal situations, the judgment of the relevance of a rule can be viewed as an act of subsuming an action under the intended scope of operations of the rule. Where an action overtly falls within the normal operation of the rule, no question of justification need arise. When an agent is challenged, he need only offer a deductive form of reasoning in response to any query. The normality of the situation in which an action is performed, if accepted by the audience, is understood as part of the constitutive content of moral practice. The use of moral notions is thus tied to a common background in which they are regarded by the agents as in some fashion a definitive expression of a communal way of life. The particular contexts of the uses of moral notions may be regarded as a partial articulation of the aspects of the background shared by both the speaker and his audience. The puzzling case arises with rulings in exigent cases in which an agent is called to vindicate himself without an appeal to preestablished rules. Here, the Confucian stress on *chün-tzu* as a reasonable agent has a peculiar role to play. The invocation of various moral notions may well figure in a piece of persuasive discourse without regarding these notions in any rule-like fashion. In Section II, we shall further pursue this theme of Confucian notions.

It has been recently maintained that there is a distinct sort of non-deductive reasoning in ethical justification. Carl Wellman discusses what he termed "conductive reasoning." "Conduction" is defined "as that sort of reasoning in which (1) a conclusion about some individual case (2) is drawn nonconclusively (3) from one or more premises about the same case (4) without appeal to other cases." Wellman continues: "Perhaps the most striking feature of all the examples I have given is that they all deal with particular cases."[22] Two of Wellman's examples are: (1) "You ought not to have spoken so harshly because your words hurt her deeply," and (2) "Martin Luther King is a fine man because, inspite of occasional arrogance, he is an unselfish and courageous worker for his fellowman." These examples do illustrate Wellman's point about the particularity of discourse, but they appear to be mere fragments rather than characteristic of argumentative situations. Their persuasive force depends on the shared background of the speaker and his audience in which such notions as "fine man," "courageous worker," "hurt," and "harsh words" are viewed as part of a common way of life.

22. Wellman, 52.

In abstraction from particular discursive contexts, these notions may have varying imports for different moral agents; their use may in part depend upon their actuating or transforming significance in the lives of different commitive agents. In dialogic situations, such notions have undoubtedly a persuasive role to play; but they need not be construed solely as sophistical tools for achieving the adherence of the audience. Although their force, as Wellman has pointed out, depends on subject matter, one need not accept the thesis that "conductive reasoning" as such "shows how factual information can be relevant to ethics."[23] A Confucian agent would insist on the exercise of *i* (rightness, righteousness) in the judgment of relevance of these notions to particular situations. Of course one can formulate a theory of moral justification, but any such theory, if it is deemed relevant to an agent's way of life, ultimately requires the judgment of the individual moral agent. The judgment may be arbitrary but it is subject to challenge, thus opening dialogic vindication within the context of reasonable persuasion. A seemingly arbitrary individual judgment need not on that account be a mere display of personal taste or sentiment. In this light, moral agents who feel the need to vindicate their peculiar judgments would continually engage in meeting challenges. Wellman's discussion of the model of challenge and response is in this way an illuminating perspective from which to view moral justification.

The particularity of the sort of reasoning discussed by Wellman is reminiscent of I. A. Richards's comments on some of the arguments in *Mencius* in the dispute between Mencius and Kao Tzu. Richards notes the general marks of these arguments:

(a) They are dominated by suasive purpose. (b) The purpose of eliciting the point of difference is absent. (c) The form of the opponent's argument is noticed, in the sense of *being used* in the rebuttal, but not *examined* so that the flaw, if any, may be found. (d) The movement is entirely concrete—from example to example.[24]

The first three features display the general aim of a speaker engaged in argumentation. Richards's insightful remarks should be noted: "Kao Tzu and Mencius appeal instead to instances of universally recognized correct behavior. Their doctrines gain authority by fitting what is 'done' not by internal clarity, precision, and consistency."[25] This may be judged to be a defect from the logical point of view, but it does throw

23. Ibid., 54.
24. I. A. Richards, *Mencius on the Mind* (London: Kegan Paul, Trench, & Trubner, 1932), 55.
25. Ibid., 57.

light upon the aim of dialogic vindication. It is noteworthy that "its movement is entirely concrete—from example to example"; the examples are not subsumed under classificatory principles. This is an aspect of Confucian argumentation that is considered to have a suasive power for the participants in discourse. Arguments, of course, can be deductively assessed, but they are subordinate to the suasive purpose of vindication of actions that appeal to the recognized *li* or rules of proper conduct. Confucian notions do have such suasive force for Confucian agents. This important truism is a useful reminder that dialogic vindication is distinct from rational justification. There is no need to downgrade the importance of vindication, because it serves a different purpose. And this different purpose requires dimensions of assessment that may not figure in an overall logical pattern of rational justification.

II

Guided essentially by the *Analects*, we shall now attempt an informal reconstruction of the role of Confucian moral notions as factors in argumentation. We shall map these factors in the spirit of the classical doctrine of rectification of names *(cheng-ming)*,[26] adopting schemes similar to Searle's for what he calls "institutional facts." Searle distinguished between "brute" and "institutional" facts. The latter "are indeed facts; but their existence, unlike the existence of brute facts, presupposes the existence of human institutions. It is only given the institution of marriage that certain forms of behavior constitute Mr. Smith's marrying Miss Jones." We can also cite such institutions as baseball and money, which give significance to certain forms of behavior. According to Searle, these "'institutions' are systems of constitutive rules. Every institutional fact is underlain by a (system of) rule(s) of the form *X counts as Y in context C*."[27] We shall shortly suggest that each appeal to a Confucian notion may be construed in a similar way, however, without claiming that we can set forth a set of "constitutive rules" in Searle's sense. The reason for not making this claim lies in the following consideration: the "institutional facts" in Confucian

26. For an exposition of the classical doctrine, see Chung-ying Cheng, "Rectifying Names *(cheng-ming)* in Classical Confucianism," *East Asian Occasional Papers* (I), ed. H. J. Lamley (University of Hawaii Asian Studies Program, Honolulu, 1969), 82–96. For my later work, see *Ethical Argumentation: A Study in Hsün Tzu's Moral Epistemology* (Honolulu: University of Hawaii Press, 1985), chaps. 3 & 4.

27. John Searle, *Speech Acts: An Essay in the Philosophy of Language* (Cambridge: Cambridge University Press, 1969), 51–52.

moral practice are the ones incapsulated in *li* or ritual rules, and other Confucian notions do not behave in any rule-like fashion in possessing, as it were, a set of criteria that governs their correct application. We leave open the question of explication in terms of rules. No attempt shall be made here. Nor do we suggest that such a task can be meaningfully carried out for reflective Confucian agents. Following Pepper, we shall assume in our discussion the distinction between *communal* and *functioning* institutions as applicable to a society that can be characterized in terms of the Confucian moral practice.

Communal institutions may be distinguished from functioning institutions in that they do not distribute specific functions among particular persons. They set up areas of mutual understanding. A common language is a ready example, or common customs, manners, faiths. A common area of understanding does not institute a society. Only functioning institutions can do that.[28]

For the Confucian, the *li* belong to functioning institutions which specify functions and obligations contingent upon the social roles and positions occupied by the agents. Searle's examples may be regarded as functioning rather than communal institutional facts. Most Confucian notions belong to a vocabulary of communal language. They presume a common understanding of their proper application, but these notions are not learned as governed by rules of application. The cultural way of life provides the background of their intelligibility without the necessity of spelling out their uses in rule-like terms. However, these moral notions are learned as having an authoritative and actuating force in conduct.

We shall discuss the various factors in Confucian argumentation in terms of the different types of appeal in various speech situations. If we use the term "validity" in the broad sense as embracing both deductive and non-deductive arguments, we may say that each appeal has a validity-value,[29] which may be challenged in a particular discourse. Using the *Analects* as our main guide, we may in general, distinguish the following sorts of appeal:[30]

28. S. C. Pepper, *Sources of Value* (Berkeley: University of California Press, 1958), 582.
29. See Wellman, chap. 11.
30. This list is not intended as a hierarchical order. We have suggested in the essay cited in n. 9 that "the Confucian moral point of view may be formally characterized as a morality of righteousness (the basic meaning of *i*) as contrasted with egoism, but substantively defined in terms of the ideal of *jen*." In this essay, we focus on another meaning of *i* as an act of judgment that establishes the contact between actions and actual situations. In our list we purposely omitted two crucial notions, *tao* and *te*, for it seems to us that these terms do not in general figure as specific argumentative factors. If they do appear, they do so as a general appeal to a way of morality and virtue that needs to be "cashed" into the other notions. The emphasis on concrete values in Confucian ethics,

1. appeal to moral notions of particular virtues
2. appeal to *li* or ritual rules
3. appeal to *jen* or human-heartedness
4. appeal to living or historical persons
5. appeal to *sheng-jen* or sage
6. appeal to *chün-tzu* or superior man
7. appeal to the *time* in exigent situation.

We shall assume that the agent who makes use of any of these appeals is primarily interested in vindicating himself for an action which he has performed, in the face of a challenge or charge by a fellow agent. For (1), (2), and (3), we may schematically represent each appeal as follows:

Schema B: "*A* (the action in question) is to be done, because *A* is properly called *n* in a situation *S*."[31]

This schema is derived from an interpretation of the doctrine of rectification of names *(cheng-ming)*. In (1), the appeal to moral notions of particular virtues involves such notions as *hsiao* (filiality), *hsin* (trustworthiness or truthfulness), *chih* (uprightness), *i* (righteousness), and *jen* (human-heartedness).[32] The schema formulates a peculiar feature of Confucian ethics in its stress on the "correspondence" between words and things (i.e., actions, persons, and states-of-affair). A Confucian agent would prefer the language of *calling* things by their right or proper "names" *(ming)* rather than the language of criteria, unless the context is explicitly regarded as a ritual one, as in the second type of appeal. Moral notions do not point to precisely formulable criteria. Their uses depend on communal institutional facts or the common understanding of *tao* and *te* (virtue) as signifying a moral way of life and not on an explicit code of moral conduct. The *li* or rules of ritual propriety, as we have previously noted, form a special category, but they are not regarded as co-extensive with the whole domain of morality. The use of the schema B with Confucian notions as substitution in-

---

we believe, is best understood in terms of the notions discussed. Our list inevitably represents a selective decision. The suggested equivalents in English are offered as rough guides for locating the foci of Confucian notions. For textual references, the reader may consult the index in James Legge's *Chinese Classics*, vol. I (Oxford: Clarendon Press, 1893). These remarks also apply, with minor qualification, to other Confucian notions omitted in the essay.

31. For *n* we may substitute any Confucian notion. The proposed account is an "ideal" explication.

32. *Jen* is occasionally used in *Analects* as a "name" of a particular virtue. What we single out for separate consideration in (3) relates to its general rather than particular use. See W. T. Chan, "The Evolution of Confucian Concept *Jen*," *Philosophy East and West* 4 (1955), and the essay cited in n. 1.

stances for *n* may be regarded as a sort of "criterion-claim," but such a claim, even if it is accepted by the audience as having a validity-value or persuasive force, does not by itself establish a criterion in the universal sense. On our proposed schema, each use of a moral notion as a "name" of an action is a ruling on the relevance of the moral notion as applicable to a particular context.[33] In normal situations, the agent does not invent a new "name" for his own purpose. His ruling on the application of a moral notion may set up a paradigm for future applications. When this ruling is widely accepted by the fellow members of the community, it can acquire a status of a criterion; but its universal function, apart from the original context in which ruling is made, is a consequence of the paradigm approbation, and not a logical or conceptual feature of the ruling. To call an action *X "hsiao"* is to rule on the relevance of *hsiao* as having a proper application in the context of the situation *S*. It is to present a claim to a legitimate application of *hsiao* in *S*. This claim can be challenged by the audience. The speaker needs to appeal to particular concrete cases in support of his claim. Thus what Richards notes to be a "concrete movement" from particular example to example is an important feature in Confucian argumentation. In the language of rulings, we may say that this amounts to the appeal to other paradigmatic rulings. When a ruling is challenged, Confucian ethics does not present any second-order principles or criteria for resolution of disputes. Thus the emphasis on the peculiar appeal to *chün-tzu* as a paradigmatic standard for guidance. In part the appeal to *chün-tzu* is an appeal to his rulings as a paradigmatic guide. We shall later say more on this sort of appeal. For the moment, let us simply stress the possibility of disagreement in an argumentative situation which presupposes a consensual background that gives intelligibility to the uses of moral notions. But these moral notions do not by themselves provide rules of application. Consequently, they are thus subject to ruling in particular cases.

33. This point is originally suggested by Gasking. We follow Gasking in using "rulings" in a semantic context to refer to the particular applications of words. Gasking remarks: "We say that a ruling for a word in a particular case 'follows from' or 'is determined by' a general rule if people who understand that rule apply the word in that particular case according to that ruling. But the *criterion* for whether a person understands a general rule for a word is that he always uses it according to such and such rulings—namely, the rulings that we say follow from it. What the general rule *means* depends on what rulings we admit as correct application of it." [D. A. T. Gasking, "Mr. Williams on the A Priori," *Analysis* 6 (1939): 74–75]. We do not claim that this is an adequate explanation for the uses of all Confucian notions. But it appears that Gasking's point is quite in line with what we take to be the significance and spirit of the doctrine of rectification of names *(cheng-ming)*, which we employ in discussing Confucian argumentation.

In the case of Confucian notions, with the exception of *li* as a code of rites or rules of proper conduct, we seem to be dealing with what Kovesi recently terms "open" rather than "complete" notions. According to Kovesi,

> when a notion is not formed completely from the moral point of view (e.g., 'killing') then it includes both morally right and wrong acts and in these cases the words 'right' and 'wrong' are used for selecting from a mixed class the types of acts that are different from the moral point of view. When a type of act selected completely from the moral point of view receives its own term (e.g., 'murder') then the words 'right' and 'wrong' are used only as reminders, they remind us what was the point of forming such notions. I would like to call such notions complete notions.[34]

No doubt some of the Confucian moral notions can function as reminders especially in situations of advice and instruction. But if we view them apart from rulings in particular situations they remain "open" rather than complete notions. Rulings or individual judgments are required for them to function as discriminators of the sorts of acts to be performed.

Let us turn to *jen* in its general interpretation as an ideal of moral excellence rather than *jen* as a particular virtue. It is difficult to explain the force of this appeal. We shall suggest a distinction between two different interpretations of moral ideals from the point of view of a commitive agent. In the one case, a moral ideal is viewed by the agent as a *norm* by which individual conduct may be *measured*. In this sense, an ideal can provide directive guidance in particular cases of moral problems and dilemmas. An ideal in this way is taken as a *norm* for measuring moral achievement. *Jen* may be taken in this way as an ideal norm. In another case, an ideal may be construed as a sort of *theme* that endows the life of a commitive agent with a certain quality of excellence. In this sense, it offers not normative or preceptorial guidance, but a focal point of orientation for conduct. It is a perspective that gives a significance or quality to an individual's life. *Jen* may be taken thus as an ideal theme, as a focal point of attention for achieving a meaning or significance in an agent's life. In either case, the appeal to *jen* has validity-value for a Confucian agent. The stress on self-cultivation in accordance with *jen* is a central feature in Confucian ethics.[35]

34. J. Kovesi, *Moral Notions* (London: Routledge & Kegan Paul, 1967), 109. Compare G. Berkeley, "Passive Obedience," in *The Works of George Berkeley*, ed. A. A. Luce and T. E. Jessop (London: Thomas Nelson & Sons, 1953), 6:34.
35. We believe that it is more compatible with the spirit of the *Analects* to regard *jen* as an ideal theme. However, on this matter of moral commitment, we cannot prescribe for other Confucian agents on a univocal rendering of *jen*.

In the light of its pervasive focus on *jen*, the appeals to (4) living or historical persons, (5) *sheng-jen*, and (6) *chün-tzu* depend on the degree of commitment to *jen*. The appeal to *sheng-jen* is an appeal to a sage who perfectly embodies *jen*. This appeal, however, does not seem to possess a validity-value, for sagehood is not regarded as an attainable ideal by Confucius, though Mencius, Hsün Tzu, and later Confucians in Sung and Ming are confident of the possibility of its attainment. In practice, a Confucian would appeal to (6) *chün-tzu*. This appeal has force, since a *chün-tzu* is a paradigmatic individual who embodies *jen*, *li*, and other Confucian virtues. He represents the living possibility of Confucian moral achievement as attainable by men of ordinary ability and capability. The appeal to (4) living or historical persons gives vivid representations of *chün-tzu*, but it is not its substitute, since the appeal to (4) is an appeal to a living embodiment of particular virtues or to personal models. It cannot take the place of *chün-tzu*. For moral instruction, the appeal to (4) would have an important role to play. These three sorts of appeal [(4), (5), and (6)] may be represented in the following form:

Schema C "*A* is to be done in *S*, because so-and-so would do *A* in *S*."

Again, *A* stands for the action to be vindicated, and *S* for the particular situation. "So-and-so" is a stand-in for *sheng-jên*, *chün-tzu*, or actual proper names of particular persons. This is a prominent feature of Confucian ethics to be explained in terms of the absence of moral rules that classify acts in different categories. The only rules are ritual ones, but the significance of the *li* depends on its connection with *jen*. One of the aims of Confucian ethics is to endow *li* with a *jen* quality. Persons who embody *jen* and related virtues can function as action-guides, and an appeal to them has a validity-value in argumentation. For some reflective agent, an appeal to *chün-tzu* may simply be a disguise for a linguistic ruling, for the intent may be better understood in this form: "*A* is to be done in *S* because a *chün-tzu* would make a ruling that applies a certain virtue notion to *A* in *S*." We think that this sort of appeal must ultimately be specified in terms of moral notions. An appeal to *chün-tzu* can thus be construed in part as an appeal to a *chün-tzu's* ruling, which can be contested in the context of argumentation. However, crucial for understanding such appeals is an appreciation of the fact that such appeals are not intended as illustrations of general rules.

We shall now turn to the last sort of appeal (7), to the *time* in an exigent situation. As an addition to our discussion in Section I, our remarks here will be brief. The appeal to what is timely and the fitting thing to do in a particular situation presupposes that the situation falls outside the normal application of *li* and other notions. In the light of the doctrine of rectification of names, we may say that exigent situations have no names or tags attached to them. They are not a problem for building-in exceptions to the application of moral notions, but a problem for *new* linguistic "legislations." Here linguistic ruling can be a creative contribution to the character and function of an established moral practice, for when such rulings are accepted by fellow members of the community, they may become part of the constitutive content of a morality. An ethics of reasonable actions is a focus on the importance of rectifying names.

The key notion that underlies our discussion of the factors in Confucian argumentation is the concept of *paradigmatic* ruling as distinct from that of *universalizable* ruling. A ruling in its concrete occurrence is a particular judgment on the relevance of rules and moral notions to particular circumstances. In any situation, it has a function in the context of judgment. But it may function as a paradigm for future judgments and conduct. Even if intended as a paradigm, it still remains a particular ruling that presents a sort of criterion-claim which may be defeated or contested by other agents. Rulings accepted by others as paradigmatic are also subject to defeat in particular cases. One peculiar feature of Confucian ethics is this stress on the *defeasible* character of rulings. Of course, the rulings of agents remain devoid of paradigmity. But when the rulings of some individuals are accepted by fellow agents, these individuals may acquire a paradigmatic status within the moral practice. This at any rate seems to be true to the spirit of the Confucius's emphasis on *chün-tzu*. Although such an ethics does not provide an epistemology of morals or a theory of moral justification, it can possess a theoretical value in contributing to our understanding of one dimension of moral creativity, i.e., to a focus on the possible contributions an agent can make to the content and function of his moral practice.

In our discussion of Confucian argumentation, we do not intend to suggest that the various sorts of appeal are independent of one another, nor to claim that these constitute distinct patterns or species of reasoning. What we aim to offer is a selective map of factors that may figure in a piece of Confucian dialogic vindication. These are the sorts of considerations to which a Confucian agent may appeal in vindicating his action in a particular situation when such an action is challenged by a fellow agent as being "improper" or "unreasonable." We have suggested that these different sorts of appeal may be understood through the doctrine of "calling things by their right names" inspired by the classical Confucian doctrine of rectifying names. In concluding our essay, we shall briefly, but tentatively, state certain features of this normative doctrine in a general form, without attending to its problematic features. The problematic features we leave to future inquiry. We hope that these brief remarks will open a discussion on the adequacy and promise for developing a Confucian doctrine of moral notions.

To call things (in the broad sense inclusive of objects, persons, situations, or states-of-affair) by their right names is to endow these things with a normative character by a speech-act. This speech-act may be of two different sorts. In one sort of cases, i.e., where the names or descriptions for things are recognized as having proper usages and are fittingly applied to normal cases, the speaker is warranted to apply them. To do so, to borrow a phrase from Austin, is to *suit* the things to the words or the speech-act.[36] We suggest that it is more plausible to regard *ming* ("names") as having both a descriptive and a normative import. Titles of roles and persons, like normal situations, are describable in terms of established linguistic expressions or labels. Application of these established "names" depends on ruling that they are so applicable to particular cases. When this ruling is a commonly recognized or accepted ruling, the understanding of the function of the normative labels and expressions is not thereby affected by the application. In normal cases, moral notions, in general, may be regarded as "bills to be filled." They have validity apart from their applications to particular cases. This is the *conventional* character of one species of rectifying names *(cheng-ming)*. The right names are thus the established descriptions that apply to normal cases. The linguistic ruling in normal cases cannot be properly termed 'linguistic legislation,' since the constitutive content of a morality remains unchanged. The ruling on an application of an established term does not amount to a conceptual revision, for in ruling, the agent is still operating within an established conceptual framework.

The more interesting sort of rectifying names concerns cases where the established names or descriptions are ruled irrelevant to the things-at-hand, to what the speaker regards as an exigent situation. In this sort of context, the speaker needs to search for proper names to describe his situations or actions. To rule that an apparently relevant notion is inapplicable to one's present case is to do two things: (a) to restrict the applicability of established moral notions, and (b) to describe the situation in new terms. Both these activities represent conceptual revision in the normative sense. In exigent situations, a moral

---

36. J. L. Austin, *How to Do Things with Words* (Cambridge: Harvard University Press, 1962), 81–82.

agent may be regarded as engaging in a process of *reconstituting* the content and function of his moral practice. In Confucian ethics, instead of insisting on (b) or the necessity of establishing new names, it focuses on an appeal to *chün-tzu* or paradigmatic individuals in argumentation. *Prima facie,* this is a plausible strategy, for if all agents were allowed to make rulings in exigent situations, moral practice would become unmanageably complex. Also, there is no security against arbitrary intrusions into moral practice. The strategy is to maintain the simplicity of moral practice, but at the same time allow rulings in exigent situations to have a projective function in the case of paradigmatic individuals. Other moralities may opt for a different strategy—for example, some concept of exception in relation to the uses of moral notions. In Confucian ethics, the doctrine of *ching-ch'üan* (the normal and the exigent), in conjunction with the doctrine of rectifying names *(cheng ming),* may be seen as attempts to cope with the same problem of moral change.

Essay 2   Confucian Vision and Experience of the World

A dialogue between Chinese and Western philosophies is both profitable and illuminating when it can perspicuously exhibit more than surface similarities and differences of ideas and problems. Initially such a project encounters a familiar difficulty that is not peculiar to discourse on Chinese philosophy. The difficulty, in part, arises from the nature of the language and the tendency of philosophical notions to vary among writers, even when they belong to the same philosophical tradition. However, this feature is a pervasive one in Chinese philosophy that displays a distinctive linguistic temperament. William Theodore de Bary justly remarks that "for the Chinese the idea is not so much to analyze and define concepts precisely as to expand them, to make them suggestive of the widest possible range of meaning. Generally, the more crucial or central the concept, the greater the ambiguity."[1] This linguistic temperament, in part, can be explained in terms of concrete rationalism or the felt-affinity of reason and experience that pervades Chinese thought in general. Even when these thinkers discourse on the nature of reality employing such terms as *t'ien* (Heaven) and *tao* (the Way), these terms, as Chung-ying Cheng points out, "are not general and abstract terms capable of logical definition, but terms with a universal yet concrete content, to be understood by means of direct and diverse experience."[2] This initial difficulty in appreciating the Chinese perspective may be converted into a virtue in developing a basis for a beginning dialogue with Western philosophy. For one thing, if a dialogue is not to be merely an exchange of ideas, the par-

---

1. William Theodore de Bary, ed., *Self and Society in Ming Thought* (New York: Columbia University Press, 1970), v.
2. "Chinese Philosophy: A Characterization," in *Invitation to Chinese Philosophy*, ed. Arne Naess and Alastair Hannay (Oslo: Universitetsforlaget, 1972), 160. See also my "The Logic of Confucian Dialogues," in J. K. Ryan, ed., *Studies in Philosophy and the History of Philosophy* (Washington, D.C.: The Catholic University of America Press, 1969), 4:15–33.

ticipants must play an active and creative role in recasting and refining the ideas and problems in a form amenable to understanding in the idioms of another philosophical tradition. Even relatively determinate philosophical notions within one tradition are subject to conceptual transformation in this process. This is particularly the case when the dialogue is dominated by a philosophical aim. This manner of proceeding is also conducive to self-understanding. I share Cheng's confidence on this point: "If it is one of the functions of philosophy to uncover presuppositions of an accepted view and to explore new ways of thinking and argumentation, the dialogue in question will certainly provide new light for discovery and exploration. No improvement in self-understanding is possible without such a discovery and exploration."[3]

Within the Confucian tradition in Chinese thought, the plurisignative feature of discourse is united in a common perspective or presupposition. This perspective is a recurrent theme that focuses upon a vision and experience of the world as a central harmony or unity of man and nature. The topic for this symposium provides an occasion for offering, in an experimental spirit, an expanded and reconstructed account of the Confucian conception of the world as a case for Western philosophical understanding and assessment. Robert A. McDermott, our symposium coordinator, has suggested that the dialogue be conducted within the scope of Milton K. Munitz's essay "The Concept of the World." This indeed is a happy decision, since a dialogue requires a well-defined context in which the participants can usefully perform their roles. I shall comply with this suggestion with inward assent. In reading Munitz's essay and his book *The Mystery of Existence*, I am consistently impressed with, and also learn with delight, Munitz's profound concern with human existence—a concern that is characteristic of major Chinese philosophical thinkers.[4] However, Munitz's concern appears to be a large one. In selecting what I regard as an illuminating basis for the dialogue, I am inevitably attracted to two key, but related, notions: the mystery of existence and the transcendence of the world. These two notions have drawn my attention to the classic expression of

3. Ibid., 142. For more discussion of the role of conceptual revision, see my "Reflections on Methodology in Chinese Philosophy," *International Philosophical Quarterly* 11, no. 2 (1971): 236–48.

4. Milton K. Munitz, *The Mystery of Existence: An Essay in Philosophical Cosmology* (New York: Appleton-Century-Crofts, 1965), and "The Concept of the World," in *Language, Belief, and Metaphysics*, vol. 1 of Contemporary Philosophy Thought, ed. Milton K. Munitz and Howard Kiefer (Albany: State University of New York Press, 1970); hereafter cited as *ME* and *CW*, respectively.

the Confucian view in *Chung Yung (The Doctrine of the Mean)*.[5] I have thus chosen *Chung Yung* as the basis of discussion.[6] Moreover, in the course of the discussion I have occasionally made use of certain remarks of Wang Yang-ming without the pretense of ascribing notions and distinctions to Wang's basic philosophy.[7] Nor do I intend to imply an evaluation regarding the complex issues that divide the rationalistic and idealistic wings of Neo-Confucian philosophy. My sole aim is to exhibit the notions implicit in Wang as having a significant bearing on our understanding of the Confucian theme of central harmony. These notions may thus serve as focal lenses through which to appreciate the Confucian vision and experience of the world.

This article is divided into two parts. Part I is devoted to a self-consciously inadequate statement of Munitz's notions of the mystery of existence and transcendence of the world. Part II presents a discussion, à la Munitz, of the Confucian theme of central harmony as an elaborate root-metaphor for Chinese metaphysical speculations.

I

Cut off from its earlier theological associations, the term "mystery," according to Munitz, has two basic uses in ordinary discourse. In the

5. *Chung Yung*, trans. by James Legge as "The Doctrine of Mean" and by Hung-meng Ku as "Central Harmony." The essay is originally a chapter in *Li Chi* [Book of rites]. According to Wing-tsit Chan, "the *Li Chi* evidently existed in the early Han dynasty (206 B.C.–A.D. 220)." All my textual references are to Chan's translation in his *Source Book in Chinese Philosophy* (Princeton: Princeton University Press, 1963). Legge's translation is found in his *Chinese Classics*, vol. 1 (Oxford: Clarendon Press, 1893). Ku's translation is included in Lin Yutang's *Wisdom of Confucius* (New York: The Modern Library, 1938).

6. Aside from being a principal Confucian classic, the importance of *Chung Yung* lies in its being a bridge between Taoism, Buddhism, and Confucianism (see Chan, *Source Book*, 95). For a more recent and sustained discussion of the significance of the theme of central harmony, see Thomé H. Fang, "The World and the Individual in Chinese Metaphysics" and T'ang Chün-i, "The Individual and the World in Chinese Methodology," in *The Chinese Mind*, ed. Charles A. Moore (Honolulu: East-West Center Press, 1967). My own approach differs from that of the authors of these two essays. I have construed the doctrine of central harmony as a metaphysical theme rather than a metaphysical thesis. This explains in part my choice of *Chung Yung*, since this work is less a metaphysical treatise (in the sense of a theory supported by arguments) than a treatise on a relatively elaborate root-metaphor for possible metaphysical constructions. The two major movements in Neo-Confucian philosophy, commonly referred to as Ch'eng-Chu School and Lu-Wang School, may be regarded as divergent attempts to develop the same root-metaphor. I owe this notion of root-metaphor to Stephen C. Pepper, who expounded it in his *World Hypothesis* (Berkeley and Los Angeles: University of California Press, 1948), chap. 5.

7. Wang Yang-ming (1472–1529), *Instructions for Practical Living and Other Neo-Confucian Writings*, ed. W. T. Chan (New York: Columbia University Press, 1963); hereafter cited as Wang, *Instructions*.

first, the term is used in cases where we intend to refer to "some secret kept by men from men." Crucial to this use, I suppose, is the action of keeping secrets, essentially an activity of men in relation to one another. The term "keeping secrets" would then belong with a family of such related notions as "hiding information" and "concealing knowledge." From the epistemic point of view, what is a mystery in this sense, in principle, can be disclosed by the avowal of men who keep the secret. In general, anything may be said to be "secret" when it is kept from observation, discovery, or understanding. The second sense of "mystery" generally refers "to any matter for which we do not have any requisite knowledge or information and more particularly, for something for which we do not have an *explanation*" (*ME*, 26). In this sense, I suppose the distinctive use of "mystery" has a connection with matters which are *unexplained* or *inexplicable*. Both these uses have contemporary lexical support. Thus the *American Heritage Dictionary* reports, under the term "mystery": (1) "Anything that arouses curiosity because it is unexplained; inexplicable, or secret," and (2) "the quality of being inexplicable or secret." Munitz rightly points out that his second meaning is neutral regarding the epistemic issue on the possibility or impossibility of knowledge. It is in the second sense that Munitz wants to rehabilitate the term as having "a *philosophically warrantable use,* namely, as standing for an in-principle unanswerable question" (*ME,* 27).

The term "mystery of existence" is thus to be understood in a philosophical way. What follows from this linguistic observation is that the question about the mystery of existence signifies a curiosity that cannot be logically satisfied. The profound, but meaningful, philosophical question "Why is there something rather than nothing?" is clarified, through a series of transformations, in terms of "Is there a reason-for-the-existence-of-the-world?" In this last formulation, the question turns out to be an unanswerable question, for it demands a sense of reason that falls outside the range of the major uses of "reason" in ordinary discourse. There is not, nor can there be, any known rational method for satisfying our quest (*MS*, chap. 10). What is crucial in the acceptance of Munitz's thesis depends, in large part, on his analysis of the notions of the world and its existence.[8] In what follows I shall con-

---

8. Regrettably, I cannot here enter into Munitz's sustained and detailed arguments for this general thesis. Munitz's notions of mystery of existence and transcendence of the world, I assume, as a Confucian, are intelligible and explicable independently of his arguments and conclusions. I am here mainly interested in the notions and theses as providing a contemporary context for understanding the Confucian theme of central harmony.

centrate on these notions before examining their relevance to my discussion of the Confucian theme of central harmony. Quite unlike his analysis of the term "mystery," Munitz's remarks on the meaning of "the world" do not seem to derive from any of the ordinary uses. In ordinary discourse, we use "the world" in a variety of contexts. In the more impersonal contexts, we tend to use the term to refer to the earth; the universe (not necessarily in the cosmological sense); the earth and its inhabitants, collectively. We also use the notion in talking about the public, or an individual state of being or an individual way of life. What interests Munitz is the philosophical question, whether the notion of the world is a referring expression. Thus in "The Concept of the World," Munitz states the main issue: "Everything in our present enquiry . . . hinges on whether or how we treat the phrase 'the world' as a referring expression" (CW, 193). His detailed discussion points to a negative answer. Munitz rejects a number of standard metaphysical theses that construe "the world" as a referring expression. As standing for a whole or a totality in the sense of everything, "everything" is a place holder that has no referring role. In the sense of being a totality of either a class or group of objects, events, or facts, the term has no meaningful use (CW, 199–218). When referring to an individual, the notion of the world seems to be a misapplication of the term "individual thing," for "to be an individual thing is, in its paradigm meaning, to be a particular that we are able to pick out and identify in various degrees of resemblance or similarity" (CW, 223).

What emerges from Munitz's discussion is that the notion of the world is a unique, nonempirical concept—a concept, as it were, that refers, in some peculiar sense, to a unique collective totality. We are here confronted with a "unique, irreducible and primitive idea" (CW, 219). In other words, the world is a unique concept in that no ordinary linguistic rule for specifying meaning applies to it. We need to presuppose some sort of an act of awareness, some "contact with that which is the unique existent exemplification of the concept" (CW, 227). "The world" may thus be construed as a *transcendent* notion, in the special sense of being a notion that transcends all other concepts. The world is transcendent "because it does not lend itself to description by other concepts, by concepts, that is to say, that may at least successfully apply to classes, objects, or entities 'within' the world but that do not apply to the world itself" (CW, 228). Munitz suggests that this unique, transcendent notion points to, or reminds us of, an experience or awareness that is distinct from that which is readily intelligible in ordinary discourse. In speaking about the world, we may stretch such ordinary terms as "knowledge" or "thought," but these uses do not convey to us any descriptions or information about the world. "All of which is simply another way of saying that the world as 'experience' is wholly unique, and cannot therefore in any ordinary sense be verbalized or conceptualized at all" (CW, 232).

From the preceding, Munitz concludes that the mystery of existence is an aspect of the transcendence of the world. We are here confronted with "an absolutely unique subject matter." Like the mystery of existence, the question "What is the world?" in the final analysis is an unanswerable question. This negative paradoxical result of philosophical examination of the concept of the world, however, does "yield thereby the occasion for a deeper insight into what the world is" (CW, 198). The insight is an insight into the logic of the notion of the world (CW, 198): (1) The notion of the world cannot be assimilated to "any of the standard and familiar ways we have of classifying terms as, for example, a name for a class, a proper name for an individual, a definite descriptive phrase, and so on"; (2) there can be no valid distinction between meaning and application of the notion of the world; and (3) more importantly, the notion is not used but "had"—it has no function in "propositional context either as a subject or as a predicate; and therefore is not part of an argument-chain in which we can undertake to set out knowledge-claims of a metaphysical sort about the world" (CW, 232–33).

In *The Mystery of Existence*, Munitz appears to maintain that, in spite of the unanswerability of the question concerning the existence of the world, we can still derive some insight from our intellectual frustration. The unanswerability of the question is said to point to a "primordial experience" of the world that is uniquely "directed to its own object, namely, to the world as existing" (*ME*, 79). The nonpropositional nature of the insight into this mystery is thus alleged to be an outcome of philosophical analysis. We are also told that the mystery of existence in some way, reveals not simply something about ourselves but "something about ourselves responding to the existence of the world in a special way, in terms of an unanswerable question. The mystery, so to speak, is in relation, or interaction, between the puzzled mind and the existence of the world, not in either one, taken separately" (*ME*, 258). I presume this insight also derives from the transcendence of the world, since the mystery of existence is but an aspect of transcendence of the world. Munitz, however, does not elaborate on the nature of this experiential insight, except to note that it has affinity with "religious experience and mysticism" (CW, 198). Perhaps Munitz is barred by his logical thesis about the world from saying anything meaningful about the other aspects of transcendence of the world. My principal concern is whether one can say anything intelligible and significant about this insight without any pretense to offering any knowledge-claims about the nature of the world. In particular, I wish to inquire whether the Confucian conception of the world can have a useful contribution to make on this question without being a target of Munitz's searching critique of various metaphysical views. This concern quite naturally lays aside the large question of whether there can be a philosophically interesting and important use of the notions of the world and its existence. But perhaps our restricted inquiry will throw some light and offer some independent grounds for accepting some version of Munitz's general theses.

II

In offering an account of the Confucian theme of central harmony in terms of Munitz's notions, one has first of all to note a linguistic problem. In Chinese, there appear to be no literary equivalents of the notions of the world or of the existence of the world. A number of Chinese terms such as *t'ien-ti, wan-wu, shih-chieh, yü-chou* seem to correspond to the English word "world" in ordinary uses.[9] Quite obviously, to talk about the Confucian theme requires one to have recourse to a *philosophical reading* of the classic *Chung Yung* [The doctrine of the mean]. A Munitzean reading is quite possible. Without giving an exegesis of the text, my reading is mainly supported by the following consideration. Although philosophically, *Chung Yung*, in the light of later Neo-Confucian thought, is a main source of Chinese metaphysical speculation, by itself the text does not appear to be a metaphysical treatise in any systematic sense, at least, in G. E. Moore's sense of being an attempt "to give a general description of the whole of the universe, mentioning all the most important kinds of things which we know to be in it."[10] Thus we meet with no description or classification of the types of entities in the world, nor do we encounter the notion of the world as a name, referring, or descriptive expression. Instead, we are given a sort of *theme,* a vision that can be developed in a number of ways. I suggest that the notion of central harmony of men, nature, and things in the world be taken as an elaborate root-metaphor. According to Pepper, "A man desiring to understand the world looks about for a clue to its comprehension. He pitches upon some area of common sense

---

9. See *A New English-Chinese Dictionary,* ed. Cheng Yi-li (Hong Kong: Kwang Tai Publishers, 1966).

10. Moore, *Some Main Problems of Philosophy* (London: George Allen & Unwin, 1953), 1.

facts and tries if he cannot understand other areas in terms of this one. This original area becomes then his basic analogy or root-metaphor."[11] I do not intend to suggest here that one can develop a definite set of philosophical categories out of the root-metaphor. What is important to note is that *Chung Yung* presents us an elaborate root-metaphor in terms of a vision rooted perhaps in some elementary experiences of man's harmony with the world.

In *Chung Yung* what appears to correspond closely to Munitz's notion of the world is the notion of *t'ien-ti*, commonly translated as "Heaven and Earth." Thus in one statement on the main theme—that *t'ien-ti* and men form a trinity—the term *"t'ien-ti"* seems to refer to something unique (sec. 22). Also, the notion of *tao* (the Way) is frequently used in the text. We find such expressions as "the *tao* of Heaven and Earth" (sec. 26), or *"tao* of Heaven" (sec. 20), "the *tao* of superior man" (sec. 15), and "the *tao* of the sage" (sec. 27). My "reading" of the text suggests that this notion of *tao* is functionally, though not literally, equivalent to Munitz's notion of existence as a verbal noun (CW, 230). In the *Mystery of Existence*, Munitz distinguishes two different senses of "exist." In the first sense, it is used as equivalent to "there is an instance of so-and-so." In the second, as used in the expression "the World exists," it describes the unique activity of the world (*ME*, 98). This special sense designates *"what the world does"* (*ME*, 93). We may say the *tao* of Heaven and Earth exists in this second sense, as long as we do not claim to offer any special knowledge when we replace the notion of *tao* of Heaven and Earth with the notion of existence (in the special sense) as its synonym. As Munitz succinctly states, "in using the term 'existence' as synonym for 'the world' we are not advancing our insight into what the world is, nor giving any analysis of the meaning of this term" (CW, 230). There are problems that we shall consider later, since the term "know" *(chih)* does occur in the text, suggesting, as it were, that the sage or a man of sincerity *(ch'eng)* has some sort of "knowledge." However, what the theme of the central harmony of man and the world points to is precisely the ceaseless, creative, and transformative character of the *tao* of Heaven and Earth (sec. 22) in relation to the *tao* of man. The relation is intrinsic to the nature of each. Man, Heaven, and Earth form a unity—a dynamic creative unity that admits of no special description nor categorization. In this sense, we may also regard the notion of *tao* of Heaven and Earth as *transcendent.* However, the notion is more a *reminder* than a *discriminator* enabling us to discern the special prop-

---

11. Pepper, *World Hypotheses*, 91. For more discussion, see my "Basic Metaphors and the Emergence of Root Metaphors," *Journal of Mind and Behavior* 3 (1982): 251–58.

erties of individual objects and persons in the world.[12] It reminds the Confucian of the possibility of an experience that is embedded in a basic perspective of human life—of the Confucian "form of life" that renders its moral and intellectual striving intelligible and significant.

Section 1 of the *Chung Yung* announces the Confucian theme. It begins with a sort of conceptual recommendation for some basic terms: "What Heaven *(t'ien)* imparts to man is called human nature *(hsing)*. To follow our nature is called the Way *(tao)*. Cultivating the Way is called education. The Way cannot be separated from us for a single moment. What can be separated from us is not the Way." This opening remark stresses the intrinsic connection between the Way of Heaven and the Way of man. That man can deviate from the Way is recognized. The purported stress is on the *ideal* connection (sec. 13). From the point of view of this ideal of inseparability of man and the Way, the world is essentially a human world. Things in the world exist as objects of human intention and actions. In this sense what the world does is ideally connected with what men do. As Wing-tsit Chan points out, "The Chinese make no absolute distinction between physical things and human activities, both being represented by the word '*shih*'."[13] *Shih* can also be rendered as "event" or "affair." In Wang Yang-ming, *shih* is construed as having the same meaning as "*wu*" or "thing." "Wherever the will is directed is a 'thing'. For example, when the will is directed toward serving one's parents, then serving one's parents is a 'thing'."[14] This proposed semantic equivalence of *shih* and *wu*, though not accepted by all Chinese thinkers, is significant in that it focuses in a perspicuous way on the underlying Confucian motif in reflecting and discoursing about the world. The world and the Way are seen as a setting for moral striving. The focus on the Way as a human Way is essentially an ideal focus. It is the Confucian ideal of *jen* (humanity) that furnishes the context for rational discourse about the world (sec. 25).[15]

The next paragraph in Section 1 of the *Chung Yung* announces the

12. See Julius Kovesi, *Moral Notions* (London: Routledge & Kegan Paul, 1967), 26–27.
13. "Chinese Theory and Practice," in *Philosophy and Culture: East and West*, ed. Charles A. Moore (Honolulu: University of Hawaii Press, 1962), 83.
14. Wang Yang-ming, *Instructions*, sec. 6. See also secs. 78, 137, 201. Two remarks of Wang's "idealistic" precursor Lu Hsiang-shan (1139–93) are worthy of note: "The affairs of the universe *(yü chou)* are my own affairs. My own affairs are the affairs of the universe"; "The universe has never separated itself from man. Man separates himself from the universe." See Chan, *Source Book*, 580, 582.
15. For a discussion of this notion of *jen* in relation to *li* (ritual propriety), see my "Reflections on the Structure of Confucian Ethics," *Philosophy East and West* 21, no. 2 (April 1971): 125–40; or *Dimensions of Moral Creativity*, chap. 3.

theme of central harmony. Significantly the theme is stated in psychological language.

Before the feelings of pleasure, anger, sorrow, and joy are aroused it is called equilibrium (*chung*, centrality, mean). When these feelings are aroused and each and all attain due measure and degree, it is called harmony *(ho)*. Equilibrium is the great foundation of the world *(t'ien-ti)* and harmony is its universal path. When equilibrium and harmony are realized to the highest degree, heaven and earth will attain their proper order and all things will flourish.

While the opening remark stresses the ideal connection of the way of life of man and the way of Heaven or Nature, this passage articulates the vision of central harmony as a realistic objective of human endeavor, assuming that the agent can discipline and harmonize his conflicting emotions. As Wang Yang-ming explains, equilibrium and harmony are not to be regarded as contrasting mental states,[16] for equilibrium, so conceived, easily suggests a static rather than a dynamic state. While the distinction is recognized, it is not to be construed as a dichotomy. "It should not be said that all ordinary persons have attained the state of equilibrium before the feelings are aroused. For 'substance and function come from one source.'[17] Given the substance, there is function, and given the equilibrium before feelings are aroused, there is the harmony in which the feelings are aroused and all attain due measure and degree."[18] The point seems to be this: unless a man possesses a disposition to achieve harmony, he cannot be said to have attained the state of equilibrium, or to be at peace within himself. And if he is not at peace within himself, he cannot attain harmony when he is in any of the emotional states. In other words, equilibrium as an achieved state is a result of harmony; harmony as an achieved state is a result of the activation of the incipient tendency toward equilibrium. Thus a superior man *(chün-tzu)*, who embodies the central harmony (sec. 2), "can find himself in no situation in which he is not at ease with himself." He is a man who "lives peacefully and at ease and waits for his destiny" (sec. 14).[19] Confucius is supposed to have said: "In archery we have something resembling the Way of the superior man. When the archer misses the center of the target, he turns around and seeks for the cause of failure within himself" (sec. 14). What the remark on central har-

16. Wang, *Instructions*, sec. 307.
17. A famous saying of Ch'eng I (1033–1107).
18. Wang, *Instructions*, sec. 45.
19. For a discussion of the notion of superior man *(chün-tzu)* as a paradigmatic individual in Confucian ethics, see my "Concept of Paradigmatic Individuals in the Ethics of Confucius," *Inquiry* 14, nos. 1–2 (1971). Reprinted in A. Naess and A. Hannay's *Invitation to Chinese Philosophy*, 41–55.

mony announces is thus a vision of the harmony of man's inward states and actions and the "things" and events in the world. When the vision is realized, all things will attain their proper order. Man and nature will thus flourish or act in harmony. From the Confucian moral point of view, this vision is an ideal theme that allows of polymorphous development contingent upon the will, capacity, and circumstance of individual agents. The central harmony is a creative, transformative harmony. It is achieved by way of sincerity *(ch'eng)*, that is, an unwavering commitment to the possibility of realizing the Confucian vision of central harmony.

In the context of practical actions, sincerity is a step in the personal cultivation of Confucian virtues (for example, humanity, righteousness, ritual propriety, and wisdom), as it is stressed in *Ta Hsüeh (The Great Learning)*. In *Chung Yung*, while these virtues are equally stressed (sec. 20), "sincerity" acquires a deeper signification and importance. It becomes the link between Heaven and Earth and man. The notion is first introduced in Section 20. This passage runs:

Sincerity is the Way of Heaven. To think how to be sincere is the way of man. He who is sincere is one who hits upon what is right without effort and apprehends without thinking. He is naturally and easily in harmony with the Way. Such a man is a sage. He who tries to be sincere is one who chooses the good and holds fast to it.

Again, the emphasis is on man's being at ease with things in the world. The vision of central harmony is thus a matter of self-realization, an experience that results through the attainment of sincerity rather than primarily by way of intellectual competence and achievement. Both are emphasized. The superior man *(chün-tzu)* "honors the moral nature and follows the path of study and inquiry" (sec. 27; see also sec. 20). However, the principal intent is a moral one. The vision is primarily one of moral achievement. This point is brought out by the following:

Sincerity means the completion of the self, and the Way is self-direction. Sincerity is the beginning and end of things. Without sincerity there would be nothing. Therefore the superior man values sincerity. Sincerity is not only the completion of one's own self, it is that by which all things are completed. The completion of the self means humanity *(jen)*. The completion of all things means wisdom. These are the character of the nature, and they are the Way in which the internal and the external are united. Therefore whenever it is employed, everything is done (sec. 25).

Sincerity is a creative and transformative force in uniting the Way of the world and the Way of man. Man forms a triad with Heaven and Earth through assisting in the nourishing and transforming process of

Heaven and Earth. He develops and completes his nature as a precondition for developing and completing the nature of other men and the nature of things (sec. 22). The Confucian world *exists* as a ceaseless world of activities. Sincerity is no ordinary moral virtue, it is "creating and accomplishing oneself and all things of the world."[20]

Let us consider the epistemic status of the passages discussed. I have suggested that the notion of central harmony be construed as a vision in the sense of its being a sort of ideal theme. An ideal, William James insightfully points out, "must be something that is intellectually conceived . . . and it must carry with it that sort of outlook, uplift, and brightness that go with all intellectual facts." Also, an ideal, aside from being a novel one to those who are attracted to it, must have a certain depth that gives rise to the active will.[21] In this sense the notion of central harmony, to the Confucian, is not a mere object of intellectual possession or entertainment. The focus on the importance of sincerity brings out the ingredient feature in any commitment to an ideal. To understand the Confucian vision as an *ideal theme*, we need to contrast it with an *ideal norm*. This distinction is offered as a way of understanding moral ideals from the point of view of a commitive agent. When an ideal, as a standard of moral excellence, is regarded by the agent as a *norm*, the agent attempts to view his ideal as admitting of programmatic articulation. An agent may work out his vision in terms of one or many specific tasks that conform to his ideal. His vision serves as a sketch, so to speak, for developing blueprints for the actualization of the ideal. The ideal, in effect, functions as a norm for evaluating conduct in terms of the requirements set forth in his vision. A different interpretation lies in conceiving the ideal as a *theme*. If we regard an ideal norm as a *telos* of a way of life, an ideal theme is a conception of a quality of life that forms the *telos* of a style of life. An ideal theme is neither a typal conception nor an archetype that establishes a pattern of behavior. It is a vision that focuses upon the gestaltlike character of a way of life. It functions as a standard of inspiration, not by providing an articulate norm or set of action guides to be complied with, but by providing a point of orientation. The achievement of an ideal theme does not depend on prior knowledge of directives that issue from it. One can comport to an ideal theme in various ways. Much depends on the creative development of the individual in his life and conduct. It is the action and experience of individual agents that furnish the content of the ideal theme.

20. T'ang Chün-i, "The Individual and the World in Chinese Methodology," 284.
21. William James, *Essays on Faith and Morals* (New York: Longmans, Green & Co., 1949), 304–5.

Characteristically, Confucian ethics does not provide a set of invariable rules or principles. Though it attempts to promote various virtues, these virtues, and moral notions in general, are not explained in anything that can be construed as analytical definitions. This lack of precise definitions can now be partially understood in the light of the Confucian vision or theme of a creative and transformative universe. Achieving harmony with the world is a temporal fitting of one's action to what is required by the actual, particular situation. The implicit concrete rationalism is a form of *reasonableness* rather than abstract *rationality* that complies with logical canons.[22] The vision as an ideal theme thus admits of divergent creative developments. Commitment to the ideal of central harmony does not, therefore, logically entail a similar commitment to what the agent takes as the epistemic ingredients implicit in the ideal.

Nevertheless, one may properly raise the question "How does one know what the ideal theme requires?" A Confucian of the *Chung Yung* would respond that the answer is a mystery in Munitz's sense. It is an unanswerable question, for no rational method can enable us to answer it in any satisfactory way. In terms of the vision of central harmony, such a question cannot be intelligibly raised, for the Confucian world is a world of ceaseless transformation. If the world is envisaged as a unique activity that endures without rest, any attempt to spell out the nature of the world is doomed to failure. A Confucian of the *Chung Yung* may happily endorse Kierkegaard's remark: "It is perfectly true, as philosophers say, that life must be understood backwards. But they forget the other proposition, that it must be lived forward. And if one thinks over that proposition it becomes more and more evident that life can never be understood in time simply because at no particular moment can I find the necessary resting place from which to understand it—backwards."[23] And if the ongoing activity of human life and the world occur ceaselessly, all things undergo transformation from one moment to the next, our reason and reflection cannot comprehend this world in its unity and totality, nor can we have rational knowledge of its basic characteristics or properties. But what we lack in intellectual comprehension is compensated by the moral intent that embeds the vision. The vision becomes a challenge for the creative development of an ideal theme, the focal point of reference and orientation for prospective action and experience. What we do by way of sincerity, "with-

22. For further discussion, see Essay 1.
23. Søren Kierkegaard, *Journals,* ed. and trans. Alexander Dru (New York: Harper & Row Publishers, 1959), 89.

out any doubleness" and/or self-deception, becomes an ingredient in
the achieved state, whatever it may be. The ideal theme remains a target
of our moral striving, an apex of our moral achievement without prior
specifiable content. If we wish to speak of "knowledge" here, this form
of knowledge is an achievement in action, something that is *posterior*
rather than *anterior* to our moral performance.[24] Perhaps this is the
heart of Wang's doctrine of unity of knowledge and action *(chih-hsing
ho-i)*.[25]

There are passages in the *Chung Yung* that appear to suggest the
sense of the *mystery* of the Way, a sense close to Munitz's "mystery of
existence." One passage runs: "The Way of the superior man functions
everywhere and yet is hidden. Men and women of simple intelligence
can share its knowledge; and yet in its utmost reaches, there is something which even the sage does not know" (sec. 11). Section 26 makes
the similar point: "the Way of Heaven and Earth may be completely
described in one sentence: they are without any doubleness and so they
produce things in an *unfathomable* way. The Way of Heaven and Earth
is extensive, deep, high, brilliant, infinite, and lasting." Section 32 exalts the Way of Heaven and Earth as "deep and unfathomable." These
three passages convey the sense of the secret, the hidden, the inexplicable, and yet the Way is supposed to be manifest and to function everywhere. If mystery is an aspect of transcendence, we have here a hint
that the Way transcends ordinary concepts. One difficulty arises with
Section 12, for it also states, in fairly categorical fashion, that "the Way
of the superior man has its simple beginnings in the relation between
man and woman, but in its utmost reaches, it is clearly seen in Heaven
and Earth."

In this connection we must attend to the distinction between a superior man *(chün-tzu)* and a sage *(sheng-jen)*. The first is the notion of
a Confucian paradigmatic individual who embodies the traditional

24. One passage in the *Chung Yung* contradicts my present reading. Sec. 24 attributes
foreknowledge to the man of absolute sincerity. But in the light of other remarks that
focus on the "unfathomable" way of sincerity (see, for example, secs. 26, 32), the passage
in question appears to be out of place. As Wang Yang-ming said, "The sage does not
value foreknowledge. When blessings and calamities come, even a sage cannot avoid
them. He only knows the incipient activating force of things and handles it in accordance
with the circumstance" (Wang, *Instructions*, 225). As we shall shortly take up, the circumstance is what is crucial for our present interest. Circumstance cannot be known in advance of its occurrence. Though we may have knowledge of "the incipient activating force
of things," we have no prior rational knowledge of the circumstance in which they are
actualized. For the distinction of these two senses of knowledge, see my "Problem of
Moral Actuation," *Man and World* 4, nos. 3 and 4 (1970): 338–50.

25. For some relevant passages, see Wang's *Instructions*, secs. 5, 26, 132, 133, 226,
and 291.

Confucian virtues, such as humanity, righteousness, wisdom, and ritual propriety. These traditional virtues are objects of knowledge in the ordinary sense. To become a sage, one must fully develop the dispositions for virtue. Sagehood does not seem to be an attainable ideal. Confucius once remarked that he could not hope to meet a sage *(sheng-jen)*, but only a superior man *(chün-tzu)*.[26] But even these traditional virtues are *known* in the practical sense as *posterior* to performance. This is, I believe, the distinguishing feature of the Confucian notion of moral knowledge as I suggested in the preceding paragraph. What concerns me now is the notion of the sage's lack of knowledge. "The sage does not know" may be construed, I believe, quite properly as "the sage has no intellectual knowledge" in the propositional sense. He presents no truth-claims, but simply acts in a manner that befits the circumstance he confronts. The world goes on ceaselessly, and things are transformed by the Way or the world's activity. The recognition of the mystery and transcendence of the world does not lead to abulia or to the lessening of the commitive agent's confidence in the transformative significance of the ideal theme of harmony of man with things and events in the world. The philosophical questions on the nature of the world and its existence, from this moral point of view, have no practical actuating import. However, in another sense, if these questions are taken in the nonpropositional sense of being perplexities that resist problematic formulations—that is, as questions that call for answer in terms, for example, of an experience of moral achievement of the vision as manifest in the lives of those who can easefully respond to the changing conditions in the world—then they have answers that pretend to no epistemic status and authority.[27] Wang, echoing Chuang Tzu, compares the mind of the sage to a clear mirror that responds to changing conditions.[28] The Way, at the end, is a matter of personal experience and realization, and not an object of intellectual search and articulation. Moral principles, if we have them, "exist in no fixed place and are

26. *Analects*, VII, 25. See my essay "Concept of Paradigmatic Individuals in the Ethics of Confucius."

27. For a further discussion of this distinction of two attitudes toward questions, see sec. V of my "Relevance of Moral Rules and Creative Agency," *New Scholasticism* 47, no. 1 (1973): 1–20.

28. Wang, *Instructions*, secs. 21, 148, and 167. This idea appears to be Taoistic in origin. In the *Chuang-tzu*, we find the following: "The Perfect Man uses his mind like a mirror going after nothing welcoming nothing, responding but not storing. Therefore he can win over things and not hurt himself." See Burton Watson, trans., *The Complete Works of Chuang Tzu* (New York: Columbia University Press, 1968), 97. See also Cheng Hao's remarks in A. C. Graham, *Two Chinese Philosophers: Ch'eng Ming-Tao and Ch'eng Yi-ch'uan* (London: Lund Humphries, 1958), 104–5.

not exhaustible."[29] True Knowledge, in the commendatory sense, is a matter of personal experience, not a matter acquired through listening to intellectual discourse about the world.[30] One is here humbled by the sense of mystery that can only be quieted by experience as a product of the *sincerity* that pervades the life and character of one's moral life.

One puzzle remains: if my philosophical reading of the *Chung Yung* is deemed correct and plausible, what, it may be asked, is the status of the various predicates that we find in Section 26? The Way of Heaven and Earth is said to be "extensive, deep, high, brilliant, and lasting." One way of handling this question is simply to remark that these are metaphorical expressions of the same theme of central harmony. But metaphors, if they are to be insightful, must draw our attention to things that are hidden or concealed, to the mystery of existence and transcendence of the world. Munitz lays his stress on the insight into our responsive relation to the world. In one sense, then, we may take these metaphors as indicative of our response to the mystery and transcendence of the world, as revelatory of what we are in our puzzle over our own existence. These metaphors can thus be construed as *responsional characterizations* of the world with no pretension to offering knowledge-claims. These are the metaphors akin to Wang's "clear mirror" of the sage. Perhaps we can best regard them as metaphors, which are essentially *amphibious* notions that straddle two different domains of discourse.[31]

Perhaps the notions of mystery and transcendence of the world can also be construed as amphibious notions. In one foot, the amphibious notions are anchored in the world. In a paradoxical way, the notions purport to tell us something about the world. In another foot, they rest on our response to the capacity of these notions to throw light upon the questioners. They disclose what we are rather than describe the nature of the world. If we insist that the two domains of discourse be rigidly distinguished in the interest of philosophical clarity, we deprive ourselves of focal lenses in which to locate the profound and persistent concern with perplexities that seems to frustrate analytic treatment.

29. Wang, *Instructions*, sec. 22.
30. Ibid., sec. 211.
31. This idea suggested itself to me as I was reading Robert J. Fogelin's treatment of amphibious statements in *Evidence and Meaning* (London: Routledge & Kegan Paul, 1967), 42–43, and Part II of Karl Aschenbrenner's *Concepts of Value: Foundations of Value Theory* (Dordrecht-Holland: D. Reidel Publishing Company, 1971). After writing the article I discovered that Rescher has used the term "amphibious notions" in some of his recent writings. I am uncertain, however, whether he would agree to my explanation and suggestion of its use in this article. See Nicholas Rescher, *Primacy of Practice* (Oxford: Blackwell, 1973), 3f.

When these domains of discourse are abstractly considered, they appear to have no meeting place, nor do they offer us insight into the underlying motives for the questions. Quite evidently, amphibious notions have no unvarying epistemic contribution to human knowledge. Their paradoxical uses, however, do not prevent them from offering insights in some nonpropositional sense. As long as human beings experience the compulsion to ask about their existence in questions that cannot be illuminated by any scientific, analytical, or metaphysical method, the experience itself can only be marked as a peculiar but significant characteristic of the perplexed mind. For the vision of the world cannot be understood in abstraction from man as a questioning animal in search for meaning in his life as he lives in the world of other men and things in general.

Amphibious notions have a legitimate role to play in the articulation of this vision. This, at any rate, appears to be a crucial feature of many of our moral, as distinct from scientific, notions.[32] What is philosophically important about the exploration of these amphibious moral notions is that they draw our attention to the inadequacy of conceptual analysis apart from having closely considered their relation to man's desires, ideals, and aspirations, in particular, apart from man's interest in characterizing their response to the world. The Chinese fondness for amphibious notions is perhaps best understood in the light of this interest. The theme of central harmony in the *Chung Yung* is stated, as I have previously noted, in psychological language with its overall moral intent. This is part of the reason why Chinese thinkers, in general, do not pay attention to the distinction between normative and descriptive statements. This feature of Confucian ethics may be considered a defect or a virtue, depending on a philosopher's viewpoint. The defect lies in the Confucian neglect of the importance of conceptual clarification; the virtue, in its unwavering moral concern with man as inherently capable of responding to the world, of harmonizing his actions and intentions with things and events in the world. The theme of central harmony thus deeply imbues the lives and thought of the Confucian thinkers and agents. It is a sort of "a primitive idea" or "a primordial experience" in Munitz's sense. If we are skeptical whether Confucian thinkers in fact possess this unique experience, we can at least appreciate their effort in articulating the vision as an object of possible experience. This issue is bound to be an unsettling one. We feel philosophically uneasy in indulging in this sort of discourse about human vision or wisdom, lest we utter nonsensical remarks that offend

32. Kovesi, *Moral Notions*, 53–58.

our contemporary analytical canons. But I believe that conceptual analysis in a broader sense can have a role to play in attending to the paradox that is inherent in amphibious notions, at least in an effort to make sense of the Confucian vision in the *Chung Yung* without making use of essentially contestable philosophical theses. In this way, we may have to content ourselves with *understanding* what the discourse is about without explaining its logic and ultimate bearing on philosophical problems. This would add a wider, though less secure, dimension to the philosophical enterprise. In Chinese thought this sort of effort is specially relevant to understanding Taoism and Ch'an (Zen) Buddhism.

Let me end my experiment in dialogue with Munitz with a note of appreciation. His conception of the mystery and transcendence of the world provides an occasion for my reflections on the significance of the Confucian ideal of central harmony. I do not know how far I have succeeded in establishing a modest base for a profitable dialogue. For the attempt, as I have mentioned at the beginning, is also an experiment in Confucian self-understanding. I should be content if I have given a plausible and interesting reading of the Confucian classic the *Chung Yung*.

Essay 3   Forgetting Morality
Reflections on a Theme in *Chuang Tzu*

The notion of *wang* or forgetting occupies a central place in *Chuang Tzu*.[1] Of interest to both reflective moral agents and philosophers is its emphasis on the necessity of forgetting moral distinctions in the attainment of *tao*. The principal aim of this essay is to offer a constructive explication of this theme from the point of view of a commitive moral agent, i.e., an agent committed to a moral practice or normative ethics. We shall offer a philosophical reconstruction of Chuang Tzu's view as compatible with Ryle's claim that it is absurd to speak of someone's forgetting the difference between right and wrong.[2] We believe that Chuang Tzu's notion, far from suggesting an anti-moral attitude, may be seen to embody a distinct meta-moral attitude that can have a practical import to a commitive agent, particularly to an agent's concern with the ideal dimension of moral experience.

I. THE ROLE OF FORGETTING IN TAOISM

Before proceeding to our exploration, let us briefly take cognizance of the role of the notion of *wang* or forgetting within the larger context of the philosophy of Chuang Tzu. The various occurrences of this notion may quite properly be construed as attempts to convey or depict, though not to describe, the nature and process of the experience of *tao*. The various uses of *wang* may thus be regarded as expressions of a doctrine that embodies fundamental ideas of strategy regarding the *tao*-experience. Since the *tao*-experience is non-intellectual, distinctions

1. Unless otherwise indicated, all references and translations used are based on Burton Watson, trans., *The Complete Works of Chuang Tzu* (New York: Columbia University Press, 1968). Hereafter cited as *Chuang Tzu*. For convenience I shall refer to Chuang Tzu as the author of the passages on *wang* found in *Chuang Tzu*. Since the relevant passages portray a fairly coherent viewpoint I have not observed the widely accepted distinction between the "inner" and "outer" chapters.
2. Gilbert Ryle, "On Forgetting the Difference Between Right and Wrong," in A. I. Melden, ed., *Essays in Moral Philosophy* (Seattle: University of Washington Press, 1958).

between things, in the broad sense as inclusive of objects, persons, actions, events, or states of affairs, are in some sense absent or blurred. The *tao*-experience is an experience of a unique, harmonious totality. As Fung points out, because of its concern with "pure experience," Taoism disparages knowledge.[3] In this state of pure experience, "there is an unbroken flux of experience, but the experiencer does not know it. He does not know that there are things, to say nothing of making distinctions between them."[4] There is no distinction between self and others. Thus it is said in *Chuang Tzu:* "the Perfect Man has no self; the Holy Man has no merits; the Sage has no fame."[5]

To forget distinctions is to enmesh oneself in experiencing the harmonious union of things, in Chuang's picturesque language, to have "mounted on the truth of Heaven and Earth, ridden the changes of the six breaths, and thus wandered through the boundless."[6] Forgetting distinctions is in this way a strategy, or more accurately, a *constitutive means* for attaining the *tao*-experience. It is a constitutive rather than a mere instrumental means that contributes to *tao*-attainment, and also in retrospective characterization, an ingredient feature in *tao*-experience itself.[7] It is one of "the arts of the Way *(tao-shu)*."[8] As Suzuki points out, the uses of such notions as *hsiang-wang* (mutually forgetting), *liang-wang* (both forgetting), and *tzu-wang* (self-forgetting) suggest that the person forgetting "absorbs both terms of the dichotomy [distinction?] completely in itself, and yet each retains its individuality." The character of *wang* consists of two components: *wang*, meaning "to lose," and

3. Fung Yu-lan, "Introduction," *Chuang Tzu: A New Selected Translation with an Exposition of the Philosophy of Kuo Hsiang* (New York: Paragon Book Reprint Corp., 1964; 1st ed. published in Shanghai, 1933), 15. Fung borrowed the term "pure experience" from William James's use in *Essays in Radical Empiricism.*

4. Fung, *Chuang Tzu,* 16–17. As Fung later points out, this "no-knowledge" is distinct from ignorance. "The fruit of discarding knowledge is no-knowledge, but this kind of no-knowledge comes from having passed through a stage of knowledge. It is not the no-knowledge of original ignorance." See Fung Yu-lan, *The Spirit of Chinese Philosophy* (London: Routledge & Kegan Paul, 1962), 78.

5. *Chuang Tzu,* 32.

6. Ibid.

7. In more standard idiom, forgetting distinctions is a "contributory" as distinct from a mere extrinsic or instrumental means, in that it contributes or is a part of *tao*-experience deemed as intrinsically good. [See C. A. Baylis, "Grading, Values, and Choice," *Mind* 67 (1958), no. 268.] Here I adopt Lau's terminology of "instrumental" and "constitutive" means, since it brings out more clearly the possibility of the internal connection between ideal and means within the life of some reflective agents. The notion of constitutive means is also crucial to understanding the Confucian strategy for ideal achievement, a point noted by Lau. This topic is worthy of further exploration. See Lau, "On Mencius' Use of Analogy in Argument," *Asia Major*, N.S. 10 (1963), reprinted as Appendix 5 in D. C. Lau, trans., *Mencius* (London: Penguin Books, 1970).

8. See the use of this expression throughout *Chuang Tzu,* chap. 33.

hsin, meaning "mind." "Thus 'to forget' is 'losing one's mind,' 'being freed from a consciousness of duality,' 'not being tied down to the idea of opposition,' 'transcending the sense of subject and object.'"[9]

It is important to note that the notion of *wang,* far from condemning distinctions, actually embraces them in *tao*-experience. Read in this way, many passages in *Chuang Tzu* have the purport of urging persons to forget distinctions, not in the sense of eliminating them, but in the sense of not being "tied down" or being obsessed with the importance commonly attached to them. We are urged to *forget* all distinctions, to engage in "the fasting of mind" and dwell in emptiness alone.[10] To attain *tao,* we are to forget the self, even forget life itself, and become one with Heaven.[11] Just as "the fish forget each other in the rivers and lakes, men [of *tao*-experience] forget each other in the arts of the Way."[12] Chuang Tzu focuses thus on his *master concern* with *tao*-experience. However, an exclusive emphasis on the character of *tao*-achievement may suggest an uncompromising negative attitude toward morality. The Perfect Man, according to Chuang Tzu, "can put Heaven and earth outside himself, forget the ten thousand things, and his spirit has no cause to be wearied. He dismissed benevolence *(jen)* and righteousness *(i),* rejects rites *(li)* and music, for the mind of the Perfect Man knows where to find repose."[13] It is this sort of passage that clearly portrays the mystical and religious aspects of Taoism. But the negative attitude at issue need not be construed as incompatible with an acceptance of a Confucian or other moral practice—a theme to which we shall return in subsequent exploration.

In understanding *Chuang Tzu* one cannot thus ignore this central theme of *tao*-experience, for the work does prominently display what Creel termed "contemplative Taoism," i.e., a doctrine favored by the mystics who are "desirous only of contemplating the universe and achieving inner peace."[14] However, it is less a theoretical doctrine than an *attitude* toward human affairs and nature, of unconcern with happenings and human actions aiming at the resolution of moral problems and dilemmas as confronted by ordinary commitive agents. Viewed in this way, forgetting distinctions has no peculiar import for commitive agents, though for the Taoists who aimlessly enjoy the free and easy

9. D. T. Suzuki, "Introduction" to James Legge's *Texts of Taoism* (New York: The Julian Press, 1959), 35.
10. *Chuang Tzu,* 58, 135.
11. Ibid., 60, 112, 133, 197–98, 372.
12. Ibid., 87.
13. Ibid., 151. See also 155, 207.
14. Herrlee G. Creel, *What Is Taoism? and Other Studies in Chinese Cultural History* (Chicago: University of Chicago Press, 1970), 44.

wandering, it is a constitutive strategy for *tao*-experience. In this view, morality seems to be relegated to the limbo of the meaningless, of the region of insignificance, for what is prized by these Taoists is the experience of the purity of the mystic vision itself.[15] Forgetting distinctions is a constitutive strategy, but when the *tao* is achieved, one forgets even the strategy of forgetting; one simply enjoys in free wandering, unmindful of the distinctions themselves.[16]

In the following exploration we shall not be concerned with the role of *wang* or forgetting in depicting a constitutive strategy for the attainment of *tao*-experience. We have "bracketed" from our concern the quasi-metaphysical and mystical aspects of Taoism to focus on the significance and plausibility of this notion for reflective moral agents.

II. CHUANG TZU AND PROFESSOR RYLE

At the outset we assumed that Chuang Tzu's notion of *wang* or forgetting is an intelligible notion. This assumption appears unproblematic, since we were concerned with a coherent statement of its role in the nature and process of *tao*-experience. In terms of Ryle's claim that

15. The Confucians of *Chung Yung*, and Neo-Confucians in general, share with Taoists the vision of *tao* as creative harmony. In Essay 4, I contrast the Taoist and Confucian perspectives as two distinct but complementary responsive attitudes toward the import of *tao* as an ideal theme. For the Confucian articulation of this vision in *Chung Yung* and the problem of actualization, see "Practical Causation and Confucian Ethics," *Philosophy East and West* 25, no. 1 (1975), 1–10.

16. I am not concerned with what Creel called "purposive Taoism," which seems to "have arisen from the attempt [of some men] to utilize an essentially mystical doctrine for the furtherance of personal ambitions and political purposes" (Creel, pp. 44–45). However, though Creel's distinction is a useful one as a logical dichotomy, it seems to preclude any intelligible concern with the moral significance of contemplative Taoism. What Creel regards as contemplative Taoism is deeply rooted in a more basic Taoist attitude toward meditation as a state of mind, of "free and easy wandering." Since contemplation carries the suggestion of an attentive state of mind directed to certain focal objects or ideas, it is perhaps better to characterize classical Taoism as meditative Taoism. The religious attitude at issue is an attempt to free the mind from preoccupation with any matter whatsoever—inclusive of objects of contemplation—in order to allow the person to meander through the flux of nature. The Taoist meditation is wandering with no directive aim. It is more a "vacuous" state of mind in which the person simply *lets* things be. It is of course not a passive state but a cultivated responsiveness to the presence of things. In this way, the aim of meditation is freedom from all attachment. distinctions between things may appear but they have no hold upon the meditator. This is suggested by the analogy of mind and mirror, which I shall later discuss. More important, perhaps, is the recognition of the possibility that a meditative Taoist may take a practical turn without being a "purposive" Taoist in Creel's sense. This possibility permits exploration of the ethical significance of classical Taoism, for which is needed a distinction between "meditative" and "practical" Taoism. In this distinction (not an exclusive disjunction), "purposive" Taoism so-called can be regarded as an example of abuse of practical Taoism.

it is absurd to speak of someone's forgetting the difference between right and wrong, our inquiry into the significance of the notion of *wang* may be questioned. We can meet this challenge by insisting quite properly that Chuang Tzu's remarks should not be construed as literary uses of language. They may appear to embody conceptual absurdities, but a deeper analysis reveals that they are illuminating conceptual distortions or oddities. It is acknowledged in one chapter that Chuang Chou [Chuang Tzu] expounded the Taoist views "in odd and outlandish terms, in brash and bombastic language. . . . He believed that the world was drawn in turbidness and that it was impossible to address it in sober language."[17] This suggests that the remarks in *Chuang Tzu* are to be seen as paradoxical ways of expressing the Taoist views, as attempts to use "bombastic language" or conceptual distortions, in lieu of "sober language" or ordinary literary language, in order to convey certain insights. However, this approach to the problem of intelligibility leaves open a further question: Granted that Chuang Tzu's remarks on *wang* or forgetting are intelligible, how is this notion to be explicated? If we follow Suzuki in remarking that *wang* is "to forget" and "to forget" is "to lose one's mind," "being freed from a consciousness of duality," "not being tied down to the idea of opposition," etc.,[18] we leave unanswered the question of how these phrases are to be construed, in particular, when one is said "to forget the difference between right and wrong." Far from being clear, all these phrases appear to be in need of further explanation. A Taoist philosopher may rejoin that our question involves the exposition of the entire text of *Chuang Tzu,* that no simple answer can be given. We shall not pursue this reply here, for our immediate purpose lies in the possibility of reconciling Chuang Tzu and Ryle on the idea of forgetting moral distinctions.

We shall assume that *wang* is equivalent to "forgetting," and that Chuang Tzu and Ryle appear to hold opposing views on the idea of forgetting moral distinctions. Then, acknowledging the paradoxical character of Chuang Tzu's remarks, we shall attempt a reconciliation. If we are successful, we need not be bogged down by the question of proper analysis. So long as some sense can be given to Chuang Tzu's uses, we are content to proceed further and elaborate our reconstruction. As Waismann points out, "language is plastic, yielding the will to express, even at the price of some obscurity."[19] So long as we can dispel

17. *Chuang Tzu,* chap. 33, p. 373.
18. Suzuki, 35.
19. F. Waismann, "How I See Philosophy" in H. D. Lewis, ed., *Contemporary British Philosophy,* 3d ser. (London: George Allen and Unwin, 1956), 472.

the obscurity embodied in Chuang Tzu's remarks, we shall have obtained a ground for their plausibility.[20]

"What is the absurdity in the idea of a person's forgetting the difference between right and wrong?" This question formed the central topic of one of Ryle's insightful essays. This question assumes outright that the idea of forgetting moral distinctions is absurd, and this naturally raises the question on the meaning of "forgetting." We shall follow Ryle's exploration of *his* question. Ryle suggests that we approach the question of absurdity of the idea of forgetting the difference between right and wrong by considering the question of teaching or learning that distinction, in particular, with the learning of taste. "Taste is educated preference, preference for recognized superiorities. To be able to recognize superiorities is to know the difference between good and bad."[21] However, "learning to enjoy, to love, or to admire is not acquiring a skill or a parcel of information. Nonetheless it *is* learning."[22] It is learning to appreciate or care for the difference in the quality of the objects of taste and preferences. Likewise, when we turn to the notion of moral knowledge, in particular to the distinction between right and wrong, some notion of care is involved. For instance, if a person is totally indifferent to the keeping or breaking of his promise, or to kindness or cruelty, we are quite unwilling to allow that he has learned the difference.[23] In this way we can see why it is ridiculous to say that one can forget the difference between right and wrong, for:

> To have been taught the difference is to have been brought up to appreciate the difference, and this appreciation is not just a capacity to do things efficiently. It includes an *inculcated caring*, a habit of taking certain sorts of things seriously.[24]

It cannot be denied that Ryle's insight lies in pointing out a basic characteristic of moral agency. Part of being a moral agent is to exemplify a basic attitude of care for the distinction between right and

20. In view of our limited aim we have focussed only on some philosophically relevant passages. Thus we make no pretense to offering an adequate account of all of Chuang Tzu's uses.

21. Ryle, 151.

22. Ibid., 153.

23. Ryle continues: "This caring is not a special feeling; it covers a variety of feelings, like those that go with being shocked, ashamed, indignant, admiring, emulous, disgusted, and enthusiastic; but it covers also a variety of actions, as well as readiness and proneness to do things, like apologizing, scolding, praising, persevering, praying, confessing, and making good resolutions" (ibid., p. 155). In other words, we have here a notion of care that embraces a variety of the feelings and actions that appear to embody a basic *attitude* characteristic of a moral agent as distinct from an indifferent or amoral agent (ibid.).

24. Ibid., 156. Italics mine.

wrong. Being brought up as a moral agent is being *inculcated* with this basic attitude rather than just having imparted to one a set of moral rules or principles. This attitude of caring is basic in the sense that it renders intelligible a variety of agent's reactive feelings and actions toward its object, not just in the sense of a fundamental principle, but in the sense of exemplifying that attitude of seriousness toward the objects deemed to have moral import. If this point is granted, one can appreciate that moral teaching is not just imparting of moral requirements, a teaching of know-how or techniques for the solution of problems, but also, an inculcation of caring. Since caring is an attitude rather than a principle, different persons may express their care in different ways. In this sense, there are different ways of caring and these ways depend on the import of the content of the moral practice for individual agents. Thus a commitment to moral principles or rules does not necessarily imply a determination of their import to individual agents. The different ways of expression of caring may portray idiosyncratic concerns quite independent of the content of the moral practice and, consequently, independent of the content of one's moral knowledge.

Having now acknowledged Ryle's insight into the importance of inculcated caring in moral learning or teaching, let us turn to his claim on the absurdity of the idea of forgetting moral distinctions. Some notion of forgetting is essential to supporting Ryle's claim. Consider the following:

Ceasing to care is not forgetting, any more than ceasing to believe something or mistrust someone is forgetting. "Forget" is reserved, apparently, mainly for the nonretention of information and loss of skills through desuetude, though it is also used for ceasing to notice things, e.g., for the oblivion brought by sleep or distractions.[25]

Ryle thus recognizes two different senses of "forgetting." A primary sense that occurs in contexts of loss of memory or inability to do things that one has previously learned to do. If a person's forgetting moral distinction makes use of this primary sense, the absurdity is obvious. However, in another sense, it seems intelligible to use the notion of forgetting for ceasing to care for moral distinction, which parallels ceasing to notice things. Ryle's remark seems to rule this out, but the absurdity at issue depends on the insistence on the sole propriety of the primary sense of "forgetting" in moral contexts. It appears to be quite proper to use "forgetting" for contexts in which one treats matters with inattention or neglect, as in cases when one is said to be inattentive to or

25. Ibid.

unmindful of things which one is supposed to do—keeping an appointment or paying one's bills on time. In this use, one can forget the difference between right and wrong in the sense of not paying attention to the difference. One ceases to care for moral distinctions just as one ceases to notice certain things. What is crucial for Chuang Tzu is this sense of ceasing to care, and not the sense of losing one's memory or skill through desuetude, for to attain the *tao*-experience, one has to cease to care for distinctions. Admittedly, there is a conceptual oddity involved in this notion of forgetting, but it can be rendered intelligible without absurdity. For passages relevant to our concern, one can describe Chuang Tzu's intent by saying that he was attempting to erect a secondary sense of "forgetting" as a significant notion without usurping the legitimate function of the primary one. Thus in the passage we have previously quoted: "The fish forget each other in the rivers and the lakes, men forget each other in the Arts of the Way," we can simply substitute "do not pay attention to," or "ceasing to care" for the term "forget" without losing the purport of the passage.

Bearing in mind the second sense of "forgetting," Chuang Tzu's notion of *wang* seems an intelligible notion. To forget moral distinction, in this sense, is to cease to care for the distinction, though the notion easily suggests an attitude of indifference. To avoid this misleading suggestion, one can treat the expression "ceasing to care" as an elliptical way of saying "ceasing to care in a certain way." Thus to forget moral distinction is to cease to care for that distinction in certain ways. This notion of ceasing to care is quite compatible with Ryle's stress on learning moral distinction as including an inculcated caring, for what is important to Chuang Tzu is not the basic attitude of caring, but the *way* of caring. "Ceasing to care" for distinction in certain ways is to be construed as *being free* from certain ways of caring, and this freedom from care is not a denial of care in the sense of not-caring or indifference. As White points out, "the carefree child may or may not give his attention to something; when he does, he is not worried by it."[26] It is this freedom from care that seems important to Chuang Tzu's notion of *wang*, which we have equated with the notion of forgetting as ceasing to care in certain ways. To "forget" moral distinctions is to cease to pay attention to the ways in which ordinary moral agents care for them. "Forgetting" in this sense implies a cultivated attitude that is exemplified in a sort of intentional, but non-deliberate response to objects, sit-

26. Alan White, *Philosophy of Mind* (New York: Random House, 1967), 79. For the image of infant in *Lao Tzu*, see chaps. 10, 20, 28, 49, 55; and Chuang Tzu's image of a newborn calf, *Chuang Tzu*, 237.

uations, and states of affairs. This is suggested by the following passage:

The fish trap exists because of the fish; once you've gotten the fish, you can forget the trap. The rabbit snare exists because of the rabbit; once you've gotten the rabbit, you can forget the snare. Words exist because of meaning; once you've gotten the meaning, you can forget the words. Where can I find a man who has forgotten words, so I can have a word with him?[27]

"Forget" in this passage has the force of "not paying attention to," but it does not imply the sense of loss of memory. The purport of passages of this sort seems to lie in redirecting the attention of men from their normal preoccupation with distinctions or matters deemed important. Chuang Tzu realizes that it is difficult to inculcate this carefree attitude toward matters of ordinary concerns. He focusses on the importance of this attitude in self-transformation. Thus he could agree with Ryle that "ceasing to care" has to do with self-transformation[28]— that when I have ceased to care for moral distinctions, I have changed. Chuang Tzu wishes to inculcate an attitude or perspective to assess rather than to abolish moral distinctions. This attitude, to be intelligible, presupposes the existence of moral distinctions. To put it in a different way, "forgetting" moral distinctions is a way of experiencing the import of the distinction. The importance of moral distinction is recognized, but it is regarded in a certain light, and in the case of Chuang Tzu, in the light of *tao*. Consider the following:

Tao is obscured by partiality. Speech is observed by eloquence. Therefore, these are the contentions between the Confucians and the Mohists. Each one of these two schools affirms what the other denies, and denies what the other affirms, there is nothing better than to use clarity *(ming)*.[29]

27. *Chuang Tzu*, 302. The last occurrence of the notion of forgetting in this passage seems puzzling. But since Chuang Tzu purports to inculcate the attitude of ceasing to care, we can bring out his point by construing his remark with an interpolation: "Where can I find a man who has ceased to care for (or ceased to pay attention to) words (without regard to their meanings) so I can have a word with him?" So construed, this is not a denial of the importance of words, but a criticism of obsession with words without regard for their meanings. Since we are not concerned with all the uses of *wang* in *Chuang Tzu*, we do not pretend to offer an account of all of Chuang Tzu's uses. However, we believe that a coherent account of such uses must involve a recognition of the basic attitude which we attempt to elucidate in this essay.
28. Cf. Ryle, 156.
29. Fung, *Chuang Tzu*, 49. This is Fung's translation with the substitution of "clarity" for "*ming*" rather than Fung's "light of reason," for the latter suggests the notion of *logos* or reason, whereas what seems intended is a sort of enlightenment or understanding that results from seeing opposing moral views or judgments as complementary rather than exclusive. We have thus followed Watson in rendering *ming* as "clarity." And this, as we noted in Section I, is a matter of experience rather than intellectual knowledge.

Kuo Hsiang explains this passage thus: "That there is a distinction of right and wrong is what the Confucians and Mohists affirm. That there is no such distinction is what they deny. To affirm what they deny and to deny what they affirm is to show there is no such distinction [in the dichotomous sense]."[30] This is what is called embarking upon two courses at once, or equalizing opposites or opposing views by regarding each as a legitimate expression from its point of view of right and wrong. The recommended attitude here is not one of unqualified rejection of the distinction, but a proposal to use *ming* or clarity as a way of dealing with exclusive claims to insight into the nature of morality.[31] To Chuang Tzu, the ideal sage is one who moves like water, is still like a mirror, and responds to things and events like an echo.[32] His mind is like a *clear mirror* responsive to changing events.[33] The attitude at issue does not imply an unqualified rejection of legitimacy of moral distinctions or notions. This Taoist attitude is very clearly stated in *Lieh Tzu:*

Nowhere is there a principle which is right in all circumstances or an action that is wrong in all circumstances. The method we use yesterday we may discard today and use again in the future; there are no fixed right and wrong to decide whether we use it or not. The capacity to pick times and snatch opportunities, and be never at a loss to answer events belongs to the wise.[34]

This critique of moral views does not imply that they are wrong or that a form of ethical skepticism or relativism is to be preferred. It is rather a critique of the tendency of moral theories to construe moral distinctions in some exclusive way, thus enunciating what appear to be unvarying or fixed principles of conduct. The critique, we suggest, draws attention to the importance of an attitude rather than implies an ethical theory.

However, it may be queried whether Chuang Tzu and other Taoists were suggesting a form of perceptual intuitionism in Sidgwick's sense, i.e., the intuitivist doctrine which holds that the rightness of an action is always determined by a particular context or situation, rather than

30. Ibid. The bracketed expression is our interpolation to indicate Chuang Tzu's view on the relativity of moral distinctions.
31. In one passage, this clarity of mind is said to be inherent in each man's nature (*Chuang Tzu,* 38–39). But this seems inconsistent with the general tenor of his notion of *wang,* since the attitude at issue is a result of cultivation rather than an expression of one's inborn nature.
32. Ibid., 374.
33. Ibid., 97.
34. A. C. Graham, trans., *Lieh Tzu* (London: John Murray, 1960), 163–64. For a discussion of a parallel theme in Confucian ethics, see my "The Concept of Paradigmatic Individuals in the Ethics of Confucius," *Inquiry* 14, nos. 1–2 (1971): 41–55.

by rules or principles.[35] In other words, the view that right action is an *occasional* determination within a particular concrete circumstance rather than a matter of principles. It is interesting to note that Chuang Tzu's "clarity of mind" seems to suggest a theory of perceptual intuition, but his point is perhaps best construed in a non-epistemic way. The point of harmonizing opposing views on right and wrong does not necessarily presuppose a superior faculty of cognition, but of a sense of at-one-ness or at-home-ness in the world. Thus the sage "harmonizes with both right and wrong and rests in Heaven the Equalizer. This is called walking two roads."[36] It implies an attitude that can be elucidated by viewing opposing moral theories, opinions, or judgments as displaying complementary rather than contrary or contradictory theses. Each view can properly be deemed acceptable within a certain domain of experience or contexts or problems, given certain assumptions that define the nature of the point of view at issue. A Confucian, for instance, given his preoccupation with personal cultivation and well-ordered society, is quite properly insistent upon *jen*, *li*, and other virtues. The "partiality" lies in its tendency to the exclusive founding of the significance of morality upon its favored moral notions.

We can also appreciate the Taoist attitude if we construe it as having relevance to moral theories and conventional morality, that is, in terms of its insistence upon the "cash value" of moral notions such as right and wrong, *jen* and *li* in the concrete contexts of live problems and perplexities. From the point of view of a reflective agent, the difficulty of accepting, with no qualification, any moral doctrine lies in its almost unavoidable tendency to regard all human actions and affairs as subsumable within a corpus of moral principles and rules, thus blinding us to the heart of moral experience as a live and significant experience. To abide by moral distinctions, whether they are embedded in moral tradition or a product of reflective analysis, is to fall into the trap of words, contentions, and disputes which bear little relevance to the experience of problems and perplexities. This is a Taoist critique of an insidious tendency of many moral thinkers and agents to be obsessed by their own views of moral distinctions. Thus, Chuang Tzu can be said to urge us to "forget" these views and the distinctions so construed.

35. See Henry Sidgwick, *Methods of Ethics*, 7th ed. (London: Macmillen), 1972, bk. I, chap. VIII. Note that this view need not be construed as incompatible with the acceptance of moral principles. For further discussion, see my *Reason and Virtue: A Study in the Ethics of Richard Price* (Athens: Ohio University Press, 1966), chap. 7.

36. *Chuang Tzu*, 41. So also: "The torch of chaos and doubt—that is what the sage steers by. So he does not use things but relegates all to the constant. This is what it means to use clarity" (ibid., 42).

From the conceptual point of view, this need not be construed as a recommendation to eliminate our moral vocabulary, but as a way of making us aware of our general tendency to erect distinctions into exclusive disjunctions, thus blinding us to appreciating the character of moral situations as we experience them in our own lives.

In responding with a clear mind to what the situation demands, we must first attend to every situation as if it were a new situation in order to appreciate its character. Of course what the situation demands depends on our judgment, but the judgment at issue is an *occasional* exercise of our "clarity of mind" and not determined *a priori* by our principles and rules. And the best way for us to attend to the situation, paradoxically, involves a sort of inattention to moral principles and rules. Thus we have "forgotten" our conceptual distinctions in the sense of holding in abeyance our readiness to apply them. In this way, "forgetting" moral distinctions, far from condemning them, is a way of appreciating or caring for them, for their import lies in concrete situations seen with "the clarity of mind." What moral knowledge we have is learned through the process of moral growth, through the application of moral notions to appropriate cases. But this knowledge does not dictate all our future actions. The point of forgetting distinctions is, as we have previously noted, not of ceasing care, but of ceasing to care for distinctions in a certain way, in the light of seeing these distinctions as capturing merely aspects of moral experience. The notion of rightness of action, for a commitive agent, remains an open term. Moral issues are not foreclosed by a commitment to principles. Thus "right" is a term open to judgment in particular contexts. The notions of right and wrong as expounded by various moral doctrines, in this way, possess merely "credit value." They are bills to be filled. And these bills can be filled in an appropriate setting without prejudging the question of what a moral agent ought to do in a particular circumstance. They may be regarded as complementary in the sense of completing a "more adequate view" that embraces the significance which each legitimates. This is *tao* as a sort of *ideal theme* (as distinct from an ideal norm with preceptive implications, a vision of an excellent way of life, and not a holistic doctrine that synthesizes opposing viewpoints of morality).[37] "Forgetting" morality exemplifies this attitude toward an ideal theme— an ideal for which no knowledge is claimed, no action proclaimed to be right or wrong in advance of moral experience. It is a matter of

37. I do not mean to preclude such quasi-metaphysical interpretation. We are merely concerned to point to the Taoist attitude construed as having a moral import. For a further discussion, see essays cited in n. 15.

responding to changing events with clarity of mind, and not a denial of moral knowledge.[38] The clarity of mind is a state of "heightened perceptiveness and responsiveness"[39] sometimes called a state of "true forgetfulness."[40] Thus Chuang Tzu does not reject moral knowledge in Ryle's sense. It is a proposal to view moral distinctions in a certain way. Chuang Tzu's notion of forgetting is thus compatible with Ryle's stress on moral knowledge as including an inculcated caring. In the next section, we shall offer an elucidation of the practical significance of this attitude.

III. A META-MORAL ATTITUDE

In the preceding discussion we have attempted to show that Chuang Tzu's notion of forgetting moral distinctions can be plausibly construed as embodying a distinct moral attitude. To "forget" moral distinctions is, in a basic sense, *to be free from* certain ways of caring rather than to be indifferent to moral requirements. It is, in effect, to be free from care, and yet, when one attends to matters-at-hand, to be without worry or anxiety. This attitude is congenial to Confucius. It is said in the *Analects* (14:30) that "a man of wisdom is free from perplexity; a man of *jen* from anxiety; a man of courage from fear."[41] What then appears as distinctive in Taoism is its focus on the achievement of *tao*. This contrasts with the more homely concern of the Confucians with the relevance of this attitude to the normative management of moral problems and human affairs. However, the Taoist attitude is not devoid of practical significance. Detached from its role as a constitutive strategy for

38. This point seems to be suggested in the following: "Where there is recognition of right there must be recognition of wrong; where there is recognition of wrong there must be recognition of right. Therefore the sage does not proceed in such a way, but illuminates all in the light of Heaven. He too recognizes a 'this,' but a 'this' which is also 'that,' a 'that' which is also 'this.' His 'that' has both a right and wrong in it; and his 'this' has both a right and wrong in it. So, in fact, does he still have a 'this' and 'that'? Or does he in fact no longer have a 'this' and 'that'? A state in which 'this' and 'that' no longer find their opposites it called the hinge of the way. When the hinge is fitted into the socket, it can respond endlessly. Its right then is a single endlessness and its wrong too is a single endlessness. So I say, the best thing to use is clarity" (*Chuang Tzu*, 40).
39. Graham, *Lieh Tzu*, p. 7.
40. "When men do not forget what can be forgotten, but forget what cannot be forgotten—that may be called true forgetting" (*Chuang Tzu*, 75). This passage seems to equivocate between two senses of "forgetting," but the point seems clear, "true forgetting" lies in being mindful of things that can be easily forgotten (in the sense of not remembering) and in forgetting (in the sense of being free from care for) what one remembers. Thus true forgetfulness is a state of freedom from attachment to things one cannot fail to remember, and not a failure of memory.
41. "If we use the unperplexed to dispel perplexity and return to unperplexity, this will be the greatest unperplexity" (*Chuang Tzu*, 279).

pure experience, the Taoist attitude stresses freeing oneself from ex-
cessive preoccupation with praise and blame,[42] beauty and strength,[43]
and poverty, titles, and stipends.[44] The adoption and cultivation of this
attitude is more like an acquisition of an ability or a knack for doing
things. In response to the question "Can a person learn how to handle
a boat?" we get this reply: "Certainly. A good swimmer will in no time
get the knack of it . . . , that means he's forgotten the water."[45] One can
acquire the attitude or the ability to "forget" by discipline and practice,
but it cannot be acquired as a skill. In this sense, the Taoist notion of
forgetting is like the notion of noticing. As White explains, "although
appropriate schooling and practice can put us in a certain condition to
notice what we used to miss, people cannot be taught nor can they learn
how to notice, as they can be taught or can learn how to detect. Noticing, unlike solving, is not the exercise of a skill."[46] One can be taught,
in a sense, how to swim; but to be a good swimmer is to be able to
acquire the knack of managing oneself in water, "forgetful" of the
water itself. One does it spontaneously and effortlessly. And in the case
of morality, one can exemplify this attitude without conscious deliberation, though this is a result of discipline and persevering practice.
Nevertheless, one can acquire the attitude as one can acquire moral
traits or dispositions—for example, conscientiousness, goodwill, and
integrity. The significance of Chuang Tzu's notion of forgetting thus
lies in the inculcation of a moral attitude rather than the teaching of a
skill.

Let us now turn to an elucidation of this moral attitude. Chuang
Tzu's notion of forgetting moral distinctions embodies an evaluative
attitude toward human appraisals in general, but it does not deny the
importance of ordinary moral appraisals. Confucian virtues, for example, need not be condemned, but rather viewed in a *new light* furnished by this attitude. One passage in *Chuang Tzu* bears this point:

The sage contemplates Heaven but does not assist it. He finds completion in
virtue but piles on nothing more. He goes forth in the Way but does not scheme.
He accords with benevolence (*jen*) but does not set great store by it. He draws
close to righteousness (*i*) but does not labor over it. He responds to the demands

42. Ibid., 80, 297–98.
43. Ibid., 89–90.
44. Ibid., 218. And we may add that, for contemporary moral philosophers, this is
a reminder of the danger of being excessively preoccupied with language without attending to the speaker's deeper intention in the use of words (*Chuang Tzu*, 152, 302).
45. Ibid., 200. See also the nice story of Cook Ting's use of butcher's knife (ibid.,
50–52).
46. White, 69.

of ritual *(li)* and does not shun them. He disposes of affairs and makes no excuses.[47]

The point, then, is to accept these moral virtues with a spirit of detachment, or better, with a spirit of non-attachment to the intrinsic importance commonly ascribed to them. The attitude is not one of indifference, but focuses upon the necessity of a perspective of *tao* or an ideal which ultimately renders these virtues significant for the commitive agents.[48]

For the non-Taoist agents, this attitude of "forgetting" can be rendered plausible for adoption, if we regard it as a moral attitude, more properly, a *meta-moral* attitude within the realm of moral concerns rather than an attitude that ontologically transcends or absolves all moral distinctions. It is a "meta-moral" attitude, that is, a second-order rather than a first-order moral attitude—an evaluative attitude that pertains to first-order moral appraisals.[49] But unlike other second-order moral attitudes or dispositions, such as conscientiousness, respect for relevant facts, and moral autonomy, our meta-moral attitude pertains more to the region of moral perplexities than to the region of moral problems. Thus it is a meta-moral attitude toward moral principles, rules, and virtues. We shall call it a "*tao*-attitude," since this attitude expresses a distinctive Chinese ideal theme of *tao* as harmony.[50] The adoption of this attitude can free moral agents from wearied engrossment in moral thinking in solving problems, not by suggesting a norm nor a supra-moral norm, but by suggesting the import of an ideal orientation or perspective for conducting moral thinking. For agents in search of life's meaning or personal identity, an understanding of the *tao*-attitude offers a possible answer to their perplexity. It is germane, in particular, to the moral dilemmas that arise out of a reflection on commitment to moral principles and on the readiness to apply moral

47. *Chuang Tzu*, 125. Italics mine.
48. "Look at words in the light of the Way *(tao)*—then the sovereign of the world will be upright. Look at distinctions in the light of the Way—then the duty of sovereign and subject will be clear. Look at abilities in the light of the Way—then the officials of the world will be well-ordered. Look everywhere in the light of the Way—then the response of ten thousand things will be complete" (ibid., 126).
49. For a discussion of this distinction between first-order and second-order virtues, see William K. Frankena, *Ethics*, 2d ed. (Englewood Cliffs: Prentice Hall, 1973), 68–70.
50. It may be called a "Taoistic attitude" in the sense of a meta-moral attitude inspired by reflections on the significance of a theme in *Chuang Tzu*. For a contrast with the Confucian attitude, see Essay 2. We may also note here that the *tao*-attitude bears a close affinity to Royce and James's stress on the "higher vision of inner significance" as basic to being a moral person, or in Frankena's words, as "part of what is involved in taking the moral point of view." This attitude involves a recognition and appreciation of the needs and interests of others, an awareness of others as persons (Frankena, 69–70).

notions without regard to the possibility of embedding these notions with an ideal theme.[51]

The *tao*-attitude elevates rather than depreciates or abrogates the importance of moral distinctions. We may elucidate the significance of the *tao*-attitude by comparing it to an ideal of forgiveness. Strawson points out:

> To be forgiven is something that we sometimes ask, and forgiveness is something we sometimes say we do. To ask to be forgiven is in part to acknowledge that the attitude displayed in our action was such as might properly be resented and in part to repudiate that attitude for the future (or at least for the immediate future); and to forgive is to accept that repudiation and to forswear the resentment.[52]

But suppose that the wrongdoer does not ask for forgiveness, and yet the person who suffers from the wrong still forgives. The wrongdoer's own repudiation is deemed irrelevant to our agent's act of forgiveness. We shall suppose that our agent espouses an *ideal of forgiveness* quite independent of the wrongdoer's repudiation of his deed. In this act of our supposed agent, who is a victim of a wrongdoing of another, his act of forgiveness, far from repudiating the distinction between right and wrong, preserves the import of the distinction in the light of an ideal perspective. Here what is *transcended* is not the distinction but the normal focus on the notion of blame that commonly attends the judgment of wrongdoing.

However, transcendence should not be interpreted in an ontological way, for the import of the ideal of forgiveness is sublunary rather than otherworldly. In this ideal sense of forgiveness, the agent redirects his normal attitude toward the act of wrongdoing as an act of a responsible agent, to another attitude toward the wrongdoer. Instead of a vengeful response or a feeling of resentment toward the wrongdoer, our agent forgives him. To forgive the wrongdoer is, in this sense, to *accept* him without regard to his deed. In a sense, he *transcends* moral judgments. But for this act of transcendence to be intelligible, our agent must be supposed to have made a moral judgment on a fellow agent's act as an act from which he suffers injury. In other words, this ideal of forgiveness presupposes rather than abolishes moral distinction. The forgiv-

---

51. For an insightful discussion of moral principles as a source of moral dilemmas, see D. Z. Phillips and H. O. Mounce, *Moral Practices* (London: Routledge & Kegan Paul, 1969), chap. 8. For a discussion of moral perplexities that resist problematic treatment, see Section V of my "Relevance of Moral Rules and Creative Agency," *The New Scholasticism* 47, no. 1 (1973): 1–21.

52. P. F. Strawson, "Freedom and Resentment," *Proceedings of British Academy* 48 (1962): 191.

ing act thereby preserves the distinction by endowing an ideal significance to the wrongdoer as a person. In a way, our forgiving agent is
upholding and withholding moral distinctions at the same time. The
fact that an act has been judged to be wrong implies an upholding of
a distinction between right and wrong; but the act of forgiveness is
withholding any further consequences that normally attend the application of moral distinctions. The forgiving act withholds in the sense
of suspending any further acts as a direct response to wrongdoing as,
for example, resentment or a demand for sanctions; in other words,
suspending any further significance attached to the application of
moral distinctions.

The ideal forgiving attitude we have characterized above bears a
close affinity to our *tao*-attitude. We may even regard it as a possible
expression of the *tao*-attitude. For in forgiving, in our ideal sense, we
accept the wrongdoer as a person in spite of his deed. To accept an agent
as a person in this light is to embrace or regard him as possessing the
same moral status of agency—that status which the wrongdoer occupied prior to his wrongdoing. It is as if we have *forgetten*, in the sense
of ceasing to care for, his deed and are now ready to enter into a relationship with him as a moral agent *qua* moral agent. When we forgive
him, we regard him as a moral agent *de novo*. He is, as it were, a moral
agent again capable of relating to us on the *status of equality*. As victims,
we have transcended by ceasing to care for his past deed. We have now
accepted him as a person whom we are to deal with anew—in a new
light that "forgets" his past. The practical import of ceasing to care for
a man's past conduct thus involves a recognition of the importance of
regarding men as persons possessing equal status. The *tao*-attitude further stresses the *harmony* between persons. It involves an attitude toward human beings—an attitude of *taking* humans as persons rather
than as things.[53]

When one *takes* another as a person rather than as a thing, one is
not supposing or assuming that he or she possesses a peculiar descriptive property. Thus the notion of assessment in terms of truth or falsity
seems out of place. Taking someone, *A*, to be a person is more like
adopting a moral attitude that forbids one to treat A in ways in which
one normally treats material objects or animals. We can of course re-
fuse to take *A* as a person, and in doing so, perhaps feel justified in
treating *A* with total moral indifference. Thus we can insult *A*. And to
insult *A* is to debase him in some way. But this debasement seems pos-

53. Readers may note this Wittgenstenian inspiration. See *Philosophical Investigations*
(New York: Macmillan, 1953), I, #281 and II, 178.

sible because of a prior acknowledgement of A as a person to be dealt with in some morally decent way. Likewise, the ascription of dignity to a man is a moral ascription, and not an empirical description. It is taking a normative stance toward him, exemplifying an attitude toward men as persons rather than as things.

We can also appreciate the significance of the tao-attitude in the context of moral problems that arise out of conflict between the interests of different individuals. Since the ideal theme of harmony involved in the tao-attitude does not provide a principle or norm for adjudication, it cannot resolve the issue of conflicting interests. However, in stressing the harmony between persons, it can offer a perspective for reconciliation by addressing the practical possibility and importance of persons living in harmony. To reconcile persons, in this sense, is to make them aware of the importance of living together in spite of their differences. It is, so to speak, to join them in friendship. The differences remain the subject of moral appraisal, but whatever principle of appraisal one espouses, the ideal perspective, if recognized by the persons in dispute, can lighten the burden or the task of resolution. One can, of course, espouse an ideal norm or principle of harmony that aims at inclusively integrating individual interests, as for example, in the case of James and Perry, but this notion of harmony is quite distinct from that of tao.[54] For the tao-attitude is essentially a person-directed rather than a subject-directed attitude. It focuses on the persons-in-dispute rather than on the subject-matter of dispute. Thus the notion of harmony involved is what we call an ideal theme rather than an ideal norm. Seen in this way, the tao-attitude offers an ideal perspective for any normative settlement of conflicting interests without providing an adjudicating principle of resolution.[55]

IV. CONCERN AND TRANSCENDENCE

In this closing section we shall reflect on the more personal significance of the tao-attitude for moral agents committed to a moral practice. Most moral agents acquire a respect for a moral practice in the process of being taught to discriminate between right and wrong ac-

54. See William James, "The Moral Philosopher and The Moral Life," in Essays on Faith and Morals (New York: Longmans, Green and Co., 1949), 208–10; and Ralph Barton Perry, General Theory of Value (Cambridge: Harvard University Press, 1950), chaps. 21 and 22.

55. This distinction between the ideal theme and the ideal norm of harmony is not an exclusive disjunction. For a further discussion see my "On the Quality of Human Life," Proceedings of the Society for General Systems Research (1975), 64–67.

tions. Ryle has insightfully drawn our attention to moral knowledge as including an inculcated caring. The content of that moral knowledge, however, consists of norms or rules, which function as guides to the regulation and assessment of conduct. To commit oneself to a moral practice is to continue to care for these functions of moral rules in those relevant contexts of actions and situations. However, such a reflective commitment does not entail that the moral practice is itself an ideal. *A fortiori*, when a moral practice is regarded by an agent as being embedded with an ideal which he espouses, it of course possesses the status of a continuing concern. The moral rules would then be viewed as instrumental or constitutive means for the achievement of his ideal. Thus an agent may be benevolent or just, not merely because such conduct is required by moral rules, but also because benevolence and justice are regarded as an expression of his ideal theme of love or concern for the well-being of his fellows—an ideal that gives import to his commitment to a moral practice. And if all agents within a moral community share the same ideal toward the moral practice, they can experience a feeling of unity or harmony, of being members of a community of mutual care and concern. In real life, this happy situation does not always occur. Rather we witness a great divergence of ideal conceptions. Contemporary life is marked more by alienation and disaffection than by a spirit of harmony and reconciliation. Even for those who share a sense of respect for the moral practice, the moral rules are often targets of criticism in terms of a multiplicity of personal ideals. This criticism does not speak with a single voice that gives one confidence in ascribing a single way of moral concern. The notion of concern or care for the moral practice, as we pointed out in Section II, may be expressed in different ways. Even for those who may be said to share the same ideal, they have very "different ways of showing that they care."[56] We may say that they have different *styles* of concern, and these different styles may portray a great diversity with regard to the import of moral practice in the lives of commitive agents. However, the thing which renders problematic the situation of caring agents is not their difference in the style of concern; rather, it is their encounter with agents who have ceased to care for the moral practice. Unlike agents with a *tao*-attitude who attempt to transcend the moral practice by embuing it with an ideal perspective within the moral domain, these indifferent or amoral agents have ceased to care because moral rules have lost import and meaning in their lives. Can these indifferent agents be brought to appreciate the importance of the moral practice? Can these indifferent

56. Rush Rhees, *Without Answers* (London: Routledge & Kegan Paul, 1969), 97.

agents find a meaning in their lives without acknowledging the force of a moral practice? These are difficult questions for a commitive agent.

One strategy for dealing with those indifferent agents would be to remind them of the moral community as a natural habitat of meaning. Simone Weil remarks that "every human being needs to have multiple roots. It is necessary for him to draw well-nigh the whole of his moral, intellectual, and spiritual life by way of the environment of which he forms a part."[57] This "need for roots" may well be expressed in a Wittgenstenian vein: "A man's moral, intellectual and spiritual life is *not even conceivable* in the absence of the ways of living in which he participates—ways of living, many of which could not have developed apart from language."[58] And as Wittgenstein points out, "to imagine a language means to imagine a form of life."[59] It is thus the form of life in which human beings live that gives them a sense of community, a background that provides intelligibility to the use of moral notions. The indifferent agent is in effect opting out of the living community in which moral practice provides a setting for the regulation of conduct. And if the indifferent agent takes leave of the community and isolates his existence, his loses an anchorage of his identity. He may find a meaning in his life, but this meaning cannot be deemed to have an interpersonal import. The more difficult question concerns those indifferent agents who live within a moral community. This question can in part be answered by an insistence on the force of the moral practice regardless of the particular views of the indifferent agents. These indifferent agents are still subject to the regulation of moral rules whether they like them or not. Their conduct is subject to this piece of moral regulation regardless of their idiosyncratic concerns. Perhaps more to the point is to ask the indifferent agent whether he cares for anybody, whether there is somebody whose suffering or distress would affect him.[60] Unless he is mad or psychopathic, he is unlikely to offer negative answers to our questions.[61] And if he does care for somebody, we can perhaps succeed in making him see the importance of caring for a moral practice that concerns interdependent human behavior. To appreciate this point is to see the possibility of extending his care for

57. Simone Weil, *The Need for Roots* (New York: Harper and Row, 1971), 43.

58. Iliam Dilman and D. Z. Phillips, *Sense and Delusion* (London: Routledge & Kegan Paul, 1971), 7.

59. See Wittgenstein, *Philosophical Investigations*, I, #19.

60. Bernard Williams, *Morality: An Introduction* (New York: Harper Torchbooks, 1972), 8–11.

61. Ibid., 8.

somebody to the care for human beings in general. The *tao*-attitude in effect offers a perspective for moral caring in the light of personal ideal concerns. But if an indifferent agent remains unmoved by our argument, there seems to be no recourse except to insist upon the impersonal operation of the moral practice. This is of course a tough-minded answer, though a genial suasion on the importance of our *tao*-attitude is to be preferred.[62]

However, there are times in which a commitive agent may be perplexed by the import of the moral practice to his own life. While acknowledging that the moral practice is rooted in a form of life, he may still be desirous of some form of understanding the nature of the form of life itself. The commitive agent may experience a disparity between the aim of the moral practice and his own ideal concerns. No perplexity, however, need arise for agents who regard the moral rules as a definitive expression of the form of life, particularly if these agents regard these rules as being embued with an ideal norm of harmony, say, the utilitarian ideal of greatest happiness. But for our perplexed agent there appears a dissociation of the moral practice from his struggle for a meaning in *his own life*. The notion of a form of life is more illuminating as a focus upon a common background of a moral practice than as a description of the nature of morality. An appreciation of a form of life is a recognition of the presupposition of the intelligibility of moral discourse and conduct; it signifies a recognition of an "atmosphere" or "horizon" in which commitive agents live—an anchorage that satisfies the need for roots. This leaves open the question of personal import, its significance for self-transformation. The import of the form of life, in the final analysis, lies in the style and ideal expression of the individual's conduct rather than in a common stance that defines the content of this concern.

In the light of the *tao*-attitude, the perplexed committed moral agent may find an answer, not as a solution to a problem, but as a possible easing of his predicament. For the *tao*-attitude points to a rationale for freedom from the objects of moral concern. It is one thing to take seriously the objects of the moral practice, another to take oneself seriously in engaging in a serious occupation. A moral agent may respect his moral practice without taking himself seriously in doing so. In this manner, the moral practice cannot be the whole story of the life of a

62. In this light the Confucian *jen* (human-heartedness) as *tao* can be considered an expression of extensive caring for persons, though the Confucians are more likely to stress the importance of *li* or ritual context for the successful effectuation of the *tao*-attitude. For the connection between *jen* and *li*, see my "Reflections on the Structure of Confucian Ethics," *Philosophy East and West* 21, no. 2 (1971): 125–40.

commitive moral agent. His care for the moral practice may lie precisely in seeing to it that its demands are satisfied, in order that he may devote himself to his ideal pursuit. When he thus comfortably fulfills his obligations, he may then direct his actions to ideal achievement. Whereas a concern for a moral practice perhaps expresses a *need* for roots, the concern with one's ideal theme, one's mode of existence, may well express a need to *transcend* the moral practice. This is the force of the adoption of the *tao*-attitude as a meta-moral attitude. Chuang Tzu bids us to "forget," in the sense of freedom from care for moral distinctions and other matters that pertain to our bodily existence, and to feel comfortable in what we do. "You forget your feet when the shoes are comfortable. You forget your waist when the belt is comfortable. There is no change in what is inside, no following that is outside, when the adjustment to events is comfortable. You begin with what is comfortable and never experience what is uncomfortable when you know the comfort of forgetting what is comfortable."[63] The *tao*-attitude is thus germane to the perplexity of our commitive agent. A man with a *tao*-attitude would have advised our perplexed friend to ease his predicament by transcending the terms set by moral distinctions, to enjoy a kind of freedom that transcends his serious concern for moral practice. Through the adoption of an ideal theme or the vision of *tao*, the agent may transform his value-crisis into an issue of personal vision. The point, in nonmystical terms, is not to cease one's respect for a moral practice, but to place it in a proper perspective within the orbit of one's ideal concern. The moral practice in this way ceases to be something of supreme importance to an individual moral agent. And if we broaden our notion of morality to include both respect for a moral practice and respect for personal ideal commitments, the transcendence of a moral practice is properly a *moral* rather than a supra-moral transcendence. In this way a reflective moral agent can learn from Chuang Tzu without embracing contemplative or meditative Taoism.

63. *Chuang Tzu*, 206–7.

Essay 4 Chinese Moral Vision, Responsive Agency, and Factual Beliefs

The principal aim of this essay is to offer a plausible basis for a philosophical appreciation of the Chinese vision of *tao* as creative harmony of man and world.[1] I present in Section I a distinction between ideal norm and ideal theme and suggest that the Confucian and the classical Taoist points of view may be regarded as encapsulating distinct but not necessarily incompatible moral attitudes. Section II develops this contrast through two different conceptions of responsive agency. In Section III, the final section, I turn to the problem of the characterizing moral vision in relation to the role of factual beliefs.

I. VISION OF *TAO* AS AN IDEAL THEME

If a moral ideal is to have an import or transformative significance for a commitive agent, he must see it as in some fashion relevant to his management of desires and emotions.[2] In its inception, the vision of a state of moral excellence is an imaginative construct. It simply bespeaks an interest of the conceiver in giving meaning to his impulses and activities. In the more specific contexts of performance, a moral agent may have a plurality of ideals for dealing with different situations without an overarching conception of unity. In this case, we may ascribe to the agent a plurality of first-order aims or plans without a second-order ideal that provides a unitary point of reference. This distinction may

---

1. To some extent this essay overlaps three of my recent studies: Essays 2 and 3 and "Practical Causation and Confucian Ethics," *Philosophy East and West* 25, no. 1 (1975): 1–10. The present essay, however, develops and supplements some of the notions adumbrated there. As in most of my Confucian essays, I have assumed the position of a reflective commitive agent in search of a philosophical explication of Chinese ethics. For methodological considerations, see my "Reflections on Methodology in Chinese Philosophy," *International Philosophical Quarterly* 11, no. 2 (1971): 236–48.

2. In Section 1 of *Chung Yung*, the idea is expressed in terms of equilibrium *(chung)* and harmony *(ho)*.

be elucidated by Parker's distinction between focal self and matrix self.[3] The *focal self*, according to Parker, refers to "the total ongoing purse of experience which is always centered on some desire or appetition, some activity or passivity seeking assuagement." The activity is a highly organized system in which lower impulses are under the control of the higher. Parker gives the examples of the total ongoing activity of writing a sentence or a "tennis player as he returns the ball directed to a certain spot on the court." A *matrix self*, on the other hand, is "a basis of personal identity." One can think of it as a life plan. "It overrides long stretches of our experience the way a plan overrides and is carried through and gives sense to the activities that fulfill it, as for example, the plan of this book is carried along from sentence to sentence or chapter to chapter, or as the conductor's knowledge of a composition continues through and survives each note, each figure, each phase and movement of the whole."

On the basis of Parker's distinction, we may say that an agent's performance that aims at an ideal achievement is possessed of a focal self, which is simply a unitary "telos" that gives a meaning to a specific moral performance. Unlike Parker, I shall construe the distinction as one between the ideal aspects of moral performance. To him the focal self is a matter of empirical description, whereas for our concern, it is a matter of ascription of ideal intention. I shall henceforth use this notion of focal self in the ideal rather than the empirical sense. Regarding the matrix self, the notion of a life plan represents only one possible interpretation of unitary ideal. In either case, both the matrix and focal selves may be viewed as targets of moral achievement. The former, an overarching, the latter a specific, ideal tied to particular circumstances of moral performance. We may view the focal self as a policy of action. Insofar as an individual has merely a focal self in each situation, he may be said to have a plurality of policies without forming them into some sort of hierarchical organization. Such persons live, so to speak, from moment to moment, flowing in the stream of experiences without feeling the need to integrate these moments into some coherent whole. We may regard a matrix self as an overarching ideal which can serve as an answer to an agent's quest for the unity of life.

The above distinction has an important bearing on understanding the experience of moral perplexities of individual agents. If we regard an agent engaged in reflection on the meaning of his life, occasioned, say, by a dissatisfaction with his state of being as merely an aggregate

3. Dewitt H. Parker, *The Philosophy of Value* (Ann Arbor: University of Michigan Press, 1958), 125–26.

of focal selves, then we may construe his quest as a quest for a matrix self that would provide some sort of coherent unity to his focal selves. Assuming that an agent succeeds in his quest, the matrix self, the over-reaching moral ideal, may take two different forms. The nature of the ideal in question depends on the attitude of the agent toward his original question. If the question about the meaning of his life is taken as a perplexity that can be problematically formulated, i.e., as an articulatable problem for which a solution may be forthcoming, the matrix self at issue may be regarded as an *ideal norm*. In this case, the matrix self is a life plan dominated by a single norm that gives unity to the focal selves by providing a measure or standard of achievement. In this way the more intellectually inclined agents would develop certain rules or precepts in accordance with the ideal norm. On the other hand, an agent may view his perplexity as not subject to a problematic formulation. The agent here may not be concerned with solving problems. In this case, his matrix self may be regarded as an *ideal theme*.[4] This ideal theme provides a life unity without a life plan. The plurality of focal selves form a coherent unity, not by being organized according to some structural order or hierarchical system, but by being infused with a quality of moral excellence. This quality gives meaning to an agent's life and diffuses like light through a variety of policies of actions without necessarily blurring the distinct individual properties of actions.

I suggest that we construe the Chinese vision of *tao* as an ideal theme, and that we distinguish the Confucian and the classical Taoist's attitudes in this light. For a Taoist like Chuang Tzu, the response to meaning or significance of life is essentially one of a response to a diffusive quality of excellence, sufficient unto itself, without any thought of its relevance to moral discrimination. Thus the diffusion of an ideal theme may appear to blur the moral distinction between individual actions. Lao Tzu urges us to minimize the importance of moral virtues, and Chuang Tzu wants us to "forget" *(wang)* them.[5] This attitude toward *tao* as an ideal theme is deemed unacceptable by the Confucians. Perhaps here lies the heart of the distinction between the mystical and practical moralist. For the former, the experience of an ideal theme endows life with a quality of excellence, blurring the distinction of focal selves or policies of action. The latter, on the other hand, may view the ideal theme as a prospective point of orientation in forming individual

4. For a further discussion of the distinction between problems and perplexities see my *Dimensions of Moral Creativity: Paradigms, Principles, and Ideals* (University Park: Pennsylvania State University Press, 1978), chaps. 5 and 8.

5. I do not intend to suggest here that this Taoist attitude is irrelevant to the status of the distinction between right and wrong. For a further discussion, see Essay 3.

policies of action. The Confucians view this ideal theme as embedded in an existing system of moral regulations expressed in terms of *li* or ritual rules. In either case, the unitary import of the ideal theme does not lie in some sort of hierarchical organization, e.g., in the subordinate or superordinate relation between focal selves. Mystical moralists tend to locate this quality of excellence within an inner mental state and attitude, a light of mind. Possessing this inner light seems to them sufficient to preserve the purity of heart and meaning in one's life. Spontaneity of response with a cultivated inner self appears sufficient in itself to guarantee moral achievement. Thus the Taoists stress *wu-wei* or negative actions as an exclusive strategy in preserving the *tao*. The Confucians, on the other hand, with their interest in the stability of social organization, typically take the *tao* as an ideal theme with prospective significance for coping with live situations. Significantly, major Neo-Confucians equate *tao* with *jen* (human-heartedness). *Jen* is an ideal theme to be developed more in positive rather than in negative performance. It is an ideal to be developed in connection with an existing moral tradition, not an inner state to be experienced as self-sufficient endowment of meaning.

The notion of *tao* is often expressed in Chinese philosophy as harmony of man and the world. In Western ethics, this notion of harmony is liable to be conceived as an ideal norm rather than an ideal theme. Thus William James and Ralph Barton Perry construe harmony in the context of individual interests, which function as a criterion of inclusive integration. This interpretation does not apply to the ideal theme. If my suggestion on *tao* is deemed plausible, then the Confucian and Taoist viewpoints may be deemed significant without providing an epistemology of moral justification. For the ideal theme, as a vision of moral excellence, does not function as a criterion for assessment of actions. It is a standard of inspiration rather than aspiration—a posture of orienting one's life and conduct without issuing preceptorial guidance or principle of justification. The notion of harmony need not be taken in the normative sense. This, at any rate, seems to be a reasonable interpretation of the Confucian conception articulated in the *Doctrine of the Mean*. Perhaps the Christian *agape* can be similarly construed.

For the mystical moralists like Lao Tzu and Chuang Tzu, the problem of practical causation does not arise. The mystical moralist is concerned with preserving his inner mental state rather than with actions that have causal consequences within the natural order of events. If the person be a Taoist, like the mythical Lieh Tzu, he would be more concerned with riding with the wind rather than with changing the direction of the wind. If he be a Christian mystic, his life may be overflowed with *agape* or love for God's creation, and his love of God cannot be otherwise expressed apart from his love of all creatures. His experiences of the ideal then appear to be quite sufficient to secure a firm foothold in the world. Because of his lack of concern for change in the natural world, his experiences of the ideal theme justly arouse the feelings of awe and admiration, but can hardly serve other agents in search of answers to their moral problems. The practical moralist with an ideal theme—a Confucian, for instance—would behave quite differently. The relation between his matrix self and the natural world does pose a problem of practical causation. So also with moral agents who have ideal norms, though this is a problem of a different kind. In either case the problem is the relation between the ideal and the actual world, i.e., how a human being can mold the natural world closer to his vision. This, then, is the heart of the problem of practical causation, as distinct from the theoretic problem of causal explanation. It is a problem for the actualization of moral vision within the natural world.[6]

For the Confucian agent with a matrix self or an ideal theme, the problem of actualization is to produce effects, by way of action, that endow the natural order with a diffusive quality of excellence. But not the whole of the natural world is a felicitous or genial setting amenable to ideal-embedded actions. The agent here is primarily concerned with that segment of the natural world that is subject to alteration by his actions, as productive of states of affairs that comport with his vision. His actions, in turn, are subject to the limitations of natural laws and the existing moral tradition. In a way his aim is, strictly speaking, not to change the world, but to relate himself to the world by responding to its scenes as required by his ideal theme. So long as the agent's actions comport with his ideal theme, the natural world may remain unchanged in substance. The discernible changes would pertain to the agent's angle of vision, the light in which he understands and conducts his life. Practical causation need not, in this way, pose an insurmountable problem. At worse, the agent can retreat to the light of inner vision, and like the Taoist, be content with living in harmony with nature.

However, this retreat to an inner sanctuary cannot be a live option for the practical Confucian, for his *jen* (human-heartedness) as an ideal theme is a prospective action-guide. Although it issues no precepts for action, the theme endows an existing moral order of *li* (ritual rules) with its ideal quality. The Confucian agent cannot content himself with *wu-wei* (negative actions) and leave nature to take its own course oblivious of human wants and aspirations. A Confucian would orient his life

6. For a further discussion see the third essay cited in n. 1.

and conduct toward *jen*-achievement that results from positive efforts and performances rather than from refraining from responsible participation in the communal setting. His actions may result in substantive changes not in the natural world, but in that segment of the natural world that intimately concerns interpersonal relations, e.g., the framework of social and political institutions, where there is much that he can accomplish. This segment is deemed subject to ideal transformation in its qualitative texture, though not always in descriptive content. To say this is not to deny the necessity of coping with exigent circumstances of human life not prefigured in *li*. We need not follow the general conservative attitude of classical Confucian thinkers in maintaining the absolute character of *li*-requirements. But one can appreciate the attitude toward the ideal theme of *jen* as providing a light in which one can meaningfully feel at home in one's moral tradition without feeling the need for structural reorganization. Detached from the setting of existing moral requirements, the ideal theme would be more at home with individual idiosyncratic perplexities, though its significance in affording individual solace and satisfaction cannot be denied. What I would like to stress is that for a moral ideal to have an import to a commitive agent, it may be taken as a theme without functioning as a sort of supernorm. Moreover, having an ideal theme is not incompatible with having an ideal norm. A Confucian committed to *jen* is free to explore alternative normative ideals, whether utilitarian or Kantian, to implement this ideal theme. The point is to appreciate their difference without construing them as exclusive ideals. Likewise, the difference between the Taoist and Confucian responses to *tao* as an ideal theme need not be construed as a dichotomy of moral attitudes that precludes any possible relation. To some reflective Chinese moral agents, the two are more complementary than contradictory attitudes. True to the spirit of *tao*, the two contrasting attitudes abide in harmony like *yin* and *yang*, each potentially generative of the other.

There is no necessary connection between ideal theme and ideal norm. An agent may espouse one without the other. In order to accommodate both moral problems and perplexities, from the point of view of a philosophy of vision, it is important to recognize the distinction and explore the connection between ideal theme and ideal norm. It is also important to inquire into the question of priority, i.e., in a context of relevance, whether one should assign priority to an ideal norm or an ideal theme. Perhaps, in the last analysis, the question can be settled only by personal decision. As a moral agent, I am more inclined to the priority of an ideal theme, particularly the Confucian *jen*, than to an ideal norm, say, the utilitarian ideal of greatest happiness.

One need not commit oneself to Confucian *jen* by adopting a conservative or ideological posture. One need not advocate conventional wisdom as a way of actualizing one's moral vision. Different ways of life and social structures are possible within an active concern for an ideal theme. In Confucius's conception of *chün-tzu* (superior man), there is implicit a conception of flexibility of agency in coping with the problem of moral change.[7]

What I have suggested thus far is a distinction between Confucian and Taoist attitudes toward a common ideal theme of *tao*. In doing so, I have assumed that the notion of *tao* as a vision of man and the world can be independently characterized apart from its uses in Confucian and Taoist literature. This assumption is, I believe, useful and relatively harmless so long as contrasting ways of thinking can be rendered intelligible without confusion. Two different agents may be said to have shared the same ideal when both positively assent to the same abstract statement about the ideal.[8] But this uniform assent does not entail that the statement in question can be characterized and understood in terms of further statements about the content and import of the ideal. Two different agents may be committed to the same ideal where it is abstractly stated and yet develop their practical import and content in different ways. This difference in import can be exhibited in different attitudes and performances toward a variety of topics. The contrast between Confucian and Taoist ways of thinking thus need not be regarded as an exclusive difference in attitude. Our assumption of a common theme thus allows us to see them as possible complements rather than exclusive attitudes toward the moral life. As the term "theme" suggests, a theme admits of polymorphous development. An abstract statement of an ideal theme, in this light, does not prejudge its content and import for a commitive moral agent. As I shall suggest in Section III, the question concerns characterization rather than description of moral vision.

II. TWO CONCEPTIONS OF RESPONSIVE AGENCY

Let us now develop further the contrasting positions of the Confucian and the Taoist (henceforth, *C* and *T*) as reflected in their diver-

7. For a discussion of this topic, see my "The Concept of Paradigmatic Individuals in the Ethics of Confucius," *Inquiry* 14 (1971): 41–55; or *Dimensions of Moral Creativity*, chap. 4.
8. I am not suggesting here that Taoists would agree with me. The philosophically interesting question is whether one can understand Lao-Tzu and Chuang Tzu without some notion of creative harmony.

gent conceptions of responsive agency, i.e., the way in which moral agents respond to the changing scenes of the natural order. Initially the difficulty lies in the notion of agency, for it is not clear whether one can legitimately ascribe this notion to T. We have suggested that the notion of *wu-wei* is a notion of negative action rather than no-action or inaction, i.e., pure passivity. As Danto has plausibly argued in his *Analytical Philosophy of Action*, doing not-*a* is distinct from not doing *a*.[9] *Wu-wei* focuses on doing not-*a* rather than inaction. Chan translates that notion as "taking no action."[10] Note that "taking no action" is an action that is intentional in character. Thus we can quite properly ascribe the notion of agency to T. However, the agent in performing a negative action need not be aware of the intention. Lao Tzu emphasizes natural spontaneity, innocence, and simplicity. In each case, the state of mind is a product of consciously cultivated attitude that leads to the sort of intention an agent might have without being aware of it. Lao Tzu urges the cultivation of an attitude that leads to spontaneous negative actions without the necessity of thinking or deliberation.[11] The T's attitude is an accomplished and not an untutored state of moral agency. Lao Tzu exalts weakness, simplicity, withdrawal, and having few desires, and he condemns Confucian virtues.

Perhaps we would do better to avoid the term "agency," and adopt a term like "person." In this way, the attitudes of C and T need not be regarded as exclusive. For the Neo-Confucians like Ch'eng Hao and Wang Yang-ming have no trouble in assimilating Chuang Tzu's metaphor of mind as mirror responding to the changing scenes of the natural world.[12] The contrast between C and T may thus be elucidated by their different conceptions of person as responsive mind.

The question at issue is the moral significance of personal cultivation *(hsiu-shen)* deemed essential to the realization of *tao*. Though the term "personal cultivation" is a Confucian one, the T's emphasis on mind as a mirror reflecting changing events can plausibly be construed as a *con-*

9. Arthur Danto, *Analytical Philosophy of Action* (Cambridge: Cambridge University Press, 1973), 167ff. See also Jeremy Bentham, *An Introduction to the Principles of Morals and Legislation* (New York: Hafner Publishing Company, 1948), 72.

10. W. T. Chan, *The Way of Lao Tzu* (Indianapolis: Bobbs-Merrill, 1963); A glossary of Chinese Names, 271.

11. For a discussion of cases of intentional acts that are not deliberate, see J. L. Austin, "Three Ways of Spilling Ink," *Philosophical Papers*, 2d ed. (New York: Oxford University Press, 1970), 276–77 and 283ff.

12. See Burton Watson, trans., *The Complete Works of Chuang Tzu* (New York: Columbia University Press, 1968), 97; A. C. Graham, *Two Chinese Philosophies: Ch'eng Ming-tao and Ch'eng Yi-ch'uan* (London: Lund Humphries, 1958), 104–5; and Wang Yang-Ming, *Instructions for Practical Living and Other Neo-Confucian Writings*, trans. W. T. Chan (New York: Columbia University Press, 1963), secs. 21, 148, and 167.

stitutive strategy for moral achievement. For our present purpose, the question concerns the character of responsive mind and its import in relation to the human and natural order of things, and not the methodology of practical knowledge. The answer in part deals with the person's psychological preparation for living in *tao*. In *C* this answer takes the form of cultivating one's heart or mind *(hsin)* or rectification of mind *(cheng-hsin)*. Significantly personal cultivation is seen in *Ta Hsüeh (The Great Learning)* as a foundation for the achievement of moral excellence, in the sense that it is a prelude to both positive and negative actions. A *C*-person, as we have pointed out, is a problem-oriented actor. He cultivates his single-mindedness, sincerity *(ch'eng)*, or seriousness *(ching)* so as to engage in actions that meet problematic cases. The ideal of *jen* as a theme is not a method for resolving problems but more like a light or perspective for dealing with problems. The moral person, for *C*, is an actor who attempts to resolve problems in the light of *jen* whenever he confronts abnormal or exigent circumstances. Normal circumstances fall with in the scope of *li* (ritual propriety). A moral person thus possesses a mind responsive to changing events and things. His responsive mind is tied to actions in accord with his judgment of *timing* of the situation. The concern with the condition of one's self is viewed as an essential quality for coping with change.

For *T*, on the other hand, the responsive mind is more than a preparation, it is an inwardly directed attitude. *Tao* is achieved when this inner attitude is preserved in response to outward events by way of negative actions. But negative actions are not aimed at resolving problems. They concern only the person's own condition of moral excellence. Strictly speaking, *T* sees no gap between his mental states and outer events and things. In this way the main concern centers on the "polishing" of mind to achieve clarity of vision. The responsive mind is thus like a mirror that reflects without obscuring the changing things and events. Here we have a sort of focus on "the purity of heart" that is deemed sufficient for moral achievement, there being no necessity for intervention from deliberation and judgment. There are no exigent situations in the strict sense. Neither is there in *T*'s conception a concern with the problems that appear to *C* to infect the human world. We have here an exclusive concern with a person's interior life. Such an inward purity is assumed to be harmonious with *tao*.

In sum, *C* and *T* differ in their conception of the import of responsive agency. But they appear to be in unison on the quality of mind as responsive to changing events. The crucial difference may further be brought out in this way. For *C*, moral excellence is always a product of constructive response of the actor in the light of the natural and existing moral order. To live in harmony, man creatively participates in the transformations of the world. Thus in *Chung Yung (The Doctrine of the Mean)* we have a stress on man as "assisting the creative transformation of Heaven and Earth." To be responsive to changing events, the person must engage in both positive and negative actions. Moreover, responsiveness to things implies for C a *responsibility* for what he does in the light of *jen* as an ethical expression of *tao*. In contrast, for *T*, the responsive mind aims simply at reflecting, in the literal sense, like a mirror, the changing scenes of the world. It is a "natural" response in which the thinking faculty is deemed inoperative. *Wu-wei* is simply a negative response that varies from case to case. *Tao* as creative harmony requires no assistance from man. There is, strictly speaking, no human as distinct from the natural order. To Lao Tzu the ideal of harmony is a natural constancy *(chang)*. To be responsive to this natural constancy is to be in some sort of intimate or caring relationship, but this relationship carries no responsibility in the moral sense.[13]

We may begin explicating this notion of care by remarking that it involves the recognition of the integrity of the situations, events, and persons within the natural order. Recognizing this integrity, the responsive mind is prepared to accept it. Acceptance involves *wu-wei*, Chuang Tzu's term for "letting things be," lest our positive actions disturb the inherent harmony in the natural world. In this sense, we can, perhaps, get a glimpse of care as an intimate relation without responsibility and emotional attachment. In *C*'s view, however, this relation is tied to the performance of social roles and obligations within the moral order of *li* (ritual propriety).[14]

The Taoistic way of caring is basically one of appreciation; it resembles the passivity of an instinctive response to stimulus. But the affinity ceases in that negative action, as we have often stressed, is a product of conscious cultivation. *Innocence* is a refined rather than a primitive state of mind.

Here we may make some suggestions on the notion of *hsin*, which can be rendered as "heart," "feeling," or "mind." In all these renderings we must always remind ourselves of the conative and affective

13. I admit that the point here is more an inspiration derived from reading and reflection than a faithful rendering of texts. For a further discussion, see my "Uses of Dialogues and Moral Understanding," *Journal of Chinese Philosophy* 2 (1975): 131–48.
14. I agree with Fingarette that Confucius did not elaborate the language of choice and responsibility. But as he correctly observes, "the absence of a developed language of choice and responsibility does not imply a failure to choose or to be responsible." See Herbert Fingarette, *Confucius: The Secular as Sacred* (New York: Harper and Row, 1972), 18.

character. The responsive *hsin* of *T wills* to have the object of its experience to remain in the state in which it appears; thus it lets things be. This state of appreciating the object has an affective aspect: the attitude of the will, in some way, brings a delight and ease to the appreciating person. The responsive *hsin* of *C*, on the other hand, strives to make the object of his response amenable to some sort of a fitting relation. The appreciation of the object is always a prelude to this relation and never an intrinsic end of response. Success yields delight, ease, and tranquility and equilibrium. Thus the affective dimension is also present as a consequence of achievement. The *hsin* in both *C* and *T* are ways of minding or being aware of objects, and in each case this expresses a "heart" for the objects; and in each case this "heart," if successfully expressed, yields certain feelings or affects. Put in another way, to *mind* an object is to have a *feel* for the object, and this presupposes a *heart* or respect for its integrity—the heart here is a state of mind predisposed to minding its objects. If we regard this as a feeling for the object, then we need to distinguish this feeling *antecedent* to action and the feeling *consequent* to the relation with the object. Interestingly, if *hsin* is minding which has a feeling for the object, this *hsin* always has a cognitive aspect not dissociated from the noncognitive ones. In neither *C* nor *T* do we have a dualism of body and mind. If being aware of an object is knowledge in some sense of Russell's "Knowledge by Acquaintance," we have in both *C* and *T* kinds of knowledge by acquaintance. The one *(T)* yields appreciative knowledge, the other *(C)* yields practical knowledge. Stated in another way, we have a knowledge by acquaintance that yields two different kinds of consequences, the one appreciative, the other practical. The former is an insight into the object by seeing and embracing its integrity, the latter an insight into a consequence of practical causation. Quite sensibly the *hsin* of *T* is the *hsin* of the Chinese artists. The *hsin* of *C* is the *hsin* of the man of action. These two *hsin* need not be incompatible—we do have artists who are men of action also!

For a commitive *C* or *T* agent, *tao* as creative harmony is a target of moral striving. Living in accord with *C*'s or *T*'s construal of the vision may be portrayed as living with different styles of life. From the philosophical point of view the question properly arises: What notion of moral creativity lies at the heart of their difference? If *tao* is creative harmony, what creative role, if any, does a moral agent possessing a responsive mind *(hsin)* have in the world of dynamic change? How do *C* and *T* differ here, and what significant consequences do their conceptions have with respect to a moral philosophy that aims at an *understanding* rather than assessment of moral experiences?

We may approach the above questions by explicating two complementary conceptions of the world and their import for understanding moral experiences. Two conceptions of the world (world$_c$ and world$_t$) are involved in C and T. World$_c$ is essentially a human world, i.e., the world of human affairs, to borrow a phrase from Dewey, of doings, sufferings, and enjoyings. For C, Tao as creativity, seen from the point of view of achievement, is realizable in a world$_c$ in which human performance figures prominently. The world of moral excellence is thus a world$_c$ of human achievement. The responsive agent is a creative partner in the natural order. Whatever cannot be achieved is consigned to the domain of fate or mandate of Heaven (tien-ming). The trinity of Heaven, Earth, and man signifies the creative partnership. This point of view is unabashedly anthropocentric, for the natural order is always potentially subject to practical causation and thus conformable to moral wishes and desires. Failure in practical causation is assigned to tien-ming, but this again requires self-examination of where the failure lies. Recall the remark attributed to Confucius in Chung Yung: "In archery we have something resembling the Way (tao) of the superior man. When the archer misses the center of the target, he turns around and seeks for the cause of failure within himself."[15] Thus "the Way cannot be separated from us for a moment. What can be separated from us is not the Way."[16]

The world$_c$ is, in this Confucian vision, the human world, the world of practical causation. Tao as creativity is thus not separated from the human tao. The vision is one of unity of the tao of heaven and the tao of man. Man is a creative agent within the world$_c$. His doings, as a paradigmatic individual, can form part of tao in creative harmony.[17] The force of cheng (sincerity) lies here, for the world$_c$ is a moral world. The view appears to be quite plausible in an obvious way. What can count as a moral consideration for men must be something which they can do something about. What does not count will be assigned to that region of the natural order that has just to be accepted as a matter of fate (ming). Tao as an ideal theme can only be developed by deliberate human effort and performance. This obviously is a continuing process of moral achievement and not something that can be attained once and for all times. This perhaps explains the historicist attitude that is presupposed in Confucian creativity, for the development of the ideal

15. Chung Yung, sec. 14.
16. Ibid., sec. 1.
17. For the significance of this notion, see my "Morality and Paradigmatic Individuals," American Philosophical Quarterly 6, no. 4 (1969): 324–29; or Dimensions of Moral Creativity, chap. 3.

theme can only occur in human historical situations. The creative agent aims at historical immortality of words and deeds.[18]

World$_t$, by contrast, is the world of a Taoist artist seeking to create conditions for the full expression of the natural order as he views it. Here the descriptive content of the natural and human order remains unchanged. Note here, creativity of the responsive agent also figures prominently in *tao* as creative harmony. For even if the world remains undisturbed by human effort, human beings still play a role in providing the conditions for preserving the world's natural processes. To *let* things be is also to guard against any unnatural intervention into a thing's development. Guarding, *wu wei*, is a human action. Guarding natural processes is a way of conserving nature. Man himself has no intrinsic characteristics that affect the world. His creativity lies in this refraining from positive actions. He has no special world of his own except the world of his experiences of *tao* which he seeks to express in his life. He is an artist faithful to his own understanding of the world around him.

The world$_t$ is the mood of a Taoist artist. The artist seeks to make manifest the hidden without disturbing the hidden itself. He wants appreciative knowledge as an intrinsic end. The artistic mood is relevant to our moral life, for there are moments in which we feel that to do something is to do violence to the object of our attention. Particularly in the case of persons, one can, by seeking to change a person too much, ruin his character and personality. And when we regard a person as a friend, one basic attitude is to leave him or her alone and contemplate our friendship quite independently of our ordinary evaluative attitude. Our ordinary evaluative attitude toward the conduct of other persons often prevents us from seeing what is good and beautiful in them.

The artistic mood of *T* is one of *innocence,* the innocence hard won by self-conscious cultivation of *wu-wei.* It is a mood of indifference to the valuative processes of other persons. The Taoist artist does not bring to this world$_t$ a judgment on what the natural or human order ought to be. He seeks to create, by way of the medium and materials, the conditions in which the world can unveil itself in clear vision. His creativity inevitably affects or transforms the nature of his subject. Since he is not describing but expressing the subject's nature, his expression creatively enters into his understanding and experience of his subject. In this way he can transform, in some sense, the nature of his subject by transcending our ordinary conceptual scheme. *Tao* as creative harmony is thus a transcendent world$_t$, not another world different

18. See W. T. Chan, *A Source Book in Chinese Philosophy* (Princeton: Princeton University Press, 1963), 13.

from that of our ordinary experiences, but this same world seen from our artistic mood. The world$_t$ points to the aesthetic dimension of moral experience. Our world$_c$ would be quite impoverished without an occasional effort at seeing it also as world$_t$. World$_t$ and world$_c$ are thus complementary lenses for understanding moral creativity and experience. World$_t$ is a transcendence of the moral world of judgment. It remains a *human* world, for the world$_t$ is always dependent for its intelligibility upon the attitude of the person. C and T can be reconciled by seeing their worlds as displaying the two different modes of human experience and existence. An appreciation of T's world does not entail an endorsement of the mystical way of life alienated from the human world$_c$. This view expresses a *Confucian bias*. But how else can we distill T's insight apart from our ordinary moral concerns? The transcendence of these concerns does not mean entering into another world, but seeing these concerns as subject to transformation in the light of the Taoist vision. Although this attitude does not resolve problematic encounters in our life, our life can be transformed because we can display the attitude in an appropriate setting. Silence and *wu-wei* make sense only within the world, where we live in relation to others. We have no ontological transcendence here.

Perhaps we can now look in a different way at T's disparagement of C's attachment to an existing moral practice *(li)*. A moral practice, whatever its nature, can only be seen as significant from the standpoint of an ideal theme. A moral agent perplexed by the meaning of his life can view existing moral practice only as a precondition, not a presupposition, of moral achievement. The need for moral anchorage in a common way of life makes sense only because this anchorage is simply a recognition of our humanity. The T-bias is the bias of an individual man in search of a meaning of his life to quiet his perplexity. Even if one lives in the world of other men, his relation to them need not always be relevant to his quest for a meaningful existence. The context of interpersonal relations is something to be transcended for an individual to live his own life and not to be accepted as a determinant of moral excellence. Tying one's ideal theme to an existing morality may even hamper one's self-development. As reflective agents, we sometimes fall into these moods exemplified in C and T's conceptions of the world. These are not incompatible attitudes, though when we attempt to generalize them into programs of action, we encounter conflict and paradox. How that conflict is to be resolved is a matter of individual decision and judgment.[19]

19. Thus I agree with Danto on that peculiar conception of knowledge "seen as a product of a certain kind of transformation," that "it is a living through of what seems

III. CHARACTERIZATION OF VISION AND FACTUAL BELIEFS

In this final section, I take up the problem of communication of one's vision as an ideal theme and the role of factual beliefs.[20] For the classical Taoists this is a pseudo problem. A Lao Tzu would prize "wordless teaching" and urge us to "use words but rarely."[21] For the most part he may content himself with *indirect* communication by way of images, metaphors, paradoxes, or fictional stories familiar to the readers of the *Works of Chuang Tzu*. Factual beliefs, however, have no role to play. As indicated in Section I, the Taoists are mystical moralists concerned primarily with self-transformation rather than with the transformation of the actual world. The problem of communication is an important concern for Confucians, and more generally for reflective commitive agents, who desire to render their vision both intelligible and credible. Since the problem pertains to persuasive discourse, it may be of philosophical interest to inquire into the role of factual beliefs.

A moral vision of the relation of man and his world is basically an imaginative conception of an ideal state of affairs—a state of moral excellence.[22] The vision implies some notion of *ought-to-be*. We may suppose that an agent envisaging an ideal theme is responding to an ex-

---

to be a transformation of the world but is really only a transformation of oneself." But unlike Danto, I believe that this conception of knowledge is not without moral significance. "Appreciative knowledge by acquaintance" may be a misapplication of the concept of knowledge embedded in our standard conceptual framework, but it can be rendered intelligible and significant for commitive agents with ideal themes. In a way, the issue concerns our notion of morality. If we confine its applicability only to interpersonal contexts of good and evil, we cannot make sense of the Taoistic attitude as a moral one. I much prefer the broader notion that allows one to speak of personal morality. It remains for moral philosophy to relate these two senses of morality in a coherent scheme. See Danto, *Morality and Mysticism: Oriental Thought and Moral Philosophy* (New York: Basic Books, 1972), 18–19, 64, 95.

20. For an ideal norm, there appears to be no peculiar problem of communication, since it can be analytically articulated in terms of the standard conceptual scheme of moral rules and principles. A matrix self is to the agent a sort of life plan that can be conceptually described in standard terms. Thus its practical import can be elucidated in preceptorial form.

21. See *Tao Tê Ching*, trans. D. C. Lau, chaps. 2 and 23. This, of course, does not imply an impossibility of communication. A Taoist, after all, engages in discourse. Though he may point to the inadequacy of our language, he nevertheless speaks. And if he wishes to be understood, his speech must be capable of being understood in conventional terms even if such terms have to be stretched to accommodate his purpose. For more extensive discussion, see Essay 5.

22. This and the following remarks are not to be taken as proposing a thesis on the psychogenesis of moral ideals, but as suggestions embodying a model for rendering intelligible and plausible a vision of ideal theme. Some of my remarks are indebted to William James's essay "What Makes a Life Significant?" in *Essays on Faith and Morals* (New York: Longmans, Green and Company, 1949).

perienced predicament which he deems undesirable. His response embodies a judgment of undesirability, and the vision itself must be espoused as desirable, as a way to remedy his predicament. Since this judgment is occasioned by reflection, we may term it a "judgment of reflective desirability." For this response to a predicament not to be an empty gesture or a mere intellectual act, the agent's judgment of reflective desirability must have practical import. The response is, of course, not unconnected with his interests, desires, and aspirations—in general, with what he wants himself to be. The situation as he experiences it is unwanted. Instead of resigning himself to living in the situation as he finds it, he wants to do something to it, to change it to some state of affairs which he thinks will be satisfactory. The ideal envisaged, as an answer to his predicament, thus embodies an active intention to transform the actual world. The ideal, in this way, implicitly contains two features: a judgment of reflective desirability and a practical intention. Should he want to engage in discourse in communicating his vision, we can plausibly suppose that the language he uses will contain two features, and may be said to be *amphibious*.[23] On the one hand, it indicates the speaker's appraisive response to the actual world; and on the other, it purports to say something that will have a persuasive effect upon his audience. We may say that the speaker here is engaged in a *characterization* rather than a description of his vision.[24] The notion of characterization, I suggest, can be used in the context of speech-acts uttered by the speaker for the purpose of articulating *persuasively* his moral vision or ideal theme. To characterize a vision, in this sense, is to provide an audience with an understanding of the vision

23. In Essay 2, I attempted to show how some passages in *Chung Yung* may be construed in terms of amphibious notions. The following sketchy remarks on the use of language in articulation of vision require further development to be used as a basis for textual interpretation. There are problems inherent in this line of approach. For example, how is this use of language related to the use of metaphors, analogies, and paradoxes in general? For our present concern with the role of factual beliefs, I hope the remarks present a useful context for discussion. At the moment, I am less concerned with presenting a philosophical thesis than I am with the possibility of constructing focal lenses for understanding ideal commitments. Thus I have not made any excursion into the ontological import of vision. I do not deny that a vision can be regarded as a sort of "root-metaphor" (in Pepper's sense) that can be construed as a basis for developing categorical systems. See S. C. Pepper, *World Hypotheses* (Berkeley: University of California Press, 1948), chap. V.

24. This notion of characterization is owed to Karl Aschenbrenner, *Concepts of Value* (Dordrecht-Holland: D. Reidel, 1972), 117. It should be noted that Aschenbrenner uses this notion only in connection with characterization of man by man. I have in effect stretched his notion in applying it to the context of communicating vision. For a characterization of Wang Yang-ming's language of moral vision as involving amphibious notions, see my *The Unity of Knowledge and Action: A Study in Wang Yang-ming's Moral Psychology* (Honolulu: University Press of Hawaii, 1982), chap. 4.

that prospectively guides the latter's conduct. Unless characterization is viewed as an expressive or a purely perlocutionary speech-act, the speaker cannot ignore the question of cognitive significance of his utterances, particularly the factual beliefs implicit in the articulation of his vision.[25]

Before proceeding to a discussion of the role of factual beliefs, let us observe that characterization can have an important function in a critical self-understanding of ideal commitments, for in attempting to articulate his vision, the reflective agent thinks through the significance and the plausibility of his ideal commitment. When the process is conducted in solitude, it can serve as a self-examination of conduct. Moral thinking can hardly be severed from moral performance—an important insight of Wang Yang-Ming in his insistence on the unity of moral knowledge and action *(chih-hsing ho-i)*. So also, reflection on the character of one's moral knowledge can affect conduct. As Chu Hsi remarked: "The efforts of both knowledge and action must be exerted to the utmost. As one knows more clearly, he acts more earnestly, and as he acts more earnestly, he knows more clearly. Neither of the two should be unbalanced or discarded."[26] Moral knowledge and action thus have a mutual dependence, or in terms of *kan-ying*, mutual influence and response.[27] We should further take note of the nature of our discussion presented in Section II. Our discussion there attempted to *characterize* the contrasting Taoist and Confucian attitudes toward *tao*. We have not tried to be faithful to the corpus of relevant texts, for our principal concern has been with a plausible explication of these attitudes from the point of view of a commitive and reflective moral agent. Just as all forms of characterization are subject to critical assessment, ours claims no exception to this rule.

Our discussion will take the form of ascription rather than description of the sorts of factual beliefs involved in characterization. Since characterization aims at achieving a reasonable persuasion of the audience, there obviously is involved a speaker's belief in the efficacy of articulating his vision. Since the vision embodies a judgment of reflective desirability, the recommended moral attitude must be viewed as reasonable. We may term this a belief in the reasonableness of the moral attitude at issue. As we have previously remarked, characteriza-

25. Austin's notion of perlocutionary speech-acts refers to those that aim at producing "certain consequential effects upon the feelings, thoughts, and actions of the audience, or of the speaker, or of other persons." See J. L. Austin, *How to Do Things with Words* (Oxford: Clarendon Press, 1962), 101.
26. Chan, *Source Book in Chinese Philosophy*, 609.
27. For a development of this notion of *kan-ying*, see the second essay cited in n. 1.

tion aims at a practical and not merely an intellectual understanding of the vision, i.e., vision as a prospective guide to conduct. More precisely, the general belief of the speaker may be represented in the form of a conditional proposition: "If my audience attends to what I say and reflects upon the desirability of the moral attitude in question, they will achieve a practical understanding of my vision." It is assumed then that the particular audience in context is reasonable, for, as I suggested, characterization is a form of reasonable persuasion. A successful characterizing speech-act thus depends on the force of its appeal. Where consensus is not obtained in a particular discourse, characterization fails in reasonable persuasion. Of course, the background of the audience may vary from case to case. What is reasonable in one discursive context may not be so in another. This is part of my reason for using the notion of reasonableness rather than rationality, which is often tied to noncontextual canons and criteria.[28]

Characterization may also involve particular factual beliefs expressed as moral notions. For a Confucian, there are such notions as *li* (ritual propriety), *i* (righteousness), *hsin* (faithfulness), *chung-shu* (loyalty and consideration). The application of these notions in appropriate contexts presupposes certain factual beliefs which do not involve an appeal to moral rules or principles. However, pending argumentation, we cannot rule out the possibility of a rationalistic construal of Confucian ethics as a system of rules and principles.[29] In general, we may group together all the conventional moral beliefs as factual in character. Thus in the light of *tao* as *jen,* each of the moral notions may be regarded as expressive of a factual belief, i.e., that conduct in accordance with its implied action-guide is in fact a *means* to the achievement of *jen.* This is not to suggest that moral notions are wholly descriptive in character. I shall say more on this later. For the present I would like to focus upon the factual role of, say, virtue-notions within characterization. Leaving open the question of whether they are merely instrumental, and/or contributory or constitutive means. For the Confucian, they are more plausibly constitutive means, since *jen* is said to embrace all virtues.[30] To accept virtue-notions thus is in part to acknowledge a

28. For further remarks see my second essay referred to in n. 7.

29. In the context of the *Analects*, this view is highly implausible. See my "Reflections on the Structure of Confucian Ethics," *Philosophy East and West* 21, no. 2 (1971): 124–40.

30. This is a more Neo-Confucian than classical theme. For example, Ch'eng Hao maintains that "a man of *jen* forms one body with all things without any differentiation. Righteousness, propriety, wisdom, and faithfulness are all [expressions of] *jen*" (Chan, *Source Book in Chinese Philosophy,* 523). For an insightful discussion of constitutive or con-

web of factual beliefs about conduct that contribute to achievement of moral excellence. These remarks, of course, do not apply to agents who dissociate their ideal theme from an existing moral practice.

Another sort of factual belief may be said to be implied in characterization. This belief pertains to the capability of the hearers to realize the Confucian vision of *tao*. It is not enough merely for the audience to be reasonably persuaded of the desirability of the vision; they must also possess an active will to realize that vision in their lives and conduct. This is a belief about the psychological capacity of the audience as moral agents. Where this capacity is absent, the articulation of the vision would have no point or actuating force. It can, of course, remain as a conception to be intellectually entertained rather than practically understood. Here we may note Confucius's stress on *jen* as realizable in extensive love as against Mo Tzu's "all-embracing love" without gradation. A moral vision does presuppose a general psychological knowledge about human capacity. Summing up, we may say that characterization involves three different sorts of factual beliefs: (1) a pragmatic appeal to reflective desirability of the vision, (2) conventional moral beliefs as a means to ideal achievement, and (3) a belief in human capacity to realize the vision.

What we have offered above does not resolve for the moral philosopher the connection between moral attitudes and factual beliefs—an issue raised and discussed in Danto's recent work on Oriental ethics.[31] However, while our discussion on characterization presupposes the distinction between evaluation and description, we maintain that there is a general dependence of moral attitude on factual beliefs. The factual beliefs at issue in characterization need not be construed as specific beliefs that call for special procedures of verification, but are either general or particular beliefs that can be ascertained by ordinary knowledge and understanding. In this context, the claim to factual knowledge may be challenged, but its acceptance depends largely upon the way of life of the people concerned and not on an advance in scientific and technological knowledge. This is not to deny that science may be relevant to ethics: our discussion has been restricted to moral vision as an ideal theme.

Moreover, just as certain factual beliefs may be said to be involved in evaluative discourse, certain other factual beliefs may also seem to depend on moral attitudes for their relevance to conduct. Thus some

tributory means, see C. I. Lewis, *An Analysis of Knowledge and Valuation* (La Salle: Open Court, 1946), chap. XVI.
31. See Danto, *Morality and Mysticism*.

philosophers, for example, A. I. Melden and Arthur Murphy, have pointed out that certain facts are already invested with moral import.[32] Says Murphy, a fact can have moral implication when so understood not merely as a fact but as a "ground for action." The categories of such understanding "are not those of impersonal description, but of intentional action, personal agency or freedom, and the justifying reasons that make sense of it."[33] This thesis appears plausible, for it is the moral point of view that in some way determines the relevance of factual beliefs. And where factual beliefs are relevant to the moral point of view, they may be termed "beliefs about moral facts." This thesis is readily intelligible in Confucian ethics. Being a father already implies certain obligations. (So with being a son or a sovereign.)[34] The moral attitude embedded in familial relationships renders the biological fact of parentage a relevant consideration for moral thinking. In the classical Confucian language of rectification of names, when a man does not live up to the expectations of obligatory performance, the "name" *(ming)* of being a son or a father requires rectification. Thus rectifying names is a procedure for rectifying conduct. Furthermore, we may say with Danto that the classical Confucian view here is that "misperception, especially in moral matters, rested upon misdescription" (that is, misusing "names" that require rectification), but qualify this thesis by stressing that the misperception at issue ultimately rests upon the moral point of view rather than upon isolated pieces of descriptive knowledge.[35] If this point is sound, it shows that the dependence of

32. See A. L. Meldon, *Rights and Right Conduct* (Oxford: Blackwell, 1958); A. E. Murphy, *The Theory of Practical Reason* (La Salle: Open Court, 1964). Also, R. W. Beardsmore, *Moral Reasoning* (London: Routledge and Kegan Paul, 1969); and D. Z. Phillips and O. M. Mounce, *Moral Practices* (London: Routledge and Kegan Paul, 1969). I believe the line of approach in these works offers a great deal of insight into the nature of moral agency, independent of whether they have successfully resolved the central problems of moral philosophy.

33. Murphy, *The Theory of Practical Reason*, 267. The theme runs throughout the whole book.

34. Both Melden and Murphy use this sort of example in their works cited in n. 32. Their analysis of moral notions offers a possibly insightful way for understanding Confucian ethics. A further exploration of this topic is, I believe, quite essential to the assessment of Confucian ethics, and normative ethics in general.

35. Danto, *Mysticism and Morality*, 102–3. Thus in general I agree with Danto's thesis that moral attitudes in some sense "presuppose" certain factual beliefs, but would like also to insist on a two-way dependence. What marks out the lines of dependence, I believe, rests on one's theory of the connection of fact and value. But from the viewpoint of a reflective agent, which is our main concern throughout this essay, the philosophical question, however it is decided, does not affect the practical understanding of one's commitment, particularly in the case of moral ideals as distinct from moral principles and rules. For a preliminary attempt to distinguish and relate these two domains of morality in the broad sense, see n. 4.

certain factual beliefs on moral attitudes is a truism. It is, however, an important truism in that we, as philosophers, are often disposed to construe conceptual distinctions as dichotomies. The importance of this truism lies in the reminder that, for moral philosophy, the question of the connection of fact and value is more a theoretical than a practical question of understanding one's moral commitment.

For a reflective moral agent, the question of the connection of fact and value is an internal rather than external question about morality. As addressed to a moral agent, the philosophical issue is not, however, without value in that it can act as a challenge to moral thinking. For a reasonable agent may need to ask how facts are to be considered from a certain moral point of view in the context of moral deliberation. As moral agents we may on reflection be perplexed with the sort of facts that are invested with moral import. Our doubt may lead us to divest the factual content implied in our moral attitude, thus dissociating the task of evaluation from that of description. In so doing we free our moral, evaluative attitudes from their connection with factual beliefs. But this disconnection of evaluation and description does not entail an acceptance of the distinction of fact and value as an exclusive logical disjunction and this disjunction as a prerequisite for moral thinking. In this light, the principal question concerns how the distinction can properly arise within reflection in the context of commitment, and not how the terms of the distinction can be seen to be connected without violating the logical disjunction at issue. The moral philosopher, moreover, has an important task: not to legislate how fact and value are to be rationally construed as dependent, but to elucidate the contexts in which that question can appositely arise for moral agents and to map out answers admissible within the corpus of moral commitments of the agent. The successful execution of this dual task may not provide adequate answers to standard philosophical problems, but can be of some service to the critical self-understanding of a reflective agent. This essay has been written in that spirit, though we have largely confined it to a discussion of Chinese moral vision.

Essay 5   Opposites as Complements
Reflections on the Significance of *Tao*

The notion of *tao* as harmony of opposites is a pervasive feature of Chinese philosophy. An early succinct statement of this notion is found in Chapter 2 of *Tao Tĕ Ching*. Such contraries as good and bad, beautiful and ugly, high and low, and generally, something *(yu)* and nothing *(wu)*, are regarded as inherently complementary terms.[1] By taking this holistic view, the sage is said to practice *wu-wei* (taking no action) and engage in teaching without words *(pu-yen chih-chiao)*. From a metaphysical perspective, the notion of harmony suggests a basic idea that admits of categorial development of methodological or dialectical principles. In a recent essay, Cheng Chung-ying offered a systematic treatment of this topic, in both Taoism and Confucianism.[2] Such a valuable reconstruction and development quite clearly display the "logical powers" of a cardinal idea. In this essay, I explore, instead, the "practical powers" of the idea of opposites as complements by assuming a moral perspective independently of the metaphysical significance of *tao* in classical Taoism.[3] My reflections on *tao* are principally addressed to this question: For a reflective moral agent who is metaphysically innocent, what is the practical significance of *tao* as a moral vision or ideal, that is, as having a role to play in his moral life?[4] For this purpose, I shall assume

---

1. The occurrence of a large number of pairs of contraries in the text presents an interesting case study for exploring the theoretical significance of Taoism as a moral theory. In the course of such an exploration, I noted some forty-two (explicit and implicit) cases that appear to suggest different types of incompatibility of lexical items which admit of a classification in terms of epistemic, practical, psychological, and physical categories. Of particular interest are cases of juxtaposition, for example, in Chapter 81. I hope to be able to complete this project in the near future.

2. Cheng Chung-ying, "Toward Constructing a Dialectics of Harmonization: Harmony and Conflict in Chinese Philosophy," *Journal of Chinese Philosophy* 4, no. 3 (October 1977): 209–45.

3. The present essay continues a series of studies on the notion of harmony in Chinese philosophy. For a companion essay on Classical Taoism, see Essay 3. The Confucian notion is explored in Essays 2 and 7, and "Practical Causation and Confucian Ethics," *Philosophy East and West* 25, no. 1 (January 1975): 1–10.

4. Such a moral life or moral practice is here left open to alternative ethical char-

that *tao,* as a moral ideal, expresses an ideal theme of a moral life as a whole rather than a supreme norm of conduct.[5] This essay may be regarded as an "experiment" in the significance of a moral ideal. Section I shows the practical significance of *tao* as exhibited in Herman Hesse's *Narcissus and Goldmund.* This novel is taken, not as a subject of critical analysis, but as an imaginative exhibition of the significance of *tao* as harmony of opposites. Section II is devoted to the creative aspect of the commitment to an ideal theme. Section III discusses the role of doubt in ideal commitment. Section IV concludes with some reflections on the significance of "wordless teaching."

I. THE SIGNIFICANCE OF *TAO*

Before embarking upon the exploration, a fuller explanation of the nature of my task is essential to appreciating my choice of a novel for elucidating the significance of *tao.* Initially, the construal of *tao* as an ideal theme presents a problem. Unlike a supreme norm of conduct which admits of articulation by a set of principles and rules, the *tao* in classical Taoism is more of an orientation toward such action-guides. At the outset, one is warned by *Tao Tĕ Ching* against naming the *tao;* thus a theoretical route of exposition appears to be inappropriate to understanding the significance of *tao.* The only viable option is to attempt a more practical way of exhibiting its significance independently of one's theoretical and normative commitments. The aim is to make sense of the notion of *tao* by constructing plausible devices for *representing* the significance of an ideal theme. In this spirit, we abstain from the use of mediating principles.[6] Without denying the utility of theo-

---

acterizations. How in detail my remarks relate to specific normative ethics remains an independent question to be explored.

5. An extensive discussion of this distinction between ideal norm and ideal theme may be found in my *Dimensions of Moral Creativity: Paradigms, Principles, and Ideals* (University Park, Pennsylvania: Pennsylvania State University Press, 1978), particularly 133–46.

6. For Confucian ethics, the notion of *kan-ying* (influence and response) serves as a mediating principle for the concrete representation of the practical significance of *jen* as an ideal theme. A mediating principle is a theoretical device that has nontheoretical analogues. In Confucian ethics, the nontheoretical representation pertains to the notion of *chün-tzu* and historical and legendary characters. For a discussion of the former, see my "Practical Causation and Confucian Ethics." For the latter, see my "The Concept of Paradigmatic Individuals in the Ethics of Confucius," *Inquiry* 14, nos. 1 and 2 (Summer 1971). A revision of this paper is incorporated in chap. 5 of *Dimensions of Moral Creativity.* The nontheoretical devices of representation may be regarded as functional equivalents of the theoretical ones. Both sorts of devices are compatible attempts to cope with the problem of effectuation of moral ideals independently of normative ethical theory. Their adequacy is thus to be assessed solely in terms of judgments of reflective desirability of

retical elaboration, we focus on the notion of *tao* as an intuitive idea of opposites as complements.[7] The two main characters, Narcissus and Goldmund, in Hesse's novel of that title, may be offered as a dramatic representation of the idea.

A question quite properly arises on the proper function of mediating principles and their analogues. In an incisive essay on Kant's moral philosophy, Paul Dietrichson addresses this question in discussing Kant's notion of the typic of the moral law as a principle of mediation between a purely abstract conception and the phenomenal world. The typic of the moral law is a way of concretizing the practical significance of the moral law, that is, "restatement of the abstract moral law in a symbolically concrete form."[8] The typic, in this sense, is essentially a heuristic device for illustrating the concrete significance of the moral law, rather than a decision procedure or substantive moral principle.[9] Unlike the Kantian agent, a Taoist can avail himself only of nontheoretical devices for representing the concrete significance of *tao*. For this purpose, he may carry out his task with such notions as the sage *(sheng-jen)* or fictional characters for exemplifying the concrete significance of an idea and simultaneously for displaying the possibility of attaining a harmonious state of affairs or *tao*-experience. In this article, I focus on the use of fictional characters for elucidating the Taoist task, consequently, the choice of Hesse's novel as a basis of explication. Narcissus and Goldmund are here offered as an imaginary illustration of the reconciliation of opposites as complements. These characters are not to be taken as instantiations of logical or metaphysical types, but as symbolic representations of the concrete significance of *tao* as an ideal theme.[10]

---

individual commitive agents rather than in terms of criteria for the construction of moral theory. Such judgments may thus be assessed in terms of reasonableness rather than deductive or inductive rationality. For an attempt at understanding this notion of reasonableness, see Essay 1 and *Dimensions of Moral Creativity*, chap. 6.

7. Cheng offers a more elaborate explanation of the notion of harmony in this way: "For any two distinctive co-existing or succeeding forces, processes, or entities, if there are mutual complementation and mutual support between the two, so that each depends on the other for its strength, actuality, productivity, and value, then we may say that these two form a harmonious whole and an organic unity." "Toward Constructing a Dialectics of Harmonization," 211.

8. Paul Dietrichson, "Kant's Criteria of Universalizability," in *Kant: Foundations of the Metaphysics of Morals: Text and Critical Essays*, ed. Robert Paul Wolff (Indianapolis: Bobbs-Merrill, 1969), 168.

9. As Dietrichson points out, the proper function of the typic for a Kantian agent is "to supply the moral law with a *nonconstructive*, purely heuristic, illustrative mediation-principle" in order "to make use of the moral law as a practical standard for appraising [the agent's] . . . material maxims." The typic thereby serves, not as a theoretical schematization of the moral law, but as a "figurative substitute for such schematization" (ibid., 176–77).

10. In acknowledging the importance of fictional characters as a device for exem-

If the preceding observations are not far from the mark, Hesse's *Narcissus and Goldmund* provides an excellent dramatic way of portraying the significance of the idea of *tao* as harmony of opposites, or opposites as complements.[11] In reflecting on this novel, I see Narcissus and Goldmund (henceforth, N and G) as representing an extreme contrast and reconciliation or harmony of opposites.[12] I see N and G as two friends with completely different and opposed ways of life: the one the life of a person with an analytical and scholarly mind, the other the life of a man devoted to an incessant pursuit of sensuous satisfaction— an opposition of two antithetical characters and aspirations. If we take either N's life alone, or G's life alone, and abstractly write out their biographies, we see the strongest possible contrasts. It is inconceivable for Narcissus to live the life of a Goldmund, and conversely. The two ways of life represent a conflict and living in each way of life yields radically different consequences. Yet from the beginning, in reading the novel, one detects a bond, a peculiar sort of friendship and mutual

---

plifying the practical significance of *tao*, we widen our philosophical inquiry to embrace a concern with the moral function of aesthetic objects, thus suggesting a way in which art objects in general can serve as illustrative devices for the practical significance of moral ideas. A portrait, for example, can represent ideas of peace, justice, or love. A landscape painting can portray the harmony of things in nature. From the intellectual point of view, such art objects cannot serve as exclusive objects of representation of the practical significance of moral ideas, but it can hardly be denied that as a companion to conceptual representation, the art objects can be quite effective in producing plausibility or reasonable persuasion in the exposition of an ideal theme. At the end, the effectiveness of any such representation depends on the sort of agent at issue. As I see it, the philosopher's role here, to borrow a term from Stephen Körner, is to engage in a sort of "exhibition analysis" rather than in the construction of a systematic moral theory. See Stephen Körner, *What is Philosophy?* (Baltimore: Penguin Books, 1969), 25f.

11. In view of the avowed influence of Lao Tzu and Chuang Tzu in the thought of Herman Hesse, it seems not unreasonable to deal with *Narcissus and Goldmund* in a Taoist way. Although there is no evidence of any direct influence of Lao Tzu in the writing of this novel, Hesse explicitly avowed his appreciation of Lao Tzu and Chuang Tzu. Without embarking upon the problem of Hesse's scholarship, my reflections on his novel are quite in the spirit of his thought. In an essay "A Bit of Theology," Hesse remarks: "Just as the pious genius and the genius of reason know each other very well, secretly love each other, are attached to each other, so too the highest spiritual experience of which we human beings are capable is always a reconciliation between reason and reverence, a recognition that the great contradictions are one and the same thing." See Herman Hesse, *My Belief: Essay on Life and Art*, trans. Denver Lindley (New York: Farrar, Straus and Giroux, 1974), 199. For appreciative remarks on Lao Tzu and Chuang Tzu, see 139, 190, 191, 218–20, and 262. For an informative biographical study, see Janet Walker, "Herman Hesse and Asian Literature," presented at the Seventh Annual Meeting of the Mid-Atlantic Region of the Association for Asian Studies, at George Washington University, Washington, D.C., October 28–29, 1978.

12. All my textual citations from Hesse's novel are taken from *Narcissus and Goldmund*, trans. Ursula Molinaro (New York: Bantam Books, 1971). Page numbers of this edition are followed by a slash and the page numbers of the original Farrar, Strauss, and Girard, Inc., 1968 edition.

care in the relationship between G and N. It is this bond that prevents N and G from regarding each other with indifference, thus opening up a possibility of mutual appreciation and complementation. The friendship between N and G does not involve a condemnation of a way of life, however objectionable it may appear from either N or G's point of view. As a matter of fact, it was N, the allegedly rigorous analytical mind, who awakened G to freedom to pursue a way of life opposed to his own. From the beginning of their encounter, N sees G an opposite but a complement. N thought that he wanted G as a friend: "He wanted the bright boy as a friend. He sensed him his opposite, his complement; he would have liked to adopt, lead, enlighten, strengthen, and bring him to bloom" (16). And as he later explicitly said to G: "No road will bring us together . . . I am serious. We are not meant to come together, not any more than sun and moon were meant to come together, or sea or land. We are sun and moon, dear friend; we are sea and land. It is not our purpose to become each other; it is to recognize each other, to learn to see the other and honor him for what he is; each the other's opposite and complement" (40–41/42–43).

The friendship between N and G is, in effect, an acceptance of and recognition of each other's integrity with no thought of influence or attempt at molding or altering one another's character or way of life. We have no trouble understanding the opposition of character of N and G, but their alleged complement is puzzling. For G to complement N, G must possess certain features which N lacks. To complement N is in some sense to complete N, and G complements N by making up a lack or deficiency in N. But for this to be possible, it must be assumed that N's way of life is in some sense incomplete, and that G completes it, and conversely. The puzzle is: What does G complete? Perhaps, to make sense of N's thought, we need to get away from the literary sense of "completion." Perhaps the complement at issue is essentially a form of learning from each other's life, not in mere acceptance of each other's integrity, but also in the appreciative experience and learning of the practical significance of a shared ideal theme. The complementation is thus achieved, not by mutual adjustment of segments in two opposed ways of life, nor by recognition of their common and intersecting elements to form a coherent way of life. Rather, it is achieved by a reciprocal appreciation and learning. The appreciative experience and learning pertain to the realization that an ideal theme admits of different concrete expressions of developments. In retrospective characterization, such a form of learning points to the mutual completion of deficiencies which may not have been felt as such in the course of living out the transformative significance of the ideal theme. The realization has also a prospective aspect, for it can function as a point of orientation for future actions and for the deepening of personal relationship.

N and G each believe in something; their "somethings" go by different names for each. For G, it is "the universal mother." This figure or image "consists of a fusion of the greatest contrasts of the world, those that cannot otherwise be combined that have made peace only in this figure. They live in it together: birth and death, tenderness and cruelty, life and destruction" (183/185).[13] For N, it is the Christian "God" for whom he lives his monkish existence and which serves at the same time as a subject for theological disquisition. N's belief in God as a perfect Creator is regarded as compatible with his belief in original sin (266–267/268–269). Both "the universal mother" and "God" have different cognitive references, but as ideal perspectives for orienting one's way of life, these references have import in providing a directional signal rather than in their capacity to serve as ideas for developing abstract conceptions or theories. From the point of view of their practical significance, the references converge on a common theme. Both the universal mother and God *care* for their offspring. Caring appears thus to be a common theme that exemplifies itself in the friendship between N and G. And this ideal theme of caring may be regarded as a sort of "hidden meaning" in the friendship between N and G—a friendship that each needs to develop and strengthen in the manner congenial to each personal character.

Both in abstract conception and in concrete experience, N and G radically contrast in their ways of living. In his own way, each believes in love, and in his own way each has to live out the full significance of this love and the caring involved and accept whatever fruits result as well as unwanted consequences. Caring appears to be an ideal theme. And it is the friendship between G and N that unites the opposite ways of life as complementary ways in which each idiosyncratically constitutes the significance of care. Even if two persons share the same commitment to an ideal theme, each can only live and develop this theme in his own life. However, the friendship that unites the two contrasting ways of life involves an acceptance of the integrity of personal existence, and it is this acceptance that enables one person to learn from another's life. Even in the course of his sensuous escapades, G has learned to think through their transitory nature, and to think through suffering,

13. Goldmund thought of this figure, strangely, as an image rather than an idea. But the fact that this thought can be expressed in my quotation clearly shows an articulation of an idea, though what Hesse wanted to emphasize is its *lived* character rather than its appearance as a mere abstract conception (*Narcissus and Goldmund*, 183).

doubt, and anguish, the meaning of his way of life. G learns from N how to think and reflect, and N learns from G also. Hesse writes: "Goldmund has shown him that a man destined for high things can dip into the lowest depths of the bloody, drunken chaos of life, and soil himself with much dust and blood, without becoming small and common, without killing the divine spark within himself" (298/301). Now it seems that learning from the life of another is not a matter of acquisition of knowledge or conviction, but of a realization of the significance of a way of life as a unique constitutive expression of an ideal theme.

Friends who cannot learn from one another have a transitory bond. The possibility of enduring friendship in part lies in learning, and this learning does not entail a conversion to a way of life opposed to one's own. The capacity to learn makes it possible to see opposites without blurring their distinctive characters. This notion of friendship appears to be different from the Taoist attitude of nonresponsibility and nonattachment. But if we suppose that the Taoists are capable of becoming friends, to make sense of the significance of this sort of friendship, some element of care must figure in as an essential ingredient. However, Hesse's depiction of the friendship between G and N seems in part Taoistic, at least in the manner in which G and N accept one another's integrity with deliberate noninterference and noninvolvement in pursuing their contrasting ways of life. Such an attitude is portrayed in the openness of the relationship—an openness to rendering assistance in G's moments of need and distress; and the relationship that endures is on the whole free from emotional involvement in each other's activities.

We may note that in learning from another person's life, whether that of a friend or a complete stranger, one also learns about oneself. The recognition of a difference in personal character and way of life can make one aware of one's own difference, of one's own defects and virtues. To borrow the language of kan-ying, there is mutual influence and response in learning from one another's life. Such learning involves not merely mutual understanding and empathy, but also an expansion of intellectual horizon and a restructuring of one's vision of life. If such learning does not lead to a change in one's way of life, it can at least divest one of cherished beliefs and biases. If N loves G, he also learns what love is as he confesses at the end when G is dying: "Let me tell you how much I love you, how much you have always meant to me, how rich you have made my life. It will not mean very much to you. You are used to love; it is not rare for you, many women have loved and spoiled you. For me it is different. My life has been poor in love; I have lacked the best of life. . . . It is thanks to you alone that my heart has not dried up, that a place within me has remained open to grace" (306/310). Indeed, we can learn much from one another concerning what love is; and friendship, in the ideal sense, is a process of learning within the setting of mutual care and respect. It is not judgment alone that makes men better but friendship and the capacity to learn from one another.

II. *TAO* AND CREATIVITY

The preceding reflections on Narcissus and Goldmund provide a way of representing the concrete significance of *tao* by opposites as complements. Narcissus and Goldmund, in spite of their differences in wants and aspirations and ways of life, have become friends. It is friendship as a form of care or love that unites these opposite characters or ways of life. What emerges from our discussion is the notion of love or caring as an ideal theme. The love experienced in the form of friendship is a personal relation that rests on a recognition and acknowledgment of the integrity of person; this acknowledgment at once embraces an attitude of acceptance and a mutual concern and is unaccompanied by any desire of a friend to alter a way of life incompatible with his own. This in turn involves a suspension of judgment on another's life and conduct. Thus two incompatible characters and ways of life are reconciled in friendship or love without a change in the descriptive content of their ways of life. Conflict between ways of life is a brute existential encounter. From the Taoistic point of view, the conflict is resolved, but not by compromise; consequently, no sacrifice of interests and aspirations is involved in personal relationship. From the practical point of view there is, strictly speaking, no problem of intellectual reconciliation, for the conflict at issue is resolved by an act of personal acceptance and mutual respect. The parties in opposition are, so to speak, joined in a bond without any alteration of their moral opinions and views about how life ought to be lived. There is no leap to a higher plane or level that integrates interests and policies—no synthesis, since the opposition is accepted as inherently complementary, and in an important sense, each character or way of life is meaningful only in light of the other. The significance of a way of life thus radically depends for its vitality upon the contrast with another way of life.

Abstractly viewed, the two ways of life represent a cognitive contrast and have incompatible logical and existential consequences. They may be said to be in harmony when the opposition is submerged within the ambience of friendship or love as a theme that is developed in two different ways. And since the ideal theme does not issue positive precepts for guidance, there is no logical opposition between the two ways of life. In light of the theme, the opposition is transformed into a difference in expression and constitutive content. A light can shine through different objects without transforming its descriptive properties.[14] The objects are experienced in harmony by virtue of their common debt to the source of light. This is the power of an ideal theme shared by two persons without the necessity of having a desire to be like one another. A person with an ideal way of life can claim to give the ideal a personally significant expression, and, in humility, must recognize that others will give it a different expression depending on their character, dispositions, and circumstances of life. A commitment to an ideal theme thus involves an appreciation of its dispersive and diffusive significance. Each dispersion and diffusion, from the point of view of a commitive agent, is a creative development of the significance of the ideal theme in a way of life.

The case of Narcissus and Goldmund thus presents only an extreme form of learning from another person's life. Its main value lies in a dramatic portrayal of the practical significance of *tao* in focusing upon opposites as capable of personal reconciliation without undergoing change in the ways of life. As I have previously pointed out, it also portrays the significance of learning about oneself, of self-understanding of one's ideal commitment. Although one's way of life is not changed, the ideal perspective that renders it significant involves a change in attitude. In the light of *tao* the commitive agent can live and do the same thing but with a different heart and mind, and the adoption of this perspective may result in a greater or more expansive development of the ideal theme. The ideal commitment is sustained in its dedication by an expansive awareness of the indeterminate variety of its actualizing possibilities. This is an awareness that an individual man is capable of becoming a member in an ideal harmonious whole embracing a multiplicity of idiosyncratic expression.

In this light one may envisage humanity as a universal realm inhabited by men who resemble one another and yet differ in their interior lives. These contrasting privacies are opaque to empirical observation,

14. I sometimes wonder about the significance of Chu Hsi's clarification of *t'ai-chi* (The Great Ultimate) by way of moon analogy:

Fundamentally there is only one Great Ultimate, yet each of the myriad things has been endowed with it and each possesses the Great Ultimate in its entirety. This is similar to the fact that there is only one moon in the sky but when its light is scattered upon rivers and lakes, it can be seen everywhere. It cannot be said that the moon has been split.

May one also properly add that the myriad things retain their own individuality through sharing a common source of light. One may also recall Plato's analogy of the Good and the sun in Book VI of the *Republic*. See W. T. Chan, trans., *A Source Book in Chinese Philosophy* (Princeton: Princeton University Press, 1963), 638.

but as polymorphous creative expressions of a shared ideal theme they are transparent. Perhaps the practical significance of such ideals as *tao*, *jen*, or *agape*, apart from their doctrinal import, represents a common holistic ideal theme. The ideal of *tao* is peculiar in its emphasis on opposites as complements. In the language of *yin* and *yang*, *tao* points to contrasts and differences as eligible complements in a harmonious whole. Since a *yin* contains seeds for the generation of a *yang*, and conversely, *yin* and *yang* are different but not exclusive. No dichotomy is involved, or, from the practical point of view, categories for the explanation and categorization of phenomena. When we construe the practical significance of *tao* as an ideal theme, it is readily intelligible why a Lao Tzu would insist on the pointlessness of discourse. The silence, the unutterability, and the unnameability of *tao*, however, remain practically significant. For it is not speech or intellectual knowledge that brings about the experience of harmony of opposites; it is the individual commitive agent whose life is lived in the light of *tao* who can yield a verbal knowledge of what *tao* means. And this is a matter of retrospective characterization of one's *tao*-experience. When one speaks about such knowledge, one can speak only for oneself. In this sense there is no universal knowledge of *tao*, no truth that can be stated to be learned in the way in which one acquires knowledge in general. Of course, when a person is committed to *tao*, he no longer has the need to worry about the nature of *tao*. In Chuang Tzu's words, he has "forgotten" *(wang)* the *tao* as a truth to be captured in a set of propositions. Instead the commitment involves an appreciation of the living significance of a vision to be cherished and lived and savored in contentment. But the contentment is not the focal aim, but a mark of consummation of a life lived in the light of *tao*.

III. DOUBT AND IDEAL COMMITMENT

Thus far I have attempted to exhibit the practical significance of *tao* for a commitive agent. One can query whether such a commitment to an ideal theme is compatible with the experience of self-doubt. Plausibly, faith in moral achievement can sometimes be accompanied by doubt about one's ability and capacity to endure in circumstances that present obstacles for realization. Faced with this doubt an agent can perhaps derive some comfort from Chuang Tzu's emphasis on the cultivation of responsive mind, that is, a mind that readily responds to changing circumstances.[15] But at the same time one is also counseled

15. Burton Watson, trans., *The Complete Works of Chuang Tzu* (New York: Columbia University Press, 1968), 97.

about the utility of doubt: "The torch of chaos and doubt—that is what the sage steers by. So he does not use things but relegates all to the constant. This is what it means to use clarity."[16] These ideas in Chuang Tzu suggest that doubt has a proper role to play in a commitment to *tao* as an ideal theme. Doubt and clarity, somewhat in an anti-Cartesian way, are compatible states of mind. In committing oneself to an ideal theme, one commits to clarifying what the ideal means in one's way of life, and unless one experiences doubt in the process of clarification, one may be too attached to one's congenial ideas and manner of behavior, thus depriving oneself of the possibility of a fuller view of what actual situations mean in light of the ideal theme.

Developing the ideal theme in one's life thus involves doubt; clarity emerges through the experience of doubt. A reflective agent, instead of being content with his commitment, at times may question the significance of the ideal theme. If his perplexity concerns the possibility of the ideal theme offering a perduring vision, can such doubt be compatible with a sincere and continuing commitment to the ideal? I am not here thinking of the case of alternative visions, but the case of continuing to live a way of life embued with an ideal while occasionally experiencing doubt about its significance. In response, one may say that if such a doubt occurs, the agent has only a halfhearted commitment to the ideal. And one mark of such a halfhearted commitment is related to one's conception of the self as somewhat independent and external to the ideal. The self is, as it were, detached from the ideal. This sort of commitment need not be insincere, for it can be a genuine experience that sometimes infects one's ideal commitment. However, another sort of response to our question brings out a different sort of doubt: The response here lies, not pointing to the distinction between the self and the ideal, but focusing upon a self in relation to the ideal or an ideal-embedded self. If one is genuinely committed to an ideal, one cannot at will detach one's self from such a commitment. A commitment to an ideal is, in this view, a commitment to an ideal self, and such a situation would preclude doubt about the significance of the ideal as an integral part of the commitment itself. It would seem then that doubt about the ideal while living by it is somewhat foreclosed by the nature of the commitment itself.

The foregoing responses to our query do bring out the distinction between actual and ideal self. Although neither response by itself can do full justice to our question, together they suggest a third response, which brings out more clearly what I regard as the most interesting

16. Ibid., 42.

case of self-doubt in the midst of an ideal commitment. Beginning with the distinction between actual and ideal self, one may regard the commitment to an ideal theme as a commitment to a meaningful connection between the actual and the ideal self. Sincere doubt can occur in this sort of context when the significance of an ideal theme is considered or reconsidered in light on one's changing needs, desires, and circumstances of life. Doubt here points to the capacity of the agent to *reflect* upon what the ideal means as a continuing concern with living. Whether such a reflection will result in a change of heart is a question only the agent can answer. But if a commitment precludes reflective reconsideration, it cannot be viewed as a reasonable commitment. And reflection on the continuing significance of an ideal theme throughout one's life is a integral part of the commitment. A sincere agent can, in this way, experience doubt while living in the light of his ideal theme. Doubt has thus a proper role in the growth and development of one's ideal commitment. It accentuates one's overall quest for the actuating import of the ideal theme. It may be regarded as an expression of the desire for the ultimate harmony of apparently discrepant experiences in the agent's relation to other men and to natural events and human affairs.

The preceding excursion into an aspect of moral psychology assumes the internal point of view of a commitive agent. The complexity of the nature of ideal commitment is hinted at rather than resolved in manageable items. What is interesting for my present purpose is the role of doubt as compatible with a commitment to *tao* as an ideal theme. From an external point of view, such an approach may appear problematic, for the issue of commitment pertains primarily to the epistemic components, to beliefs and attitudes that can be articulated clearly in order that one may properly assess the rationality of the commitment. It may be said that what is at issue, prior to proper assessment, concerns the role of choice in commitment. In other words, in what sense can a person choose his ideal theme? For a rational agent, this question is important, because there clearly are alternative visions competing for his attention. Unless he can opt for one with good reasons, exploration of cases of self-doubt in the midst of commitment is simply an interesting aside rather than an illumination on the nature of choice. I do not intend to deal here with this complex issue, which pertains to the epistemology rather than the psychology of morals. However, apart from the question of assessment of moral beliefs and attitudes, the question of the role of choice in commitment cannot be set aside as irrelevant, for it seems particularly puzzling in the case of *tao* as an ideal theme. Pondering this question is important in two ways: as a further elucidation of the nature to *tao* commitment and as a rectification of some possible misunderstandings concerning the nature of Taoist ethics or, for that matter, Confucian ethics.

Obviously, if one conceives of choice or decision as a consequence of a process of deliberation or calculation in the presence of options, choice must precede action. This standard notion of choice is particularly germane to the case of an ideal norm. In this context, one can regard the norm as relevant to policies of action or life plans. If a way of life is governed, as a matter of commitment, by an ideal norm, then such a commitment may be characterized as an outcome of the agent's choice. A choice can, in this way, be an intellectual exercise of moral agency. With an ideal theme, since we are not clearly presented with principled components, choice in this sense does not seem intelligible. Even if we suppose that one can clearly articulate the cognitive components involved in say, *tao*, choosing the *tao* as an ideal way of living does not seem to make good sense. Further, our quandary is compounded by the Taoist insistence on the unutterability of *tao*. Thus it seems that one cannot intelligibly choose to live by *tao*.

Tao, as an ideal theme of harmony of opposites, has a vague and minimal cognitive content. We are offered no guiding principles for articulating clearly its specific or detailed practical import. It is as if the commitive agent knows what it is not and not what it is in itself. He knows, for example, that opposites are not what they seem to be, but he can hardly formulate positive criteria for distinguishing genuine from pseudo complements. A commitment to *tao* is more a resolution to view things in a certain way than a knowledge of the nature of things. In this regard, a Confucian agent has an advantage with *jen* as an ideal theme. For part of *jen's* cognitive content can be positively understood in terms of *li* and other virtues which, collectively, may be construed as constitutive means for the realization of *jen*.[17] Such virtues, however, are not acceptable to the Taoist as proper means for attaining *tao*. One may say that the Taoist is more oriented toward moral perplexity that resists problematic formulation than toward problems that are solved by conscious efforts at cultivating virtues. Even when *tao* can be appreciated as a harmony of opposites, a Chuang Tzu would insist that such a minimal cognitive content eventually should be discarded or forgotten.[18] He would even go further, pointing to the unutterability of

17. For an account of *li* in terms of moral, aesthetic, and religious values, see my "Dimensions of *Li* (propriety)," *Philosophy East and West* 29, no. 4 (October 1979): 373–94; and "*Li* and Moral Justification: A Study in the *Li Chi*," *Philosophy East and West* 33, no. 1 (1983): 1–16. For a more general discussion of the basic functions of *li* and its connection with *jen* and *i*, see Essay 13.

18. For an extensive discussion of this notion, see Essay 3.

tao. In such a situation, no clear notion of choice seems intelligible or possible.

Of course, if the agent persists in demanding a fuller understanding of *tao,* a Lao Tzu would be quite prepared to offer "makeshift description."[19] Thus, a way is suggested to help the agent out of his quandary. This suggestion may be appreciated by attending to a distinction between two senses of understanding: the intellectual and the practical.[20] In the intellectual sense, one can understand, say, a subject-matter by comprehending what it is about. This ordinary sense of understanding involves descriptive knowledge. To understand the significance of *tao* in Taoism is to be able to produce a description of Taoism in terms of a set of propositions. All of us are quite familiar with the large number of books and articles on Taoism. The characteristics of the Taoist *tao* in this way can be displayed for objective examination and evaluation. Here, should a reader succeed in comprehending such books, he himself need not be committed to *tao.* And our exploration of the question of practical significance would be quite irrelevant to his understanding. However, there is another sense of understanding relevant to Taoism. For if we take Lao Tzu seriously about the "makeshift descriptions" of *tao,* an intellectual understanding would be completely alien to the insights intended in the text. Here we may attempt to engage in a task of practical understanding, and understanding the significance of *tao* consists essentially in trying to elucidate the nature of the commitment to *tao* from an internal point of view of a Taoist moral agent. To understand *tao* in this way is to embrace it. As D. Z. Phillips points out:

There is a use of 'understanding' which is synonymous with 'caring', 'loving', etc. Thus it might be said that only the humble man possesses understanding. Here, the understanding is inseparable from humility, and is almost a synonym for it. When we say that a man who lacks humility lacks understanding, we are saying that he lacks the understanding that humility brings, which is a roundabout way of repeating the assertion that he is not humble.[21]

In light of the practical sense of "understanding," the notion of choice has no place, since choice quite properly pertains to intellectual understanding. Looking back to my remarks in Section I, Narcissus and

19. D. C. Lau, trans., *Leo Tzu: Tao Te Ching* (Baltimore: Penguin Books, 1963), chaps. 15 and 25. All my quotations are taken from this translation.

20. I am here pointing to a distinction without suggesting a dichotomy. As a matter of fact, the connection between these two sorts of understandings does pose important problems for moral philosophy. I offered some tentative methodological suggestions in "Tasks of Confucian Ethics" and "Some Responses to Criticisms," *Journal of Chinese Philosophy* 6, no. 1 (1979) and 7, no. 1 (1980).

21. Ilham Dilman and D. Z. Phillips, *Sense and Delusion* (London: Routledge and Kegan Paul, 1971), 102–3.

Goldmund did not choose to become friends. The care they showed for one another and the learning involved are not a by-product of deliberation in the midst of options. To embark upon the task of practical understanding, whether in the care of a person or of his belief in a way of life, involves a *concern* with them as objects of practical understanding. It is practical rather than intellectual understanding that is at issue for a reflective Taoist. And if one understands *tao* in this sense, one embraces *tao* as an ideal perspective for orienting one's thought and action. No choice is present in this sort of understanding. Consequently, a commitment to *tao*, quite in the spirit of classical Taoism, is not a product of choice. Therefore, it makes no sense to speak of choosing to live by *tao*. And to be concerned with the significance of *tao*, is, in this way, in part to be committed to *tao* as a subject of elucidation. My excursion into cases of self-doubt has been to articulate the nature of *tao*-commitment. Understanding *tao* in this sense is to embrace it, even if doubt inevitably occurs in the course of its elucidation. If my remarks thus far have successfully conveyed the nature of the *tao* commitment, one may regard the discussion of the case of Narcissus and Goldmund as a collection of "makeshift descriptions" for acquiring an actual experience rather than a set of manageable cognitive items to be more carefully dissected for the sake of intellectual understanding. Although I am not a sage, I do steer by "the torch of chaos and doubt," in Chuang Tzu's sense. In drawing attention to the need of practical understanding, naturally more doubts must remain, not only intellectual puzzles, but also practical ones that are oriented toward moral problems and issues.

IV. "WORDLESS TEACHING"

The use of "makeshift descriptions"[22] in the practical understanding of *tao* is intimately connected with the notion of "teaching without words." In Chapter 43, *Tao Te Ching*, we find the following:

---

22. I have followed Lau's renderings of *ch'iang wei chih jung* and *ch'iang wei chih ming* as "makeshift descriptions," as they occur respectively in chap. 15 and chap. 25 of *Tao Te Ching*. As I understand them, these expressions suggest "being compelled to name, describe, or speak on what in reality cannot be so named, described, or spoken." I take them to refer to an activity of a teacher engaging in discourse for showing the significance of nondiscursive phenomena. Consequently, sentences occurring in this sort of discourse are not to be construed as naming or referring to propositions or propositional attitudes. I take this to be one proper use of practical discourse in nonargumentative contexts. Such a use of practical discourse, I believe, requires serious exploration. Although the remarks that follow are not intended as an exegesis of the notion of "wordless teaching," they are quite in line with the plausible interpretation of this notion in terms of non-

The most submissive thing in the world can ride roughshod over the hardest in the world—that which is without substance entering that which has no crevices.

That is why I know the benefit of resorting to no action. The teaching that uses no words, the benefit of resorting to no action, these are beyond the understanding of all but a very few in the world.

This passage suggests that "wordless teaching" is a paradoxical expression that draws attention, not to the impropriety or disutility of employing language, but to the *peculiar* attitude involved in communicating the significance of the *tao*-experience. Such an attitude may be said to be "submissive" or "soft" in that the teacher aims not at imparting doctrines or precepts, but at conveying something that cannot strictly be formulated in assertions or propositions. "Makeshift descriptions" have a role to play, but they are not to be taken as assertions. Consider Chapter 81: "Truthful words are not beautiful; beautiful words are not truthful. Good words are not persuasive; persuasive words are not good." These remarks, if construed as assertions, are obviously subject to counterexamples. The problem, however, is to pin down more clearly the status of such "makeshift descriptions." Hobbes states that "words are wise men's counters; they do but reckon by them; but they are the money of fools."[23] If such "makeshift descriptions" are to be regarded as counters, one must be able to distinguish the wise from the foolish. A Lao Tzu would be quite content to be called a "fool," but as philosophers, we can hardly accept this ascription. At the same time, we can hardly pretend to possessing the wisdom of a Taoist sage. If we are sympathetic to Taoism, we appear to have no recourse except to focus on a principal function of religious discourse. In a recent essay on the ineffability of *tao*, after traversing several conceptual routes, Danto offers this conclusion:

> The office of religious language is precisely to dramatize the limits of our understanding to a point beyond which we cannot proceed except by changing our lives; and having changed them the utterance has no point, the incomprehension it induces no longer being of moment, its role being that of a linguistic sacrifice which is achieved when we discard the utterance as transformed persons.[24]

---

preceptive, or more generally, the nonassertive use of words. For the former, see Ch'en Ku-ying, *Lao Tzu chin-chu chin-i* (Taipei: Commercial Press, 1970), 54; for the latter, see Sung-peng Hsu, "Two kinds of Changes in Lao Tzu's Thought," *Journal of Chinese Philosophy* 4, no. 4 (1977): 350.

23. Thomas Hobbes, *Leviathan* (Oxford: The Clarendon Press, 1952), pt. 1, chap. 4, p. 29. For a perceptive discussion of this epigram in connection with visual language, see C. M. Turbayne, *The Myth of Metaphor* (New Haven, Connecticut: Yale University Press, 1962), chap. 5.

24. Arthur Danto, "Language and the Tao: Some Reflections on Ineffability," *Journal*

Danto's remark is reminiscent of Chuang Tzu's: "The fishtrap exists because of the fish; once you have gotten a fish, you can forget the trap. . . . Words exist because of meaning, once you have gotten the meaning, you can forget the words. Where can I find a man who has forgotten words so that I can have a word with him?"[25] Both Chuang Tzu and Danto stress the point of self-transformation. But if "make-shift descriptions" are necessary for this purpose, these "descriptions" must be more than temporary expedients for teaching the audience *something* about the significance of self-transformation. One way to render this form of teaching intelligible is to draw a distinction between *insight* and *truth.* Characteristically, truths are imparted by way of statements whose claims to knowledge can be assessed, while insights are tied to their capacity to illuminate the shifting scenes of human life. An insight, in this sense, does not consist in an intuition or immediate apprehension of a new truth, but an awareness and adoption of a new perspective for appreciating the significance of objects, facts, or states of affairs in ordinary life. An insight can lead to a discovery of unfamiliar facts or provide an occasion for exploring the plausibility of truth-claims; but it has an independent practical import. The expression "wordless teaching," when taken literally, is self-contradictory; but when it is taken as an unconventional way of focusing on teaching insights rather than truths, the expression can be rendered intelligible. The "makeshift descriptions" employed in such a teaching can be regarded, *à la* John Wisdom, as illuminating paradoxes that have a practical import for the appreciative audience. If such a teaching on the practical significance of *tao* as harmony of opposites is successful, the audience may be said to have acquired an ideal perspective for viewing opposites as complements. Such an insight may yield novel ways of thought, decision, and action, particularly on the occasion of perplexity of a reflective moral agent concerning the significance or meaning of his life.

The words used in communicating insights are a vehicle in the activity of a teacher, but the teacher can have no assurance that his words will always succeed in fulfilling his intention. This is especially evident when the insights conveyed are construed by the teacher and his audience in doctrinal terms. On this point, Otto Neurath's fictional character Ku-Lu-Ling put it well:

of Chinese Philosophy 1, no. 1 (1973): 55. It is interesting to compare Danto's reflections to Seng Chao's. See Chang Chung-yuan, trans., "Nirvana is Nameless," *Journal of Chinese Philosophy* 1, nos. 3/4 (1974): 247–74.
    25. Watson, *The Complete Works of Chuang Tzu*, 302.

There are many schools and many doctrines. It is the way of a doctrine that it passes through the skies like a cloud bank, visible to all but meaning different things to different people. The doctrine is one thing to him who gives it and another to him who receives it.[26]

On the part of the teacher, his failure represents a lapse from his intended objective. A teacher may be so excited with an insight that he couches it misleading doctrinal form. On the part of the audience, different appreciative responses are to be expected in view of their varying backgrounds, needs, desires, and aspirations. So also, even if words serve their purpose well, the teacher can have no confidence that the insights will be received in accordance with his intention. The reason, I think, lies in the flexible character of the words used in conveying insights. In the manner in which they adjust to different contexts and occasions of use, the words appear as "makeshift descriptions," since they admit of no determinate formulation. These words, however, are constitutive of the attempt on occasion to clarify the nature of the insight—consequently, constitutive of an attempt at self-understanding. An insight, by its nature, is a vague and inchoate conception. To convey it by means of language is to articulate clearly one's own understanding. In this regard, the task of the teacher is analogous to that of a creative artist seeking an expression of his emotions in works of art. In the words of Collingwood,

the act of expressing is . . . an exploration of his emotions. He is trying to find out what these emotions are. There is certainly here a directed process: an effort that is directed upon a certain end; but the end is not something foreseen and preconceived, to which appropriate means can be thought out in the light of our knowledge of its special character. Expression is an activity of which there can be no technique.[27]

Similarly, a teacher of insights is engaged in an activity of clarification of his thought, not just for the sake of conveying something to his audience, but for the sake of self-understanding. Insights provide answers to perplexities rather than solutions to problems. Unlike truths or truth-claims, they also need to be recast for the audience in order to perform their functions in varying contexts of communication. In this way, self-understanding is a process of growth or continuing enrichment of a polymorphous creative experience. Teaching insights may thus be regarded as an activity of both communication and self-understanding.

26. Otto Neurath, "The Little Discourse on the Virtues," in *Empiricism and Sociology*, ed. Marie Neurath and Robert S. Cohen (Dordrecht-Holland: D. Reidel Publishing Co., 1973), 92.
27. R. G. Collingwood, *The Principles of Art* (Oxford: The Clarendon Press, 1938), 111.

To say that the words are a vehicle for communicating insights is to point to their function in showing the intended insights. Say that I am genuinely committed to the significance of *tao* in *Tao Tê Ching*. To convey the insight that I have learned from my own reading and reflection, by necessity I have to engage in discourse, thus making use of words to fulfill my teaching function. However, there is a radical contingency in this use of speech. For my words, in the final analysis, are makeshift instruments. I am engaged in a sort of "wordless teaching." There appears to be nothing paradoxical about this notion, for it is a *focal* notion that draws our attention to the importance of showing the significance of a perspective in the teaching activity. But in a way, it is misleading to call these words "makeshift instruments" to be discarded when they have served one's purpose in *showing* insights. This is, I think, the *force* of Chuang Tzu's remark on "forgetting words." Recall that after urging us to forget words after we have got the meaning, Chuang Tzu ends with the question: "Where can I find a man who has forgotten words so that I can have a word with him?" This remark suggests that words used in conveying insights are more than just contingent instruments to be ignored after we have used them. For assuming that one sometimes succeeds in this task, the words used are constitutive of one's understanding of the insights. In the abstract, these words may appear as heuristic devices or "makeshift descriptions," but in a concrete setting of discourse, they are constitutive of the understanding of the speaker.

To engage in "wordless teaching" is in effect to *experiment* with constituting the nature of the insight. When such an experiment is successful, the teacher is also an accomplished learner. The teacher, so to speak, achieves self-understanding in experimenting with words in conveying insights. When he fails, this failure provides a further setting for another experiment. The contingency involved in "wordless teaching" in part relates to the context-dependent character of these experiments. Although in context the successful words constitute the insight, one has no assurance that in another context they can function in the same way. Perhaps one's insights have undergone transformation through the process of reflection. If this happens, it appears that the more effective way is to employ words that can adjust themselves to various settings of discourse. In appearance, these words are context-invariant; in an occasion of use, they flexibly adapt themselves to changing circumstances. Thus metaphors, symbols, anecdotes, and the like convey insights better than do literal or context-independent uses of language.

Teaching, in the sense I have been trying to articulate, is a struggle with self-understanding. The vital sense of failure in sincere communication becomes an occasion for continuing one's experiments with "wordless teaching." Quite expectedly, the experienced moments of success provide no assurance that the insight at hand will be expressed in the same way by the student or the audience. Chuang Tzu's "forgetting words" makes sense also in reminding us of an aspect of the audience's response. The constitutive instruments of the teacher can at best serve as a paradigm for the learner's own self-understanding. The learner has to reconstitute the insight in his life and thought. In communicating his insight, the learner, in effect, takes on the role of the teacher. As a teacher, he is then prepared to receive a disparate variety of responses.

The notion of "wordless teaching" in *Tao Te Ching,* if it be intelligible, has nothing to do with communicating knowledge or truth. As I have suggested, it is best rendered as a form of teaching connected with the conveying of an insight or perspective for viewing the significance of familiar facts or states of affairs in human life. When one appreciates such a perspective, one in effect embraces it. In this sense, the perspective has now a transformative significance in one's life. *Tao* as a perspective for viewing opposites as complements can thus be appreciated as an insight. The "makeshift descriptions" are thus more than expedient instruments for conveying the insight or for achieving self-transformation; they are themselves constitutive of the insight that inspires such a transformation.

Essay 6   Morality and Human Nature

Enquiry into the nature of human beings has been an enduring preoccupation of both Eastern and Western philosophers. The underlying question concerning man's basic nature as a repertoire of powers and tendencies and its manifestations in human conduct, is amenable to different interpretations and answers, all of which reflect, as it were, proposals of conflicting descriptions and/or visions or ideals of humanity. The question is a large one. Insofar as moral philosophy has a place in the inquiry, instead of dealing with the more general and perhaps more fundamental question about the essence of human nature, it is more manageable to focus on a narrower question about the connection between morality and human nature. This narrower question is particularly important for normative ethical theory, since philosophical and moral doctrines, and "all practical suggestions about how we ought to live, depend on some belief about what human nature is like."[1] Our question, however, presupposes that the notions of morality and of human nature are distinct, and at the same time are intimately connected with each other. Without taking the distinction as an exclusive logical disjunction, or the connection as a logical or conceptual one, the understanding of the question depends on how the distinction is to be construed, and the construal may well reflect a certain way of answering the question concerning their connection.

For a preliminary clarification of our question, it is useful to attend to a classical Chinese formulation. Wang Chung (27–100? A.D.), in his essay *On Original Nature*, offers the following:

Man's natural feelings and dispositions are the root of government and the source of rules of proper conduct *(li)* and music. Therefore as we investigate the matter, we find that rules of proper conduct are employed to check the excesses of dispositions and feelings and that music is used to regulate them. In man's natural dispositions there are qualities of humbleness, modesty, deference, and compliance. In men's natural feelings there are the qualities of

---

1. Mary Midgely, *Beast and Man: The Roots of Human Nature* (Ithaca, N.Y.: Cornell University Press, 1978), 166.

likes and dislikes, pleasure and anger, and sorrow and joy. Hence music has been created to enable their feeling of reverence to be expressed everywhere. Natural dispositions and natural feelings are therefore the reason why systems of rules of proper conduct and music have been created.[2]

If we set aside the peculiar Confucian moral concern with music, Wang Chung's statement presents a relatively clear view of our question. Put in more general form, morality as a system of rules of proper conduct has an intimate connection with man's basic motivational structure, which consists of feelings, desires, and dispositions. Morality so construed pertains not to the whole nature of man, but only to a certain aspect of this nature. The aim of the inquiry, in other words, is directed toward a plausible explication or understanding, rather than an explanation of the nature of morality.[3]

In this essay, I focus on two different sorts of extreme theories that give us some insights into the nature of morality as a subject matter of ethical inquiry. What I call Externalism, as the term suggests, construes the connection between morality and human nature as essentially an external affair. On this view, morality is in some sense *alien* to human nature. The very existence of morality, consequently, points to certain problematic aspects of man's basic motivational structure. As opposed to this view, what I call Internalism construes the connection as an intimate and internal one. On this view, morality is in some sense *inherent* in human nature. More fully, there are in man's basic nature certain feelings and dispositions, which, if unimpeded in their expression and development, will attain fulfillment in human conduct. In the critical discussion of these two views, I am more interested in their general assumptions and presuppositions rather than in the adequacy of specific versions of each theory. However, it is difficult to discuss these views without sometimes invoking some familiar conceptions of human nature and conduct. Typically, for instance, Externalism is associated with the conception of man as in some basic sense bad, aggressive, and destructive; Internalism is perhaps more frequently associated with the

2. Wing-tsit Chan, trans., *A Source Book in Chinese Philosophy* (Princeton, N.J.: Princeton University Press, 1963), 293. The passage quoted contains minor emendations for convenience of the present exposition. For the notion of *hsing*, following Forke, I render it as "natural disposition," and *li*, following Dubs, as "rules of proper conduct." See Alfred Forke, trans., *Lun Heng, Part I: Philosophical Essays of Wang Chung* (New York: Paragon Book Gallery, 1962), 384; Homer H. Dubs, trans., *The Works of Hsüntze* (Taipei: Ch'eng-wen Publishing Co., 1966), 213.

3. For this distinction, see Henrik von Wright, *Explanation and Understanding* (Ithaca, New York: Cornell University Press, 1971); Nicholas Rescher, *Conceptual Idealism* (Oxford: Basil Blackwell, 1973), 189–94; and my "Tasks of Confucian Ethics," *Journal of Chinese Philosophy* 6, no. 1 (1979): 55–67.

conception of man as naturally good, compassionate, and cooperative.[4] In these typical versions of the theories, quite obviously some normative ethical doctrine is taken for granted. On the face of it, there would not appear to be any genuine issue if the parties to the dispute clarify their assumptions and central concerns. And when the assumptions and the underlying concerns are elucidated, both types of theory, far from being mutually exclusive claims to insights, may in fact turn out to be complementary lenses for understanding two principal aspects of morality. In this spirit, I shall first present Externalism and Internalism and then consider the possibility of their reconciliation, and, ultimately, their significance for moral philosophy.

I. EXTERNALISM

Externalism implicitly conceives of morality as adjudicating conflicts between interests of different human beings. In the now familiar notion of the moral point of view, morality represents "a point of view which is a court of appeal for conflicts of interests. Hence it cannot (logically) be identical with the point of view of self-interest."[5] But this conception of morality presupposes that man, in terms of his basic motivational structure, is in some sense a self-seeking or self-interested animal. His feelings and desires demand satisfaction. The natural propensity toward such satisfaction, however, need not be construed in the narrow sense of preoccupation with self-interest which excludes any concern with other people's feelings and desires. In other words, the propensity is not necessarily selfish as opposed to altruistic. Rather, it is more of an inclination toward *partiality* to the things wanted. This propensity is in some way "bad." For, as Hsün Tzu points out, what is good is that which is "upright, reasonable, and orderly," and what is bad is "that which is prejudiced, irresponsible, and chaotic." Were man's basic motivational structure good in the sense defined, there would be no need for rules of proper conduct, nor would there be need for moral education.[6] Less misleading is Hume's remark on the con-

4. For a variety of versions, particularly in social sciences, see John J. Mitchell, ed., *Human Nature: Theories, Conjectures, and Descriptions* (Metuchen, N.J.: The Scarecrow Press, 1972).
5. Kurt Baier, *The Moral Point of View* (Ithaca, N.Y.: Cornell University Press, 1958), 190.
6. Burton Watson, trans., *Hsün Tzu: Basic Writings* (New York: Columbia University Press, 1963), 162. For an attempt at a plausible explication of this aspect of Hsün Tzu's ethics, see my "The Conceptual Aspect of Hsün Tzu's Philosophy of Human Nature," *Philosophy East and West* 27, no. 4 (1977); "The Quasi-Empirical Aspect of Hsün Tzu's Philosophy of Human Nature," *Philosophy East and West* 28, no. 1 (1978); and "Dimen-

fined generosity of men: "Now it appears, that in the original frame of our mind, our strongest attention is confined to ourselves; our next is extended to our relations and acquaintance; and 'tis only the weakest which reaches to strangers and indifferent persons. This partiality, then, and unequal affection, must not only have an influence on our behaviour and conduct in society, but even on our ideas of vice and virtue."[7]

Man's basic motivational structure is thus, from the moral point of view, *problematic*. Compounded by the condition of scarcity of resources to satisfy individual desires, men are inevitably impelled to compete against one another. In the succinct words of Hsün Tzu, "desires are many but things are few."[8] This condition necessitates some form of regulation of human behavior. Morality in this light is a regulative system. In one Chinese form of Externalism, it is *li* or rules of proper conduct that regulate human strife. In contemporary Western moral philosophy, a similar view may be expressed by saying that law and morality must have a certain content because of certain natural facts about us, e.g., facts pertaining to limited resources and limited altruism;[9] or that the "'general object' of morality, appreciation of which may enable us to *understand* the basis of moral evaluation, is to contribute to betterment—or non-deterioration—of the human predicament, primarily and essentially by seeking to countervail 'limited sympathies' and their potentially most damaging effects."[10]

But as I have construed it, the focus on partiality in man's basic and premoral motivational structure is not logically tied to any conception of selfishness as opposed to altruism. There is, of course, a problem of filling in the details in our sketch of Externalism, for how one fills in the details of the motivational structure is highly problematic. In large part, the difficulty in specification of the content of such a structure is contingent upon the nature of the occurrent feelings and desires and the circumstances in which individuals pursue their satisfaction. Plausibly, the specification may point to a diversity of content depending on the cultural context that renders the specification meaningful. If man's basic motivational structure, in its problematic aspects, requires regulation, it does not follow that such a regulation in terms of moral rules can be logically derived from these aspects.

------

sions of *Li* (Propriety): Reflections on an Aspect of Hsün Tzu's Ethics," *Philosophy East and West* 29, no. 4 (1979).

7. David Hume, *A Treatise of Human Nature* (Oxford: Clarendon Press, 1951), Book III, pt. II, sec. 2.

8. Dubs, *The Works of Hsüntze*, 152.

9. See H. L. A. Hart, *The Concept of Law* (Oxford: Clarendon Press, 1961), chap. 9.

10. G. J. Warnock, *The Object of Morality* (London: Methuen & Co., 1971), 26.

The preceding observation immediately raises, for some philosophers, the issue of relativism. A just Externalist response here would draw attention to its central concern, i.e., the problematic character of man's basic motivational structure. And such a concern and its conceptual articulation do not entail, as in the case of egoism versus altruism, ethical relativism. Concerning the issue of cultural relativism and its implications for human conduct, the Externalist can accept some anthropologists' emphasis on cross-cultural universals as formal or conceptual categories rather than specific content universals. As Murdock points out, rarely do the universal similarities found among different cultural patterns "represent identities in specific cultural contents. The true universals of culture, then, are not identities in habit, in definable behavior. They are similarities in classifications, not in content."[11] Of course, the issue remains whether such moral rules are "true" universals. And this question is difficult to answer. Moral rules, as a device for dealing with human conflict, may vary in accordance with their respective purposes. Where purposes differ, rules may also differ. Moreover, even with respect to the same purpose, one may still implement the purpose with different rules. This latter consideration is particularly relevant to the conception of morality as a regulative system. Here, as a general point, a single purpose is assumed. And this purpose can be implemented by different rules as evident, for example, in the difference between the Decalogue and the Confucian *li* or rules of proper conduct. A general conception of a purpose, in its concrete import, can vary with the particular circumstance of the cultural group or individual in question. Different cultures may be said to share the same formal ideal, for example, of justice. Macbeath justly reminds us that "the starting point, the problem and the goals are the same for all. But between the starting point and the goals there are solutions at which different peoples have arrived in their attempts to give concrete expression to the ideal, and to embody it in a way of life. It is these concrete and detailed articulations of the formal ideal, that is operative of embodied ideals, which provide practical guidance and prescribe detailed duties and obligations of moral agents."[12] Thus we can understand how two different cultures, while "agreeing" on the "object" of morality, to use Warnock's term, differ in their ways of implementing the object. In this sense, relativism does infect our moral understanding.

The above, however, cannot be completely persuasive without a de-

11. George Peter Murdock, "The Common Denominators of Culture," in Mitchell, *Human Nature*, 416. Similar views are held by Ralph Linton and Clyde Kluckholn. See Mitchell, *Human Nature*, chaps. 40 and 41.
12. A. Macbeath, *Experiments in Living* (London: Macmillan & Co., 1952), 68.

fense of an assumption of *conceptual relativism*, for Externalism assumes that conceptual agreement at the abstract level does not entail a uniform substantive moral consequence. Further, apart from the issue of their logical derivation, moral concepts have their "cash value" only in actual circumstances. That is, they are in some sense culture bound. And for recent moral philosophy of the objectivist persuasion, this implicit assumption raises questions, for comparative moral evaluation is not only intelligible and possible, but also quite rational, in that such an evaluation makes a legitimate claim to validity. Of course the claim may be mistaken, but the possibility of a mistake here presupposes that there is a correct answer, which it is the task of moral philosophy to uncover.

There is a twofold rejoinder to this "objectivist" objection. In the first place, if one adopts a skeptical posture, the Externalist can point out that the objectivist claim implicit in our comparative evaluation is an expression of ethnocentrism,[13] or else an objectification of a deeply entrenched proclivity owing primarily to one's philosophical education. It is arguable that the philosopher's preoccupation with moral notions reflects more of an interest in the philosophical than the ordinary uses of the terms in question. As Rorty recently maintained, "Words like 'good,' once they have been handled in the way that the philosophical tradition has handled them, acquire a sense in respect to which this is so."[14] More to the point, perhaps, the issue raised may be construed as a challenge to the Externalist pretension to rationality. A proper response, and a plausible one, is to disclaim rationality as tied to logical canons of the inductive or the deductive variety, and to be content with reasonableness as distinct from rationality as it is standardly conceived.[15] And reasonableness here pays heed to convention, though not uncritically. Logical consistency is, of course, adhered to, but only if the situations at hand are adjudged to be relevantly alike so as to sanction the same assessment. Moreover, reasonableness addresses itself more to the sense of concrete significance of rationality in actual circumstances. Consistency is no doubt a value in abstract discourse, but its value presupposes significant similarities among actual situations for it to have a concrete import. Reasonableness, though obviously tradition or culture bound, is not a matter of arbitrary subjectivity, for it is open

13. This appears to be implicit in Richard Rorty, "Pragmatism, Relativism, and Irrationslism," Presidential Address to the American Philosophical Association, Eastern Division, December 29, 1979. See *Proceedings and Addresses of the American Philosophical Association* 53, no. 6 (1980): 719–38.

14. Richard Rorty, *Philosophy and the Mirror of Nature* (Princeton, N.J.: Princeton University Press, 1979), 306 (italics omitted).

15. See Ch. Perelman, "The Rational and the Reasonable," *The New Rhetoric and the Humanities* (Dordrecht: D. Reidel Publishing Company, 1979), 117–24.

to discursive argumentation and justification.[16] Reasonableness can, whenever appropriate, make claim to objectivity. For, after all, it is an impartial exercise of reason. As much as rationality, it is an exercise of a distinctive human capacity. But such a capacity in the absence of man's motivational structure is hardly problematic in practical contexts. I am not here maintaining Hume's thesis that reason is slave of the passions, but rather that without passion reason is hardly problematic for conduct.

II. INTERNALISM

My characterization of Externalism is, I hope, a clear reconstruction of a plausible position on the connection between morality and human nature. The plausibility rests roughly on several dimensions of assessment of the conception of human motivation which point to its problematic character and the necessity of appropriate remedy in terms of rule-regulation. As we have noted on the issue over the essence of man, much has been left out regarding other aspects of man. But what is left out is not necessarily the result of any negative evaluation, for obviously the problematic motivational aspect can only be intelligibly handled because of man's mental capacity or power of mind to overcome the disastrous consequences that may ensue from the operation of the motivational structure. In a real sense, it is our motivational structure that poses problems for moral regulation.

In this conception of morality and human nature, one may properly raise two questions from the Internalist point of view. In the first place, it may be said that the problematic situation arises out of the occurrent strength of some of our dispositions. It may well be that the neglected factors are the ones that possess the authority of moral regulation, though not the power in actual exercise. One can recall Butler's conception of conscience as a reflective faculty or Mencius' unequivocal emphasis on four moral beginnings or seeds of virtue, i.e., the hearts of compassion, shame, courtesy and modesty, and right and wrong.[17] The Externalist, however, may grant the existence of these dispositions and yet point to their possible problematic consequences. Depending on situations of human intercourse, our dispositions are appraised in terms of their beneficial and harmful consequences. Take compassion; as in the case of Mencius or Rousseau,[18] it can be morally problematic without reflective guidance. A blind compassionate act may well lead

16. See Essay 1.
17. D. C. Lau, trans., *Mencius* (Baltimore: Penguin Books, 1970), 82–83.
18. See J. J. Rousseau, "A Discourse on the Origin of Inequality," in *The Social Contract and Discourses* (New York: E. P. Dutton and Co., 1950).

to human ills or misery. And if we insist that there is still a reflective capacity (Butler) or a sense of distinguishing right from wrong conduct (Mencius), then again it must be pointed out that such a reflective capacity is a non-moral capacity. For in the absence of moral commitment, we have no assurance that it will pay heed to moral demands. Moreover, an Externalist will remark that though the Internalist's focus on our native capacity for morality or moral motivation is quite to the point, this does not establish that human nature is inherently good. For such a moral motivation is plausibly an outcome of moral cultivation or development of second-order moral desires mediated by both thinking and will, and is informed by a regard for the importance of moral considerations.

But it may be said that the Externalist still neglects one major aspect of morality. Granted that morality is a basically regulative system, which it unquestionably is, there is still the question about the *value* of this regulative system. Unless we value regulation, we are not likely to endorse it. But then if we value it, still we must value it for a reason.[19] An Externalist could reply: were human intercourse immune to conflict, we would not value regulation. It is hardly intelligible to justify regulation of human conduct when this conduct displays nothing but harmony.

The Internalist, however, can still insist that the substantive aspect of morality cannot be accounted for by Externalism. In the first place, not all of morality, whether Jewish, Christian, Confucian, or Buddhistic, is concerned merely with regulation. Although different moralities have their different contents, there is still a wider concern with the good life on the whole. A distinction needs to be drawn between the broad and narrow senses of morality. Externalism focuses merely on the narrow sense of morality as a system of constraints. In the broad sense, however, morality deals with principles and/or ideals which a person accepts as defining his conception of proper conduct and of the good life on the whole.[20] The question "what is man?" may well be a question of "what is fitting to the dignity of man?" or "what it means for a man to deserve the title of manhood or humanity."[21] It is quite proper to regard this question as the main focus of Mencius's ethical doctrine. And the thesis compendiously, though misleadingly, formulated in terms of the *goodness* of human nature answers this proper question. It

19. Ian Gregory, "Psychoanalysis, Human Nature and Human Conduct," in R. S. Peters, ed., *Nature and Conduct* (New York: St. Martin's Press, 1975), 114.

20. For a parallel distinction, see J. L. Mackie, *Ethics: Inventing Right and Wrong* (Baltimore: Penguin Books, 1977.), 106.

21. Renford Bambrough, "Essay on Man," in Peters, *Nature and Conduct,* 7.

is a question of human dignity or, in Mencian terms, what it is to be a moral agent.

The substantive content of morality has to be seen in this light. Focusing on innate compassion or commiseration, or on our capacity to respond to the needs of others in distress, is a way of pointing to the *humanity* of human beings. The Externalist would agree on the importance of this concern for humanity. Hsün Tzu, for example, acknowledges the narrowness of his Externalist focus on the problematic human predicament. Since morality has its basic and preeminent function in regulating human conduct, if it is not joined with an ideal function, i.e., an ennobling function, it may appear to individual agents a mere system of formal constraints without the depth of personal significance. Even if human conflict can be resolved or averted by *li* as a system of rules of proper conduct, it is the task of a moral teacher, apart from inculcating respect for these rules, to "nourish" our basic motivational structure. After all, this motivational structure is the "raw material" for moral transformation. In Hsün Tzu's words, "The original nature of man is the beginning and material; acquired characteristics are the beautification and glorification of the original nature. Without original nature, there would be nothing to which to add acquired characteristics; without acquired characteristics, the original nature could not become beautiful of itself."[22]

The problematic nature of our basic motivational structure does not point to its intrinsically evil character. When our basic motivational structure is subjected to moral regulation and ennobled by a regard for moral virtues, it deserves the title of moral structure. Thus when moral transformation, in accord with an ideal of humanity, is successful, the resulting character can also be properly viewed as our nature. Morality, in the broad sense, must point to some ideal of humanity which renders meaningful the compliance with a regulative system. On this Internalist conception, one must appreciate the claim that "unless there existed some sentiment on the part of man, there would never be any motivation to be moral."[23] But it must be noted that such a sentiment is itself either a reflective sentiment, that is, a sentiment mediated by reflection, or else an *extension* of the scope of operation of the sentiment owing to experience and reflection. The latter is more particularly a Confucian focus developed by Mencius.[24] In this light an

22. Dubs, *The Works of Hsüntze*, p. 130. For an axiological approach to *li*, see my "Dimensions of *Li* (Propriety): Reflections on a Theme in Hsün Tzu's Ethics," *Philosophy East and West* 29, no. 4 (1949): 373–94.
23. Gregory, "Psychoanalysis," 111.
24. For a recent explication of this theme, see David S. Nivison, "Two Roots or One?"

Externalist cannot deny that morality—in the broad sense of embracing the ideal of humanity—is an outgrowth of certain seeds or beginnings found in man's basic nature. Properly nourished and gently cared for, these seeds would grow into the virtues which we ascribe to persons of moral attainment. Moreover, as the scope of these sentiments extends, the problematic motivational structure focused on by the Externalist can be gradually overcome. But nourishing these sentiments also guides them reflectively toward proper channels. A morality of the *ideal* of humanity or of virtues can thus be seen as firmly rooted in human nature.[25]

For this view to be plausible, we need to adopt a retrospective view of moral achievement. While the rules that govern our problematic motivation are essential, in retrospect, compliance with these rules also displays personal virtues or merits. We have here an internal connection between ideal morality and achievement. Virtues are not the direct targets of moral endeavor but characteristic achievements of personal styles of performance that extend the range of the seeds of moral sentiment. Faced with a stranger in distress, a benevolent man engages in helpful conduct, not in order to display his benevolence, but in order to help remedy the distressful situation. When he succeeds, he acts benevolently. The virtue is as it were an *adverbial* qualification of his performance.[26] Of course our notions of virtue can also be deployed in the statement of principles, for example, the principle of justice or benevolence. This distinction, of course, does not imply that the two have no connection of any sort, for we do expect a just man to act in accord with the principles of justice, and conversely. But it is quite possible—moreover it is actually the case in Confucian ethics—that one can espouse an ethics of virtues without an ethics of principles. This raises, of course, the issue of reductionism. What is at issue for the Internalist position, like that of Mencius, is the ideal of humanity, and this ideal can be stated in terms of the possession of virtues rather than rule-like principles of conduct. All virtues are personal achievements grounded

---

Presidential Address to the American Philosophical Association, Pacific Division, March 28, 1980. See *Proceedings and Addresses of the American Philosophical Association* 53, no. 6 (1980): 739–61.

25. For more discussion of this view, see my "Confucian Vision and the Human Community," *Journal of Chinese Philosophy* 11, no. 3 (1984): 227–38.

26. As Dewey remarks, "To say that a man seeks health or justice is only to say that he seeks to live healthily or justly. These things, like truth, are adverbial. They are modifiers of action in special cases. How to live healthily or justly is a matter which differs with every person. It varies with his past experience, his opportunities, his temperamental and acquired weaknesses and abilities." John Dewey, *Reconstruction in Philosophy* (Boston: Beacon Press, 1957), 167.

in the extension of certain basic dispositions such as compassion, modesty, shame, and the sense of the distinction between right and wrong. And in the last case it is not always a spontaneous response but a reflective assessment of what the situation requires. As Mencius once remarked, reason and righteousness (i.e., the sense of what is right as distinct from wrong conduct) are common to all men.[27] Reason is reasonableness in judgment appropriate to what the situation demands, rather than a consultation with prior principles assented to by the agent. Reasonableness is sentiment informed by experience and reflection rather than compliance with canons of inductive or deductive logic. On this, Mencius and the Externalist Hsün Tzu seem to agree, though unlike the latter, Mencius hardly pays any attention to the problematical features of man's basic motivational structure.

III. A CONCEPTUAL REORIENTATION

The notion of human nature may be deployed to ask questions that may offer some insights into the regulative and the ideal aspects of morality. Seen in the light of the distinction between the ethics of principles and the ethics of ideals, the issue may appear contestable. But morality itself is an essentially contestable concept.[28] What sense we appeal to must depend on what we have in mind, on what sorts of questions that occupy our inquiry. If we ask why we need regulation in the first place, we are bound to be attracted to Externalism. For regulation is a way of dealing with problems that arise out of human intercourse. The language of rules and principles has here its indispensable employment in discourse on morality. Were we not beset by problems in our dealings with one another, we would hardly have the need of rules or principles. Rules and principles are ways of dealing with human problems that arise out of our encounters with one another. This capacity of formulating rules and principles is quite justly an exercise of reason. And here our reason can also serve a second-order function by critically assessing rules and principles in dealing with particular cases. When internalized, these rules and principles also serve as internal monitors of one's conduct, for they are also ways of dealing with internal conflicts.

The basic questions about human beings are, so to speak, *problem-indicators*. They indicate problems to be resolved. Rules and principles

27. Lau, *Mencius*, p. 164.
28. W. B. Gallie, "Essentially Contested Concepts," *Proceedings of the Aristotelian Society* 56 (1956); and Dorothy Emmet, *The Moral Prism* (London: Macmillan Press, 1979), chap. 1.

offer procedures for dealing with them. The rules and principles of morality, however, unlike ordinary rules, are not just rules of thumb or heuristic devices which may be discarded when they are deemed inefficacious in resolving problems. For, since they possess moral import, they can become objects of commitment, and consequently, constitutive means for realizing an ideal way of life. The concept of human nature in this way is amenable to at least a partial explication of morality as a regulative system constitutive of the ideal way of life of a people. Humanity, in this sense, is a rule-making as well as a rule-constituted animal. In this way, one can now appreciate the insight of Internalism. For as objects of commitment, rules are no longer matters of external imposition, but objects of internal assent constitutive of what it is to be a human being. Coupled with the ideas of virtue and an ideal vision of the whole of human life, human nature is no longer a matter of external description, but an internal characterization. In this way, while appreciative of the problematic orientation of moral rules, our focal concern is the concern of *being* a worthy human being. And the questions quite justly arise: What is it to be a moral agent? What capacity do we possess for such a moral accomplishment?

In some basic sense, the question about the nature of man is a question that man addresses to himself. If rules are constitutive of the nature of social intercourse, equally these rules are deemed important because they themselves are constitutive means for the realization of the ideal of humanity. Man is a self-defining animal. Perhaps, in the end, it is his own interpretation of his humanity that counts as his essence. Plausibly, it is this basic capacity that is inherent in "man as a self-interpreting animal." It may be said that "he is necessarily so, for there is no such thing as the structure of meanings for him independently of his interpretation of them, for one is woven into the other. But then the text of our interpretation is not that heterogeneous form that is interpreted: for what is interpreted is itself an interpretation; a self-interpretation which is embedded in the stream of action."[29] Herein perhaps lies the strength of Internalism, but this need not commit one to the claim that there is a single source of man's moral motivation that attains its flourishing when unimpeded by external circumstances. We need not follow Mencius in accounting for the existence of evil as due largely to the uncongenial influence of external circumstances, nor with Rousseau's explanation of the existence of evil

29. Charles Taylor, "Interpretation and the Sciences of Man," *Review of Metaphysics* 25, no. 1 (1971), reprinted in Roger Beehler and Alan R. Drengson (eds.), *The Philosophy of Society* (London: Methuen, 1978), 167–68.

as due to the corruption of civilization. On this issue we are more inclined to the more reasonable position of the Externalist Hsün Tzu and
Hume. The fact of scarcity of resources to satisfy individual wants
poses problems in human intercourse. Even if we have regard and affection toward others, we are more likely to be partial toward our kin
or friends. And in the absence of a regard for moral regulation, our
partiality is more likely to be displayed in our conduct than extensive
benevolence. Hsün Tzu would concur with Hume in focusing upon the
problematic character of our "natural temper" and "outward circumstance" which give rise to the necessity of moral rules.

Of course, Externalism and Internalism need not be in genuine conflict if they are regarded as characterizations of the external and internal points of view of morality.[30] Seen as exclusive doctrines, they do
conflict and have quite radically distinct consequences for human intercourse. As points of view, they are complementary, for they do disclose
to us two aspects of morality in the broad sense. From the external point
of view, we see morality as a regulative system of rules or duties. One
can hardly deny this function in any established morality. But from the
internal point of view, the same rules and duties have their peculiar
import for the commitive participants. The two points of view are complementary though not simultaneously relevant to the same situation.
This complementarity is best seen when a commitive agent shifts from
the internal to the external point of view for the purpose of critical
assessment of the rules themselves. Likewise, an observer of a moral
system may come to appreciate what it means to be committed to the
moral system that he observes, thereby coming to experience the concrete import of commitment. Here the first is transformed into the
second point of view. In abstract discourse, the two are logically dichotomous, and coupled with a specific normative doctrine of human
nature, the dichotomy is complete; hardly any bridge is possible without taking sides. But as beings engaged in reflection in concrete contexts, we need no *a priori* decision on the soundness of either Externalism or Internalism in the exclusive sense. We take them as different
points of view relevant to different circumstances in our moral life.
Here as self-interpreting animals we may well need to adopt one view
rather than another, but these views are more like suggestions for
understanding the human predicament and aspirations than presentations of premises for practical reasoning.

30. See Hart, *Concept of Law*, 84, 244; and my *Dimensions of Moral Creativity: Paradigms,
Principles, and Ideals* (University Park, Pennsylvania: Pennsylvania State University Press,
1978), chaps. 1 and 6.

IV. FOUNDATIONS OF MORALITY

The above quasi-pragmatic move toward reconciling Externalism and Internalism may be deemed unsatisfactory, for what it assumes is the position of a reflective agent. Morality from this vantage point is an object of self-understanding. Externalism and Internalism are not doctrines to be adhered to but insights into the aspects of morality as a matter of personal commitment. But for a moral philosopher there is the question of the *foundation of morality*. And this classic question in moral philosophy may be said to lie at the heart of the dispute between the two conceptions of morality and human nature. Perhaps by reflecting upon this classic problem, we can also gain some insight into the tasks of moral theory. Let me reiterate here that I have not meant to present the two conceptions as doctrines of normative ethics, for such an interpretation quite easily gives rise to the controversy between Kantian formalists and teleologists. There is no denying that both these competing doctrines are in some sense concerned with the question of the foundation of morals. But this question, though apparently a single question, actually conceals a cluster of distinct questions. It is like asking the question "what is man?" apart from any commitment to a specific normative ethics. As Bambrough recently observed: "What is man? What is a man? There is a plurality and variety of men, but also a plurality and variety of questions about men. 'What is man?' is itself many questions, and questions of different kinds."[31]

Let me here follow the lead of Richard Price in clarifying the question on the foundation of morals without being biased by the Kantian conception of pure moral philosophy.[32] In the first place, the question may be construed as "what is the *true account* or *reason* that such and such actions are *right*, or appear to us under this notion?" In this light, the question belongs to moral epistemology, for it addresses the nature of moral knowledge, that is, whether or not, as in the case of the eighteenth-century British moralists, moral justification is founded on reason or sentiment. On this question, both Externalism and Internalism as I have presented them may appear to contribute indirectly to moral epistemology. An Externalist epistemology of morals is bound to stress the problem of human conflict, and to regard moral justification as an appeal to principles and rules. However, we cannot deduce from the theory the nature of these principles or rules without cou-

31. Bambrough, "Essay on Man," 6.
32. Richard Price, *A Review of the Principal Questions in Morals* (Oxford: Clarendon Press, 1948), 233–35. It must be noted here that Price's terms are "foundations of virtue" rather than "foundation of morals."

pling the theory with a specific normative ethical doctrine that gives it a substantive content. The nature of the moral epistemology at issue remains an open question. So also with Internalism. While it may stress the problem of understanding moral commitment and the role of an ideal in such a commitment, an open question remains: What is the best explication of the nature of this ideal as befitting humanity and its relation to rules and principles acknowledged as a component of the moral commitment? For such an understanding, a specific normative ethical doctrine is required to give an Internalist moral epistemology substantive content.

In the second place, the question on the foundation of morals may mean, "What are the *primary principles* and *heads* of virtue; or the considerations inferring obligations in particular cases and rendering particular actions right?" This question belongs to the province of normative ethics and the theory of moral reasoning. Again, Externalism and Internalism are not very helpful unless we combine them with specific doctrines of moral principles or virtues and an account of moral reasoning in particular situations. However, the respective conceptions may well influence a philosopher in formulating his normative theory. At any rate, our characterization offers no guide to answering the problems of moral epistemology, nor does it offer an adequate formulation of a normative ethics or a theory of moral reasoning.

A third construal of the question on foundations of morals is an inquiry into "the *motives* and *reasons*, which lead us to it, and support the practice of it in the world." This question properly belongs to what may be called moral psychology. However, we need not follow Price in construing this inquiry so narrowly as one that aims primarily at an account of moral action in terms of motives as extrinsic aids or instruments for the sole support and practice of morality. For as Price himself recognizes, there are other factors, such as liberty or self-determination, intelligence, and a "consciousness of rectitude."[33] And when we focus on the 'consciousness of rectitude', if it is meant as an emphasis on moral concern, it is itself a powerful motivating force in moral conduct. But unlike extrinsic motives, the concern itself, for the commitive agent, has an intrinsic moving force in moral performance.

On the question of the foundation of morals as a question of moral psychology, Internalism has much to contribute vis-à-vis its stress on personal moral achievement as a realization of the concrete import of moral comitment. As a personal achievement, morality is a concrete expression of a personal aspiration. A man's moral nature is quite

33. Ibid., 181–84.

properly the basis for his moral attainment. The common capacity for moral achievement can be properly viewed as morally significant. Imbued with the ideal of humanity, it may be seen as a native sentiment that can well operate quite independently of external circumstances. And this point is not unconnected with our proposal of a conceptual reorientation for the sake of self-understanding. What is it to be a moral agent? Unless we see what we achieve as *internally connected* with our moral motivation, with our moral sentiment that has an affinity with our basic nature, can we properly understand ourselves as moral agents? When morality is invested with an ideal of humanity that has an intrinsically actuating force for a committed agent, our nature is an ideal nature, i.e., an expression of an aspiration for human excellence. If this aspiration is shared by all commitive agents, we can endorse Hume's remark that "the notion of morals implies some sentiment common to all mankind, which recommends the same object to general approbation and makes every man, or most men, agree in the same opinion or decision concerning it."[34] But as a common sentiment, it has both an affective and a cognitive aspect. And the latter is implicitly an ideal of human excellence seen as a light that illuminates human agency as moral agency. Perhaps more persuasively, we can view our ideal of humanity, insofar as it has an intrinsically moving import, both as "a sentiment of the understanding" and as "a perception of the heart." This Butlerian characterization does appear to do justice to our understanding of moral agency.[35]

For a commitive agent, the ideal of humanity is an object of sentiment as well as an object of volition. This moral ideal furnishes a way of seeing persons as having a moral import. It is a perspective, a point of orientation, what I elsewhere call an *ideal theme* rather than a norm for assessing conduct.[36] Given the commitment to the ideal, morality cannot be regarded simply as compliance with rules and principles, but must be regarded as compliance with them insofar as these rules and principles are invested with the ideal of humanity. For this sort of moral achievement, morality can have nothing to do with benefits extrinsic to personal commitment. In this sense, it has nothing to do with personal advantages accrued in the realization of particular purposes. Plausibly, as it is recently pointed out, "when Socrates says that the right act is the advantageous act, he is insisting that you cannot understand what

34. David Hume, *An Inquiry Concerning the Principles of Morals* (Indianapolis: The Library of Liberal Arts, 1957), 93.
35. Joseph Butler, "A Dissertation Upon the Nature of Virtue" in *Five Sermons* (Indianapolis, Indiana: The Library of Liberal Arts, 1950), 82.
36. See *Dimensions of Moral Creativity*, chap. 8.

is to your advantage until you understand what rightness is."[37] This emphasis is also present in Confucian ethics. *The Great Learning* reminds the Confucian agent that rightness *(i)* is the real profit.[38] One cannot expect payments or rewards extrinsic to actions that aim at the realization of the ideal of humanity. Of course a concern with human excellence is quite properly a concern for human welfare, i.e., a concern with those requisites or preconditions for the achievement of moral excellence. For an Internalist, human welfare is a necessary, but not a sufficient, condition for moral performance. As Aristotle points out, "it is impossible or at least not easy to perform noble actions if one lacks the wherewithal."[39] Morality, in this light, has no "object" external to itself. Although moral evaluation may be a device or human invention for dealing with the human predicament, "it does not follow, however, that it must have an object or end wholly beyond itself, in the sense of its being itself simply a way of trying to bring such an external object into existence."[40] In a deeper sense, the Externalist conception of morality as a mere instrument for resolving the problem of human conflict cannot do justice to the practice of morality seen from the point of view of a commitive moral agent.

What more can be said about Externalism? It also has important contributions to make to moral psychology. For after all, even if morality is quite properly a matter of personal commitment, it is, at least in its origin, a social institution. The rules and principles, as objects of serious commitment, must have their significance apart from such a commitment. There must be some independent account for the existence of these rules and principles in the first place. At least a partial account in terms of man's problematical motivational structure is quite in order. For an elucidation of an aspect of moral conduct moral psychology is undeniably a legitimate inquiry, but such an inquiry cannot be pursued oblivious to that aspect of social theory that has a contribution to make to an understanding of morality as a social institution. Moreover, the problematical motivational structure that leads to the establishment of a morality must at least be presupposed to make sense of morality as a system of rules that has its import apart from personal commitment to an ideal of humanity. When an Internalist attempts to

37. D. Z. Phillips and H. O. Mounce, *Moral Practices* (London: Routledge and Kegan Paul, 1969), 31.

38. Chan, *A Source Book in Chinese Philosophy*, p. 94.

39. Aristotle, *Nicomachean Ethics*, Martin Ostwald, trans., (Indianapolis: Bobbs-Merrill, 1962), Book I, 1011a.

40. William K. Frankena, *Thinking about Morality* (Ann Arbor: University of Michigan Press, 1980), 30–31.

account for the *content* of morals, inevitably a regard must be paid to the point of the moral rules. Even if these rules are not espoused as personal rules of conduct or as strategies for achievement of the ideal of humanity, they nevertheless remain in force for regulating moral conduct. Moral psychology cannot be dissociated from social psychology. But then, there need be no contestable issue here so long as moral psychology, aiming at an elucidation of the internal aspects of moral agency, is considered a legitimate field of inquiry.

Externalism and Internalism are not incompatible conceptions of the connection between morality and human nature. Each draws attention to certain facts about human or moral motivational structure. Any issue here does not admit of empirical resolution, for both are normative lenses for understanding morality. The Externalist draws attention to the point of morality as a social institution or an institution of human life. It would offer no insight if human beings were unconcerned with problems that beset their intercourse. Nor is the Internalist focus of much interest unless our attempt at understanding moral psychology is imbued with a concern for human beings in the way that, undeterred by difficult circumstances besetting their lives, they aspire to ideal achievement. We need both Externalism and Internalism to understand ourselves, to *interpret* our own actions and those of others. The pragmatic tone of our earlier proposal for conceptual reorientation is in fact a way of expressing this reconciling move. What is meaningful depends much on our understanding of morality. There are times when we need to focus on morality in the narrow sense as dealing with human conflict, but there are other times when we need to focus on the ideal of reconciliation. Each bespeaks the necessity of understanding the problematic and non-problematic aspects of motivational structure, making us appreciate better, not the whole of common humanity, but those aspects that indicate the necessity of a reflective understanding of one as well as the other aspect of morality.

The question of human nature and morality appears to be a single question, but, as we have pointed out, it is a cluster of questions that no doubt has a unity,[41] but the unity depends on how we view the component questions, independently of one another and in mutual connection. For our answer to one does affect our answer to another. At least we must be clear that the question pursued may point to a valuable insight, even if this insight, pending further inquiry, is irrelevant to what appears to be a connected question. Externalism and Internalism, as we have insisted throughout this paper, are plausibly incisive answers

41. Bambrough, "Essay on Man," 6.

to different, but not unconnected, questions. In closing, however, we may quite properly observe that the questions with which they are concerned are questions of *human* concern. Whether or not one accepts any reconciling attempt, the two conceptions of the connection of human nature and morality offer a challenge to our understanding of ourselves as human beings. And if we take up this challenge, we inevitably confront ourselves as questioning animals and realize that the question of the connection between morality and human nature is a question of objective characterization as well as a question of interpreting the conduct of present humanity in the light of our ideals and current information derived from the human sciences. The views depicted here are therefore a challenge to *redefinition of human beings.* In this light the problem of morality and human nature is a continuing *human* concern. It is a burden to be borne by reflective persons who seek to understand both *de facto* and ideal humanity.

Harmony and the Neo-Confucian Sage

Owing largely to the influence of Confucius, the history of Chinese ethical thought assigns a special role to exemplary individuals in the elucidation of moral notions. In the *Analects* Confucius spoke often on the contrast between the superior man *(chün-tzu)* and the small-minded man *(hsiao-jen)*. A closer study of his remarks reveals a conception of paradigmatic individuals as concrete embodiments of Confucius's ideal of *jen* (humanity). For Confucius, the ethically superior persons in the community are not mere custodians of a cultural tradition or models of emulation; they are the ones invested with an action-guiding function by virtue of their flexibility in dealing with exigent situations of the moral life.[1] Ordinary persons are deemed capable of becoming paradigmatic individuals. Although Confucius believed that only a sage *(sheng-jen)*, a perfect man of *jen*, can establish a harmonious social order, he did not uphold sagehood as a practical objective for ordinary moral agents. He once said that he could not hope to meet a sage, but would be quite content with meeting a superior man.[2]

Subsequent Confucian thinkers like Mencius and Hsün Tzu, however, expressed great confidence in sagely attainment. To Mencius, *jen* (humanity) is "the distinguishing characteristic of man."[3] All men are capable of becoming sages so long as they cultivate, with tender care and nourishment, their originally good nature.[4] Hsün Tzu, though holding a contrary view on human nature, shared the same sentiment.[5]

1. For a detailed discussion of this topic see my *Dimensions of Moral Creativity: Paradigms, Principles, and Ideals* (University Park: Pennsylvania State University Press, 1978), chap. 5 and 6.
2. *Analects*, 7:25.
3. D. C. Lau, trans., *Mencius* (Baltimore: Penguin Books, 1970), 7B:16.
4. Ibid., 2A:6, 6A:6; and 4:32, 6B:2.
5. Burton Watson, trans., *Hsün Tzu: Basic Works* (New York: Columbia University Press, 1963), sec. 23, p. 167. For a study of Hsün Tzu's theory of human nature see my "The Conceptual Aspect of Hsün Tzu's Philosophy of Human Nature," and "The Quasi-Empirical Aspect of Hsün Tzu's Philosophy of Human Nature," *Philosophy East and West* 27, no. 4 (1977), and 28, no. 1 (1978).

In the *Doctrine of the Mean*, sagehood becomes a luminous theme. We are presented with a view of the sage as a man of sincerity *(cheng)* who can "assist in the transforming and nourishing process of Heaven and Earth," thus "forming a trinity with Heaven and Earth" (C108).[6] The sage is seen to be a supreme embodiment of *tao* or *jen* (humanity)—the vision of harmony of man and nature.[7] As Chan points out, this vision of harmony "eventually assumed the greatest importance in Neo-Confucian philosophy" (C108). In this essay, I offer some reflections on the significance of the Neo-Confucian conception of sagehood in relation to their vision of harmony. I focus primarily on a narrow but important aspect of their moral thought. In particular, I want to inquire into their conception of sagehood and its significance for Confucian agents, i.e., the agents committed to the realization of the vision of harmony. Although I concentrate on some remarks of certain thinkers generally regarded as belonging to the idealistic wing of Neo-Confucianism, I believe that my reflections border on "a central thread" in Confucian moral theory.[8]

I. THE TASK OF SAGEHOOD AND THE IDEAL OF HARMONY

In the *Doctrine of the Mean*, the Confucian vision of harmony is notably expounded in psychological language. The sage is regarded as one who abides by the Mean. The Mean is explained in terms of *chung* (centrality, mean) and *ho* (harmony). *Chung* refers to the state prior to the arousal of such feelings as pleasure, anger, sorrow, and joy; *ho* to the harmonious expression of these feelings as they are experienced in

6. Abbreviated textual references are used for three frequently cited works: (1) "C" for W. T. Chan, ed. and trans., *A Source Book in Chinese Philosophy* (Princeton: Princeton University Press, 1963); (2) "C&L" for Chu Hsi and Lü Tsu-ch'ien, eds., *Reflections on Things at Hand: The Neo-Confucian Anthology*, trans. W. T. Chan (New York and London: Columbia University Press, 1967); and (3) "W" for Wang Yang-ming, *Instructions on Practical Living and Other Neo-Confucian Writings*, trans. W. T. Chan (New York and London: Columbia University Press, 1963). Page number follows each abbreviated citation.

7. For a discussion of the contemporary significance of this essay for moral theory independently of its metaphysical and religious import, see Essay 2; and "Practical Causation and Confucian Ethics," *Philosophy East and West* 25, no. 1 (1975): 1–10.

8. For the most part I rely on Chan's *Source Book* and Chu Hsi and Lü Tsu-Ch'ien's *Reflections on Things at Hand*, particularly on selections from Ch'eng Hao's works. I have also made use of the relevant remarks of Wang Yang-ming for a clearer elaboration of certain Neo-Confucian themes pervasive throughout the history of Chinese moral thought. As often noted by scholars, the Neo-Confucian philosophy, while rejecting Taoism and Buddhism, assimilates certain insights from these schools. The conception of sagehood, as I shall have occasion to observe, reflects the influence of Taoism. Since the Confucians and the Taoists share a common ideal of harmony, it should not be surprising to note their common attention to the problem of sagehood. For an attempt to characterize their contrasting responses to a common ideal, see Essay 4.

man's daily activities (C98). The *tao* or the Way is the vision of the grand harmony of man and nature. The cultivation of *tao* is "to be done through humanity *(jen)*." Echoing Mencius, *jen* is said to be "the distinguishing characteristic of man" (C104). And man can realize this *tao* or *jen* if he "honors the moral nature and follows the path of study and inquiry" (C110). The sage is described as a man who "hits upon what is right without effort and apprehends without thinking," who lives "naturally and easily in harmony with the Way *(tao)*" (C107).[9] The practical import of these themes receives a much clearer articulation in Neo-Confucian philosophy.

In spite of their preoccupation with metaphysical speculations, major Neo-Confucian philosophers from the eleventh to the sixteenth century were deeply committed to the actualization of the classic vision of harmony of man and nature. This vision has been rendered as an ideal of universal fellowship of all things. In the influential and inspiring words of Chang Tsai's *Western Inscription:*

Heaven is my father and Earth is my mother, and even such a small creature as I finds an intimate place in their midst. Therefore, that which fills the universe I regard as my body and that which directs the whole universe I consider as my nature. All people are my brothers and sisters and all things are my companions. (C&L 76–79, C497)

The character of the sage is said to be identical with that of Heaven and Earth (C&L 77). To Ch'eng Hao, Chang Tsai's statement expresses the substance of *jen* (C&L 79–80).[10] The man of *jen* is one "who forms one body with all things without any differentiation" (C523). Moral learning, for the Neo-Confucian, is essentially a process of becoming a sage. Self-cultivation with reverent seriousness *(ching)* in the pursuit of *jen* or the Mean is considered essential. The problem of becoming a

9. For the purposes of this essay, I use the notions of *tao* and *jen* interchangeably, though these terms have a history of conceptual evolution and metaphysical significance in Neo-Confucianism. However, the points I wish to make are quite independent of their metaphysical thought. Where seemingly metaphysical terms unavoidably occur, I attend primarily to their significance as moral notions. But it must be noted that for a comprehensive understanding of Neo-Confucian philosophy, particularly the key notion of *li*, one needs to appreciate the conceptual apparatus deployed in their ontological discussions. For insightful studies on the notions of *li*, *jen*, and other Neo-Confucian notions, see the following articles of W. T. Chan: "Neo-Confucianism: New Ideas in Old Terminology," *Philosophy East and West* 17, nos. 1–4 (1967): 15–35; "The Evolution of the Neo-Confucian Concept *Li* as Principle," *Tsing Hua Journal of Chinese Studies*, NS IV, no. 2 (1964): 123–49; "The Evolution of the Confucian Concept *Jen*," *Philosophy East and West* 4, no. 4 (1955): 295–319; and "Chinese and Western Interpretations of *Jen* (Humanity)," *Journal of Chinese Philosophy* 2, no. 2 (1975): 107–29.

10. As Chan points out, Chang Tsai's *Western Inscription* becomes the basis of Neo-Confucian ethics (C498).

sage, quite in the spirit of the *Doctrine of the Mean,* poses a dual task. On the one hand, according to the *Great Learning* it is the task of practical methodology concerning the proper steps in moral self-cultivation. On the other hand, it is a task in the inward recognition of the significance of the vision within the moral life. Although the major Neo-Confucians differed with respect to their conception of the former task, largely because of their opposing interpretations of "investigation of things" or the role of study and inquiry in the process of moral cultivation, they seemed to agree on the nature and importance of the second task. Influenced by Mencius, they devoted a great deal of attention to the nature and development of *hsin* (mind-heart). In this essay I focus on the second task.

The problem of becoming a sage has less to do with the acquisition of factual knowledge than with constituting, by thought and action, the content and import of the vision of harmony of man and nature. The problem of sagehood is concerned not with extrinsic strategies or instruments, but with the development of a character or quality of mind capable of realizing the ideal of harmony. The Confucian classics have a role to play. But when the Neo-Confucians dealt with these classics, they were primarily interested in articulating the insights implicit in these classics. In Kierkegaardian language, they were not "objective thinkers" concerned with elaborating a general ethical theory or doctrine extrinsic to Confucian morality; they were *committed* thinkers interested in the possibility of "subjective appropriation" of classical Confucian ideas.[11] The question of sagehood, for them, seems largely a question of "How can a person become a Confucian moral agent?" i.e., a man of *jen*—a question somewhat parallels Kierkegaard's "How can one become a Christian?" It is a question of being personally transformed by the Confucian vision.

As Ch'eng Hao remarked, "A student should understand the substance of *jen* and make it concretely part of his own self. Then all that is necessary is to nourish it with moral principles *[li]*. All such things as seeking the meanings of the classics are meant to nourish it" (C531). It is said that Ch'eng Hao "considered memorization, recitation, and acquiring extensive information as trifling with things and losing one's purpose" (C&L52). Understanding the Confucian classics is thus not a matter of discovering precepts, but a discernment of the nature of things in the form of *li* (principles or rationales).[12] To understand the

11. See Søren Kierkegaard, *Concluding Unscientific Postscript* (Princeton: Princeton University Press, 1941), pt. 2, chap. 2.
12. Owing to the influence of the Ch'eng brothers, Ch'eng Hao and Ch'eng I, the

li of a thing is to appreciate its actuating significance in one's own life. To understand *jen* is to embrace *jen* as one's own task. *Understanding*, in this sense, is not a product of constructing a moral theory external to one's moral commitments but a product of contemplating and pondering the living significance of moral ideas in human life. Understanding is a form of self-knowledge—a form of experiencing the import of one's learning within one's life.[13] In this light, the problem of becoming a sage is a task of *practical understanding*. Intellectual understanding can aid but cannot replace this task. From the Confucian point of view, moral theory is essentially a task in practical understanding. This form of moral theory has problems quite distinct from those in standard Western moral philosophy.[14]

II. THE COHERENCE OF THE CONFUCIAN VISION

A question justly arises concerning the coherence of the Confucian *tao* or *jen* as an ideal of harmony. Unless one can render intelligible the coherence of the Neo-Confucian's vision, it appears quite pointless to pursue further their conception of sagehood. It is helpful to view the Confucian *tao* as a coherent notion of harmony of man and nature in the *non-systemic sense*. Although the Neo-Confucians intended their vision as a comprehensive conception that comprises all things in the universe, they did not develop a systematic ontology with a categorical scheme for the classification of existing entities and their relations to one another. In particular, we are offered no "chain of beings" or a hierarchy of entities in superordinate or subordinate relations. The *li* (principle/rationale) is regarded as inherent in all things. In Ch'eng I's

---

notion of *li* becomes a key notion in Neo-Confucian philosophy. Although the term has metaphysical significance, *li* is not viewed by the Ch'eng brothers as an abstract concept: "It is both natural and moral." Moreover, there is no dichotomy between the natural (or metaphysical) and moral interpretations. See the insightful study of this notion Chan's "Evolution of Neo-Confucian Concept *Li* as Principle," and A. C. Graham, *Two Chinese Philosophers: Ch'eng Ming-tao and Ch'eng Yi-Ch'uan* (London: Lund Humphries, 1958), pt. I, sec. 1.

13. The Confucian conception of the relation between moral knowledge and action receives an incisive and original articulation in Wang Yang-ming's doctrine of unity of knowledge and action. [See my *The Unity of Knowledge and Action: A Study in Wang Yang-ming's Moral Psychology* (Honolulu: The University of Hawaii Press, 1982)].

14. It may be observed that the notion of practical understanding does not play an important role in contemporary moral philosophy, with the possible exception of A. E. Murphy, *The Theory of Practical Reason* (LaSalle: Open Court, 1965), and A. E. Melden, *Rights and Right Conduct* (Oxford: Basil Blackwell, 1958). These two works, I believe, are quite helpful in a contemporary explication of Confucian moral thought. For some methodological suggestions on this topic, see my "Tasks of Confucian Ethics," *Journal of Chinese Philosophy* 6, no. 1 (1979): 55–67.

famous saying, *Li* is "one but its manifestations are many" (C550). There is no doubt that they were concerned with the problem of one and many. The notion of *li*, in particular, suggests a conception of organic unity. As Needham points out, "there is 'law' implicit in it, but this law is the law to which parts of wholes have to conform by virtue of their very existence as parts of wholes."[15] For the present, let us just note that the Neo-Confucians proposed no categorical systems in the sense familiar to students of Western philosophy.[16]

It seems that the coherence and import of the Confucian vision as a moral vision does not depend on having a systematic ontology. Seen in the light of their concern with moral theory as a task of practical understanding, the absence of a categorical scheme does not affect the coherence of the vision. From this point of view, *tao* or *jen* is best construed as a coherent *ideal attitude* or perspective for organizing or unifying the diverse and conflicting elements of moral experience. Elsewhere I have termed this an *ideal theme.*[17] The notion of *ho* or harmony in the *Doctrine of the Mean,* for instance, is expressive of an ideal attitude toward one's feelings, ultimately, a way of looking at all things inclusive of human affairs and natural events. The comprehensive attitude at issue does not necessarily involve a systematic theory or a clear and precise idea that unveils the constitutive elements of thought and action. In short, the ideal attitude has a significance quite apart from the ability of the agent to articulate its nature and import in terms of a coherent system of propositions. To adopt *tao* or *jen* as a governing ideal of one's life does not imply a determinate conception of the ideal to be realized. It is to adopt an attitude and to resolve, with one's heart and mind *(hsin),* to look at things and events in such a way that they can become constituents in a harmonious unity without the unity being specified in advance of experience of man's confrontation with the changes in the natural world. Thus, to adopt this ideal attitude is to see human life in its morally excellent form, as possessing a coherence in which apparently conflicting elements are elements of an achievable harmonious order. The presence of conflicting elements is in experience a fact to be acknowledged. Acknowledgement brings with it a task of reconciliation. As Cheng rightly points out, the adoption of the ideal of harmony, together with the view of opposites as complements, paves

15. Joseph Needham, *Science and Civilization in China,* vol. 2 of *History of Scientific Thought* (Cambridge: Cambridge University Press, 1962), 567.
16. A more detailed discussion on *li* as a moral notion will be given in Part III of this essay.
17. See the first essay cited in note 7 above and chap. 10 of my *Dimensions of Moral Creativity.*

the way to a dialectics of harmonization in Chinese philosophy.[18] Since the desired coherence of the moral order is not spelled out *a priori*, harmonization of conflicting elements in experience is essentially a *creative* endeavor on the part of both the Confucian moral theorist and the agent. The ideal of harmony is an ideal of the dynamic interplay of man and nature. The discordant notes in experience set a *challenge* to man's efforts in the actualization of his vision of excellence. In terms of this vision the world of man and nature is not a static order with implications to be discerned by a process of logical inference. Consequently, a commitment to the Confucian vision carries a great burden, a *creative* burden calling for persevering sincerity *(cheng)* and seriousness *(ching)*. As Wang Yang-ming incisively observes, moral learning, the learning of becoming a sage, is a creative process; it is "the task of creating something from nothing" (W72–73).

In the light of *tao* or *jen* as an ideal theme, sagehood can be attained by ordinary agents in varying degrees and circumstances of their lives. Except perhaps for a few individuals, attainment of sagehood does not appear to be an enduring state, for the harmony experienced is something that occurs at a particular moment in time and place. Such an experience cannot by itself foreclose the possibility of future issues or problems. The *tao* as an ideal attitude has thus a continuing relevance throughout the course of the commitive agent's life. It may be noted, however, that a particular experience of harmony is not without its charm and significance. Typically, such an experience gives rise to a sense of satisfaction indicative of a supervenient quality of moral achievement. In the manner of Aristotle, we may say that it is a quality of pleasure that "completes an activity not as a characteristic completes an activity, but as a completeness that superimposes itself upon it, like the bloom of youth in those who are in their prime."[19] As a quality of moral achievement, such a sense of completion of one's own being is bound to differ from one agent to another. In this manner, two different agents may share the same vision and yet experience its import differently. And in different ways the experience of the quality of achievement increases the confidence of the commitive agents in search of future experiences of harmony.

Thus far we have focused on *ho* or harmony in the *Doctrine of the Mean*. The notion of *chung* (equilibrium, mean, or centrality) appears to be another aspect of that Confucian classic. The two words *chung*

18. See Cheng Chung-ying, "Harmony and Conflict in Chinese Philosophy," *Journal of Chinese Philosophy* 4, no. 3 (1977).

19. Aristotle, *Nichomachean Ethics*, trans. Martin Ostwald (Indianapolis: Bobbs-Merrill Co., Inc., 1962), 1174b.

and *ho* together may be regarded as the ideal of central harmony. *Chung* or equilibrium is said to be the state of mind prior to the arousal of emotions, suggestive of a state of calmness unperturbed by the experience of emotions. We have here a distinction that is not a dichotomy. As Wang points out, equilibrium *(chung)* and harmony *(ho)* are not contrasting states (W263). The distinction pertains to two complementary mental states in the experience of *tao*. When emotions are aroused and expressed in concord *(ho)*, one naturally experiences a state of equilibrium. Equilibrium is here a state of consummatory quiescence attendant upon a successful effort at harmonizing one's emotions as well as thoughts and actions. Like the experience of harmony, such a state is bound to be transient. As Wang puts it, "unless we are sound asleep or dead like drywood or dead ashes," we cannot avoid having thoughts (W78). To be alive is to engage in thought and action concerning one's feelings and desires. To live in the light of *tao* or *jen* is to make it a paramount perspective in dealing with conflicting elements in human life in the midst of changes in the natural world. The coherence of the Confucian *tao* thus provides only a point of orientation for meeting moral problems, not by way of a system of specific rules of conduct, but by way of a challenge to the agent to constitute the content and import of his commitment. Wang forcefully reminds one of his students, "The Way *(tao)* has neither spatial restrictions nor physical form, and it cannot be pinned down to any particular" (W46). In the final analysis, the import of *tao* is a matter of personal realization (W47).

III. THE CHARACTER OF THE SAGE

If the *tao* or vision of harmony of man and nature is ultimately a matter of personal realization, it behooves the Confucian agent to acquire an ability to cope with changing situations in his life. In the words of the *Doctrine of the Mean*, he must aspire to become a sage "who hits upon what is right without effort and apprehends without thinking" (C107). Such agility, however, presupposes the presence of a sagacious mind that embodies to some extent insight into the nature of the moral life.[20] The Neo-Confucian conception of the sage's mind, construed as

20. This notion of sagacity may be said to be present in the *Doctrine of the Mean*, sec. 31. In addition to magnanimity, generosity, benignity, and tenderness, etc., the qualities of "quickness of apprehension, intelligence, insight, and wisdom" are ascribed to the sage (C112). These various sagely qualities may be regarded as expressions of the sense of wisdom to be explained. In sec. 24 (C108), foreknowledge is also ascribed to the sage (the man of absolute sincerity). This point is inconsistent with the vision of harmony. For Wang's incisive comment, see W225.

an embodiment of wisdom, provides a further clarification of the task of Confucian agents. In general, though not in details, the Neo-Confucian would endorse Aristotle's notion of practical wisdom as a form of excellence in deliberation, i.e., "correctness in the goal, the manner, and the time" of action.[21] As Blanshard has noted recently, this notion of wisdom is "not concerned so much with the ascertainment of facts or elaboration of theories as with the means and end of conduct."[22] Before we take up this notion of wisdom,[23] let us first attend to the Neo-Confucian conception of the impartial character of sagehood.

In a somewhat paradoxical way, Ch'eng Hao characterized the sage as having no mind *(wu-hsin)* or feelings *(wu-ch'ing)* of his own and yet his mind and feelings are in accord with all things.[24] He recommended that "for the training of the superior man there is nothing better than to become broad and extremely impartial and to respond spontaneously to all things as they come" (C&L40).[25] This conception of the sage's character appears to be an ingenious appropriation of Taoistic ideas. In *Tao Teh Ching,* for instance, one finds the notion of "no mind"—"The sage has no mind of his own. He takes as his own the mind of the people."[26] In *Chuang Tzu,* the notion of "no feeling" is explained in this way: "When I talk about having no feelings, I mean that a man doesn't allow likes or dislikes to get in and do him harm. He just lets things be

21. Aristotle, *Nichomachean Ethics,* 1142b. We may note here that this concern has been a pervasive feature of Chinese moral thought.

22. Brand Blanshard, "Wisdom," vol. 8 of *Encyclopedia of Philosophy,* ed. Paul Edwards, 322.

23. For Blanshard, wisdom has two components of reflectiveness and judgments (ibid., 323–24). In my reconstruction of the Neo-Confucian notion of moral reflection in Part IV, the notion essentially involves an element of value judgment. Perhaps a single term "reflective judgment" is more appropriate as a general label for the Neo-Confucian conception. It must be noted that my present concern deals with a narrow but important aspect of Neo-Confucian philosophical psychology. An adequate discussion must take into account Wang Yang-ming's doctrine of unity of moral knowledge and action. (See my *Unity of Knowledge and Action.* In Essay 13, I have adopted Chu Hsi's broader conception of wisdom as a depository of insights derived from the exercise of *i* which involves reflective judgment.)

24. This attribution is a reading of the passage, "The constant principle of Heaven and earth is that their mind is in all things, and yet they have no mind *(wu-hsin)* of their own. The constant principle of the sage is that his feelings are in accord with all creation and yet he has no feelings of his own" (C&L40).

25. This citation immediately follows the passage in the preceding note. In the discussion I partially follow Chu Hsi's interpretation of the whole passage, viz., "To have a mind in all things and to be in accord with all creation is the same as to be extremely impartial, and to have no mind nor feelings of one's own is the same as to respond to all things as they come" (C&L40).

26. Lao Tzu, *Tao Te Ching,* trans. D. C. Lau (Baltimore: Penguin Books, 1963), chap. 49, p. 110. Note Chan's use Ch'eng Hao's remark as a comment on this chapter. See W. T. Chan, trans., *The Way of Lao Tzu* (Indianapolis: Bobbs-Merrill Co., Inc., 1963), 49.

the way they are and doesn't try to help life along."[27] Like Chuang Tzu, Ch'eng Hao would stress the importance of having a mind responsive to changing circumstances, but he would urge the agent to engage in positive actions rather than "taking no action" (wu-wei) or "letting things be."[28] Being a practical moralist, Ch'eng Hao was concerned, not so much with the fact that we have feelings, desires, and thoughts, but with the tendency we have to view their significance solely in terms of our own benefits. Impartiality of mind is thus a precondition for the attainment of tao. In his words, "Everyone's nature is obscured in some way and as a consequence he cannot follow the Way (tao). In general, the trouble lies in the resort to selfishness and the exercise of cunning. Being selfish, one cannot take purposive action to respond to things, and being cunning, one cannot be at home with enlightenment" (C&L40).

Ch'eng Hao's notion of impartiality is distinct from the notion of logical consistency or universalizability. Whether or not one accepts impartiality as a fundamental moral principle,[29] one can hardly dispense with the notion in characterizing "the moral point of view."[30] While the notion of universalizability of moral principles appears to be subject to a trivialization argument,[31] the notion of impartiality seems quite secure as depicting a basic feature of the Confucian conception of moral commitment. For Confucius, moral thinking is characteristically in terms of i (rightness or righteousness) as contrasted with profit or personal gain (C28). The morally superior man (chün-tzu) is "broadminded and not a partisan"; he "regards righteousness (i) as the substance of everything" (C24, 28).[32] Ch'eng Hao's notion of impartiality may be understood in terms of the notion of i.[33]

27. B. Watson, trans., The Complete Works of Chuang Tzu (New York and London: Columbia University Press, 1968), chap. 5, pp. 75–76.

28. The Taoist attitude of "letting things be" is not without moral significance (see Essay 5). For a good and brief contrast between Ch'eng Hao and Chuang Tzu on emotions, see Fung Yu-lan, A History of Chinese Philosophy (Princeton: Princeton University Press, 1953), 2:526.

29. D. H. Munro, Empiricism and Ethics (Cambridge: Cambridge University Press, 1967), 206.

30. For examples, Kurt Baier, The Moral Point of View (Ithaca: Cornell University Press, 1958), chap. 8, and W. K. Frankena, Ethics, 2d ed. (Englewood-Cliffs: Prentice-Hall, Inc., 1973), 110–14.

31. See Don Locke, "The Trivializability of Universalizability," Philosophical Review 78 (1968): reprinted in Wilfred Sellars and John Hospers, eds., Readings in Ethical Theory (New York: Appleton-Century Crofts, 1970), 517–28.

32. This theme is the main focus in Mencius.

33. For a more extensive discussion on this aspect of the notion of i (rightness, righteousness), see my Dimensions of Moral Creativity, chaps. 5, and C. Y. Cheng, "Yi as a Universal Principle of Specific Application in Confucian Morality," Philosophy East and West 22 (1972): 269–80. (For a later study, see Essay 13.)

The notion of impartiality is particularly important to the Neo-Confucian vision of harmony. As we have seen in Part II, a commitment to *tao* or *jen* involves the adoption of an all-embracing perspective for dealing with one's own mental states. The ideal perspective is obviously incompatible with a narrow preoccupation with personal gain and calculative thought. A constant engagement in calculative thought quite obviously distracts the agent's attention from the import of the vision. In pursuing the vision, it is thus essential to cultivate one's mind by avoiding "selfishness and cunning." This emphasis does not imply that no benefit is to be obtained in self-cultivation, but the benefit so obtained is intrinsic rather than extrinsic to morality.[34] Selfish thoughts *(ssu-i)* and selfish desires *(ssu-yü)* are to be feared because they are "impurities of mind" that blur the ideal objective.

Thus far we have focused on the negative aspect of impartiality. The positive aspect belongs to the correct manner in which the sage expresses his feelings in varying situations of his life. For Ch'eng Hao, "the sage is joyous because according to the nature of things before him he should be joyous, and he is angry because according to the nature of things before him he should be angry. The joy and anger of the sage do not depend on his mind but on things" (C&L41).[35] This remark suggests that impartiality involves the notion of rectitude or correctness of emotions. With Brentano, we may say that the correctness of emotions "consists in a kind of correspondence between the emotion and its object." For example, "One loves or hates correctly provided that one's feelings are adequate to their objects—adequate in the sense of being appropriate, suitable, or fitting."[36] The correct expression of the sage's emotions thus lies in their being the fitting or suitable responses to the objects or situations he confronts in his immediate experience. However, this correctness of emotional expression presupposes that the sage has an insight into the nature of *li* or organic unity of all things. The impartial mind of the sage is a positive feature of the highest moral attainment. Thus, impartiality is not only a precondition (in the neg-

34. As Ch'eng I remarked: "To a sage, righteousness *[i]* is profit. Whenever he is at ease with righteousness, there is profit for him" (C&L195). In the *Great Learning*, the contrast between "real" and mere profit is explicitly recognized: "Righteousness is considered to be the real profit" (C94).

35. Again, "Among human emotions the easiest to arouse but the most difficult to control is anger. But if in time of anger one can immediately forget his anger and look at the right and wrong of the matter according to principle *[li]*, he will see that external temptations need not be hated, and he has gone more than half way toward the way *(tao)*" (C&L41).

36. Franz Brentano, *The Origin of Our Knowledge of Right and Wrong* (London: Routledge and Kegan Paul, 1969), 76.

ative sense, as contrasted with egoism) but a constitutive characteristic of sagehood.

Apart from its metaphysical significance, the Neo-Confucian notion of *li* (principle) as suggestive of a conception of organic unity has interesting implications for elucidating a form of moral thinking. Graham's examination of this notion in Ch'eng Hao and Ch'eng I points to the use of *li* as accounting "not for the properties of a thing but for the task it must perform to occupy its place in the natural order."[37] In this conception, "each thing has a principle *(li)* to follow; fathers should be compassionate and sons filial, fire should be hot and water cold."[38] No distinction is made between the descriptive and the normative uses of *li*.[39] Although Ch'eng Hao did not develop a systematic doctrine of *li*, he believed that ultimately, there is only one *li*, self-sufficient and unchanging (C534). It seems clear that "*li*" is a universal term, but in the moral context, the *li* of actions cannot be construed in terms of moral principles in the sense of universal rules of conduct. For in the Neo-Confucian conception, moral thinking is not a subsumptive process consisting in the application of a universal rule to a particular case. As a universal term, *li* is perhaps more plausibly explicated in terms of the *conceived likeness of status*. This is Abelard's conception of "common reason" or "common cause."

According to Abelard, Socrates and Plato are alike in being men, not because they possess a common essence, but because they share in the status of man. "We call it the status itself of man to be man, which is not a thing and which we also called the common cause of imposition of the word on individuals, according as they themselves agree with each other."[40] To say that a universal word imposes a common cause is the same as to say that the user of the word conceives the likeness of the things. This conception, however, pertains to the shared status of the things called by the same name. This sharing of status does not imply the sharing of the same descriptive properties. In this sense, a universal term can be used to refer to the common status of things that are quite radically unlike in descriptive properties. This status, however, is a conceptual imposition. In an analogous way, we may say that two or more things possess the same *li* insofar as they share the same

37. Graham, *Two Chinese Philosophers*
38. Ibid.
39. Ibid.; see also Chan, "The Evolution of Neo-Confucian *Li* as Principle," 139. For a later study, see my "Reason and Principle in Chinese Philosophy," in Eliot Deutsch and Ron Bontekoe, eds., *Blackwell Companion to World Philosophy* (Oxford: Blackwell, 1997).
40. A. Hyman and J. J. Walsh, eds., *Philosophy in the Middle Ages* (Indianapolis: Hackett Publishing Co., 1973), 179–80.

normative status. In this sense, the *li* of a thing is its ought-to-be status within the natural order. And since the natural order, in the light of the Neo-Confucian vision, is also a moral or ideal order of *jen*, the *li* of all things would signify the shared *jen*-status. This *jen*-status is dues to the "imposition" of the Neo-Confucian vision. Tautologically, in the light of the vision, the *li* is inherent in all things. We may then say with Ch'eng Hao that there is only one *li* in the world. The self-sufficient and unchanging character of this *li* in effect signifies a *moral necessity* in the *jen*-order. Ultimately, every individual thing possesses *li* or the status of being a part of the *jen*-order. Whether or not this explication of *li* can be properly ascribed to the Neo-Confucians or resolve the problem of universals, it appears to comport with the spirit of their moral thought. The account is compatible with the view of *li* as a conception of ontological status.

IV. MORAL REFLECTION

The sage, with his insight into the *li* of things, can respond "spontaneously to all things as they come." Unlike the sage, the ordinary Confucian agent has to engage in moral thinking. In the spirit of Mencius, Ch'eng Hao urged the preservation of his mind and nourishment of his originally good nature (C&L125). The process of self-cultivation quite naturally involves self-mastery in the discipline of the agent's feelings and desires (C&L161). However, at the heart of the moral life lies the activity of thinking that aims at a harmonious integration of the agent's inner states with outward events. This form of thinking does not require the calculation of consequences of actions except insofar as they are parts of the *jen*-achievement. Nor does the thinking require a set of standard recipes or hierarchy of values to be applied in different circumstances.[41] Moral thinking is essentially a response to a concrete situation. Thus the Confucian agent must cultivate a mind responsive to all changes that may occur in his life. The question of what to do in such and such a circumstance cannot be answered by merely consulting established rules or precepts. An appropriate answer depends primarily on thinking in a particular setting. In Chinese terms, *chin-ssu*, it is "reflection on things at hand."[42] Thinking necessarily in-

41. This point is explicit in a passage attributed to Ch'eng Hao. "Generally speaking, if one can achieve learning so naturally so to be beyond words [i.e., experience of *jen*], he will really achieve it in a natural way. If one schematizes or makes deliberate arrangements, he does not achieve it in a natural way at all" (C&L57–58). See also (W42–43).

42. Although the words *chin-ssu* occur in the title of Chu Hsi and Lü Tsu-ch'ien's influential Neo-Confucian anthology, only two terse passages explicitly deal with this no-

volves an element of reflection. It is a "mind-in-action." Further discussion on this notion of moral thinking should provide a deeper understanding of the task of Confucian agents. I shall take the suggestive mirror metaphor as a point of departure.[43]

Wang Yang-ming compares the sage's mind to a clear mirror. "Since it is all clarity, [the sage's mind] responds to all stimuli as they come and reflects everything. There is no such case as a previous image still remaining in the present reflection or yet-to-be reflected image already existing there. . . . [The] sage does a thing when time comes. . . . The study of changing conditions and events is to be done at the time of response" (W27). If one takes this mirror metaphor seriously, it suggests two different features of moral reflection. In the first place, the moral mind-in-action reflects like a clear mirror, receiving impressions or objects without pronouncing any judgment. In the second place, the mind-in-action engages in reflection in the sense of thinking about what ought to be done. The first sense of reflection focuses on the receptive or passive capacity of the mind. In terms of impartiality we have discussed in Part III, the mind-in-action is open to the reception of any changing events which it confronts. This state of readiness, however, is a prelude to reflection in the second sense, i.e., thinking at a particular time and place with respect to the appropriate course of action to be taken. Moral reflection proper pertains to this thinking in an occurrent situation.

Since the sage perfectly embodies *tao* or *jen*, his moral reflection and his response can hardly be distinguished. He spontaneously responds to "all things as they come." This spontaneous response is natural or immediate in the sense that it is unmediated by judgment. The sage, representing the ideal case of the moral life, may be said to have "no mind or feelings," since his mind embodies the *tao*. He engages in no appraisive activity. But for ordinary agents, reflection on "the changing conditions and events" is indispensable. Moral reflection is essentially an appraisive activity. What the agent ought to do finally depends on

---

tion. The following explication is basically a partial and incomplete reconstruction of this important notion largely inspired by Chan's rendering in terms of "reflections of things at hand."

43. The use of the mirror metaphor in depicting the sage's mind is a favorite among Chinese philosophers. Chuang Tzu seemed to have originated the use. For some of its occurrences, see the "mirror" index in Chan's *Source Book*. Brief discussions of Ch'eng Hao's use are found in Fung, *History of Chinese Philosophy*, 2:525–26, and Graham, *Two Chinese Philosophers*, 105. We may also note that to some extent, the common use of "still or clear water" serves much the same purpose. My choice here is based on convenience in illustrating a pervasive feature of Chinese moral thought. It may be noted that even a conservative moral theorist like Hsün Tzu found a Confucian use of "clear water" in his discussion of sagehood (Watson, *Hsün Tzu*, p. 131).

his judgment of the case at issue. In the normal course of human life, the judgment is made without much effort and deliberation, in view of the fact that the ordinary agent is equipped with moral learning, i.e., an established or conventional set of rules and precepts. Whether or not the established rules in one's moral community are relevant to a case at hand is a question to be decided after "study of the changing conditions or events." In other words, the decision rests on a judgment of relevance of rules to a particular circumstance; in Confucian language, the exercise of *i* or one's sense of rightness. When the situation is an unfamiliar or exigent case, moral reflection requires some effort to appreciate the situation before judgment. In either normal or exigent cases, appreciating the situation is an essential component of moral reflection.[44] Put another way, moral judgment is mediated by an *appreciation of the situation*. The stress on "the time of response" focuses on the necessity of making an *independent* judgment adequate to the case at hand. In the language of *li* (reason, rationale), the *li* of each case cannot be determined a priori. As Wang Yang-ming says, "moral principles *[i-li]* exist in no fixed place and are not exhaustible. Please do not think that, when you have gotten something from conversations with me, that is all there is to it. There will be no end if we talk for ten, twenty, or fifty more years" (W28). In this view, moral reflection is clearly not a deductive process. Nor is it an inductive generalization from particular cases. Even if conventional rules are deemed relevant, their relevance to the current problem is a matter for the agent's appraisive judgment. One may, of course, raise the question of justification of moral judgments, but that goes beyond the scope of the present essay.[45]

As a mind-in-action, moral reflection is a form of mindfulness. It is selective attention to the distinctive features of a situation informed by the agent's sense of importance.[46] The appreciation of an occurrent situation presupposes an evaluative judgment. This sense of importance has been emphasized by Mencius.[47] Since moral reflection is directed to *li* as an organic unity, it is also mindful of the *gestalt* of the situation. Following Matson, we may say that it is an activity of *apperception*, i.e., the distinctive features of the organic whole are "not only perceived, but are united and assimilated to a mass of ideas already

44. For more discussion independently of Confucian ethics, see my *Dimensions of Moral Creativity*, chaps. 6 and 7.

45. An attempt to provide a Confucian answer to this question is given in Essay 1.

46. The following analysis is an appropriation, with modification, of Matson's insightful discussion of what he calls "sizing up" activity. See William Matson, *Sentience* (Berkeley and Los Angeles: University of California Press, 1976), chap. 5.

47. The sense of importance is explicitly discussed in *Mencius*, IVA:14.

possessed, and so comprehended and interpreted."[48] Given a commitment to *jen*, thinking in light of *li* is principally an apperception based on a *moral* interest. The apperceived whole is in part a construction of the agent in abstraction from his total environment. The total environment may be objectively described, but at issue is a question of acting, of wondering what is the right or appropriate response to an occurrent situation. Relevance of the situational features is determined by *jen* or moral interest, and not by an exhaustive survey or descriptive inquiry. The moral interest is concerned, not with all facts of the case, but only with those facts that are relevant to the realization of *jen*. Since an interpretative element enters in moral apperception, different agents may constitute in different ways the content and import of *jen*. As an overarching ideal theme, *jen* can be developed in various ways without losing its action-guiding function.

Moral reflection obviously carries the liability to error. Nevertheless, the judgment of importance is a *constitutive* feature of the situation. And when fellow agents regard the judgment as paradigmatic, it can, in place of a rule, serve as a guide to other's moral apperception. The notion of a moral situation is not a mere descriptive concept. For the Confucian agent, *jen* implies a moral relation between human beings. He can agree with Kovesi that "situations are not out there in the world, existing independently of us, so that human beings could just step in and out of them." "To be in a situation is to be related to other human beings in a certain way."[49] Moral situations pertain to the shared status of human beings. This shared status is one of mutual concern in different contexts of human relation. To engage in moral reflection is, for the Confucian agent, "to extend on the basis of similarity in kind" (C&L94).[50] The similarity pertains not to descriptive properties, but to the shared *moral status* in the light of *jen*.

The above discussion of moral situation recognizes the distinction between an objective characterization and the agent's own conception of "the reality of the situation."[51] Acceptance of this distinction, from

48. Matson, *Sentience*, 151.

49. Julius Kovesi, *Moral Notions* (London: Routledge and Kegan Paul, 1967), 119.

50. This interpretation of Ch'eng I's remark is consistent with Chu Hsi's. Chu Hsi said that "we must only proceed from what we understand in what is near to us and move from there." For instance, "if one understands how to be affectionate to his parents (i.e., what it is to be a son or daughter), he or she will extend this feeling on the basis of similarity in kind, to being humane (*jen*) to all people" (C&L94). For the Confucian, being a son or daughter involves parental affection. The affection is an implicit feature of the status or role within the family. The extension of parental affection is plausible only in the light of the conception of shared *jen*-status.

51. See S. C. Pepper, *Source of Value* (Berkeley and Los Angeles: University of California Press, 1958), 437f.

the moral point of view, does not imply acceptance of an exclusive dichotomy. For if there were a case in which the agent *constituted* his own situation, the situation so envisaged would also enter into an objective characterization of his situation. This is especially prominent in human affairs as distinct from mere natural events. What we experience in our life is often not just a matter of what happens to us independently of our judgment and choice but what we *make* to happen. We are responsible, moral agents. What we enjoy and suffer are very often the outcome of what we think and do. These activities are a part of the human situation that can be objectively described from an observer's point of view. What an agent thinks and does figures in as ingredients in this characterization. The agent, though he may fumble or err, contributes to the reality of the human situation. No moral theory can ignore this reality if it pretends to being an adequate account of morality.

Summing up, the Neo-Confucian conception of sagehood is a conception of wisdom or an insight into the *li* of all things. The task of a Confucian agent may thus be clarified by focusing on a form of moral reflection which is essentially an apperceptive activity in a particular, occurrent situation. To be a Confucian agent, in the light of *jen*, is to engage in moral creativity. In this conception, creative moral endeavor may be compared to the artist's grappling with the problem of clarity of his initial conception of what he wants to do, of making concrete an inchoate idea by way of action mediated through reflection. The initial knowledge of what one morally wants to do depends on action for clarification. As Chu Hsi states: "When one knows something but has not yet acted on it, his knowledge is still shallow. After he has experienced it, his knowledge will be increasingly clear, and its character will be different from what it was before" (C609).

V. CONCLUSION

Throughout this essay, emphasis was placed mainly on the Neo-Confucian conception of sagehood in relation to the task of Confucian agents in quest of realization of *tao* or *jen* as a vision of harmony of man and nature. In this role, the conception of sage's mind as an embodiment of wisdom or insight into the *li* (principle, rationale) of things points clearly to the creative character of moral agency and moral reflection as a response to an occurrent situation. However, it must be observed that the Neo-Confucian conception of sagehood has another role to play in the articulation of the practical significance of *tao* or *jen*. As suggested in Part II, *tao* or *jen* is an ideal theme, a perspective for orientation in human life, rather than a norm with preceptive implications. *Jen* is not a utopian vision, though there is an inherent vagueness in this conception of moral ideal. Some clarification is needed for appreciating the significance of an ideal theme. The Neo-Confucian conception of sagehood may be regarded as an attempt to exhibit the *concrete possibility* of the ideal, a sort of symbolic representation of the possibility of realizing the ideal in the natural order. While Confucius looked to superior men *(chün-tzu)*, who are essentially *reasonable* human beings, the Neo-Confucians aspired to a greater height. Their conception of sagehood thus provides a bridge between the conception of moral ideal and the actual world of natural events and human affairs. An inquiry into this aspect of Neo-Confucian philosophy should contribute to a fuller understanding of the issues and problems that divide major Chinese thinkers. A careful examination of such topics as the relation between morality and human nature, thought and action, and the role of investigation of things in self-cultivation, deserves attention from the point of view of contemporary moral philosophy. An adequate evaluation of Neo-Confucian moral thought depends on the outcome of such an examination. In closing, however, I hope it is appropriate to offer some suggestions on the notion of *li* in the interest of comparative moral philosophy.

The notion of *li* suggests an affinity with Moore's conception of intrinsic goods as organic wholes. This comparison, however, is highly misleading. The Neo-Confucians were not ideal utilitarians. Their notion of moral thinking or reflection does not deal with causal consequences as an aggregate of intrinsic goods.[52] The notion of *li* basically pertains to the agent's activity of fusion or integration of his inner states (i.e., thoughts, desires, and feelings) and outward events. As organic wholes, Moore's personal relations and aesthetic experiences would be acceptable to a Neo-Confucian or a classical Confucian, not because they are intrinsically good in the sense that they "are judged to be good if they existed by themselves, in absolute isolation,"[53] but because they are judged to be eligible constituents of *tao* or *jen*-experience. As a moral ideal, *jen* obviously concerns "the *best* state of things *conceivable*," but this conception falls outside the scope of Moore's investigation.[54] His notion of intrinsic good, also, cannot be properly applied to *tao* or

52. I am here thinking of Moore's remark: "In asserting that the action is the best thing to do, we assert that it together with its consequences presents a greater sum of intrinsic value than any possible alternative." G. E. Moore, *Principia Ethica* (Cambridge: Cambridge University Press, 1951), 25.

53. Ibid., p. 187.

54. Moore explicitly distinguishes this notion from that of the "human good" or "the *ultimate* end toward which our action should be directed" and the notion of what is "good in itself in a high degree" which forms the topic of his investigation (ibid., 183–84).

jen. Tao or *jen* is not something that can exist in "absolute isolation" or something to be discovered by Moore's method of isolation for intrinsic goods. Unlike utilitarians, the Neo-Confucians did not propose any general formula for guiding and assessing moral conduct. This absence of a general formula for right actions marks a distinctive feature of classical and Neo-Confucian ethics. In this respect, the conception of right action resembles the doctrine of perceptual intuitionism. In the case of Mencius, or more prominently of Wang Yang-ming, there appears a form of intuitionism in the notion of *liang-chih*, commonly rendered as "innate knowledge (of the good)." But *liang-chih* is more an innate capacity for moral discrimination than a principle of moral justification. In this respect, Wang, like Aristotle, stresses the necessity of moral thinking in particular circumstances.[55]

For comparative purpose, perhaps the best course is to attend to C. I. Lewis's conception of the good life on the whole as a "temporal gestalt." The notion of *li* in the context of *jen* as a moral ideal suggests such a conception. The Neo-Confucian would probably accept, with some modification, Lewis's account. In this view, the value characterizing a whole life is "found to be realized in the living of it. . . . The relation of good and bad experiences in constituting a good or bad life is not that of a series of temporally juxtaposed and externally related moments but is that of ingredients which affect and qualify one another; the relations of components in a temporal *Gestalt*."[56] This conception of the good life focuses on dynamic organic unity that clearly contrasts with a static inclusivistic or aggregative conception. The problem for a moral agent, seen from this Neo-Confucian perspective, is the problem of creative constitution of the import of *jen* by way of thought and action. For moral theory, this view obviously rests on an assumption of the internal relations between the means and the end— an assumption that requires further examination. For the present, let us close with a suggestion that an analysis of this Neo-Confucian problem can benefit from a study of this aspect of Lewis's theory of value, especially in relation to Wang Yang-ming's doctrine of unity of knowledge and action.

55. For a recent incisive account of this aspect in relation to Aristotle's conception of moral ideal, see David Wiggens, "Deliberation and Practical Reason," *Proceedings of the Aristotelian Society* (1975–76), 29–51. See also Stuart Hampshire, *Two Theories of Morality* (Oxford: Oxford University Press, 1977).

56. C. I. Lewis, *An Analysis of Knowledge and Valuation* (LaSalle: Open Court, 1946), 486.

Essay 8   Competence, Concern, and the Role of Paradigmatic Individuals *(Chün-tzu)* in Moral Education

From the perspective of Confucian ethics, learning to become an exemplary, autonomous moral agent, a *chün-tzu,* is a constant and unceasing process of self-cultivation *(hsiu-shen).*[1] This process involves the acquisition and critical interpretation of an established cultural tradition, seen as an embodiment of a concern for human well-being *(jen),* as well as familiarity with rules of proper conduct *(li),* with due regard to reasoned judgment concerning their relevance to particular circumstances *(i).*[2] This process also involves a daily examination of the ethical import of one's words and deeds.[3] More generally, the Confucian conception of self-cultivation may be characterized as a gradual process of character formation "by making oneself receptive to the symbolic resources of one's own culture and responsive to the sharable values of one's own society."[4]

1. Confucius once remarked, "Men of antiquity studied to improve themselves; men today study to impress others"; D. C. Lau, trans., *Confucius: The Analects* (New York: Penguin Books, 1979), 14:24. On this remark, Hsün Tzu commented, the *chün-tzu* "uses learning to ennoble himself; the petty man uses learning as a bribe to win attention from others"; see Burton Watson, trans., *Hsün Tzu: Basic Writings* (New York: Columbia University Press, 1963), 20. For original text, see Li Ti-sheng, *Hsün Tzu chi-shih* (Taipei: Hsüeh-sheng, 1979), *ch'üan-hsüeh p'ien.* For the significance of the notion of paradigmatic individuals and its application to that of *chün-tzu,* see my *Dimensions of Moral Creativity: Paradigms, Principles, and Ideals* (University Park: Pennsylvania State University Press, 1978), chaps. 3–5.

2. For the acquisition and critical appreciation of the classics in Confucian education, see my "The Ethical Uses of the Past in Early Confucianism: The Case of Hsün Tzu," *Philosophy East and West* 35, no. 2 (1985): 135–39; and "Reasonable Challenges and Preconditions of Adjudication," presented at the Sixth East-West Philosophers' Conference, East-West Center, July 30-August 12, 1989. A Chinese translation by Wang Ling-kang of the former paper appeared in *Che-hsüeh yü wen-hua,* vol. 15, no. 4 (1988). For a compendious statement of the basic Confucian notions *(jen, li,* and *yi)* and their interdependence, see "Problems of Confucian Ethics," in Lawrence C. Becker, ed., *Encyclopedia of Ethics* (New York: Garland, 1992).

3. See Tseng Tzu's remark in the *Analects,* 1:4; and Watson, *Hsün Tzu,* 15.

4. Tu Wei-ming, *Confucian Thought: Selfhood as Creative Transformation* (Albany: State

A Confucian philosopher today would appreciate Arthur Murphy's similar conception of moral learning as a continuing process throughout life. "Moral learning is not for children merely; we must go on learning all our lives if the requirements of our moral situations are rightly to be met. The point of moral training is to supply the starting point and to develop the concern and capacity with which we can thus go on. It is teaching that prepares us to go beyond our instructions and to solve a problem for ourselves." In other words, moral learning or education consists primarily in the development of *competence* in accord with the established "grounds of reason" and an inculcation of a *concern* for membership in moral community. The content of such moral training will be "the accepted moral precepts of the group in which training is given." Whether such "grounds *for* action" are sufficient for guidance in hard cases remains a question open to individual reasoned judgment. Becoming a moral person is a special kind of achievement.[5]

For a Confucian moral philosopher, training in competence ideally is the acquisition of a consummate skill in the management of one's conduct and affairs in accord with the *li*, and the inculcation of moral concern is a matter of extensive concern for humanity. Training in competence and inculcation of *jen*, the humane attitude of caring for certain matters deemed important in human relationships *(lun)*, must go hand in hand, allowing the moral learner to grow in moral understanding of other persons and in meeting problems and perplexities. The main difficulty lies, not merely in acquiring a minimum mastery of the requirements of accepted moral practice, but more fundamentally in developing a flexible attitude to deal with exigent circumstances of human life. On the whole, it seems unproblematic to instruct learners in the *li*, precepts or maxims of an established morality.[6] But the heart of the difficulty in moral education lies in helping the learner to develop a sense of autonomy informed by a concern for *jen* in response to changing situations of human life. In this essay, I offer some philo-

---

University of New York Press, 1985), 68. More fundamentally, this process involves the difficult task of transforming existing society into a human community of mutual concern or personal relationships. For further discussion, see my "Confucian Vision and the Human Community," *Journal of Chinese Philosophy* 11, no. 4 (1984).

5. Arthur E. Murphy, *The Theory of Practical Reason* (LaSalle: Open Court, 1965), 193–95. Of course, emphasis on the development of competence in accord with established precepts does not deny the important role of critical reflection in the revision of these precepts, say in eliminating inconsistency or incoherence. Also critical reflection and moral growth may yield a deeper understanding of the rationales of these precepts.

6. Such an instruction in the *li* is by no means simple or mechanical, for successful training involves a practical understanding of the delimiting, supportive, and ennobling function of *li*, as well as their justification. For extensive discussion, see Essay 13.

sophical reflections on the role of paradigmatic individuals or *chün-tzu* in moral education, centering attention on the inculcation of *jen* or concern for humanity, rather than on training in competence. More particularly, I hope to provide a tentative, though partial, Confucian answer to the question "How can humans learn to become autonomous moral agents in the spirit of *jen* in a way that can have a transformative or actuating significance in their own lives?"

I. MORAL COMPETENCE

As a preliminary to our inquiry, let me make a few observations on moral competence. Moral competence may be likened to the mastery of a skill. For the most part, the student can be taught a set of rules or techniques as efficient instruments for satisfying his or her needs, interests, or desires within the ambit of established moral practices. The Confucian *li,* as a set of formal prescriptions for proper behavior, can, like any skill or technique, be learned. I do not mean to suggest that training in a skill is primarily mechanical, for what is aimed at is more crucially a sensitivity or a *knack* in applying maxims and precepts. Constant perseverance in practice may help the learner to acquire this knack. To this extent, successful moral training entails perceptiveness or appreciation of concrete situations. For the most part, no special ability is required of ordinary agents to learn to conduct themselves in accordance with accepted moral rules or precepts.

The problem arises when the agent experiences a conflict of obligatory requirements. In principle, a moral teacher may provide guidance by way of a doctrine of rules and exceptions or a hierarchy of rules and principles. Conflict between first-order rules may be resolved by an appeal to a second-order rule. And if there is a conflict between the second-order rules, a third-order rule may be invoked in accord with the requirements of the moral theory, and so on. In this manner, exceptions may be built-in in the formulation and application of rules. If a moral teacher accepts such a doctrine, children may be taught to master it and apply it to particular situations of conflict.

Doubts have been expressed about the presumed adequacy of this quasi-legalistic doctrine of rules and exceptions. Murphy, for example, justly maintains that the doctrine is "both theoretically and practically futile." Firstly, "the complexity of specific situations is such that no list of exceptions, drawn up in advance, will actually cover all morally questionable cases." Secondly, more fundamentally, no reference to rules as directives can answer questions such as these: "When ought such exceptions to be made?" "Who's to judge?" and "How is he or she to judge?"[7] Thirdly, the doctrine implausibly assumes that situations come, so to speak, with ready labels for identification or classification. Were this view acceptable, all "practical problems would be conclusively soluble theoretical problems; . . . The crux is in the labeling, or the decision depends on how we see the situation."[8] Lastly, learning the doctrine as part of moral education requires a highly sophisticated intellectual ability. It seems that any positive social morality, as contrasted with a critical morality, exists for the sake of men and women of ordinary intelligence.[9]

As theoretical philosophers, we may find congenial Berkeley's dictum that "we ought think with the learned, and speak with the vulgar."[10] But our theoretical reflections on moral matters, especially those that are to provide some guidance to practical thinking, cannot be deemed acceptable without due regard for the capabilities of "the vulgar," the ordinary people—a respect not only for their linguistic or discursive capacity, but for what they are and what they are capable of, what they can do and understand. To impose our theoretical edifice, however coherent and systematic, upon their thinking would be to deprive them of an opportunity to think for themselves in the light of their own experience, circumstances, and aspirations. We would defeat the whole point of moral training: to provide a beginning rather than an end to the development of moral autonomy.[11] It is, perhaps, for this

7. Murphy, *The Theory of Practical Reason*, 118–19. Murphy also points out, plausibly, that respect for moral rules as reasons for action "is not to set them up as the logical requirements of games that, in the general interest, it is good to play. Their defeasibility is not that of laws with built-in loopholes (exceptions) in them. It is rather that of grounds of action with, though good as *so far* cogent, may be insufficient for the resolution of concrete problems" (ibid., 208–9). Note that this critique of the doctrine of rules and exceptions, as Murphy acknowledges, presupposes the distinction between normal and exigent situations. For further discussion and the corresponding distinction between *ch'ing* and *ch'üan* in Confucian ethics, see *Dimensions of Moral Creativity*, 72–76, 86–103. For an attempt to develop a Confucian doctrine of justification of judgments in exigent situations, see my *Ethical Argumentation: A Study of Hsün Tzu's Moral Epistemology* (Honolulu: University of Hawaii Press, 1985), 51–101.

8. Stuart Hampshire, *Freedom of Mind* (Princeton: Princeton University Press, 1971), 55–56. For further development of this point, see *Dimensions of Moral Creativity*, 12–16.

9. For this distinction see H. L. A. Hart, *Law, Liberty, and Morality* (Stanford: Stanford University Press, 1963), 17–24.

10. A remark, according to Jessop, quoted from the sixteenth century Italian Augustinus Niphus. See T. E. Jessop, ed., *The Works of George Berkeley*, vol. 2 (London: Thomas Nelson and Sons, 1949): *A Treatise Concerning the Principles of Human Knowledge*, para. 51.

11. This seems to be one motivation in the recent revival of virtue ethics and critique of moral theory. For samples of the latter, see Stanley G. Clarke and Evan Simpson, eds., *Anti-Theory in Ethics and Moral Conservatism* (New York: State University of New York Press, 1989). For the former, see Gregory Trianosky, "What Is Virtue Ethics All About? Recent Work on the Virtues," *American Philosophical Quarterly* 27, no. 4 (1990): 335–44.

reason that Confucius tailored his teachings to the character, capacity, and circumstances of individual agents *(yin-ts'ai shih-chao).*[12]

In view of the practical necessity of justifying one's moral judgments, particularly those made in exigent cases, it may be rejoined that a systematic moral theory, equipped with a hierarchy of rules and/or principles, can provide unambiguous guidance. The issue raised is much too complex to be discussed here. Let me simply indicate, on the one hand, that such an insistence seems motivated by the deductivist aspiration and, on the other, that a plausible non-deductivist approach— one, say, that emphasizes standards of argumentative competence— seems available. For example, requirements such as consistency and coherence, respect for linguistic practices, and appeal to experience or plausible presumptions may be taught as standards for reasoned justification in ethical discourse. Some of these standards may be precisely formulated for use as premises of deductive arguments in certain cases, say, to meet challenges to judgments that pertain to normal situations. However, though loose and vague as compared to principles of logical systems, they remain useful as guidelines for reasoned justification of ethical judgments, presuming of course that ethical argumentation is viewed as a cooperative enterprise for resolving common problems of the participants.[13]

II. INCULCATION OF MORAL CONCERN

Consider now the possibility of inculcating a *jen*-attitude or moral concern. Suppose that teachers have a modicum of success in moral training; can they be assured that moral concern is also inculcated in the process? This question presumes that there is a distinction between training and inculcation. While this distinction seems unimportant from the standpoint of an ethics of rules or principles, it is especially required in an ethics of character or virtues. I suggest that the distinction may be elucidated in this way. Training, as an aspect of moral learning or education, is primarily a form of teaching maxims, precepts, or rules with a view to behavioral compliance with accepted or acceptable requirements in a positive social morality. The *li*, as a set of formal prescriptions, or the Decalogue can be taught by way of train-

---

For an attempt to accommodate principles within Confucian ethics construed as an ethics of virtue, see Essay 14.

12. D. C. Lau, trans., *Confucius: The Analects (Lun Yü)* (New York: Penguin Books, 1979), 11:22.

13. For an extensive discussion of this alternative to the deductivist approach to ethical justification, see my *Ethical Argumentation*, chaps. 1–2, and Essay 10.

ing, in the hope that the pupils in due time will practice what they learn and develop appropriate habits of obedience. In principle, and in the practice of many cultures, the teacher can employ the method of reward and punishment or of all sorts of enticing and repulsive devices. It is hoped that through persistent and forceful urging, in conjunction with the use of this method, the learner will acquire the desired habit of obedience to rules. It is doubtful, however, whether such a form of teaching can succeed in imparting an understanding of the *point* or rationale of these rules; or if these rules are justifiable in terms of principles, whether the rationales for accepting them can be properly appreciated.

I do not mean to suggest that moral training cannot be successful. Rather, we have little assurance in conveying or inculcating the *importance* of these rules and principles to human life, particularly in teaching the desired moral attitudes presupposed by rules or principles. Becoming a moral agent is not merely acquiring knowledge of the difference between right and wrong conduct. It is fundamentally coming to *care* for the difference. This is Ryle's insight in reminding us that such learning includes "an inculcated caring," a basic characteristic of moral agency.[14] As I have written elsewhere: "Part of being a moral agent is to exemplify a basic attitude of care for the distinction between right and wrong. Being brought up as a moral agent is being inculcated with this basic attitude rather than just being imparted with a set of moral rules or principles. This attitude of caring is basic in the sense that it renders intelligible a variety of the agent's reactive feelings and actions toward its object, not just in the sense of a fundamental principle, but in the sense of exemplifying that attitude of seriousness toward the objects deemed to have moral import."[15]

Similarly, some of the virtues like benevolence *(jen* in the narrow sense) or courage cannot be taught without inculcating the attitude of active concern and care for the well-being of every human.[16] We need not deny that a moral teacher can successfully habituate the pupil to act benevolently or courageously, or to take benevolence or courage as a consideration in ethical deliberation. In the former case, the habit of performing benevolent acts may well be formed without an affectionate concern or care for the well-being of others. In the latter case, one must note with Williams that "the virtue term itself does not occur in the

14. See Gilbert Ryle, "On Forgetting the Difference Between Right and Wrong" in A. I. Melden, ed., *Essays in Moral Philosophy* (Seattle: University of Washington Press, 1958).
15. See Essay 3.
16. *Mencius*, 2A:6.

content of deliberation." Rarely is it "the case that the description that applies to the agent and to the action is the same as that in terms of which the agent chooses the action." Consider, for example, the benevolent or kind-hearted person, he or she "does the benevolent things, but does them under other descriptions, such as 'she needs it,' or 'it will cheer him up,' 'it will stop the pain.' The description of the virtue is not the description that appears in the consideration."[17]

Possession of the *jen*-attitude or moral concern has a Janus character. It faces on the one hand outward toward other agents, and on the other inward. The outward direction is caring for one's fellows; it involves respect for others as persons rather than things in the Kantian sense.[18] This concern is manifested in two ways: (1) a regard for other persons' exercise of moral sense or the "heart" of the distinction between right and wrong *(shih-fei chih hsin)* within the community,[19] and (2) attention to other persons' needs, feelings, desires, and aspirations as these are relevant to the realization of *jen*.[20] The former expresses a concern and respect for a community, its established standards of conduct that determine the eligibility of members' choices and actions, subject to reasoned defeasibility. To inculcate this concern is to impress upon the pupil the importance of being a member of a moral community. The attitude to be inculcated is not a blind adherence to customary standards, but one of respect for established practices. This respect is not incompatible with the agents maintaining a critical stance on issues to which existing morality does not provide ready-made solutions. The authority of standards is presumed, though it creates a burden of justification for departure. If one can reasonably show their inadequacy, say, in dealing with changing circumstances, the presumed authority is defeated, though the agent may experience regret in doing so.[21] In Hsün Tzu's words, the respect is consistent with the exercise of *i* or reasoned judgment in response to changing circumstances *(yi i pien-ying)*.[22] Thus the inculcation of respect for established morality, ideally, must also involve the inculcation of reasonableness. This is distinct from training in rational prudence or in compliance with canons of inductive or deductive logic. While the significance of prudence or satisfaction of self-interest is not denied, from the Confucian point of

17. Bernard Williams, *Ethics and the Limits of Philosophy* (Cambridge: Harvard University Press, 1985), 10.
18. See for example, R. S. Downie and Elizabeth Telfer, *Respect for Persons* (London: George Allen and Unwin, 1969).
19. See *Mencius*, 4A:17.
20. See my "Confucian Vision and the Human Community."
21. See *Dimensions of Moral Creativity*, 98–103.
22. *Hsün Tzu, pu-kou p'ien* and *chih-shih p'ien.*

view, reasonableness, characteristic of paradigmatic or exemplary persons, cannot be properly understood without *jen* or extensive concern for others, as well as the sense of appropriateness, moderation in passions and temperament, impartiality or fairmindedness, and intelligent appreciation of the actuating import of the cognitive content of ethical knowledge.[23]

The outward regard for others' mode of existence (i.e., their needs, feelings, interests, and aspirations) signifies an attitude of reciprocity or mutuality *(shu)*, acknowledging the importance of active sympathy with others' well-being as they conceive it.[24] Also, one may reformulate the Confucian insight, as Danto does: "Morality is bound up with the felicities and distractions of common life." The insight of the Confucian notion of reciprocity *(shu)* may be reformulated in this way: "How others feel about our actions toward them should be internally related to our feeling about those actions, and hence their feelings should penetrate our motives."[25] Differently put, human lives within a moral community are possible because there exists a reciprocity of individual wills oriented toward a common telos, implying an acknowledged bond. The bond is, so to speak, the intersection of individual lives, an anchorage for both personal and cultural identity. This attitude provides significance to personal lives. Respect for persons, especially in the light of *jen*, is not just a Kantian respect for persons as ends in themselves, but a respect for individual styles of life, deemed as polymorphous expressions of a common culture. As Mencius points out, there are alternative paths to the pursuit of *jen*.[26]

We may say that the reciprocity of moral wills, conjoined with the respect for established standards of conduct and informed by reasonableness, constitutes the outward direction of *jen* or moral concern. Some notion of common good may be said to be part of this concern, but this notion must not be construed as a determinate, ideal norm of moral conduct. Major Neo-Confucians, e.g., Ch'eng Hao and Wang Yang-ming, would prefer *tao* or *jen*, in the broad sense, as an *ideal theme*

23. For further discussion, see my *The Unity of Knowledge and Action: A Study in Wang Yang-ming's Moral Psychology* (Honolulu: University Press of Hawaii, 1982), 94–100. For a more general discussion of the significance of reasonableness in ethical theory, see my "Ideals and Value: A Study in Rescher's Moral Vision" in Robert Almeder, ed., *Praxis and Reason: Studies in the Philosophy of Nicholas Rescher* (Washington: University Press of America, 1982), 194–98.

24. For further discussion, see n. 20 above; A. I. Melden, *Rights and Persons* (Berkeley: University of California Press, 1977); Murphy, *The Theory of Practical Reason;* and John Macmurray, *Persons in Relation* (London: Farber & Farber, 1961).

25. Arthur C. Danto, *Mysticism and Morality* (New York: Basic Books, 1972), 115.

26. *Mencius*, 6B:8.

amenable to individual interpretation in the light of the agent's experience and understanding, rather than as a norm that provides specific prescriptions for conduct.[27] They would endorse Danto's appreciation of Confucius's insight: "No man could be counted moral who did not have that minimal concern for others that permits his felicity to vary as their does."[28] But they would add, in the spirit of Wang Yang-ming, that a commitment to *jen* as a vision of the universe as a moral community entails a concern for the well-being of all existent things. In this light, the pursuit of one's own happiness must pay heed to that of others, humans and non-humans. Of course, due allowance is made for the limitations of one's efforts in relation to natural and cultural orders.[29] Given that there are no fixed rules for inculcating the vision of *jen*, especially involving reasonableness, a person committed to *jen* would turn inward to realize the outward direction of moral concern. Inculcation of *jen*-attitude is a "heavy burden," involving not only a resolute will but also self-knowledge.[30] As Confucius once said to Yen Yuan in response to his question about *jen:* "The practice of *jen* depends on oneself alone, and not on others."[31]

The inward aspect of *jen* or moral concern is a concern for one's own moral condition, an attitude of self-regard focusing on cultivating harmonious dispositions. Respect for *li* or tradition is indispensable for self-development, or in Hsün Tzu's words, for ordering one's temperament and nourishing life *(chih-ch'i yang-sheng).*[32] For this purpose, a person committed to *jen* or *tao* as an ideal theme may adopt maxims of common morality or first personal precepts as contributory to self-cultivation.[33] A more intellectual or rational person may formulate a plan of life for securing a sense of personal identity, i.e., a sense of unity or coherence in his or her life, subject of course, to adjustment in the light of changing circumstances. Such a plan of life, as Rawls conceives it, "is designed to permit the harmonious satisfaction of his interests."[34] There is a schedule of activities so that various desires can be satisfied

27. See *Dimensions of Moral Creativity,* chap. 8, and *The Unity of Knowledge and Action,* chap. 2.

28. Danto, *Mysticism and Morality,* 115.

29. See *The Unity of Knowledge and Action,* chap. 3; and Essay 9.

30. Tseng Tzu said, "A Gentleman *[chün-tzu]* must be strong and resolute, for his burden is heavy and the road is long. He takes benevolence *[jen]* as his burden. Is that not heavy? Only with death does the road come to an end. Is that not long?" (*Analects,* 8:7).

31. *Analects,* 12:1.

32. *Hsün Tzu, hsiu-sheng p'ien;* Watson, *Hsün Tzu: Basic Writings,* 25.

33. See *Ethical Argumentation,* 100–101; *The Unity of Knowledge and Action,* 36–37.

34. John Rawls, *A Theory of Justice* (Cambridge: Harvard University Press, 1971), 91 and 408.

without interference. Presumably such a plan would yield a sense of personal identity.[35] However, as an ideal theme, *jen* is more a point of orientation, a unifying perspective for dealing with personal problems and perplexities. The coherence of one's life is a quest, a constant challenge. The ideal of *jen* allows for diversity of individual life plans as well as styles of life, so long as they pay heed to the common form of life within a moral community. It is, so to speak, an ideal of "congeniality of excellences" rather than a universally prescriptive norm for human life. The possibility of its realization depends on the growth of a moral agent in expansive awareness of and concern for all humans and nonhumans. Inculcating such a concern, as I have earlier stated, is not just a matter of developing moral competence, nor of teaching methods for securing self-realization. The problem of inculcating *jen* or moral concern may thus be characterized as a problem of developing a sense of importance of the individual quest for the meaning of life, for a personal style of life within the moral community, and ultimately for *tao* or the "unity and harmony of man and nature" *(t'ien-jen ho-i).*[36]

The inculcation of *jen* or moral concern focuses on practical understanding as distinct from intellectual understanding, for it teaches the pupil to appreciate the meaning of commitment, its actuating import in thought and action, or in Wang Yang-ming's term, the unity of knowledge and action *(chih-hsing ho-i).*[37] As with inculcation of moral sentiments in general, training in minimal competence is necessary, for moral sentiments have an intellectual component. In teaching a child, for example, what "shame" means, "we teach him to feel ashamed."[38] Moreover, in the process we also want to teach him or her to appreciate, à la Hsün Tzu, the distinction between shame and honor and how the experience of shame, owing to one's mean circumstances *(shih-ju),* say poverty, is consistent with being a person of moral honor *(i-jung).* For one who aspires to be a paradigmatic individual, a *chün-tzu,* he or she would not be distressed nor find it unacceptable to be in such a circumstance provided that the shame is undeserved from the point of view of righteousness *(i-ju).* However, a *chün-tzu* cannot have shame justly deserved *(i-ju).* For shame justly deserved is a depraved condition wrought by such acts as "licentiousness, filthiness, transgression of duty, disorderliness *(luan-li),* arrogance, oppressive cruelty, and greed."[39]

35. See Dewitt H. Parker, *The Philosophy of Value* (Ann Arbor: University of Michigan Press, 1958), 125–26.
36. For contrast between the classical Taoist and Confucian conceptions of *tao* as an ideal theme, see Essay 4.
37. See *The Unity of Knowledge and Action,* esp. chap. 1.
38. Robert W. Burch, "Are There Moral Experts?" *The Monist* 58, no. 4 (1974): 656.
39. *Hsün Tzu, cheng-lun p'ien;* Homer H. Dubs, trans., *The Works of Hsüntze* (Ch'eng-

While a *chün-tzu* may be considered a worthy person, this does not
mean that he or she possesses feats of uncommon excellence in ability,
knowledge, or skill in inquiry or argumentation. Rather, the *chün-tzu*
is distinguished in having palpable ethical integrity.[40] In the next section, I offer some reflections on the role of *chün-tzu* or paradigmatic
individuals in inculcating *jen* or moral concern. I shall assume that *jen*
cannot be construed without reference to *li* and *i*, for they are basic
and interdependent notions of virtue in Confucian ethics. Particular
notions of virtue, such as filiality, courage, and trustworthiness, are
notions of dependent virtue, in that their ethical import depends on
direct or indirect reference to one or more of the basic interdependent
virtues.[41]

III. PARADIGMATIC INDIVIDUALS: *CHÜN-TZU*

One salient feature of classical Confucian ethics is its focus on *chün-
tzu* or exemplary individuals in the elucidation of ethical notions as well
as their practical import in moral education. In the *Lun Yü (The Analects)* Confucius often spoke of the contrast between *chün-tzu* and *hsiao-
jen* (small-minded or petty person). A closer study of his remarks on
chün-tzu points to a conception of paradigmatic individuals as concrete,
exemplary embodiments of his ideal of *jen* or humanity.[42] For Confucius, the *chün-tzu* are not mere custodians of *li* or cultural tradition, nor
mere models of emulation; they are persons invested with an action-
guiding function by virtue of their flexibility and styles of life. Confucius believed that only a sage *(sheng-jen)*, a perfect man of *jen* can
establish an ethically enduring, harmonious, social and political order.
Yet, unlike Mencius, Hsün Tzu, and the Sung-Ming Confucians, he did
not uphold sagehood as a practical end for ordinary moral agents. He
once said that he had no hope of meeting a sage, but would be quite
content with meeting a *chün-tzu*.[43] He repudiated the ascription of sage-

wen, 1966), 209, with emendation. See also Hsün Tzu's essay on honor and shame *(jung-
ju p'ien)* in Dubs, 56–66. A complete translation of this essay along with a useful introduction to the background is found in John Knoblok, *Xunzi: A Translation and Study of
the Complete Works*, (Stanford: Stanford University Press, 1988), 1:182–95.

40. Ibid., *ju-hsiao p'ien;* Dubs, *The Works of Hsüntze*, 96–97. Cf. Burch, "Are These
Moral Experts," esp. 658.

41. For a compendious statement of the interdependence of *jen, li,* and *i,* see Essay
13. More detailed studies based on the *Hsün Tzu* may be found in my "The Problem of
Conceptual Unity in Hsün Tzu and Li Kou's Solution," *Philosophy East and West* 39, no.
2 (1989).

42. See *Dimensions of Moral Creativity*, chaps. 3–5.

43. For similar view on *chün-tzu* as exemplary, creative persons, but interpreted in
terms of the notion of model in depicting their role in socio-political order, see David L.

hood, perhaps in response to some people's praise: "How dare I claim to be a sage or even a man of *jen*. Perhaps, it might be said of me that I seek wisdom and pursue the realization of *jen* without slack, and teach without being weary."[44] As for being a *chün-tzu*, he said; "In unstinted effort you may compare me to others, but in becoming a *chün-tzu*, I have yet no success."[45] Even Mencius, a professed follower of Confucius's teaching, disclaimed being a sage: "A sage is something even Confucius did not claim to be. What an extraordinary thing for you to say of me."[46]

While sagehood was not in Confucius's eyes a practically attainable ideal, we may appropriate Hsün Tzu's conception in devising a mythic story for appreciating the role of *chün-tzu* or paradigmatic individuals in the inculcation of *jen* or moral concern. In this story,[47] the *li*, the right and proper rules of conduct, are an "invention" *(cho)* of a wise and benevolent sage called Kung Chih-jen [The wise and benevolent Kung]. This invention was made in response to the problem of conflict of individual interests.[48] After much reflection and thought-experiment on the possibility of resolving this human predicament, Chih-jen proposed the *li*, along with sanctions for violation. This proposal was widely accepted and put into practice, and, as a consequence, the *li* became customary rules of proper behavior *(yüeh-ting ch'eng-su)*.[49] Over

---

Hall and Roger T. Ames, *Thinking Through Confucius* (Albany: State University of New York Press, 1987), 188–92. For my comment on the notion of model, see *Dimensions of Moral Creativity*, 36, 47–49; and remarks toward the end of this paper.

44. *Analects*, 7:34. This interpretive translation of 7:34 owes to Lau, *Confucius: The Analects*, and Chien Mu, *Lun Yü hsin-chieh* (Taipei: Sheng-wu, 1965), 1:256–57.

45. *Analects*, 7:33 (Lau's translation with emendation); and Ch'ien Mu, *Lun Yü hsin-chieh*, 255–56. Perhaps, contrary to Ch'ien Mu's interpretation, these remarks of Confucius are expressions not merely of modesty, but of the difficulty in inculcation of *jen* in moral education.

46. *Meng Tzu*, 2A:2. The translation is adopted from D. C. Lau, *Mencius* (Baltimore: Penguin Books, 1970), 79.

47. For the basis of this story, see *hsing-o p'ien;* Watson, *Hsün Tzu: Basic Writings*, 160. The story may be recast for appreciating the role of Jesus in Christianity by substituting God for Kung Chih-jen, and the Decalogue for the *li* as I often told seminarians in my ethics classes in the early 1970s. In fact, this paper is based on extensive retrospective notes written in spring 1975.

48. This Hsün-tzean view would embrace the recent conception of morality as a social creation in the works of Harman and Castañeda, especially as elucidated by Wong; unlike the *Li Chi*, however, Hsün Tzu is less explicit about resolving internal conflicts within individual lives. See David Wong, *Moral Relativity* (Berkeley: University of California Press, 1984), 23–36. For a critical appreciation, see my review in the *Review of Metaphysics* 39, no. 2 (1985): 381–83. See also my "*Li* and Moral Justification: A Study in the *Li Chi*," *Philosophy East and West* 33, no. 1 (1983): 1–16.

49. See *Cheng-ming p'ien;* Watson, *Hsün Tzu*, 144. For a reconstruction of Hsün Tzu's arguments for the necessity of *li* in response to the problem of human conflict, see my

a long period of time, general compliance was secured, but Chih-jen was unhappy about this situation, for people followed the *li* mainly to avoid the sanctions and not because of *jen* or mutual concern. In this situation, sanctions are heeded, but for the most part, people's activities are motivated largely by concern for personal gain. While this concern is not always unreasonable, it remains an extrinsic consideration from the perspective of *jen*.

Chih-jen realized that *jen* cannot be inculcated by way of *li* or rules of conduct. As action-guides, the rules have to be formulated in general, impersonal language. However theoretically sound and practicable, they remain abstract. Even if people recognize *jen* as *li's* implicit rationale, there is no assurance that people will learn to care for one another. Differently put, the concrete significance of *jen* or concern for one's fellows cannot be conveyed by such abstract language, or even by more specific directives aiming at promoting *jen*-realization. Chih-jen hit upon a brilliant idea. Inculcating *jen*, he thought, is basically a problem of "incarnating" *jen*, or exhibiting its possibility of attainment as an intrinsically moving or actuating force in human conduct. Again, after much thought and deliberation, Chih-jen decided to devote his efforts to cultivate some accomplished *jen*-persons and to elevate them to the status of *chün-tzu* or paradigmatic individuals.[50] In his mind, these exemplary persons, while not perfect, embodied *jen* in their lives and conduct, and thus, could serve as examples of the concrete significance of *jen*. The *chün-tzu* are the exemplars of intrinsic actuation of *jen*, not models for imitation or emulation—though in actual practice, moral teachers may center their attention on the latter as a prelude to the inculcation of *jen* or moral concern.[51]

"The Quasi-Empirical Aspect of Hsün Tzu's Philosophy of Human Nature," *Philosophy East and West* 28, no. 1 (1978): 3–19.

50. This conception of paradigmatic individuals and application to *chün-tzu* was elaborated in my *Dimensions of Moral Creativity* with a view to elucidating their role in actual moralities or moral practices. It makes no claim to the role of paradigmatic individuals in the resolution of moral disputes, a view proposed by Alderman. My own view of moral justification is given in *Ethical Argumentation*, 50–101. See Harold Alderman, "By Virtue of a Virtue," *Review of Metaphysics*, vol. 36, no. 1 (1982). For a more detailed discussion of the role of paradigmatic individuals as action-guides or standards of inspiration, see my "Some Responses to Criticisms," *Journal of Chinese Philosophy*, vol. 7, no. 1 (1980).

51. For the importance of the notion of paradigmatic individuals for moral philosophy, we may regard it as a non-conceptual analogue of Kant's notion of the *typic* of the Moral Law. Fictional characters, such as those in the *Chuang Tzu*, may serve the same non-conceptual role in clarifying the concrete significance of Chuang Tzu or Lao Tzu's notion of *Tao*. For further discussion on Kant, see Paul Dietrichsen, "Kant's Criteria of Universalizability" in Robert Paul Wolff, ed., *Kant: Foundation of the Metaphysics of Morals: Text and Critical Essays* (Indianapolis: Bobbs-Merrill, 1969). For Taoism, see Essay 5. For an interpretation of *chün-tzu* as models of emulation or moral excellence, see Donald J.

The point of our fictive story may be put in more general terms. Acknowledged paradigmatic individuals may serve as examples of the intrinsically actuating force of an existing morality. The paradigmatic individuals offer an example, so to speak, of the mediation of the ideal and the actual world: the concrete possibility for the realization of the ideal of moral concern. While they have a representative function in this way, they are neither archetypes of moral excellence nor models of imitation or emulation.[52] They show how a sincere commitment to the ideal can have a transformative significance in the agent's life and conduct and thus provide an answer to the question "How can I become a person of moral concern?" Given my commitment to a morality, how can such a commitment have a transformative significance in my life? Alternatively, this is a question of meaningful commitment.[53] For a moral teacher, the aim of moral inculcation is to supplement moral training by focusing on paradigmatic individuals as *possible* answers to this question of becoming a moral agent. Possible answers because the effective role of paradigmatic individuals is entirely contingent upon acknowledgement by agents within a morality that has a cultural history. These individuals are themselves historical creatures, though as *chün-tzu*, they are preeminently persons who possess such qualities as a sense of righteousness *(i)*, catholicity and neutrality, and harmony of words and deeds.[54]

Perhaps, more important from the point of view of the individual quest for the meaning of life within a moral community, the paradigmatic individuals, by virtue of their concern for their fellows, offer an example of how one can learn the actuating significance of moral commitment from the lives of other persons, even if these persons were mere products of literary imagination. As Dilman points out, we can appreciate what Tolstoy wrote about the peasants whom he admired and the sense in which moral agents can learn from one another. Consider the example of Ivan Illych in Tolstoy's *Death of Ivan Illych*. Ivan learned something from Gerasim, the peasant lad. "Tolstoy leaves us in no doubt that Gerasim made him see a possibility to which Ivan's way of living had kept his eyes shut, a possibility that was excluded by

---

Munro, *The Concept of Man in Ancient China* (Stanford: Stanford University Press, 1969), 114. For the relevance of the notion of intrinsic actuation to psychoanalysis, see Hugh Mullan, "Horney's Contribution to a Rational Approach to Morals," *American Journal of Psychoanalysis* 48, no. 2 (1988).

52. The Confucian notion of *kan-ying* (stimulus and response) has a similar function in providing a bridge between the ideal and the actual world. For further discussion, see my "Practical Causation and Confucian Ethics," *Philosophy East and West* 25, no. 1 (1975).

53. See *The Unity of Knowledge and Action,* 55–58.

54. See *Dimensions of Moral Creativity,* chap. 5.

the way he lived. Ivan Illych had been caught up in a way of life that excluded the possibility of care for and devotion to other people. By his example Gerasim opened up for Ivan what was a new possibility and made him realize what was wrong with his life. The possibility in question is one that is internally related to a certain way of living."[55]

Here we may recall Danto's appreciation of Confucius's insight into the reciprocity of moral wills and the Confucian respect for persons as respect for exemplary individual styles of life rather than as a respect for the generic feature of rational agency or self-determination.[56] Perhaps Confucius deserves the credit for being the first moral teacher to recognize the role of paradigmatic individuals in moral education. His conception of *chün-tzu* in inculcating *jen* or moral concern, as a partner in learning the *li*, reflects a concern with the meaning of moral commitment. While it recognizes their importance in moral education, this conception does not provide a set of principles or precepts that can serve as premises of practical reasoning. But it does point to the use of moral language as a language of serious moral commitment, as implied in his doctrine of correct use of terms *(cheng-ming)*.[57] Hume seems to express a similar view in his remark: "The merit of delivering true general precepts in ethics is indeed very small. Whoever recommends any moral virtues really does no more than is implied in the terms themselves. That people who invented the word *charity*, and used it in a good sense, inculcated more clearly, and much more efficaciously, the precept, *Be charitable*, than any pretended legislator or prophet, who should insert such a *maxim* in his writings."[58] However, emphasis on the use of moral language by paradigmatic individuals as elucidative of an aspect of moral commitment should not be construed as a metaethical thesis on the nature of moral language, for the Confucian notion of *chün-tzu* does not pretend to be a basis for conceptual analysis of ethical

55. Ilham Dilman and D. Z. Phillips, *Sense and Delusion* (London: Routhledge and Kegan Paul, 1971), 27–29.

56. Cf. Downie and Telfer, *Respect for Persons.*

57. See *The Analects*, 13:3. For my reconstruction of this doctrine of *cheng-ming*, see *Ethical Argumentation*, 101–37.

58. David Hume, "Of the Standard of Taste," *Essays: Morals, Political and Literary* (Oxford: Oxford University Press, 1963), 233–34. Aschenbrenner comments: "Hume's thesis that the very presence of a word such as *charity* in our language has a didactic or preceptive power more effective than any explicit command or exhortation can be extended to all appraisive language. To use it is to understand the implied precept if not actually to embrace it." This interpretation is more plausible if we assume the use of moral language by paradigmatic individuals in exemplifying moral language as a language of personal commitment rather than as a mere impersonal language of ethical discourse. See Karl Aschenbrenner, *The Concepts of Value: Foundations of Value Theory* (Dordrecht-Holland: Reidel, 1971), 22.

terms, but one that focuses on the inculcation of *jen* or moral concern, on learning to become a *jen*-person from the exemplary lives of other committed persons.

Such a form of *jen*-learning inevitably involves some degree of idealization of the character or virtues of *chün-tzu* or paradigmatic individuals, a sort of *projection* of desirable personal attributes. In turn, this projection involves, more fundamentally as Mencius sees it, an active sensitivity to the suffering, and we may add, to the happiness or well-being of others. In this manner, the cognitive sense or content of moral commitment to a moral tradition acquires a lively "force and vivacity," to borrow Hume's term, in the minds of the agents. Responding to a person as embodying the actuating significance of moral commitment thus involves both sense and sensibility, and the two cannot be severed if paradigmatic individuals are to play an effective role in moral education, that is, in training and inculcation of moral concern.

Conceivably, in the case of moral training, *chün-tzu* or paradigmatic individuals may serve as models of emulation or even as models of imitation. It may even be maintained that appreciating the role of paradigmatic individuals, particularly in a theory of virtues, may point to a non-mechanical "decision procedure" for resolving moral perplexities. As Alderman points out, "In this view of things, determining what one ought to do involves neither knowing and applying a rule nor specifying a good and predicting which course of action will most efficiently yield access to it. Rather one resolves moral ambiguity and makes choices by envisioning what some paradigmatic individual would do in the same situation; and knowing what he would do requires an imaginative experiment of envisioning him doing it."[59] Alderman is well aware that there is the problem of "choosing alternative characterizations of paradigmatic individuals."[60] I wonder whether this problem may not reflect, in some cases, competing characterizations derived in part from a diversity of cultural backgrounds or forms of life, which render intelligible such characterizations.[61] Also, different though not necessarily incompatible idealizations of the characters of paradigmatic individuals may well reflect quite distinct concerns of individuals in

---

59. Alderman continues, "One might prepare for these imaginative experiments by, for example, living with the paradigmatic individual, by reading characterizations of his life, or by having personal contact with one of his disciples. In either case what one would try to do is to exemplify a certain character. Aristotle, as I have noted, recognized that one acquired virtuous character by *acting like* the person who has such character" (Alderman, "By Virtue of a Virtue," 149). Some of my remarks below are indebted to Alderman's excellent paper. See n. 67 below.

60. Ibid., 148.

61. See *Dimensions of Moral Creativity*, 10–11.

their quests for styles of life, but this quest, presuming a shared concern for the well-being of the moral community, is reasonable if the priority of moral rules is acknowledged as a constraint on the pursuit of individual ideals.[62] It is the necessity of this acknowledgement that accounts for the importance of moral training, for the acquisition of minimal competence in learning and applying moral rules, at least as a guide to dealing with recurrent, though normal, problems of human interaction. Even within the personal lives of moral agents, these rules may be quite helpful, if not always necessary, in resolving internal conflicts.[63] On the more global scale of intercultural conflict, it is doubtful that characterizations of paradigmatic individuals, even if they have close affinity or functional equivalence, can help resolve the difficulty of acting ethically, unless some transcultural principles or ground rules are accepted as preconditions of adjudication.[64]

In moral instruction or training, paradigmatic individuals may quite properly play the role of models for imitation or emulation by providing standards of aspiration or examples of competence to be attained. In the inculcation of *jen* or moral concern, they serve as standards of inspiration by providing a point of orientation rather than specific targets of achievement. The notion of imitation seems out of place in characterizing this function, for it may misleadingly suggest an "unthinking imitation of the lives and conduct of certain individuals without regard to moral criteria."[65] With proper qualification, allowing for creativity, however, imitation in the sense of *mimesis* may be acceptable. As Tatarkiewicz points out, "In early Greece, *mimesis* signified imitation, but in the sense in which the term is applied to acting and not to copying."[66] As this process of *mimesis* involves imaginative experiments in "acting like the person who has such a character," it is best to use Collingwood's notion of *re-enactment* rather than imitation.[67] In "acting like" a para-

62. Ibid., 135–39.
63. Wong, *Moral Relativity*, 175.
64. For an attempt to specify these principles, see Essay 14.
65. *Dimensions of Moral Creativity*, 48.
66. Wladyslaw Tatarkiewicz, *History of Aesthetics*, ed. J. Harrell (The Hague: Mouton and Warsaw: Polish Scientific Publications, 1970), 1:17, cited in Eliot Deutsch, *On Truth: An Ontological Theory* (Honolulu: University of Hawaii Press, 1979), 26.
67. Alderman, "By Virtue of a Virtue," 149. In his letter to me (December 24, 1982), responding to my query about his use of "appropriate imitation" in the article, he stated that in the article he has in mind the distinction between "*impersonating*" and *enacting*" as in the theater, and that it may be connected with my conception of "analogical projection." I prefer "re-enactment" in Collingwood's use, though without adopting his controversial thesis that re-enactment applies only to thought and not to acts. See Alan Donagan, *The Later Philosophy of R. G. Collingwood* (Oxford: Clarendon Press, 1962), 220–22.

digmatic individual in a particular situation, the agent is trying to re-enact the *spirit* in which he or she acts, and this involves imaginatively rethinking the concrete significance of moral concern in the present. The moral agent is much like Collingwood's historian, re-enacting in his mind "the history he is studying."[68]

In Confucian ethics this historical re-enactment is the re-enactment of *jen*, the spirit of *li* as ennobling humanity.[69] The *chün-tzu*, in this way, can serve as *an* example of how the Confucian China today in Taiwan can reanimate the Confucian cultural tradition with a new character and significance, in cultivating the moral autonomy of individuals. As I see it, it is a sort of *investiture*, conferring honor upon individuals who exemplify the spirit of *jen* in relation to the Confucian tradition without slavish adherence to conventional rules of propriety. As suggested in this essay, this is a task of inculcating *jen* or extensive moral concern, rather than in training or instruction of moral precepts. For moral precepts, however effectively taught, are always subject to interpretation in changing circumstances, to the exercise of *i*, a moral agent's sense of rightness in relation to the *li* or moral tradition—the preeminent quality of a *chün-tzu* in coping with indeterminate, problematic situations of human life. In Confucian ethics, autonomy is not a given or a Kantian presupposition of rational agency, but an achievement anchored in a common form of life. It is a challenge to moral self-cultivation *(hsiu-shen)*. Moral education, in both training and inculcation, provides only a beginning and not an end. As Hsün Tzu reminds us, moral learning has no terminus, it is traveling but not arriving, which does not cease until death. Such learning requires constant effort at attaining integrity or "completeness" and "purity" *(ch'üan* and *tsui)*.[70] Pursuit of *jen* is a constant burden without assurance of attainment. Though one may experience joy in the course of persistent effort, one must not blame Heaven and one's fellows if one fails.[71] Recall Confucius's remark: "The practice of *jen* depends on oneself, not others" *(Analects, 12:1)*.[72]

68. R. G. Collingwood, *An Autobiography* (Oxford: Oxford University Press, 1964), 112.

69. See Essay 13.

70. *Ch'üan-hsüeh p'ien;* Watson, *Hsün Tzu: Basic Writings,* sec. I: "Encouraging Learning."

71. See *The Analects,* 14:36.

72. An earlier version of this paper was presented with a different title ("The Role of *Chün-Tzu* in Moral Education and Modern Life") at the International Symposium of Chinese Culture and the Modern Life, Fu Jen Catholic University, Taipei, Taiwan, December 19–23, 1989.

Essay 9

Between Commitment and Realization
Wang Yang-ming's Vision of the Universe as a Moral Community

INTRODUCTION

Any attempt to present the thought of Wang Yang-ming (1472–1529) is beset by a major problem, for the dynamic character of his works resists systematic formulation. It behooves the student to heed Wing-tsit Chan's reminder: "The philosophy of Wang Yang-ming is a vigorous philosophy born of serious searching and bitter experience. It is no idle speculation or abstract theory developed for the sake of intellectual curiosity."[1] In his letters and conversations recorded by his disciples, we find a recurrent emphasis on personal realization as a key to understanding his teachings. Indeed, it is plausible to maintain that his central teachings, such as the unity of knowledge and action and the vision of the sage as "forming one body with Heaven, Earth, and the myriad things," are intended not as theoretical doctrines but as compendious statements of the outcomes of his quest for understanding the spirit of Confucian learning. Wang's doctrine of the unity of knowledge and action, for example, may be regarded as a forceful and concise way of stating the unity of his life and teaching during his formative years.[2] As Tu Wei-ming points out, "unlike the unity of speculative construct or epistemological system, the integrity of Yang-ming's teaching is based on his life experiences rather than an objectifiable structure of propositions."[3]

1. Wang Yang-ming, *Instructions for Practical Living and Other Neo- Confucian Writings*, translated with notes by Wing-tsit Chan (New York: Columbia University Press, 1963), xix; hereafter cited as *Instructions*. The Chinese text I have consulted for this paper is Wing-tsit Chan (Ch'en Jung-chieh), *Ch'uan-hsi lu hsiang-chu chi-p'ing* (Taipei: Hsüeh-sheng, 1983). Emendations of Chan's translations are indicated by asterisks.
2. For an approach to this doctrine as a solution to the problem of moral commitment and achievement, see my *The Unity of Knowledge and Action: A Study in Wang Yang-ming's Moral Psychology* (Honolulu: The University Press of Hawaii, 1982).
3. Tu wei-ming, *Neo-Confucian Thought in Action: Wang Yang-ming's Youth (1472–1509)*

156

Wang's quest for the spirit of Confucian learning may be charac-terized as a quest for the *spirit* and *meaning* of Confucian sagehood, the ideal embodiment of the unity and harmony of man and nature. We may see this quest as the search for an answer to the question, "How can one become a Confucian sage?" in a way parallel to Kierkegaard's "How can one become a Christian?"[4] Obviously such a question is in-telligible only in light of a firm commitment to the actuating or trans-formative significance of the notion of sagehood. According to the Chronological Biography *(Nien-p'u)*, at the age of seventeen, Wang had a strong desire "to study to become a sage." Possibly his desire was fore-shadowed at an earlier age. As a precocious boy of ten, Wang asked his tutor, "What is the most important task in life?" The tutor responded, "It is to pass the civil examinations." Wang commented in a doubtful tone, "I am afraid that passing the civil examinations cannot be con-sidered as the most important task in life. Perhaps, it is to study to become a sage or a worthy."[5] The vision of sagehood seems to have acquired a definite shape at the age of thirty-three, when Wang first met his best friend, Chan Jo-shiu. The same biography informs us that both resolved "to promote and clarify the teachings of the sages."[6] In Chan Jo-shiu's epitaph of Wang, we are told that they had "agreed to adhere to Ch'eng Hao's teaching: 'the man of humanity *(jen)* forms one body with all things without differentiation.'"[7] In the *Inquiry on the Great Learning*, written a little over a year before his death, we find a comprehensive statement of this Confucian vision. It is reasonable to presume that his youthful commitment to the realization of sagehood is more a commitment to a task of clarifying the concrete significance

---

(Berkeley: University of California Press, 1976), 3. A complementary approach is to see Wang's philosophy as "a product of a living dialogue," since his doctrines "were given expression largely in response to the questions addressed to him by others." See Julia Ching, *To Acquire Wisdom: The Way of Wang Yang-ming* (New York: Columbia University Press, 1976), xvi.

   4. See Søren Kierkegaard, *Concluding Unscientific Postscript* (Princeton: Princeton Uni-versity Press, 1941). For the significance of this question to understanding moral crea-tivity in general, see my *Dimensions of Moral Creativity: Paradigms, Principles, and Ideals* (University Park: Pennsylvania State University Press, 1978), 16–19. For the significance of this question for understanding Wang's attitude toward convention and Confucian classics and the role of moral reflection, see *The Unity of Knowledge and Action*, chap. 3.

   5. *Yang-ming ch'üan-shu*, in Ssu-pu pei-yao, (Taipei: Chung Hwa, 1970), 32:3a and 32:2a. Tu's *Neo-Confucian Thought in Action* gives an incisive discussion of the character of Wang's search, decision, and experience of enlightenment that culminates in the doc-trine of the unity of knowledge and action.

   6. *Yang-ming ch'üan-shu*, 32:5a-6b.

   7. Tu, *Neo-Confucian Thought in Action*, 93. In Huang Wan's eulogy, Yang-ming is described thus: "Ernest and untiring, he counselled others to the practice of the good, desiring by *jen* to save all living beings under Heaven." See Ching, *To Acquire Wisdom*, 35.

of the vision, a sort of an ideal theme to be developed in thought and action, rather than an ideal norm that has preceptive import.[8] Ideal theme is more a perspective or point of orientation than a fixed principle of conduct.

At any rate, in Wang's teaching, the role of commitment in learning to become a sage is often stressed. In one of the instructions to his disciples at Lung-ch'ang, Wang states, "If the will is not [firmly] established [li-chih], nothing in the world can be accomplished. Though there may be hundreds of professions, there is not a single one that does not depend on such a determination." He goes on to point out, "If one establishes one's will to become a sage, one can become a sage; if one establishes one's will to become a worthy, one can become a worthy." The lack of willful commitment or decision is compared to a ship without a rudder, or a horse without a bit.[9] Elsewhere, he remarks that "the way of learning is a task of creating something out of nothing . . . all depends on making up one's mind [li-chih]. If the student makes up his mind to have one thought to do good, his mind will be like the seed of a tree." With tender care in cultivation and nourishment, the vitality of the tree "will be increasingly great and its branches and leaves more luxuriant."[10] This commitment or decision is one to be made with one's hsin (mind and heart), or in Kierkegaard's language, with the whole inwardness of one's personality.[11] The decision furnishes a basis and a point of departure (t'ou-nao) for learning to become a sage (hsüeh-sheng).[12]

The principal aim of this essay is to offer a critical introduction to some basic ideas of Wang's philosophy. After dealing with the problem of methodology (Part I), I discuss the vision of jen as an object of ethical commitment (Part II), and the nature of self-confidence expressed in Wang's doctrine of mind (Part III). I turn next to the conception of liang-chih as a mediation between the ideal of jen and the actual world (Part IV), and conclude with a brief discussion of problems that arise out of the general characterization of liang-chih. This order of exposition is adopted mainly for convenience of exposition, for in Wang's mature philosophy all these topics are interdependent and deserve a more comprehensive study.

    8. For a detailed discussion of the distinction between an ideal theme and ideal norm, see Dimensions of Moral Creativity, chap. 8; and for jen as an ideal them in Wang's philosophy, see The Unity of Knowledge and Action, 32–35, 75, and 80.
    9. Yang-ming ch'üan-chu, 26:5b. Cf. Frederick G. Henke, The Philosophy of Wang Yang-ming (New York: Paragon Book Reprint Co., 1964), 463.
    10. Instructions, sec. 115. See also, Instructions, secs. 16, 30, and 96.
    11. Søren Kierkegaard, Either/Or (New York: Anchor Books, 1959), 2:171.
    12. Instructions, secs. 31, 102, and 168.

I. THE PROBLEM OF EXPLICATION

Before proceeding to Wang's vision, let me make clear my approach by remarking on the problem of explication. In addition to the difficulty of appreciating Wang's recurrent stress on personal realization as the key to understanding his teachings, there is a fundamental problem of interpretation. Wang's own explanations of his basic tenets employ standard terms derived from Sung Confucianism and the Classics. These terms are often used in a novel way without explicit warning. It is quite possible that these terms function as "satellite notions" that revolve around the central theme of *jen* or *tao*. As satellite notions, complementary terms such as *t'ien-li* (Heavenly reason) and *hsin chih pen-t'i* (mind-in-itself)elucidate the central theme of *jen* as the ultimate concern of human endeavors.[13] These terms have no explanatory value in theoretical discourse, but are best construed as indicative of the ways of *practical understanding*. They give alternative emphases to the actuating or transformative significance of the vision of *jen*.

Aside from the difficulty of translating and interpreting major terms such as *t'ien-li* or *liang-chih*, Wang also tends to collapse the significance of various distinctions such as *wu* (things) and *shih* (affairs or events), *hsin* (mind) and *li* (reason).[14] I have chosen not to translate some of these terms, not because available translations are completely inadequate, but because such translations, as the ones given in the parentheticals of the preceding paragraph, may have connotations that mislead the readers into thinking that there exist exact English equivalents with the same philosophical import. Moreover, they appear to be somewhat contrary to my own understanding of Wang's intentions in using these terms. My uncertainty on the value of some translations possibly reflects a personal failure. In retaining the transcriptions, I believe that a coherent interpretation is possible and quite consistent with Wang's own stress on personal realization *(t'i-jen)*, though there is a special difficulty in reconciling such an attempt with Wang's claim that there is something that cannot be verbally transmitted.

Consider the following conversation recorded by Lu Ch'eng:

13. These satellite notions may also be termed "focal notions." For their significance for moral theory, see *Dimensions of Moral Creativity*, 10–15.

14. In the *Instructions*, we find various quasi-identical expressions that involve the character *chi* to indicate connection between terms, e.g., *tao chi t'ien* (Heaven), *hsin* (mind) *chi li*. These expressions tend to suggest synonyms, but more plausibly suggest some sort of non-contingent connection between meanings of terms. The issue of interpretation is difficult to deal with without understanding the language used in communicating Wang's vision. For a hypothesis to resolve the difficulty, see *The Unity of Knowledge and Action*, 79–90.

PASSAGE A:

I said, "Scholars of later generations have written a great deal. I am afraid some of it has confounded correct learning."

The Teacher said, "The human mind and *t'ien-li* are completely undifferentiated" *(hun-jan)*. Sages and worthies wrote about them very much like a portrait painter painting the true likeness and transmitting the spirit. He shows only an outline of the appearance to serve as a basis for people to seek and find the true personality. Among one's spirit, feelings, expressions, and behavior, there is that which cannot be transmitted. Later writers have imitated and copied what the sages have drawn.[15]

Or more directly, responding to a student's report of his realization of the meaning or significance of the doctrine of the extension of knowledge, Wang said,

PASSAGE B:

From this we can know that knowledge acquired through personal realization is different from that acquired through listening to discussions. When I first lectured on the subject, I knew you took it lightly and were not interested. However, when one goes further and realizes this essential and wonderful thing personally to its very depth, he will see that it becomes different everyday and [its significance] is inexhaustible.[16]

If one takes the point of untransmitability seriously, then Wang's utterances can only be construed as *pointers* toward appreciating the heart of his teachings. But at the same time, these pointers are often given in standard terminologies that require interpretation. Given the important role of self-realization, inevitably these pointers can be elucidated only in the light of *personal* understanding. Thus, while retaining the transcriptions, such as *liang-chih* and *t'ien-li,* I often present what may be called *focal indicators* for their meanings; largely to facilitate my exposition, but also to indicate ways of interpretation without ascribing to Wang theoretical or systematic doctrines or using doctrinal labels familiar to students of Western philosophy. In particular, I have refrained from ascribing metaphysical doctrines to Wang, because my own exploration of Wang's works has been guided by my own interest in moral philosophy. This is not to deny that, with respect to some of Wang's central teachings, there are metaphysical presuppositions and implications. On the whole, I believe that, in a preliminary way, Wang's insights are best appreciated without such a metaphysical focus.[17] In

15. *Instructions*, sec. 20*.
16. Ibid., sec. 211. Wang goes on to remark that the phrase "the extension of knowledge" is truly "a secret transmitted from the sages of thousands of years ago. If we realize this, [we know that] it can wait a hundred generations for a sage to confirm it without a doubt." Note that from passages like this, it is easy to ascribe mysticism to Wang.
17. Mou Tsung-san's influential thesis that Wang has a moral metaphysics must cer-

sum, what follows is a personal report of what I have learned from reflection on Wang's philosophy.

II. THE VISION OF *JEN:* THE UNIVERSE AS A MORAL COMMUNITY

Wang's adoption of Ch'eng Hao's vision of the man of *jen* as "forming one body *(yi-t'i)* with all things without differentiation" has its eloquent expression in Chang Tsai's *Western Inscription* and was endorsed by Ch'eng Hao and his younger brother Ch'eng I (1033–1107).[18] This vision is a powerful expansion of the classical Confucian ideal of man "forming a triad *(t'san)* with Heaven and Earth" in the *Doctrine of the Mean.*[19] It is significant that, for Chu Hsi (1130–1200), the statements of the Ch'eng brothers fail to provide a clear and definitive guide to the realization of *jen*. According to Ch'eng Hao, "The student must first of all understand *jen*. The man of *jen* forms one body *(yi-t'i)* with all things without differentiation. Righteousness *(i)*, wisdom *(chih)*, and faithfulness *(hsin)* are [expressions of] *jen*."[20] Chu Hsi points out that these are excellent sayings but are "too broad" and "it is difficult for the student to embark upon [the road to *jen*]." On Ch'eng I's saying that "the man of *jen* considers Heaven and Earth and all things as one body *(yi-t'i)*," Chu Hsi complains that the saying is "too profound" and "there is nothing [definite] to be grasped [as a point of departure]."[21] The statement that the man of *jen* has the same body *(t'ung-t'i)* as that of Heaven and Earth and all things is unobjectionable so long as one realizes that *jen* is something to be sought within the person himself.

---

tainly be seriously discussed as an original effort in the development of critical Confucianism. See Mou Tsung-san, *T'sung Lu Hsiang-shan tao Liu Chi-shan* (Taipei: Hsüehsheng, 1979), chap. 3. For a tentative response to the significance of moral metaphysics to moral theory, see my "Reflections on Moral Theory and Understanding Moral Traditions" in Eliot Deutsch and Gerald James Larson, eds., *Interpreting Across Boundaries: New Essays in Comparative Philosophy* (Princeton: Princeton University Press, 1988).

18. For these statements, see Ch'eng Hao (1032–1185) and Ch'ang Tsai (1017–73) in Chan's *A Source Book in Chinese Philosophy* (Princeton: Princeton University Press, 1963), 497–98 and 523; hereafter cited as *Source Book.*

19. Ibid., 107–8. Similar vision, but with different purport, is found in the *Hsün Tzu*. See, for example, Burton Watson, trans., *Hsün Tzu: Basic Writings* (New York: Columbia University Press, 1963), 44, 94–95, and 167. For an explication of the vision in *The Doctrine of the Mean* inspired by Wang Yang-ming, see Essays 2 and 4. For Hsün Tzu's version, see a preliminary explication in my *Ethical Argumentation: A Study in Hsün Tzu's Moral Epistemology* (Honolulu: University of Hawaii Press, 1985), 160–63; and "The Problem of Conceptual Unity in Hsün Tzu and Li Kou's Solution," *Philosophy East and West* 39, no. 2 (1989); and "Hsün Tzu and The Unity of Virtues," *Journal of Chinese Philosophy* 14, no. 4 (1987).

20. Chan, *Source Book*, 523.

21. See Ch'ien Mu, *Chu Tzu hsin hsüeh-an* (Taipei: San-min, 1982), 2:59–60.

"*Jen* is the character of mind and the *li* (rationale) of love." It is through the extension (*t'ui*) of this mind and love that the vision of *jen* is possible of realization. Put differently, the notion of "the same body" suggests an exclusively external rather than internal approach to *jen*-realization. Furthermore, to talk about the man of *jen* as having "the same body" as all things, "will lead people to be vague, confused, neglectful, and make no effort to be alert."[22]

Chu Hsi's dissatisfaction with the notion of "forming one body" (*yi-t'i*) or "having the same body" (*t'ung-t'i*) as a way of characterizing the vision of *jen* justly raises a crucial issue on any attempt to elucidate *jen* in general or abstract terms without a proper elaboration of its concrete significance. That is to say, the practical relevance of the vision requires an exemplification of the possibility of its realization in the actual world. Wang's own version of *jen*, though making use of the notions derived from the Ch'eng brothers, may be seen as a response to Chu Hsi's challenge. Wang's own version runs:

PASSAGE C:

The great man regards Heaven, Earth, and the myriad things as one body (*yi-t'i*). He sees (*shih*) the world as one family and the country as one person. . . . Forming one body with Heaven, Earth, and the myriad things is true not only of the great man. Even the mind (*hsin*) of the small man is no different. Only he makes it small. Therefore, when he sees a child about to fall into a well, he cannot help a feeling of alarm and commiseration.[23] This shows that his humanity (*jen*) forms one body with the child. Again, when he observes the pitiful cries and frightened appearance of the birds and animals about to be slaughtered, he cannot help feeling an "inability to bear" their suffering.[24] This shows that his humanity forms one body with birds and animals.[25]

Wang goes on to point out that the man of *jen* also forms one body with plants, stones, tiles, mountains, and rivers.[26]

22. Ibid., 2:60. It must be noted that for Chu Hsi the external approach is important to the pursuit of Confucian learning. The investigation of things stressed in the *Great Learning* consists in investigating the *li* of all things (*ch'iung-li*). The view is rejected by Wang, but largely owing to misunderstanding. The issue between Chu and Wang raises a complex question concerning their relationship. For a preceptive study, see Shu-hsien Liu, "On Chu Hsi as an Important Source for the Development of the Philosophy of Wang Yang-ming," *Journal of Chinese Philosophy* 12, no. 1 (1984). For Wang's critique of Chu Hsi on the investigation of things, see *Instructions*, sec. 135, passim.
23. *Mencius*, 2A:6. See Chan, *Source Book*, 65.
24. Ibid.
25. *Inquiry on the Great Learning* (*Instructions*, 272). (This translation in Chan's except for the substitution of "sees" for "regards.")
26. Differently stated: "Everything from ruler, minister, husband, wife, and friends to mountains, rivers, spiritual beings, birds, animals, plants should be truly loved in order to realize my humanity that forms one body with them, and then my clear character will

When we ponder this vision, we can no longer say that the notion of "one body" *(yi-t'i)* is a concept devoid of concrete significance. The use of Mencius's doctrine of innate capacity for moral feeling—in particular, the inability to bear the suffering of all existent things—gives us some sense of concrete significance. The classical ideal of the harmony of man and nature is now understood as an ideal of the *universe as a moral community.* This ideal furnishes the committed agent a unifying perspective for experiencing and dealing with all persons, things, events, and human affairs. However, as an object of commitment, the possibility of realizing *jen* within the actual world depends on extending *hsin* (mind/heart) to its utmost reaches. Love and active sympathy are characteristically the expressions of *jen*, especially within the human world. *Jen* stresses the significance of the moral vision as residing in human relationships *(lun)*, a habitat which is capable of indefinite expansion and ultimately embraces the whole universe. As Wang once rhetorically put it: "At bottom Heaven and Earth and all things are my body *(wu-shen).* Is there any suffering or bitterness of the great masses that is not disease or pain in my own body?"[27]

Since *jen* depends on extending *hsin* (mind/heart), we may say that the possibility of realizing *jen* rests on the actualization of *jen-hsin* (sometimes called *tao-hsin*). The notion of *hsin* carries the connotation of "appreciation," which suggests a range of abilities or dispositions, such as awareness, taking cognizance, perceiving, esteeming, sensibility, and responsiveness to the states or conditions of existent things. For Wang, this *hsin* is Heavenly-endowed, and one that is naturally intelligent *(ling)*, clear or shining *(chao)*. It is called the "clear character" *(ming-te)* in the *Great Learning.* So long as it is not beclouded or obscured *(pi)* by selfish desires, the clear character will manifest itself and thus will attain the condition of forming one body *(yi-t'i)* with the whole universe.[28] The intrinsic quality *(pen-t'i)* of the clear character is also called *liang-chih.*

Let us reserve the notion of *liang-chih* for Part IV and focus on the vision of *jen* in Passage C. Presumably when this vision is realized, one may also be said to have "the same body *(tung-t'i)*" as all things. But notably, our understanding of the language of vision here is largely based on the idea of *jen* as a sort of diffusive affection. Other ways of characterizing the vision are also present in Wang.[29] Later, we shall at-

---

be completely manifested, and I will really form one body with Heaven, Earth, and the myriad things" (ibid., 273).

27. *Instructions*, sec. 179.
28. *Inquiry on the Great Learning (Instructions*, 272–73).
29. For examples, *t'ien-li, tao,* and *chih-shan* (the highest good).

tend to some examples. For the present, let us explore some possibilities for further elucidation of "one body" *(yi-t'i)* or "same body" *(t'ung-t'i)*. The primary meaning of *t'i* is "the human body." *T'i* is a generic term for "the head, body, hands, and legs."[30] Wang's notion of *yi-t'i* appears to be an analogical extension of the idea of a living human body. This is suggested in his explanation of *yi-t'i* as the sharing the same *ch'i*.[31] *Ch'i* may be rendered as "vital force." Since in Chang Tsai and in Sung-Ming Confucianism, it is a technical term used, along with *li* (principle/reason/norm), to explain material things, it can also be rendered as "material force." However, Wang rarely used the notion of *ch'i*.[32] Like the *t'i* in *yi-t'i*, *ch'i* in *yi-ch'i* appears to be an analogical or metaphorical extension of *ch'i*, which is believed to pervade the living human body. As Graham points out, "*Ch'i*, a common and elusive word in ordinary Chinese speech and philosophy, covers a number of concepts for which we have different names in English or none at all. Unlike the abstract *li* (represented as veins or grain only by metaphor), *ch'i* is quite concrete; it really is, among other things, the breath in our throats. It is the source of life, dispersing into the air at death."[33]

For further reflection on the notion of *yi-t'i* (one body), particularly to stress the notion of *jen* as the *li* of creative vitality or energy,[34] let us consider Wang's response to Lu Ch'eng's query on the difference between the notion of *jen* and Mo Tzu's doctrine of universal love.

PASSAGE D:

It is very difficult to say. You gentlemen must find it out through personal realization *(t'i-jen). Jen* is the *li* of unceasing creative and vital transformation *(tsao-hua sheng-sheng)*. Although it is prevalent and extensive and there is no

---

30. *Chung-wen ta ts'u-tien* (The Encyclopedic Dictionary of the Chinese Language), (Taipei: San-min, 1976), 10:440 (entry 1).

31. *Instructions*, sec. 274*. For a complementary passage on *t'ung-t'i* (the same body), see *Instructions*, sec. 337.

32. For example, Chan's index gives only two occurrences of "material force."

33. Graham continues: "We breathe it in and out and feel it rising and ebbing in our bodies as physical energy, swelling when we are angry, failing in the limb which grows numb." See A. C. Graham, *Two Chinese Philosophers: Ch'eng Ming-tao and Ch'eng Yi-ch'uan* (London: Lund Humphries, 1958), 3. Note that the conception of *ch'i* as pervading the universe was prevalent in the fourth century B.C., which strikingly suggests that *ch'i* in the ancient Chinese cosmology has affinity with *pneuma* (breath) in Stoic cosmology. For Chrysippus, "*pneuma* pervaded the entire universe, just as bodily *pneuma* had pervaded the entire body." For a brief discussion of the ancient Chinese cosmology and Mencius's peculiar use in his notion of *hao-jan chih chi* (the flood-like *chi*), see D. C. Lau, trans., *Mencius* (London: Penguin Books, 1970), Introduction, 24–26. For Chrysippus, see Michael Lapidge, "Stoic Cosmology," in John M. Rist, ed., *The Stoics* (Berkeley: University of California Press, 1978), 170.

34. This echoes a basic idea of Ch'eng I and Chu Hsi. See Chan, *Source Book*, 560 and 632.

place where it does not exist, nevertheless there is an order in its operation and growth. . . . Take a tree, for example. When in the beginning it puts forth a shoot, there is the starting point of the tree's spirit *(sheng-i)* of life. . . . The love between father and son and between the elder and younger brothers is the starting point of the human mind's *(hsin)* spirit of life, just like the sprout of the tree. Mo Tzu's universal love makes no distinction in human relationships and regards one's own father, son, elder brother or younger brother as being the same as a passer-by. That means that Mo Tzu's universal love has no starting point. It does not sprout. We thereby know that it has no roots *(wu-ken)*. For that reason, it cannot be considered to be the process of unceasing transformation. How can it be called *jen?*[35]

Quite clearly the notion of *jen* or *yi-t'i* is not an abstract concept, but one that has a concrete significance. Wang's criticism of Mo Tzu echoes Mencius,[36] i.e., that Mo Tzu denied the special parental relationship, but more vividly and persuasively focused on Mo Tzu's lack of appreciation or neglect of that human "need for roots" which the commitment to the realization of *jen* entails. Mo Tzu's doctrine of universal love thus has "no roots" *(wu-ken)*. Unlike the Confucian ideal of *jen* as one of diffusive affection, it has no starting point in familial relationships. "It has no sprouts." How then can a purely abstract conception be understood without some exemplification of its concrete significance? *Jen*, as involving the *hsin* (mind/heart) appreciative of the integrity of every existent thing and of concern for the preservation of its continuing spirit or vitality, may properly be said to be the *li* of unceasing creative transformation. Alternatively put, it is our *hsin* that manifests the *li* of things *(hsin chi li)*—the theme we shall explore in Part III.

For a fuller appreciation of the practical import of *jen* as an object of ethical commitment, it is worthwhile to consider Wang's use of the distinction between *t'i* (inward nature) and *yung* (function/expression). The *t'i* here also appears to be a metaphorical extension of *t'i* in the sense of a living human body. Just as we cannot conceive of a body apart from its various functions, such as sensation, feeling, etc., we cannot understand the *t'i* of any concept without understanding its *yung* or operational significance. Thus for Wang, the distinction between *t'i* and *yung* is a relative distinction and not a dichotomy. In his words, "When we speak of *t'i* as *t'i*, *yung* (function) is already involved in it. When we speak of *yung* as *yung*, *t'i* is already involved. This is what is called "*t'i* and *yung* coming from the same source."[37]

35. *Instructions*, sec. 93*.
36. *Mencius*, 3B:9 (Chan, *Source Book*, 72).
37. *Instructions*, sec. 108*. The quotation is from Ch'eng I. See Chan, *Source Book*, 570.

In the *Inquiry on the Great Learning,* we find a use of the distinction between *t'i* and *yung* in connection with *yi-t'i* (one body), e.g., *yi-t'i chih t'i* and *yi-t'i chih yung.* According to Wang, in the *Great Learning,*[38] "manifesting clear character has to do with establishing *(li)* or setting forth the *t'i* of man's forming one body *(yi-t'i)* with Heaven, Earth, and the myriad things, whereas loving the people has to do with realizing *(ta)* the function *(yung)* of [the ideal of] forming one body *(yi-t'i)* with Heaven, Earth, and the myriad things. Thus manifesting clear character must necessarily involve loving people, and loving people is the way of manifesting clear character."[39] We may construe Wang to be saying that we cannot understand the *t'i* of the vision of *jen* as forming one body with all things without appreciating it as having an expressive power *(yung)* or as having an intrinsically actuating or transformative significance within the moral life. Recall that *jen* is the *li* of creative vitality and transformation and has its "root" in the experience of human relationships. The *t'i* or inward nature of the commitment to *jen* cannot thus be separated from the effort to realize its *yung* or expressive power, not only in the realm of human relationships, but also in the universe as a whole. *Jen,* the ideal of the universe as a moral community,[40] by virtue of its *t'i* and *yung,* is thus an object of ethical commitment, rather than an object of intellectual entertainment. And the realization of this commitment, while ultimately a matter of personal experience, presupposes a confidence in *hsin* (mind/heart) as a point of departure.

III. MIND AS THE LOCUS FOR THE MANIFESTATION OF *LI*

Appreciating the concrete significance of the vision of *jen* indicates only an initial understanding of the possibility of becoming a sage. For a committed agent (that is, one who is seriously committed to the vision,) the urgent task is to search for ways and means to convert the

38. Like Chu Hsi's, Wang's *Inquiry on the Great Learning* is more a philosophical than a textual commentary on the *Great Learning (Ta Hsüeh).* The opening of the *Great Learning* runs: "The Way *(tao)* of learning to be great (or adult education) consists in manifesting the clear character, loving the people, and abiding *(chih)* in the highest good." Much of Wang's exposition of his own philosophy is elucidated by way of this ancient classic, which is originally part of the *Li Chi* (Record of Rites).

39. *Instructions,* p. 273*.

40. Wang's ideal of *jen* has a close affinity with Dewey's ideal of morality as social. According to Dewey, "Within the flickering inconsequential acts of separate selves dwells a sense of the whole which claims and dignifies them. In its presence we put off morality and live in the universal. The life of the community in which we live and have our being is the fit symbol of this relationship. The acts in which we express our perception of the ties which bind us to others are only rites and ceremonies." See John Dewey, *Human Nature and Conduct* (New York: Modern Library, 1930), 331–32.

possibility into an actuality. Following Ch'eng I, Chu Hsi has taught that the starting point consists in the investigation of things *(ko-wu)*, which means embarking upon an inquiry into the *li* (principle/rationales) of each thing. For, according to Chu Hsi, the human mind is intelligent and thus equipped with a knowing ability, and there is not a single thing in the world that is devoid of *li*. When a person has exerted himself for a long time in "exhausting the *li* of things *(ch'iung-li),*" he will suddenly acquire an insight into their interconnection *(huo-jan kuan-t'ung)*. As a consequence of this experience, "the qualities of things, whether internal or external, refined or coarse, will be apprehended. Moreover, the mind's inward nature *(t'i)* and function *(yung)* will become completely perspicuous."[41]

According to the Chronological Biography, at the age of twenty Wang and his friend tried to follow Chu Hsi's advice by investigating the *li* of the bamboos in front of his pavilion, but ended up in utter frustration and sickness. Seventeen years later, while in exile in Lung-ch'ang, in the dead of night, Wang acquired an instantaneous insight *(wu)* into the true meaning of "investigation of things" in the *Great Learning*. For the first time, he realized that "my own nature is quite sufficient to attain sagehood," and that he had erred in "seeking the *li* of things and affairs from the outside."[42] In retrospect, Wang said of his sudden enlightenment:

PASSAGE E:

It was only after I had lived among the barbarians [in Lung-ch'ang] for [almost] three years that I understood the meaning [of "investigation of things"]; that fundamentally, there is not a single thing in the world that can be investigated; and that the effort to investigate things is only to be carried out with one's mind and the wholeness of one's own person. If one is firmly committed to the teaching that everyone can become a sage, he can assume the responsibility [of fulfilling the commitment].[43]

Wang's doctrine of mind as the locus for the manifestation of the *li* of things *(hsin chi li)* may be construed as a compendious expression of his own experience of the efficacy of self-reliance, that is, the mind itself possesses its own capabilities and resources for realizing the vision of *jen*.[44] The doctrine may be regarded as an *expressive symbol* of Wang's

---

41. Chu Hsi. *Ssu-shu chi-chu* (Hong Kong: T'ai-p'ing, 1980), 6. Cf. Chan, *Source Book*, 89.

42. *Yang-ming ch'uan-shu*, 32:7a.

43. *Instructions*, sec. 319*. For the faith in the ability of every person to attain sagehood, see *Mencius*, 6B:2; and *Hsün Tzu*. See Watson, *Hsün Tzu: Basic Writings*, 167–68.

44. For a justification of rendering *hsin chi li* as "The mind manifests *li*," see *The Unity of Knowledge and Action*, 87–91.

self-confidence in attaining sagehood. However, his use of *li* in stating the doctrine appears to presuppose an established usage presumed to be familiar to his audience. For clarification, it is important to explore Chu Hsi's uses, particularly in view of the fact that Wang's doctrine was taught as a direct critical response to Chu Hsi's conception of investigation of things. There is also a problem of coherent explication of the doctrine, because of a series of highly perplexing claims based on the doctrine, for example, such claims as "outside the mind there is no *li (hsin-wai wu-li)*," "outside the mind there are no things or affairs *(hsin wai wu-wu, hsin-wai wu-shih)*." More centrally, there is an apparent inconsistency between his view that "knowledge is the intrinsic quality *(pen-t'i)* of the mind" and that "the mind has no inward nature *(t'i)* of its own." While one must respect Wang's appeal to personal realization for the meanings of these tenets, such an appeal is helpful only when there is a prior discursive understanding. One must first have some idea of what Wang's teachings are about before he can tell whether or not his experience constitutes, so to speak, a personal corroboration of their acceptability. In what follows, I shall deal with these difficulties with a view of offering a coherent, though critical reconstruction of Wang's conception of mind.

Let us first attend to Wang's own explanation of his doctrine of *hsin chi li*, i.e., mind is the locus for the manifestation of *li*. According to Wang, Chu Hsi's teaching, adopted from Ch'eng I, that *li* is inherent in things external to the human mind has been obscuring people's minds for a long time. It is difficult to dispel this obscuration by a single saying such as *hsin chi li*. Nevertheless, he proceeded to elucidate this saying by way of examples.

PASSAGE F:

For instance, in the matter of serving one's parents, one cannot seek for the *li* of filial piety in the parent. In serving one's ruler, one cannot seek for the *li* of loyalty in the ruler. In the intercourse with friends and in governing the people, one cannot seek for the *li* of faithfulness and humanity *(jen)* in friends and the people. They are all in the mind. It is the mind that manifests *li (hsin chi li)*. When the mind is free from the obscuration of selfish desires, it is the embodiment of *t'ien-li* (Heavenly *li*), which requires not an iota added from the outside. When this mind is completely invested with *t'ien-li* and manifests itself in serving parents, there is filial piety. When it manifests itself in serving the ruler, there is loyalty. And when it manifests itself in dealing with friends or in governing the people, there are faithfulness and humanity *(jen)*.[45]

Note that the passage involves two distinct but closely connected terms: *li* and *t'ien-li*. *Li* appears as a generic term subject to specification

45. *Instructions*, sec. 3*.

in particular contexts, such as the *li* of filial piety or the *li* of friendship. Presumably one can also speak of the *li* of tables and chairs. *T'ien-li*, on the other hand, is there explicitly contrasted with selfish desires *(yü)*; and significantly it does not admit of specification.

For understanding Wang's use of *li* in the above passage, we may make a brief excursion to Chu Hsi's uses, some of which are also implicit in the works of Ch'eng I.[46] Sometimes Chu Hsi used *li* in the sense of "what is naturally so" *(tzu-jan)*, suggesting a descriptive use. On one occasion, responding to the query on the distinction between *tao* (way) and *li*, Chu Hsi remarked that "*tao* is a collective term *(tsung-ming)*, *li* is a term that refers to the detailed items." Differently put, "The word *tao* is all-encompassing; the *li* are so many veins inside the *tao*."[47] This use suggests the notion of pattern *(wen-li)*. Thus he also said that *li* "can be compared to the patterns *(wen-li)* of bamboos and trees."[48] In this sense, the *li* of a thing or state of affairs consists of its pattern or orderly arrangement of elements. More significantly, we have in Chu Hsi the use of *li* that is functionally equivalent to "reason," and in two distinctive ways.[49] In the one case, *li* refers to "the reason why a thing is as it is *(so-yi jan chih ku)*." In another context, *li* is said to refer to "what is right and proper *(tang-jan chih tse)*.[50] And by extension in familiar ethical contexts, that is, in contexts that involve the use of Confucian notions of virtue, we may use *li* to refer to judgments and actions. In light of some of the remarks of Chu Hsi, it seems plausible to ascribe to him a distinction between reasons for existence and reasons for action. Since the former has primarily *explanatory* force in accounting for the existence of things or states of affairs, quite properly its use conveys Chu Hsi's metaphysical interest in the nature of existence. Thus in Chu Hsi's system, *li* cannot be separated from *ch'i* in accounting for the nature of individuals. The latter, on the other hand, has primarily *normative* force. But on the whole, the ideal standard is implicit rather than explicit. Thus its justificatory force remains an important subject for further inquiry.

The foregoing sketch of Chu Hsi's uses of *li* does not pretend to ascribe to him a clarity in conceptual distinction. Because of their fun-

46. See Graham, *Two Chinese Philosophers*, chap. 1. My discussion of Chu Hsi's uses of *li* is largely indebted to Ch'en Jung-chieh's (W. T. Chan's) article entitled "*Li*" in Wei Cheng-t'ung, ed., *Chung-kuo che-hsüeh t'su-tien ta-ch'üan* (Taipei: Shui-neu, 1983), 479–86.

47. *Chu Tzu yü-lei* (Taipei: Cheng-chung, 1962), 6:1a.

48. Ibid. 6:2a.

49. For this proposal for dealing with Wang's use of *li* in various binomials, e.g., *t'ien-li, tao-li, i-li*, and *t'iao-li*, see my *The Unity of Knowledge and Action*, chap. 2.

50. See Ch'en (Chan), "*Li*," 481.

damental ethical orientation, for the most part Confucian thinkers, with Hsün Tzu as a possible exception,[51] do not clearly distinguish descriptive, explanatory, and normative uses of terms. In general, terms commonly considered descriptive, such as "father" and "son," are used with implicit normative force. As Graham justly points out, for them, "one is truly a father only if one is compassionate, truly a son only if one is filial."[52] Factual statements, in the context of ethical discourse, are generally regarded as being invested with moral import.[53]

For present purposes, our sketch of Chu Hsi's uses of *li* gives a preliminary framework for understanding Wang's doctrine of *hsin chi li* (mind). Unlike Chu Hsi, Wang has no metaphysical interest in accounting for the existence of things. Thus, the explanatory and descriptive uses of *li* do not help us in interpreting his doctrine. Only the normative use of *li* is at issue. The *li* of filial piety in Passage F, for instance, is quite properly construed as a reason for acting in accordance with the requirements or standard of filiality. *Li* in this sense is a reason for action, since it expresses an agent's active concern for his parents. The formula *hsin chi li*, which I have rendered as "the mind manifests *li*," is a concise way of stating a truism, and as we shall later see, an important truism. Alternatively, we may render *hsin chi li* as "it is the mind that renders *li* manifest." In this manner, it is absurd to say that one can "seek for the *li* of filial piety in the parents." The same truism may be stated more forcefully but provocatively in such remarks of Wang's as: "Outside the mind, there is no *li* (*hsin-wai wu li*)," "Outside the mind, there are no things *(wu)* or affairs *(shih)*."[54] In light of the vision of *jen* (Part II), we can now appreciate that Wang's quest for sagehood is basically an internal rather than an external quest. Reasons for actions *(li)* are those that are informed by the spirit of the vision, and can be sought only within oneself, or in Wang's term, within the mind *(hsin)*. Thus we may say with Julia Ching that *hsin chi-li* initially "represents Yang-ming's attempt to internalize the moral quest."[55] But ultimately, it embodies an important truism with practical import. As Wang said

51. See my *Ethical Argumentation*.

52. Graham, *Two Chinese Philosophers*, 18.

53. This is an uncommonly held view in contemporary ethical theory. See Arthur E. Murphy, *The Theory of Practical Reason* (La Salle: Open Court, 1965), 110; A. I. Melden, *Rights and Right Conduct* (Oxford: Blackwell, 1969); and D. Z. Phillips and H. O. Mounce, *Moral Practices* (London: Routledge & Kegan Paul, 1969). For the relevance of these works to the understanding of Confucian ethics, see my "Tasks of Confucian Ethics," *Journal of Chinese Philosophy* 6, no. 1 (1979): 59–61.

54. The first two phrases, for example, appeared in what preceded Passage F. For the last, see *Instructions*, sec. 33.

55. Ching, *To Acquire Wisdom*, 58.

of the basic purpose of his doctrine, it is proposed as a remedy, to rectify moral faults and misconduct.

PASSAGE G:

Why do I maintain that it is the mind that manifests *li*? Simply because people of the world have divided the mind *(hsin)* and *li* into two, thus giving rise to many defects and evils. For instance, the five despots drove out the barbarians and honored the House of Chou all because of their selfishness, and therefore they did not act, as they should, in accord with *li (pu tang-li)*.[56]

Wang goes on, as in Passage F, to invoke the distinction between *t'ien-li* and selfish desires. Let us now turn to this distinction.

Again, *t'ien-li* (Heavenly *li*), along with other binomials involving *li*,[57] e.g., *tao-li* and *i-li*, is part of the standard Neo-Confucian conceptual apparatus. But significantly, whether implicit or explicit, it is contrasted with human desires *(jen-yü)*, which are generally regarded as selfish or self-serving desires oblivious of ethical requirements. The *locus classicus* of this distinction is found in the "Record of Music" *(yüeh-chi)* in the *Book of Rites (Li Chi)*:

To be still at birth is man's Heavenly endowed nature. Man acts as he is affected by external things, and thus develops desires *(yü)* incidental to his nature. As he confronts things, he becomes conscious [of his internal states] and thereupon displays his likes and dislikes. When these likes and dislikes are not regulated from within, his consciousness [of the states] will be beguiled by external things. If he does not turn back to himself and engages in reflection, his *t'ien-li* will be eclipsed. In general, there is no end to things affecting men. But if man's likes and dislikes are not regulated, he will be subjected to transformation according to the occurrence of external things. In this manner, he will eclipse *t'ien-li* and gives free rein to his desires. As a consequence, we have rebellious and deceitful hearts, along with licentious and violent disorder. For this reason, the strong oppresses the weak, the multitude tramples upon the few, the clever deceives the ignorant and stupid, the audacious makes the timid suffer; the sick are not cared for; the old, young, orphans, and the lonely are neglected and cannot find a proper home.[58]

In this passage, it is worthy to note that the distinction between *t'ien-li* and human desires *(jen-yü)* does not strictly represent a dichotomy. Man's likes and dislikes, and the desires that arise from them, are not always problematic. Desires qua desires are not good or bad. As Hsün Tzu incisively points out: "Beings that possess desires and those that

---

56. *Instructions*, sec. 322*.
57. See n. 49 above.
58. See Wang Meng-ou, *Li Chi chin-chu chin-i* (Taipei: Commercial Press, 1977), 2:491. Cf. James Legge's *The Li Ki or Collection of Treatises on the Rules of Propriety or Ceremonial Usages* in Max Müller's *The Sacred Books of the East* series (Delhi: Moltilal Barnasidass, 1966), 2:96–97.

do not belong to two different categories—the categories of the living and the dead. But the possession or non-possession of desires has nothing to do with good government or bad."[59] The author of our passage in the *Li-Chi* was probably influenced by Hsün Tzu. What is condemned is not self-regarding desires in general, but only those desires that are not regulated. And significantly, *t'ien-li* is the standard for regulation. The problematic desires are those which are selfish and self-serving in a manner that deviates from *t'ien-li*. Thus Wang, like Neo-Confucians in general, uses the term *szu-yü* (selfish desires) in lieu of *jen-yü* (human desires), though the latter's contrast with *t'ien-li* is often sharply drawn, as for example in Chang Tsai's saying: "Those who understand the higher things return to *t-ien-li*, while those who understand lower things follow human desires."[60]

Another thing to observe on our passage from the *Li Chi* is that, as a norm or standard, *t'ien-li* is something to be discovered by reflection or introspection. There is the suggestion that *t'ien-li* is inherent in the human mind, rather than something like the Natural Law inherent in the nature of things, as these things are regarded as external to the human mind. In this way we can appreciate Ch'eng Hao's saying, "Although my learning is indebted to others, the two words *t'ien-li* represent something that I personally realized."[61] And, Wang's remark in response to the query on the meaning of *chung* (equilibrium or centrality) in the *Doctrine of the Mean*, "It *(chung)* is a matter of personal realization of one's own mind. It cannot be explained by words. *Chung* is nothing but *t'ien-li*."[62] While I do not know the reason for the use of *t'ien-li* instead of *li*, as in the *Hsün Tzu*,[63] we may properly conjecture that since *t'ien* (heavenly) in the binomial *t'ien-li* has the connotation of something supreme, vast, and awe-inspiring, *t'ien-li* may be construed as a supreme standard.

When we construe *li* as functionally equivalent to reason, *t'ien-li* is a term for "the reason for moral reasons." However, *t'ien-li*, particularly in Wang, is not a supreme standard or ideal norm as exemplified in the

59. Watson, *Hsün Tzu: Basic Writings*, 150. For further discussion, see my "The Conceptual Aspect of Hsün Tzu's Philosophy of Human Nature," *Philosophy East and West* 27, no. 4 (1977).

60. As Chan points out, "Chang was the first Confucianist to have made a clear-cut distinction between the Principle of Nature *(t'ien-li)* and human desires. The sharp distinction was maintained through Sung (960–1279) and Ming (1368–1644) Neo-Confucianism until Ching Confucianists vigorously revolted against it." See Chan, *Source Book*, 509.

61. *Erh Ch'eng ch'üan-shu* in *Ssu-pu pei-yao*, (Taipei: Chung-hwa, 1976), 12:4a; cited in Chan, *Source Book*, 520.

62. *Instructions*, sec. 76*. See also *Instructions*, sec. 96.

63. See *Ethical Argumentation*, 20–30.

familiar Western doctrine of the hierarchy of values, inspired perhaps by Plato's *Philebus*. For Wang, as I have suggested in an earlier study,[64] it is more an alternative expression for the vision of *jen* as an ideal theme (Part II), but has its special use in focusing on selfish desires as the obstructive factor in realizing the vision as evident in Passage F. Thus if "the mind is free from the obscuration of selfish desires, it is the embodiment of *t'ien-li*;" and when this mind is completely pervaded by the concern with *t'ien-li*, it will become evident in serving one's parents. Thus Passage F is accompanied by the following remark:

PASSAGE H:

If the mind *(hsin)* is free from selfish human desires and is completely invested with *t'ien-li*, and if it is the mind that is sincere in performing filial acts, then in the winter it will naturally think of the cold of parents and seek a way to provide warmth for them, and in the summer it will naturally think of the heat of the parents and seek a way to provide coolness for them. These are all offshoots of the mind that is sincere in its filial piety. Nevertheless, there must first be such a mind before there can be these offshoots.[65]

Wang's doctrine of mind as the locus for the manifestation of *li (hsin chi li)* cannot thus be understood without his conception of mind as a moral mind *(tao-hsin)*, i.e., a human mind animated by the commitment to the vision of *jen*, in the comprehensive sense, as an ideal of the universe as a moral community. In pursing its actualization with sincerity and self-examination, a commitive person will experience joy. In Wang's words:

PASSAGE I:

Joy is the intrinsic characteristic *(pen-t'i)* of the mind. Though it is not the same as the joy of seven feelings [i.e., pleasure, anger, sorrow, joy, love, hate, and desire], it is not outside of it. Although the sages and the worthies have another true joy, ordinary persons can also experience joy. Only that ordinary persons are not aware [of the ethical significance] of this experience. Instead they bring upon themselves a great deal of anxiety and suffering as well as bewilderment and self-abandonment. Even in the midst of all these, this joy is not absent. As soon as a single thought is enlightened, and one examines oneself with utmost sincerity, the joy is present there.[66]

Let us turn to Wang's tenet that "the mind has no *ti* (inward nature) of its own." Consider the following remark:

PASSAGE J:

The eye has no inward nature *(t'i)* of its own. Its inward nature consists of the colors of all things. The ear has no inward nature of its own. Its inward nature

64. See *The Unity of Knowledge and Action*, 33–35.
65. *Instructions*, sec. 3*.
66. *Instructions*, sec. 166*.

consists of the sounds of all things. . . . Likewise, the mind has no inward nature of its own *(hsin wu-t'i)*. Its inward nature consists in the right and wrong of the influences and responses of Heaven, Earth, and all things.[67]

One way to interpret this perplexing remark is to recall that for Wang, as we have indicated toward the end of Part II, the *t'i* (inward nature) of a thing cannot be conceived or characterized apart from its *yung* (function). It follows that the *t'i* of the mind cannot be grasped apart from its function. Implicit is the presupposition that any attempt to describe the nature of a thing in purely abstract or theoretical terms cannot capture its *t'i*. We may thus regard Passage J as a reminder on the inadequacy of any abstract approach to the nature of things. Wang's attitude toward any abstract inquiry is purely *pragmatic*. In light of his preoccupation with the vision of *jen* and personal realization, this attitude is intelligible. However, the appeal to the correlativity of *t'i* and *yung* (function) throws no light on the plausibility of Passage J. For even if a thing's inward nature cannot be conceived apart from its function, the latter can still be intelligently described in abstract terms. To describe a thing's function, after all, is to indicate its possible rather than its actual operation. Thus we speak intelligibly of a thing's failure to carry out its function or malfunction. But observe that in doing so, we presuppose a prior understanding of its function. Similarly the human mind can sensibly be said to have a function, quite distinct from its actualization. In terms of Wang's notion of *t'ien-li;* the mind can fail to comply with its own requirements. Wang would remind us, as in Passage H, that this is because the mind is obscured *(pi)* by selfish desires. This explanation, as we shall see in the Conclusion, is inadequate to account for moral failure. But even if the explanation is sound, it is uninformative, unless something can be said about the *t'i* of *t'ien-li* in relation to the mind. In fact, Wang explicitly maintained that *t'ien-li* is the fundamental *t'i* of the mind *(hsin chih pen-t'i)*.[68] But this tenet is inconsistent with that in Passage J.

A closer examination of Passage J reveals a deeper problem. Wang's use of *t'i* is highly misleading. If one follows his frequent insistence on the significance of the correlativity of *t'i* (inward nature) and *yung* (function), one would expect him to say that the *t'i* of the eyes and the *t'i* of the ears involve their *yung*, i.e., as consisting of seeing and hearing rather than colors and sounds, which are the objects and not the functions of eyes and ears.[69] If *t'i* is inseparable from *yung*, still *yung* cannot

---

67. *Instructions*, sec. 277*. A related passage on *liang-chih* as inherent in all things will be discussed in Part IV.

68. *Instructions*, sec. 145.

69. Chu Hsi is quite clear on this point. When queried on *tao* with respect to *t'i* (in-

be construed in terms of objects. *Yung* is a term used to indicate the capacity or ability of an object to function in a certain way, and not a term designating objects qua objects. Passage J thus contains a series of misdescriptions founded on a categorial confusion between function and object. This elementary conceptual error thus prevents us from understanding the *t'i* of the mind through the analogy with the *t'i* of the senses, i.e., that the *t'i* of the mind consists of "the right and wrong of the influences and responses of Heaven, Earth, and all things." Even independently considered, this characterization of the mind is hardly intelligible. Perhaps Wang was simply proposing another way of saying that the faith in the capacity of the mind to realize the vision of *jen* lies ultimately in the success of one's efforts. And this success would constitute the *t'i* of the mind committed to *jen*-realization. But such a restatement engenders insuperable difficulty in understanding his doctrine of mind as the locus for the manifestation of *li (hsin chi li)*. Perhaps Passage J, being a remark recorded by a disciple without any indication of its context, is an occasional remark in response to a non-serious query, and thus cannot be considered a contribution to coherent explication of Wang's conception of mind. Perhaps Passage J, being a remark recorded by a disciple without any indication of context, is an occasional remark in response to a non-serious query, and thus cannot be considered a contribution to a coherent explication of Wang's conception of mind. Passage J, in particular, is inconsistent with Wang's various characterizations of the nature of mind through his notion of *pen-t'i*, which suggests a conception of intrinsic property.[70] In the next part of this essay, I shall take up one of these characterization in connection with *liang-chih*.

The preceding exposition of *hsin chi li* in Passage F concentrates

---

ward nature) and *yung* (function), Chu Hsi replied, "Let us suppose that the ear is *t'i*, its *yung* is hearing. Likewise, if the eye is considered as *t'i*, its *yung* is seeing." For Chu Hsi, *t'i* and *yung*, while inseparable, comprise a relative distinction. "Consider our body as *t'i*, seeing and hearing, as well as the movements of our hands and legs, are its *yung* (functions). But if we consider our hand as *t'i*, then the movement of the fingers is its *yung*." Moreover, the *t'i* of a thing cannot be understood apart from its *li* in the explanatory sense, particularly in accounting for the distinction between individuals. The trouble with Wang, with respect to the *t'i-yung* distinction and relation, lies in his failure to attend to the notion of *li* as having an explanatory force, i.e., as accounting for the existence of particular things. This difficulty, I believe, is owing to his exclusive preoccupation with the realization of the vision of *jen* and thus it prevents him from seeing that one cannot appreciate the integrity of individual things without pursuing a factual inquiry into their nature. An aspect of this problem will be dealt with in the Conclusion of this essay. See Ch'ien Mu, *Chu Tzu hsin hsüeh-an*, 1:429–31. A more general discussion of the *t'i-yung* distinction is given in my "*T'i-yung* (substance and function)" in *Encyclopedia of Chinese Philosophy* (New York: Garland, forthcoming).

70. For some examples, see *Instructions*, secs. 2, 6, 101, 118, and 228.

largely on the roles of *li* and *t'ien-li*. *T'ien-li* plays the central role in Wang's teachings. He frequently uses *li* as a stand-in for *t'ien-li*. But it must be noted that the distinction is philosophically important. Whereas it is quite natural to use the locution "the *li* of *x*," one cannot sensibly employ the locution "the *t'ien-li* of *x*." "The *li* of *x*," construed as "reasons for actions," can be analyzed into different types of reason depending on the notion of virtue deemed appropriate to the context of discourse, e.g., "the *li* of filial piety" or "the *li* of loyalty" as in Passage F. *T'ien-li*, on the other hand, is unanalyzable. As we have earlier suggested, it is an alternative term for Wang's vision of *jen*, but stresses primarily, as in the *Li Chi*, its opposition to selfish desires. Thus Wang once reminded his student that *li* does not admit of "splitting up."[71]

Wang has a tendency to collapse important philosophical distinctions for fear that the distinctions can easily be converted into exclusive dichotomies. This fear is sometimes present in his strange interpretation of Chu Hsi's view. For instance, Chu Hsi's construal of the investigation of things *(ko-wu)* in terms of investigating the *li* of things to the utmost *(ch'iung-li)* was said to be a matter of abiding by *t'ien-li* at all times and places. Says Wang, "*T'ien-li* is clear character, and to investigate the *li* of things to the utmost is to manifest clear character."[72] This tendency to collapse valuable distinctions makes difficult a sympathetic appreciation of his works, but can perhaps be accounted for by his preoccupation with the realization of the vision of *jen*. In the case of *li*, he did not seem to display any interest in *li* in the explanatory sense, that is, in accounting for the existence of things *(so-i-jan)* as is evident in Chu Hsi—though it must be admitted that some of his sayings may be interpreted as having metaphysical import or even as proposing a conception of things akin to some version of metaphysical idealism.[73] But given Wang's avowed interest in the quest for becoming a sage, it is best to see his doctrine of *hsin chi li* as an expressive symbol of a culmination of a stage in his quest, that is, the human mind by itself is quite sufficient for pursuing the realization of *jen* without relying upon the quest for *li* inherent in external things. Indeed, for Wang, things *(wu)*, like affairs or events *(shih)*, are but the objects of human will *(yi)*, particularly the will to attain the highest good.[74] And the *li* of things have no intrinsic epistemic status; they are the manifestation of the mind's concern with *t'ien-li*. As we shall remark in the Conclusion of this essay,

71. Ibid., sec. 35.
72. Ibid., sec. 7.
73. See Carsun Chang, *Wang Yang-ming: Idealist Philosopher of Sixteenth Century China* (Jamaica: St. John's University Press, 1962).
74. *Instructions*, sec. 6.

this view raises an important problem pertaining to the role of factual knowledge and inquiry in his moral theory.

Given the mind's concern with the vision of *jen* or *t'ien-li*, an urgent question arises for a committed agent: "In what sense or respect can the mind attain the vision?" Perhaps, late in life, Wang realized that it is not satisfactory to answer that so long as the mind is completely free from the obscuration of selfish desires, *t'ien-li* will manifest itself (Passage H). Were this the concrete content of self-reliance, all an agent would need to do would be to perform negative actions. Something positive must be said about the characteristic ability of the human mind to realize the vision. Wang's conception of *liang-chih*, a term adopted from Mencius, is a response to our agent's question. The doctrine that the mind is the locus of *li*-manifestation *(hsin chi li)* can at most serve as an expressive symbol of self-reliance. It is useful as a word of encouragement, but it can be misleading in suggesting that sagehood is a condition of utter tranquility rather than activity. Also, it can easily be translated into a theoretical doctrine subject to analytical examination abstracted from Wang's commitment to the vision.

Before we turn to Wang's conception of *liang-chih*, something must be said about Wang's use of *tao* (the Way). Like *t'ien-li*, it is an alternative term for *jen*, the ideal of the universe as a moral community (Part II). But we have in *tao* a focus on the ongoing course of changing circumstances that requires, as we shall see, an agent's sense of rightness *(i)* in coping with changes. In Wang's words, "It *[tao]* has neither restrictions nor physical form, and cannot be pinned down to any particular."[75] As earlier suggested (Introduction), a commitment to the Confucian vision is a commitment to an ideal theme rather than an ideal norm with preceptive import. And this means that the vision itself has an inexhaustible significance within the moral life. As Wang succinctly put it, "*tao* cannot be exhausted with finality *(tao wu chung-ch'iung)*."[76] One cannot deduce from *tao* any specific precepts to guide moral perplexities. The realization of *tao* basically depends on one's effort, ultimately on extending one's *liang-chih*.

IV. *LIANG-CHIH* AS THE BASIS OF MEDIATION

According to the Chronological Biography, a year after Wang's sudden enlightenment on the meaning of "the investigation of things and the extension of knowledge," he began teaching the unity of knowledge

75. Ibid., sec. 66.
76. Ibid., sec. 64*. See also sec. 342.

and action *(chih-hsing ho-i)*.[77] His concern with this theme, independently of his later conception of *liang-chih*, may be seen as a response to the question of understanding the actuating force or transformative significance of moral knowledge as a form of practical knowledge.[78] In the light of his vision of *jen* (Part II), this teaching has a distinctive place in focusing upon the unity of self and action. A sincere commitment to *jen* involves an active will *(yi)* to self-transformation. And this means that the agent has a conscientious regard for the *quality* of his thought and interests as they affect the effective pursuit of *jen*. The ideal self to be realized is fundamentally constituted by one's acts.[79] Thus it is imperative for the agent to exercise constant vigilance in surveying his thoughts as they affect the quality of his actions. This point applies also to moral knowledge derived from learning. When asked about the unity of knowledge and action, Wang said:

PASSAGE K:

You need to understand the basic purpose of my doctrine. In their learning people of today separate knowledge and action into two different sorts of task. As a consequence, when a thought arises, although it is evil, they do not stop it because it has not been translated into action. I advocate the doctrine of the unity of knowledge and action precisely because I want people to understand that when a thought is aroused it is already action. If there is anything evil when the thought is aroused, one must overcome the evil thought. One must go to the root and go the bottom and not allow evil thought to lie latent in his mind. This is the basic purpose of my doctrine.[80]

Indeed, knowing what is good or evil, right or wrong, is an intrinsic characteristic *(pen-t'i)* of the mind concerned with *jen*. Given that the mind is the locus of *li*-manifestation (Part III), especially in the sense of *t'ien-li*, moral knowledge, in a sense, may be construed as an outcome of ideal achievement, i.e., retrospective rather than prospective knowl-

---

77. *Yang-ming ch'üan-shu*, 32:8a.

78. For an attempt at a plausible explication of this doctrine as a contribution to moral psychology, see my *The Unity of Knowledge and Action*, particularly chaps. 1 and 2. The brief account that follows summarizes some results of this work.

79. This line of interpretation is inspired by Dewey's similar doctrine (see n. 40 above). For more than a hint of affinity, we may cite the following: "The unity of self and action underlies all judgment that is distinctively moral in character;" and "The identity of self and act, the central point in moral theory operates in two directions. It applies to the interpretation of the quality and value of the act and to that of the self. . . . What makes the difference between the two [between the good and the bad person] is the *quality* of the interest that characterizes them. For the quality of the interest is dependent upon the nature of the object which arouses it and to which it is attached, being trivial, momentous; narrow, wide; transient, enduring; exclusive, inclusive in exact accord with the object." See John Dewey, *Theory of the Moral Life* (New York: Holt, Rinehart and Winston, 1960), 151 and 160.

80. *Instructions*, sec. 226*.

edge.[81] In Wang's formulation, "Knowledge is the intelligent locus *(ling-ch'u)* of *li*," or "Knowledge is the intelligence *(ling-ming)* of the mind."[82] Retrospective knowledge is the fruit of the successful exercise of intelligence, that is, the ability to take proper cognizance of matters at hand, particularly with respect to the keen discernment of the import of good and evil thoughts. In this manner, prospective knowledge informed by the vision of *jen*, via the active will *(yi)* can be translated into action, thus transforming an actual self into an ideal self, and gives rise to retrospective knowledge. In Wang's succinct words, "Knowledge is the beginning of action and action is the completion of knowledge."[83] Wang's later conception of *liang-chih*, a binomial involving *chih* (knowledge) as a component, appears as a simple linguistic modification. But this conception, while it incorporates some of the insights of this doctrine of the unity of knowledge and action,[84] furnishes the readers a deeper and firmer grasp of the concrete significance of the vision of *jen* (Part II). For in a fundamental way, *liang-chih* plays a central role in Wang's mature philosophy, especially in providing the basis for mediation between the ideal of *jen* and the actual world of human experience. Unlike his doctrine of mind as the locus of *li*-manifestation *(hsin chi li)*, which at most serves as an expressive symbol of self-confidence in one's quest for sagehood (Part III), his conception of *liang-chih* directs the commitive agent to the *seat* of self-sufficiency as a solid point of departure *(t'ou-nao)*.[85]

Again, as is the case with Wang's other doctrines, understanding his conception of *liang-chih* requires personal realization (Passage B). In the Chronological Biography we are told that at the age of forty-nine, Wang began teaching the doctrine of extension of *liang-chih*. He was reported to have made the following remarks:

PASSAGE L:

My doctrine of *liang-chih* was arrived at through a hundred deaths and a thousand sufferings. I cannot help but concisely express it by a single utterance.

81. For a detailed discussion of this distinction, see *The Unity of Knowledge and Action*, chap. 1. For its general significance apart from Wang's doctrine, my *Dimensions of Moral Creativity*, chap. 2.
82. *Instructions*, secs. 118* and 78.
83. Or differently put, "Knowledge is the direction of effort and action is the effort of knowledge." *Instructions*, sec. 5.
84. Wang is not clear about the connection between his doctrine of the unity of knowledge and action and his conception of *liang-chih*. Arguably, the former can simply be considered a component of the latter, given Wang's recurrent emphasis on extension of *liang-chih* in his later life. For some suggestive passages, see *Instructions*, secs. 140, 165, and 321.
85. *Instructions*, sec. 168. This focus on *liang-chih* as the point of departure does raise the problem of its connection with factual knowledge—the principal theme of the Conclusion of this paper.

Only I fear that when a student receives this teaching, it is all too easy for him to regard the teaching as something to play with occasionally without any real understanding, as it involves concrete and substantial effort.[86]

And yet Wang has explained the notion of *liang-chih* in a variety of ways. From the standpoint of explication, it is difficult to set forth a simple and coherent view without reconstruction. While we have no evidence that Wang would encourage such an attempt, he did admit that *liang-chih* has a diversity of compatible interpretations.[87] In what follows, I offer a general characterization of *liang-chih* under different headings. The order of exposition represents a coherent reading of Wang's varying remarks. In the Conclusion, I point to some problems that arise out of our characterization, particularly to the problem of the relation between *liang-chih* and factual knowledge.

A. Moral Discrimination

In Wang's major works, there is a recurrent emphasis on *liang-chih* as inherent in every person's mind. It is inborn rather than acquired, that is, its presence in the human mind does not depend on deliberation or upon learning.[88] It is indestructable and omnipresent,[89] though sub-

---

86. *Yang-ming ch'üan-shu*, 33:16b. See also *Instructions*, secs. 107, 280, and 312; a similar point is depicted in one of Wang's poems on *liang-chih*. A free translation runs:

Liang-chih is manifest at the moment of solitary self-consciousness.
Outside of this there is no knowledge.
Who is there devoid of *liang-chih*?
Who is there that understands *liang-chih*?
Pain and tingle are only known to oneself.
If one asks another about one's pain and tingle,
He will answer "Why is it necessary to ask about one's own pain and tingle?"

(ibid., 20:36a; cf. Ching, *To Acquire Wisdom*, 243).

87. The passage I have in mind is the following conversation recorded by Huang Mien-chih.

I said, "There is only one *liang-chih*. King Wen wrote the explanations of hexagrams in the *Book of Changes*, Duke Chou wrote the explanations of the lines of the hexagrams, and Confucius wrote the commentaries and 'Appended Remarks.' Why did each view the *li* (rationale) differently?" The teacher said, "How could these sages be confined to a rigid pattern. So long as they all proceeded from *liang-chih*, what harm is there in each one's explaining in his own way? Take for example a garden of bamboos. So long as they all have branches and joints, they are similar in general. If it were rigidly insisted upon that each and every branch or joint had to be of the same size or height, that would not be the wonderful handiwork of creation. You people should just go ahead and cultivate *liang-chih*. If all have the same *liang-chih*, there is no harm in there being different here and there. But if you are not willing to exert effort, you don't even sprout. What branches or joints are there to talk about?

(*Instructions*, sec. 293*.)

88. *Inquiry on the Great Learning* in *Instructions*, 278.
89. *Instructions*, sec. 171. See also secs. 152 and 208.

ject to obscuration *(pi)* by the insistence of one's selfish desires. Fundamentally *liang-chih* is a native ability to distinguish the right from the wrong, as well as the good from the bad.[90] However, the notion of rightness is subordinate to that of goodness. As Wang put it,

PASSAGE M:

Liang-chih is only the sense of right and wrong,[91] and this sense of right and wrong is nothing but the love [of good] or the hate [of evil]. If one has this love or hate, one can exhaust [the meanings] of right and wrong. . . . The words right and wrong refer to general standards of conduct. How to apply them [to actual situations] depends on human ingenuity.[92]

This remark applies also to such words as "should" and "must." And significantly, as we shall see in section C, moral notions do not encapsulate fixed standards of conduct.

In the basic sense, then, *liang-chih* refers to the native but peculiar ability of human beings to discern moral distinction,[93] more especially in particular situations that call for positive actions. For further elucidation on the nature of this ability and the sense of knowledge *(chih)* involved in *liang-chih*, we may consider the following:

PASSAGE N:

Knowledge *(chih)* is the intrinsic characteristic *(pen-t'i)* of the mind. The mind is naturally able to know. When it perceives *(chien)* the parents, it naturally knows that one should be filial. When it perceives the elder brother, it naturally knows that one should be respectful. And when it perceives a child about to fall into a well, it naturally knows that one should be commiserative.[94] This is *liang-chih* and need not be sought outside.[95]

This translation may be misleading in suggesting that the sense of knowledge at issue is "knowing that," e.g., knowing that a statement or proposition is true or false. Observe that knowledge *(chih)* is here closely tied to perception. But perception here is more than just sense

90. See *Instructions*, sec. 162.
91. *Mencius*, 6A:6; Chan, *Source Book*, 54.
92. *Instructions*, sec. 288*.
93. It may be noted that among classical Confucians, it is Hsün Tzu, rather than Mencius, who has developed a plausible view on the nature of the mind and its role in the acquisition of knowledge. For him, discrimination *(pien)* is a general ability—for example, the ability to distinguish objects of the senses as well as those of internal states, such as likes and dislikes, anger, pleasure, etc. Moral discrimination is a special form of the general ability, but is essentially an acquired rather than an inborn ability. For detailed discussion, my *Ethical Argumentation*, 30–37, and 138–59; and "The Possibility of Ethical Knowledge: Reflections on a Theme in the *Hsün Tzu*" in Hans Lenk and Gregor Paul, eds., *Epistemological Issues in Classical Chinese Philosophy* (Albany: State University of New York Press, 1993).
94. *Mencius*, 2A:6; Chan, *Source Book*, 65.
95. *Instructions*, sec. 8*.

perception. It is closer to recognition or acknowledgement, though it may be misleading in suggesting that past experience is required for the exercise of *liang-chih*. It is better to use Wittgenstein's notion of "seeing as" or aspect-seeing for understanding Wang's use of *chih* (knowledge).[96] The term *chien*, rendered as "perceives," can also be rendered as "sees," much in the sense in which one sees a friend in the street, or someone as a friend, as a parent, or as an elder brother in Wang's examples. Of course, one must be cautious in imputing this ability to the outcome of learning, for *liang-chih* is inborn. The use of the term *liang* in *liang-chih* clearly implies *liang* in the sense of innateness, though it also conveys some sense of goodness that cannot be understood apart from Wang's vision. We shall pursue this notion in section B. For our present purposes, in order to convey the nonpropositional character of knowledge *(chih)* involved in the exercise of *liang-chih*, it is perhaps best to adopt Russell's term "knowledge by acquaintance," but with an explicit warning against construing it as an epistemological concept. According to Russell, "we have *acquaintance* with anything of which we are directly aware, without the intermediary of any process of inference of any knowledge of truths."[97] The exercise of *liang-chih* as an ability of moral discrimination does yield knowledge *(chih)* in this sense of acquaintance. And in this sense also, knowledge *(chih)* may be said to be the intrinsic characteristic *(pen-t'i)* of the mind, and that ability to know is *liang-chih*.

In view of its close tie to sense perception and to internal perception of one's mental states, it is unsurprising that Wang, earlier in explaining his doctrine of the unity of knowledge and action, made use of what may be called aesthetic and psychological analogies. Knowing filial piety is compared to seeing and loving beautiful colors, and to one's knowledge of pain.[98] Such analogies suggest that Wang's *liang-chih*, because of its affinity with Hutcheson's moral theory, may be rendered as *moral sense;* though again, one must not ascribe to Wang any interest in moral epistemology. For Hutcheson, moral sense is a form of perception of "immediate goodness" of some actions, whether one's own or another's, completely free from any view on their bearing for self-interest or selfish desires. Moreover, this notion of moral sense does not

96. See Ludwig Wittgenstein, *Philosophical Investigations* (New York: Macmillan, 1969), pt. 2, 197f. For the use of this notion in connection with Wang's doctrine, see my *The Unity of Knowledge and Action*, chap. 1.

97. Bertrand Russell, *Problems of Philosophy* (Oxford: Oxford University Press, 1950), 48.

98. *Instructions*, sec. 5. For further discussion of these analogies, see *The Unity of Knowledge and Action*, 9–15.

presuppose any propositional knowledge, and is much akin to the aesthetic perception of objects with harmonious form or composition.[99] The affinity of *liang-chih* with Hutcheson's moral sense does suggest a topic worthy of exploration in comparative ethics.

B. Moral Consciousness

Liang-chih, in the sense of the ability of moral discrimination, although basic, cannot capture the depth of Wang's concern in his teaching of extending *liang-chih*. While the human mind is, in the rudimentary sense, consciousness,[100] without a commitment to the vision of *jen*, it would be indifferent to moral concern. Possessed of *liang-chih*, our mind as informed by the vision will be distinctively marked as moral consciousness. Moreover, the vision can no longer appear as a mere object of intellectual entertainment, though it can be a proper subject of serious discourse. As Wang once remarked, "*Tao* is public and belongs to the whole world, and the doctrine is public and belongs to the whole world. They are not the private properties of Master Chu or even Confucius."[101] A discussion of Wang's vision and the central role of *liang-chih* is thus quite consonant with this spirit of Wang's teachings.

Earlier we indicated that *liang-chih* provides the basis for mediation between Wang's vision and the actual world. *Liang-chih* is the seat of self-reliance in the pursuit of the vision. More especially, *liang-chih* renders completely perspicuous the possibility of realizing the ideal of "forming one body" will all things in the universe. As Wang was wont to say, it is *liang-chih* that manifests *t'ien-li*.[102] "*Liang-chih* is nothing other than *t'ien-li*, where our clear consciousness expresses itself. . . . [Moreover,] there is only one *liang-chih*. Wherever its manifestation and operation, it is quite self-sufficient."[103] As the intrinsic quality *(pen-t'i)* of the moral mind, *liang-chih* is "naturally intelligent, clear and unbe-

---

99. One explicit passage in Francis Hutcheson's *An Inquiry Concerning Moral Good and Evil* supports this interpretation. "We are not to imagine that this moral sense, more than any other senses, supposes any innate ideas, knowledge, or practical proposition: We mean by it only a determination of our minds to receive the simple ideas of approbation or condemnation, from actions observed, antecedent to any opinions of advantage or loss to redound to ourselves from them; even as we are pleased with a regular form, or as an harmonious composition, without having any knowledge of mathematics, or feeling any advantage in that form or composition, different from immediate pleasure." See D. D. Raphael, ed., *British Moralists: 1650–1800* (Oxford: Clarendon Press, 1969), 1:269.

100. "The mind is not a piece of flesh and blood. It is wherever consciousness is. For example, our ears and eyes can know things by hearing and seeing; our hands and feet can know itches and pains" (*Instructions*, sec. 323).

101. *Instructions*, sec. 176.

102. Or "*Liang-chih* manifest *tao*" or "*Tao* is manifested in *liang-chih*." See *Instructions*, secs. 169, 284, 165, and 265.

103. Ibid., sec. 189*.

clouded."[104] When the mind is devoid of any selfish desires, *t'ien-li* will be evident (Passage H).

This notion of *liang-chih* as the seat of moral consciousness does involve *liang-chih* in the sense of moral discrimination, and significantly stresses the exercise of clear intelligence in discerning the moral import of particular situations. As we have suggested, moral knowledge is "the intelligent locus of *li*." And when *li* is construed as a stand-in for *t'ien-li* (Part III), we have a supreme standard guiding the intelligent exercise of *liang-chih*. Inspired by the *Book of Rites (Li Chi)*, and like most of his Confucian predecessors, Wang often urged his students to get rid of selfish desires and preserve *t'ien-li*.[105] As embodying the concern for *t'ien-li*, *liang-chih* is properly considered a personal standard, that is, a standard for making autonomous judgment of the moral quality of thought and actions, as well as feelings.[106] But as we shall see in Section C, as an alternative expression for the vision of *jen*, it is a non-preceptive standard. Thus Wang's notion of *liang-chih* cannot be understood apart from his vision and confidence in the mind as possessing its own capability of realizing the vision—topics we have elaborated in Parts II and III of this study.

Before turning to the non-preceptive standard in *liang-chih*, a word must be said about its implicit volitional character. *Liang-chih*, being an active concern of the moral mind with *t'ien-li*, clearly involves the will to its actualization. Thus, in addition to the cognitive sense as moral discrimination, *liang-chih* cannot be understood apart from the earnest endeavor in actual performance. Passage N clearly points to the volitional element involved. The sense of knowledge by acquaintance is quite remote from that of passive appreciation of the situations described. And this point, given our discussion thus far, is fairly evident in the following:

PASSAGE O:

The mind is the master of the body, and the capacious and clear consciousness *(hsü-ling ming-chüeh)* of the mind is the meaning of *liang-chih*, as naturally inherent [in the mind]. When this *liang-chih*, in its capacious intelligence and clear consciousness is activated in response to external challenges, I call it the will *(yi)*, knowledge *(chih)* must be present before the will. Without knowledge, there will be no will. Is knowledge then, not the inward nature *(t'i)* of the will?[107]

104. *Inquiry on the Great Learning* in *Instructions*, 274.
105. *Instructions*, sec. 4. For numerous passages on this theme, consult Chan's index under the entry "Principle of Nature" *(t'ien-li)*.
106. Ibid., secs. 44 and 206. For Wang's discussion of *liang-chih* in relation to feelings, see secs. 8, 158, 166, 290, 292, and 297.
107. I render *hsü-ling* here as "capacious intelligence," for it suggests a sort of open-

C. Deliberation and Changing Circumstances

T'ien-li, as an alternative term for *jen,* is basically an ideal theme rather than a norm with preceptive import. As a standard for conduct, it is a unifying perspective for dealing with changing circumstances, a standard of inspiration rather than a standard of aspiration, i.e., an ideal that is animated by the commitive agent's concern for its actualization in the real world. It is the agent, by his or her active endeavor, that endows *t'ien-li* with a vital spirit. Embodying this active concern with *t'ien-li, liang-chih* cannot be rendered as "intuition" as this term is used in Ethical Intuitionism. For *liang-chih* has nothing to do with the alleged claim of immediate knowledge of self-evident propositions concerning the meanings of the terms "right," "good," or "obligation" in moral discourse.[108] As we have seen in Section A, *liang-chih* has a volitional character not present in the use of "intuition" in Western ethical theory (Section B). And especially in the context of exigent and changing circumstances of human life, *liang-chih* is not the repository of universal principles or rules to guide the perplexing moral agent. In terms of one of its functions *(yung),* it is akin to that of conscience in Butler's sense, but without the implication that human nature is a sort of an ordered system of particular passions, affections, and appetites subordinate to the governance of principles of self-love and benevolence under the supreme aegis of the authority of reflection or conscience.[109] For Wang, *liang-chih* is a supreme moral authority, but there is no suggestion that *liang-chih* occupies that preeminent position that can inform us as to how the various demands of the elements of human nature are to be met, as stipulated by a hierarchy of values intimated in Butler's moral theory. There is an agility or flexibility in the exercise of *liang-chih* that is absent in Butler's notion of conscience. For this reason, rendering *liang-chih* as "conscience" may be highly misleading, though it is useful in conveying the idea of personal autonomy. But it must be admitted that Wang, to my knowledge, provides us no clue as to how this idea is to be explicated.[110]

---

ness or open-mindedness, i.e., a flexible exercise of intelligence to deal with changing circumstances—the topic of the next section, III. See *Instructions,* sec. 137*. For further discussion on the Wang's notion of *yi* as will, see *The Unity of Knowledge and Action,* 21–28.

108. For the principal uses of the notion of intuition in ethical theory, see "The Concept of Moral Intuition," in my *Reason and Virtue: A Study in the Ethics of Richard Price* (Athens: Ohio University Press, 1966), 163–82.

109. See Joseph Bulter, *Fifteen Sermons Preached at Rolls Chapel* (London: G. Bell and Sons, 1953), esp. Sermon III.

110. This is one of my reasons for not following Professor Mou in ascribing "moral

For appreciating Wang's attitude toward the role of deliberation in the exercise of *liang-chih*, we may begin by recalling Passage M, where human ingenuity is stressed in the application of presumably established, general standards of conduct. The question of what to do can arise in both normal and changing or exigent circumstances of human life. Deliberation about the right thing to do is thus necessary, "so as to provide a basis for the proper handling of affairs."[111] For an ordinary agent the question in the normal situation can probably be answered with relative ease, so long as he or she has a good sense of what conventional morality requires. Moreover, the availability of past experience, whether one's own or another's, can provide sufficient guidance. In such a situation, *liang-chih* need not be invoked. Genuine perplexity arises in changing or exigent circumstances, where established standards do not provide clear guidance.[112] Wang mentioned two cases: Shun's "marrying without first telling his parents," and King Wu's "launching a military expedition before burying his father." Both these actions are for Wang unprecedented and represent the outcome of the direct and deliberative exercise of *liang-chih* in exigent situations. Established standards, which are appropriate to normal situations, cannot be invoked in exigent cases. Shun or Wu could not help doing what he did, given the absence of guidance from past experience of the paradigmatic actions of others in similar circumstances. He could only search into his *liang-chih* "in an instant thought in his own mind and weighed all factors as to what was proper" and acted accordingly.[113]

While *liang-chih* is inherent in all minds, the distinguishing characteristic of the sage lies in his attitude toward study and reflection. Unlike ordinary persons, he does not worry over "minute details and varying circumstances" with a view to preparing himself to deal with all possible human situations. "What he studies is precisely the extension of *liang-chih* in order carefully to examine [the import of] *t'ien-li* in the mind."[114] As invested with *t'ien-li*, *liang-chih* is indeed a standard, but it does not issue recipes for coping with changing circumstances. This is because "minute details and varying circumstances" cannot be

---

metaphysics" to Wang, since his term is derived from the critical interpretation of Kant's ethical theory. In my mind, Mou's explication of *liang-chih* is a brilliant development of Neo-Confucianism of Sung and Ming and is worthy of attention from any serious student of Chinese philosophy (see n. 17 above).

111. *Instructions*, sec. 139.

112. For the role of this distinction between normal and exigent circumstances for Confucian ethics and moral theory, see *Dimensions of Moral Creativity*, chaps. 4 and 5; for Wang in particular, see, *The Unity of Knowledge and Action*, chap. 3.

113. *Instructions*, sec. 139.

114. Ibid*.

predetermined prior to their occurrences. Indeed, moral reasons *(i-li)* cannot be categorized in advance of confrontation with particular circumstances.[115] The thing to do is to keep the mind clear as a mirror and engage in moral reflection. "The sage does a thing when the time comes. . . . The study of changing conditions and events is to be done at the time of response."[116] It is Wang's faith in *liang-chih* that it can provide *unerring* guidance without prior factual inquiry. This faith poses a problem to be taken up in the Conclusion.

D. *Extension and Achievement*

The vision of *jen* is an ideal of the universe as a moral community (Part II). For a committed agent, *"jen* is the *li* of unceasing creative and vital transformation" (Passage D). Given *liang-chih* as the basis of the mediation between the ideal and the actual world, the extension of *liang-chih,* i.e., the increasing expansion of the scope of one's concern is an urgent task. The committed agent sees his *liang-chih* as "the spirit of creation."[117] Presumably, the utmost achievement is a complete realization of the vision. This interpretation is suggested in a rather perplexing passage on *liang-chih,* as inherent not only in men but in all things in the universe.

PASSAGE P:

Liang-chih of man is the same as that of plants and trees, tiles and stones. This is not true of them only. Without man's *liang-chih* there cannot be Heaven and Earth. For at bottom, Heaven, Earth, and the myriad things form one body *(yi-t'i)*. The point at which this unity is manifested in its most refined and excellent form is the clear intelligence *(liang-ming)*. Wind, rain, dew, thunder, sun and moon, stars, animals and plants, mountains and rivers, earth and stones are essentially of one body with man. It is for this reason that such things as the rains and animals can nourish man and that such things as medicine and minerals can heal diseases. Since they all share the same *ch'i* (breath), they can penetrate into one another.[118]

We remarked earlier on the notion of *ch'i* (Part II). One way to construe this passage is to take it as a retrospective report of Wang's own experience of the extension and achievement of *liang-chih* (Passage L). Were it to be taken in the prospective sense, his notion of extending *liang-chih* as a task would seem pointless. And consistent with much of my reading, the passage can also be read as an exaltation or glorification of the vision of *jen*. But I must admit that a metaphysical reading is possible, and this sort of reading does deserve careful exploration.[119]

115. Ibid., sec. 52.
117. Ibid., sec. 261.
119. See particularly Mou's work cited in n. 17 above.

116. Ibid., sec. 21.
118. Ibid., sec. 272*.

The foregoing discussion on Wang's conception of *liang-chih* presents a sketch of its role in relation to Wang's vision and cannot pretend to be a comprehensive exposition; but I hope it serves as an introduction to further inquiry.

CONCLUSION

In this study, we have dealt with some principal aspects of Wang's philosophy. In effect, we have charted the *tao,* the journey from commitment to *jen,* the vision of the universe as a moral community, to its possible realization through the extension of *liang-chih.* For a committed agent, the path will be difficult and at times tortuous, as in Wang's own case, since *tao* is essentially a course of changing events that cannot be expressed in determinate formulas. Without persistent self-reliance and effort, the agent is bound to experience nothing but anguish and frustration. But in Wang's belief, when he becomes a sage, while equipped with no foreknowledge, he knows "the incipient and activating force of things and handles it in accordance with the circumstance."[120] For a practical student of ethics, Wang's vision may appear as moral idealism. Though lending itself to lofty and exalted redescription, it is more usefully regarded as an object of imaginative entertainment rather than a serious candidate for moral commitment.[121] For a philosophical thinker who shares Wang's vision, there is an intimation of a profound human responsibility toward the cosmos. He will, perhaps, proclaim with James, "whether we are empiricists or rationalists, we are ourselves parts of the universe and share the same one deep concern in its destinies. We crave alike to feel more truly at home with it, and to contribute our mite to its amelioration."[122] In addition to these possible responses to Wang's vision, there will undoubtedly be others, whether genial or hostile, sincere or pretentious, serious or amusing, and, of course, complete indifference.

For a contemporary Confucian philosopher, however, our study gives rise to problems that require careful consideration. By way of conclusion, I focus briefly on two problems that arise out of our general characterization of *liang-chih.* The aim is to formulate these problems and to suggest their importance for further inquiry, rather than to propose solutions. In the final analysis, these problems, along with others,

120. *Instructions,* sec. 281.
121. For a discussion of this issue on the justification of adopting Wang's vision, see my *The Unity of Knowledge and Action,* 91–100.
122. William James, *Essays in Radical Empiricism and A Pluralistic Universe* (New York: E. P. Dutton, 1971), 128.

deserve attention, not only because they are important to the evaluation of Wang's philosophy as a whole, but also because they raise disturbing questions for one, like the present writer, concerned with the critical development of Confucian ethics.

The first problem that comes to mind pertains to moral failure. Wang's insistence on selfish desires as the one and only source of the obscuration of the mind (i.e., that so long as the mind is free from the obscuration of selfish desires, *t'ien-li* will manifest itself), cannot be considered an adequate explanation of moral failure (Passage F). For the mind at issue is a moral mind *(tao-hsin)*, one that is informed by the vision of *jen* as a moral vision in that sense of moral as involving the concern for others; and thus the value of this tenet is limited to spelling out the meaning of moral commitment. As an account of moral failure, the view is simplistic. As Hsün Tzu has shown, owing to its ability to draw distinctions, the moral mind committed to *tao* as a holistic vision can be obscured *(pi)* in many different ways. In general, the mind can be obscured by distinctions such as desire and aversion, the beginning and the end of human affairs and endeavors, immediate and distant consequences of action, past and present experiences, as well as the breadth and shallowness of knowledge. Unless the mind is guided by reason *(li)*, it cannot cope with changing circumstances.[123] Because of this liability to diverse sources of obscuration, the *liang-chih* of the moral mind cannot be an unerring guidance to resolving moral perplexities and dilemmas. Wang's lack of interest in the notion of *li* in the explanatory and descriptive senses prevents him from paying close attention to Hsün Tzu's insight (Part III). More importantly, even if the mind is divested of selfish desires, for a reflective agent, this is a condition preparatory to the exercise of *liang-chih,* and not a condition of moral achievement.

As Wang is well aware, moral failure may also result from insincerity of the will. *Liang-chih* as involving will pertains quite properly to the sincerity of the will, or in Wang's words, "A sincere will is in accordance with *t'ien-li.*"[124] This aspect of Wang's philosophy deserves further study. However, it is unclear how Wang would deal with conditions of the will that may well be beyond the agent's control, for example, lack of will or weakness of will. On this question, I believe that a careful examination of the works of Mencius will provide materials toward the construction of an adequate answer. And related to these internal con-

---

123. See Watson, *Hsün Tzu: Basic Writings,* 121–38; and my *Ethical Argumentation,* 138–45.
124. *Instructions,* sec. 101.

ditions, there are external ones that affect the exercise of *liang-chih*, again, those that are not subject to the agent's control. *Liang-chih* can successfully mediate the vision of *jen* and the actual world only if both natural and cultural orders cooperate. There are natural and cultural constraints to the exercise of *liang-chih*, and these constraints may well prevent the agent from realizing that vision *in toto*. In exploring this question, again, we can learn much from Hsün Tzu and Mencius, and Confucius's attitude toward human fate *(ming)*. A contemporary Confucian must thus inquire into the connection between *liang-chih* and fate *(ming)*. This inquiry more especially involves a complex and difficult question concerning the relation between *liang-chih* and factual knowledge: in standard Neo-Confucian terms, "knowledge of moral nature *(te-hsing chih chih)*" and "knowledge of hearing and seeing *(wen-chien chih chih)*." For present purposes, I shall formulate the question as the relation between moral knowledge and factual knowledge. What Wang says on this problem is quite incisive, but rather incomplete.

According to Wang, "*Liang-chih* does not come from hearing and seeing, and yet all hearing and seeing are functions *(yung)* of *liang-chih*. Therefore *liang-chih* is not impeded by seeing and hearing. Nor is it separated from hearing and seeing."[125] Differently put, "*liang-chih* is the basis *(t'ou-nao)* of learning and inquiry."[126] This remark quite clearly points to the connection between moral knowledge and factual knowledge, but significantly assigns a secondary status to the latter. In this view, factual knowledge or inquiry is relevant to the proper exercise of *liang-chih*, and in turn can yield moral knowledge in the retrospective sense, i.e., the knowledge that an action is in accord with the *t'ien-li* of *liang-chih*. In other words, the moral relevance of factual knowledge is determined by *liang-chih*. From the moral point of view, then, inquiry has an indispensable role in the quest for factual information, and the outcome of this quest will provide the necessary data for deliberation at the time of response to changing circumstances (IV.C). However, in light of *jen*, the vision of the universe as a moral community, the secondary status assigned to factual knowledge and inquiry may well be questioned. For that vision expresses a concern for the existence of things. How then can such a concern be indifferent to the need of inquiry into their nature, even if such an inquiry has no direct relevance to moral problems and perplexities? In this connection, one would also think that prior factual knowledge is an indispensable aid in dealing with changing circumstances of human life. It is only the sage who can

125. Ibid., sec. 168.
126. Ibid., sec. 140.

dispense with such knowledge. But for ordinary committed agents, the possession of factual knowledge is an invaluable aid to dealing with exigent cases. Wang seemed to be aware of this point (Passage O), but on the whole uninterested in pursuing the problem of the connection between moral knowledge and factual knowledge. It is, however, to his credit that he suggested *liang-chih* cannot be exercised apart from factual knowledge.[127]

127. For a perceptive discussion of this problem in contemporary Confucianism, see T'ang Chün-i, *Chung-Kuo che-hsüeh yüan-lun, tao-lun p'ien,* 3d ed. (Taipei: Hsüeh-sheng, 1978), chap. 10, 340–47.

Essay 10

The Possibility of a Confucian Theory of Rhetoric

In her instructive paper "Ethical Values in Classic Eastern Texts," Helen North raises a central question for comparative East-West rhetorical studies: "The topic of *arete* and the use of *ethos* as a mode of persuasion constitute the principal debts that classical Western rhetoric owes to ethics. Is there anything comparable to be found in Eastern classical texts? Specifically, what ethical qualities seem important for the purpose of persuasion, and how are they applied in Eastern classical texts?"[1]

Any attempt to deal with such a question must pay heed to Robert Oliver's pioneering work on ancient India and China.[2] The question is especially difficult to tackle if one accepts Oliver's thesis of cultural relativism: "The kinds of ideas that interest or move people and the reasons why they accept or reject are not universals, they are particular attributes of specific cultures."[3] Moreover, the priority of topical considerations is determined by a value judgment relative to a holistic, cultural system.[4] Equipped with such a thesis, the focus would be on divergence rather than convergence of rhetorical concerns. The concluding chapter of Oliver's book presents some general crucial contrasts between rhetorics of the East and the West.

Oliver's work does provide us with a guide to comparative East-West rhetoric. Philosophical students of classical Chinese thought will certainly profit from reading his book whenever they attend to questions of rhetorical theory. Especially noteworthy are Oliver's discussions of the elements of rhetoric in the *Analects* and in the *Mencius*.[5] However,

---

1. See Helen North, "Ethical Values in Classic Eastern Texts," presented at the conference on Rhetoric: East and West, East-West Center, Honolulu, Hawaii, June 12–18, 1988.
2. Robert T. Oliver, *Communication and Culture in Ancient India and China* (Syracuse: Syracuse University Press, 1971). Hereafter cited as *Communication and Culture*.
3. Ibid., 7. Original italics deleted.
4. Ibid., 9–10.
5. Ibid., chaps. 8 and 10.

from the philosophical point of view, any approach to comparative East-West rhetoric must deal with a more fundamental question concerning the nature of textual interpretation. Concern with this question does not vitiate the insightful contributions of Professors North and Oliver.

Let us begin with the observation that, unlike in the West, there is virtually no work in either ancient China or India that is "explicitly devoted to rhetoric." Oliver explains this fact by pointing to the inseparability of philosophy and rhetoric in these cultures, and in the East in general. In his words, "the reason for this difference is greatly significant. In the West, rhetoric has been of such high importance that it has received very considerable attention as a separate field of inquiry. In the East, rhetoric has been of such even higher consequence that it never has been separated from philosophy but has received continuous attention as an essential and integral part of generalized philosophical speculation."[6]

This explanation appears to assume that the absence of independent rhetorical treatises in both ancient China and India must not be construed as an absence of rhetorical concerns. Given this assumption, the task left to scholars may be conceived as the constructive interpretation of texts important to rhetoric as an academic discipline. The explanation is also consistent with the assumption that rhetorical theory is implicit in these texts and thus the task is one of reconstructive interpretation. In either case, what is involved is a sort of creative hermeneutics or plausible explication of notions or ideas that contribute to the development of a rhetorical theory.

Such a form of philosophical interpretive inquiry is well exemplified in Ronald Dworkin's recent work in philosophy of law. According to Dworkin, interpretation of a legal practice or of social practices in general—for example, the practice of courtesy—is a constructive interpretation, "a matter of imposing purpose on an object or practice in order to make of it the best possible example of the form or genre to which it is taken to belong."[7] More perspicuously, the aim of constructive interpretation, is to present, in the best light, a coherent explanation of an object or an existing legal practice, as well as, more significantly, a sound and adequate justification of the practice.[8] Insofar as

6. Ibid., 260. According to a recent scholar of Chinese thought, there was a lost treatise on argumentation in the time of Hsi Kang (223–62 A.D.). Unfortunately, no source for this claim was given. See Robert Hendricks, "Hsi Kang and Argumentation in the Wei," *Journal of Chinese Philosophy* 8, no. 2 (1981), 214 n 35.

7. Ronald Dworkin, *Law's Empire* (Cambridge: Harvard University Press, 1986), 52.

8. This point is clear in Dworkin's recurrent stress on the dimensions of fit and jus-

epistemology is conceived as inquiry into the coherent explanation *cum* justification of any human practice, Dworkin's work may be properly described as legal epistemology.[9] Similar epistemological concern with moral practice is shown in my recent attempt to set forth a Confucian conception of ethical argumentation, based on the *Hsün Tzu*, as a study in moral epistemology.[10] The same concern with plausible explication of aspects of Confucian moral psychology is explicit in my study of Wang Yang-ming's doctrine of the unity of knowledge and action.[11]

North's paper provides an occasion for a preliminary exploration of the possibility of developing a Confucian theory of rhetoric. This exploration is an attempt to interpret the rhetorical import of Confucian ethical thought. While North's question on the use of *ethos* and *arete* as a mode of persuasive discourse will have a central role in this inquiry, I shall not approach the question by comparing or contrasting classical Greek and Chinese texts. In what follows, I am mainly concerned with laying out part of the groundwork for such a comparative study. In Part I, adopting the framework of Aristotle's *Rhetoric* with some modification and drawing from my study of Hsün Tzu's conception of ethical argumentation, I discuss the role of *ethos* and *arete*, or more generally, the style of performance, that is, the desirable qualities of participants in argumentation. Special emphasis is placed on *jen* (benevolence), *li* (propriety), and *i* (rightness, righteousness). Part II deals at length with some issues of *logos* or reasoning in Confucian argumentation. After assessing the adequacy of the deductivist approach, as suggested by Aristotle's notion of *enthymeme*, I propose two types of reasoning as distinctive of Confucian argumentation: one akin to Aristotle's argument from ex-

tification and their interaction as a test for an adequate interpretation of legal practice. See *Law's Empire*, esp. 139, 190, 215, 230–31, 239, 255, and 265.

9. Such an enterprise is both descriptive and normative as explicitly acknowledged by a recent writer on legal reasoning: "I set forth an account of certain features of legal argumentation which are actually instantiated within law reports, and explain the reasons why I think they ought to be fundamental features of legal argumentation given its function; these reasons I further offer as explaining why such features are in fact highly common in the practice of legal argumentation, as can be shown by a plethora of examples." See Neil MacCornmick, *Legal Reasoning and Legal Theory* (Oxford: Clarendon Press, 1978), 13.

10. See my *Ethical Argumentation: A Study in Hsün Tzu's Moral Epistemology* (Honolulu: University of Hawaii Press, 1985) and "Ethical Uses of the Past in Early Confucianism," *Philosophy East and West* 35, no. 2 (1985): 133–56. For a more general study in moral practices from the participant's point of view, see my *Dimensions of Moral Creativity: Paradigms, Principles, and Ideals* (University Park: Pennsylvania State University Press, 1978).

11. See *The Unity of Knowledge and Action: A Study in Wang Yang-ming's Moral Psychology* (Honolulu: University of Hawaii Press, 1982) and Essay 9; and "Reflections on Moral Theory and Understanding Moral Traditions," in Eliot Deutsch and Gerald James Larson, eds., *Interpreting Across Boundaries: New Essays in Comparative Philosophy* (Princeton: Princeton University Press, 1988), 280–93.

ample (rhetorical induction), and another, coordinative reasoning, that is, reasoning that employs a number of logically independent factors or premises, cooperatively, in producing a non-logically compelling yet reasoned conclusion. In the final part, I respond to Professor North's comparative remarks especially on Mencius and Han Fei Tzu in relation to *basilikos logos*. I suggest that Hsün Tzu's essays on the ways *(tao)* of the ruler and ministers provide a good case study, and conclude with some brief remarks on the divergent conceptions of *pathos* implicit in the works of Hsün Tzu and Mencius, and on difficulties of interrogating classical Chinese texts for comparative rhetorical inquiry.

I. CONCEPT AND CONCEPTIONS OF RHETORIC

Let me begin by reflecting on Hsün Tzu's distinction between generic *(kung-ming)* and specific terms *(pieh-ming)*.[12] To a large extent, we may for elucidation employ the recent, functionally analogous distinction between concept and conception.[13] A generic term is a formal, gen-

12. Textual references to Hsün Tzu in this paper are taken from the following: Li Ti-sheng, *Hsün Tzu chi-shih* (Taipei: Hsüeh-sheng, 1979), which is a careful and updated edition based on the standard one by Wang Hsien-ch'ien, *Hsün Tzu chi-chieh* (Taipei: World Publishing Co., 1961); H. H. Dubs, trans., *The Works of Hsüntze* (Taipei: Ch'eng-wen, 1966); and Burton Watson, trans., *Hsün Tzu: Basic Writings* (New York: Columbia University Press, 1963). Abbreviated references are used, for example, "L13," "D39," and "W22" for the works of Dubs, and Watson with their page numbers. The second occurrence of the reference indicates the translation adopted. Whenever available, a third reference is given for comparative purpose only. Minor emendations are marked by asterisks. Major emendations are explained in the notes. When only Li is cited, this indicates either my own translation or reference to a passage not found in both Dubs's and Watson's works. Asterisks are used for both emendation of translation and for distinguishing important homophones of different Chinese characters.
13. In various ways and theoretical contexts, some recent philosophers make use of this distinction. Instead of talking of two senses of "concept," the terminology of "concept" and "conception" proposed by Rawls and Attfield brings out the distinction more clearly. To my knowledge, Dworkin has given the best elaboration of the distinction. It should be noted that in employing this distinction in explaining Hsün Tzu's distinction between generic and specific terms, I am claiming only that they are functionally but not logically equivalent. For Hsün Tzu's, as I have noted elsewhere, is not a conceptual dichotomy but essentially a functional, pragmatic distinction and relative to purposes of discourse. See *Ethical Argumentation*, esp. 45, 76–78; and "The Problem of Conceptual Unity in Hsün Tzu and Li Kou's Solution" *Philosophy East and West* 39, no. 2 (1989); H. L. A. Hart, *The Concept of Law* (Oxford: Clarendon Press, 1961), 156; John Rawls, *A Theory of Justice* (Cambridge: Harvard University Press, 1971), 5–9; Robin Attfield, "On Being Human," *Inquiry* 17 (1974): 175–76; Dworkin, *Law's Empire*, esp., 71–72. For Dworkin's earlier discussions, see *Taking Rights Seriously* (Cambridge: Harvard University Press, 1978), 34–36; and *A Matter of Principle* (Cambridge: Harvard University Press, 1986), 70–73. A parallel distinction is found in Roichi Okabe, "Can the East Meet the West Rhetorically? An Overview of Rhetorical Divergence and Convergence from the Eastern Perspectives," presented at this conference.

eral, abstract term amenable to specification by other terms in different discursive contexts. These terms, used in practical or theoretical contexts, may be said to be specific terms in the sense that they specify the significance of the use of a generic term adapted to a current purpose of discourse. Alternatively, we may say that there are various levels of abstraction or specification of the use of general terms. Thus a specific term in one context may function as a generic term in another context, whenever current purpose requires such further specification. In the language of concept and conceptions, a generic term designates a *concept* that can be used in developing various *conceptions*.[14]

As Dworkin points out, this distinction between concept and conception is quite different from the familiar distinction between meaning and extension of terms.[15] However, the semantic distinction between generic and specific terms is properly between the wider and the narrower scope of application of a term. The crucial motivation for the distinction lies in the purposes at hand. Specification has to do primarily with the significant use of a concept, which may well represent, so to speak, a crystallized conception. Consider *tao;* were it to be exclusively viewed as a Confucian concept or generic term of Confucian discourses, it would be a crystallized conception of classical and Neo-Confucian thought. But for the Taoists, *tao* would represent an altogether different concept or crystallized conception of their discourses, as preeminently exemplified in *Lao Tzu* and *Chuang Tzu.* This suggests that we may quite properly speak of *tao* as representing two different concepts, each of which is a product of a crystallized conception. And in both cases, *tao* can be viewed as a generic term. In the case of Confucianism, *tao* is a generic term subject to specification by way of such general and interdependent notions of virtue (henceforth, aretaic notions) as *jen, li,* and *i,* while each of the latter in turn may be significantly specified further, as occasion arises, by way of particular aretaic notions, for example, filiality *(hsiao),* loyalty *(chung),* trustworthiness *(hsin),* consideration *(shu),* and courage *(yung).*[16]

14. For a partial justification of this conceptual interpretation, see *Ethical Argumentation,* 173–74n2.

15. Dworkin, *Law's Empire,* 71.

16. See *Ethical Argumentation,* 160–63; and "Hsün Tzu and the Unity of Virtues," *Journal of Chinese Philosophy* 14, no. 4 (1987), 381–400. For a study of *li* (propriety) as a generic term subject to specification of its significance in response to certain critical questions concerning its subject matter, scope, purposes or functions, see "The Concept of Li Confucian Moral Theory" in Robert Allinson, ed., *Understanding the Chinese Mind: The Philosophical Roots* (Hong Kong: Oxford University Press, 1989). For a similar study of i (rightness), see my "Hsün Tzu and the Unity of Virtues," *Journal of Chinese Philosophy* 14, no. 4 (1987). [Essay 13 incorporates with revisions the relevant materials from these

In light of the foregoing, we may distinguish the concept of rhetoric from various conceptions of rhetoric. With Aristotle, we may say that the concept of rhetoric pertains to the study or discovery of the means of persuasion "coming as near such success as the circumstances of each particular case allow."[17] A rhetorical theory, I suggest, is a systematic conception of rhetoric. The possibility of a Confucian rhetorical theory thus concerns the systematic development of a conception of rhetoric. A recent rhetorical theorist maintains: "Rhetoric proper starts with Aristotle. All rhetoric is in some way—more or less—derived from Aristotle."[18] While this claim may be questioned from the standpoint of the history of rhetoric, for a moral philosopher the claim is unproblematic if it is a claim to Aristotle as a guide for exploring the relation between ethics and rhetoric, a claim that seems to be attested by Aristotle's remark that "rhetoric is an offshoot of dialectic and also of ethical studies."[19] Moreover, it is to Aristotle that we are indebted for providing us a philosophical framework for any rhetorical theory informed by ethical theory. For a Confucian ethical theorist, especially, Aristotle's framework of *ethos*, *logos* and *pathos* offers an illuminating way of interpreting the rhetorical import of Confucian ethics. In Aristotle's own words, "rhetorical study, in its strict sense, is concerned with the modes of persuasion."[20] "Of the modes of persuasion furnished by the spoken word there are three kinds: The first kind depends on the personal character of the speaker; the second on putting the audience into a certain frame of mind; the third on the proof, or apparent proof, provided by the words of the speech itself."[21]

In view of Perelman's works on rhetoric as a general theory of argumentation and some recent contributions to informal logic,[22] I shall

---

papers.] For the relation between Confucian general and particular aretaic notions, see the insightful work of Ch'en Ta-ch'i, *Kung Tzu hsüeh-shuo* (Taipei: Chung-hua wen-hua she, 1954); and Yeh Ching-kuei, *Kung Tzu te tao-te che-hsüeh* (Taipei: Cheng-chung, 1977).

17. Or in the words of Professor Okabe of this conference: "Rhetoric as a discipline [is] . . . an established field of study whose concern is the art of informative and suasory discourse. This concept is applicable to all times, to all cultures, and to all peoples. It is thus a generic term of universal application." Okabe contrasts this with rhetoric as "an approach to resolving human problems." We have here a practical conception of rhetoric rather than a representative of all conceptions of rhetoric. For Aristotle, see *Rhetoric* (translated by W. Rhys Roberts) in W. D. Ross, ed., *The Works of Aristotle*, vol. XI (Oxford: Clarendon Press, 1952), 1355a. For Okabe, see n. 13 above.

18. W. Ross Winterowd, *Rhetoric: A Synthesis* (New York: Holt, Rinehart and Winston, 1968), 18. See also, Hoyt Hudson, "The Field of Rhetoric," in Maurice Natanson and Henry W. Johnston, eds., *Philosophy, Rhetoric and Argumentation* (University Park: Pennsylvania State University Press, 1965), 21–22.

19. Aristotle, *Rhetorica*, 1355b.

20. Ibid., 1355a.   21. Ibid., 1356a.

22. I have in mind the following: Ch. Perelman and Anna Olbrechts-Tyteca, *The New*

not follow Aristotle in assigning rhetorical deduction or enthymeme a central place.[23] If rhetorical theory is conceived, à la Perelman, as a systematic theory of argumentation, a general deductivist approach does not seem adequate, as we shall see in Part II. In general, argumentation is a dialectical rather than a demonstrative activity or a deduction. As Perelman points out, "the aim of argumentation is not to deduce consequences from given premises; it is rather to elicit or increase the adherence of the members of an audience to theses that are presented for their consent. Such adherence never comes out of thin air; it presupposes a meeting of minds between speaker and audience."[24] In *Ethical Argumentation*, much along the same line, though paying no heed to its rhetorical aspect *per se*, I viewed Confucian argumentation as a reasoned persuasive discourse, a cooperative enterprise aiming at a solution to a problem of common concern among participants. Presupposed in this conception is an operative ethical tradition as a background for explanation and/or justification of normative claims or value judgments. A profile of argumentation is presented, consisting of a characterization of the desirable qualities or *ethos* of participants, standards of competence, phases of discourse embracing both explanatory and justificatory activities, diagnosis of erroneous beliefs, as well as ethical reasoning and uses of definition in overcoming difficulties in communication. In what follows, adopting Aristotle's tripartite scheme of *ethos, logos,* and *pathos,* I shall sketch a Confucian conception of rhetoric by developing certain aspects of Confucian argumentation. At the outset, it must be noted that the conception proffered is *one* possible way of interpreting Confucian moral thought and practice. Given that morality is a concept amenable to competing theoretical employment, it is, in Gallie's term, an "essentially contested concept."[25]

Rhetoric: A Treatise in Argumentation (Notre Dame: University of Notre Dame Press, 1969); Perelman, *The New Rhetoric and the Humanities* (Dordrecht: D. Reidel, 1979); Perelman, *The Realm of Rhetoric* (Notre Dame: University of Notre Dame Press, 1982); Stephen Toulmin, *The Uses of Argument* (Cambridge: Cambridge University Press, 1958); Stephen Toulmin, Richard Rieke, and Allan Janik, *An Introduction to Reasoning* (New York: Macmillan, 1979); Paul Taylor, *Normative Discourse* (Englewood Cliffs: Prentice-Hall, 1961); Robert H. Fogelin, *Understanding Arguments: An Introduction to Informal Logic* (New York: Harcourt Brace Jovanovich, 1978); and Stephen Nalor Thomas, *Reasoning in Natural Language,* Third Edition (Englewood Cliffs: Prentice-Hall, 1986). My approach in *Ethical Argumentation* is largely inspired by Perelman's works, though no attention is given to the rhetorical aspect of Hsün Tzu's moral epistemology.

23. For a perceptive study of the key role of enthymeme in Aristotle's *Rhetoric,* see William M. A. Grimaldi, *Studies in the Philosophy of Aristotle's Rhetoric* (Wiesbaden: Franz Steiner Verlag, 1972).

24. Perelman, *The Realm of Rhetoric,* 9–10.

25. W. B. Gallie, *Philosophy and Historical Understanding* (London: Chatto and Windus,

Style of Performance

Confucian argumentation is a cooperative activity of reasonable persuasion addressed to a particular rather than a universal audience.[26] Apart from the requirement of satisfying certain standards of competence such as conceptual clarity, consistency, coherence, respect for linguistic practices, and accord with reason and experience, it is expected that participants possess and display certain qualities of character conducive to the proceeding. Ideally, these are the qualities of a *chün-tzu* (an ethically superior person) or paradigmatic individual who governs his or her life by *tao*, the ideal of the good human life as a whole. The *tao* of the *chün-tzu* is the *tao* of humanity embodying *jen*, *li*, and *i*. Says Hsün Tzu, "The superior man is not called a worthy because he can do all that men of ability can do. The superior man is not called wise because he knows all that the wise men know. The superior man is not called a dialectician because he can dispute concerning all that the dialecticians dispute about. The superior man is not called an investigator because he can investigate everything investigators investigate into. He has his standard *[tao]*" (*ju-hsiao*, L131, D96).

Because of the ethical responsibility involved, the *chün-tzu* will refrain from engaging in contentious discourse.[27] For contention is liable to transform argumentation into an adversarial proceeding and thus obstruct rather than promote the cooperative undertaking. Instead of addressing a problem of common concern, a contentious person is more often motivated by the desire to win an argument. Were such a desire intense, issues pertaining to right and wrong or to the actual matters are bound to be ignored (*hsing-o*, L557, W170, D316). Moreover, a contentious person will lack the patience for explaining the reasoned support of his thesis (*jung-ju*, L57). Even if he offers explanations, they are likely to be hasty and inadequate to do full justice to the issues at hand. As Hsün Tzu points out, "When one discourses on one's ideas, one should give a complete explanation of one's reasons" (*cheng-*

1964), chap. 8. See also Dorothy Emmet, *The Moral Prism* (London: Macmillan, 1979), chap. 1. This is a recurrent theme of Dworkin's *Law Empire* in proposing his conception of "law as integrity."

26. With somewhat different emphasis, what follows is a brief summary and supplement of the discussion of the notion of *chün-tzu* regarding style of performance based on *Ethical Argumentation*, 8–14. A more extensive study of this notion in the *Analects* is given in *Dimensions of Moral Creativity*, chap. 4–5. As in *Ethical Argumentation*, the discussion is indebted to Ch'en Ta-ch'i, *Hsün Tzu hsüeh-shuo* (Taipei: Chung-hua wen-hua she, 1954), chap. 6. For the distinction between particular and universal audience, see Perelman and Tyteca, *The New Rhetoric*, 31ff.

27. See *ch'üan-hsüeh*, L17, W22, D39; *pu-kou*, L42.

ming, L521, W147, D291). More importantly, as Ch'en Ta-ch'i remarks, contention is a sort of agitating passion that disturbs the calmness of mind,[28] and thus deprives the participant of the clarity of mind essential to the exercise of sound judgment. Hsün Tzu compares the human mind to a pan of water.

If you place the pan on a level and do not jar it, then the heavy sediment will settle to the bottom and the clear water will collect on top, so that you can see your beard and eyebrows in it and examine the lines in your face. But if a faint wind passes over the top of the water, the heavy sediment will be stirred up from the bottom and the clear water will become mingled with it, so that you can no longer get a clear reflection of even a large object. The mind is the same way. If you guide it with reason *[li*]*, nourish it with clarity, and do not allow external objects to unbalance it, then it will be capable of determining right and wrong and of resolving doubts. But if you allow petty external objects to pull it about, so that its proper form becomes altered and its inner balance is upset, then it will not be capable of making even gross distinctions (*chieh-pi*, L490, W131–132, D271).

Along with composure and clarity of mind, a *chün-tzu* will engage in discourse with dignity, seriousness, and sincerity (*fei-hsiang*, L88). As a person imbued with a *jen*-mind, an active and affectionate concern for the well-being of his fellows, he will be circumspect in explaining his ideas to others, while guarding against the possibility of injuring others' sense of self-respect (*fei-hsiang*, L86). "The humane man (*jen-che*) loves others, hence he hates what injures others" (*i-ping*, L328, D168*, W69). In general, "words of praise give more warmth than clothing and silk; words of injury are more piercing than a spear or two-pronged lance" (*jung-ju*, L55). Whether or not he desires association or dissociation, the man of *jen* must respect others. However, not all expressions of respect are prompted by the same feeling. In the case of the worthy, he will respect and value their association. In the case of the unworthy, he will also respect them but with apprehension. In confronting the worthy, he will show his respect and try to be intimate. In confronting the unworthy, he will still show respect but keep them at a distance. "The outward expression of respect is the same, but one's inner feeling is different" (*ch'en-tao*, L298).

Characteristically, the *chün-tzu* is magnanimous *(k'uan)*. He practices the art of accommodation *(chien-shu)* (*fei-hsiang*, L86). Respect for both the worthy and the unworthy exemplifies such a practice, in accord with rules of civility or proper conduct *(li)*. Observance of these rules is a matter of decency. As an appropriate requirement of discourse, the *li* provide a way of promoting argumentation as a cooperative enterprise,

28. Ch'en Ta-chi'i, *Hsün Tzu hsüeh-shuo*, 91.

ensuring an open and orderly forum for airing differences in opinion. The *li* are, so to speak, diplomatic protocols facilitating the expression and consideration of competing views proffered as solutions to a problem of common concern. They provide acceptable channels for satisfying the desires of the participants. Much like our law of contracts and law of wills, they enable us to carry out our wishes effectively.[29]

Apart from the concern with *jen* and *li*, a *chün-tzu* is a man of *i*, who desires to arrive at a sound and reasonable judgment in response to changing circumstances of human life *(i-yi pien-ying)*.[30] An exercise of *i* requires an attitude of *kung* (impartiality). *Kung* is opposed to partiality *(p'ien)* in two different ways. As an expression of fairmindedness, a *chün-tzu* will discount his own personal interest or preference *(szu-yü)* in favor of what he deems to be right and reasonable from an impersonal standpoint *(hsiu-shen,* L36, D53, W32). This attitude also involves patience or receptivity *(hsüeh-hsin)* in listening to competing opinions before arriving at a reasoned judgment. Argumentation, as we have seen, is not a prudential discourse engaged in for the purpose of personal gain. Preoccupation with personal interest, in another way, will also lead to aspect-obsession, while *tao* is, by contrast, a holistic and unifying perspective for dealing with problems of human life *(chieh-pi,* L472, D258, W120). Partiality in this way may lead to beclouding the mind *(pi)* in dealing with exigent situations; thus it is obstructive of argumentation as a cooperative enterprise.[31] In sum, a *chün-tzu* is a man of integrity *(te-ch'ao),* who cherishes purity *(ts'ui)* and completeness *(ch'üan).* Given his dedication to *tao,* to *jen, li,* and *i,* he will not allow his ethical will to be subverted by power or profit, or by the sway of the masses *(ch'üan-hsüeh,* L19, W23, D40–41). For him, discourse is an avenue for expressing concisely and coherently his ethical commitments, with due attention to relevant facts *(cheng-ming,* L525, W149, D292). Unlike the sage, he has no comprehensive knowledge of the rationales *(li*)* of facts or events that affect human well-being. He can only rely upon his deliberation and planning, informed by extensive learning *(fei-hsiang,* L89).[32]

29. For distinguishing *li* (rules of proper conduct, ritual rules, propriety) from its homophone (which is variously translated as "principle," "rationale," "pattern"), I introduce an asterisk for this graph, eg., *li**. The *li* also have delimiting and ennobling functions. For more discussion, see Essay 13.

30. See *pu-kou,* L43; and *chih-shih,* L306. For other senses of *i,* see Essay 13.

31. These remarks are indebted to Dahlstrom's critique of certain aspects of argumentation: see Daniel Dahlstrom, "Tao and Ethical Argumentation," and my "Some Aspects of Ethical Argumentation: A Reply to Daniel Dahlstrom and John Marshall," *Journal of Chinese Philosophy* 14, no. 4 (1987). For further discussion of *pi,* see *Ethical Argumentation,* chap. 4.

32. See also *fei shih-erh tzu,* L102; *hsing-o,* L555, W168–69, D315.

The foregoing discussion of the desirable qualities of *chün-tzu* pertains, so to speak, to the *style of performance* of participants in argumentation. As Oliver has noted, echoing Buffon, if style is the man himself, "there must be as many different styles as there are speakers or writers. . . . Style is everywhere highly individualistic."[33] As an individual expression of ethical commitment, of the exercise of the virtues of *jen*, *li*, and *i*, it is a unique ethical expression. The style of a man, à la Schopenhauer, may be said to be an expression of "the physiognomy of the soul." As Danto insightfully remarks, the style represents the qualities of the man himself, "seen from the outside, physiognomically." There are no rules for self-representation in ethical discourse. Following Aristotle, Danto reminds us that the exercise of virtues is not rule-governed. "To be kind is to be creative, to be able in novel situations to do what everyone will recognize as a kind thing. A moral person is an intuitive person, able to make the right judgments and perform the appropriate actions in situations in which he or she has perhaps never been before."[34] In argumentation, apart from possibility of misunderstanding, a *chün-tzu*, because of his open-mindedness, is willing to run the risks involved in lending a receptive ear to others *(hsüeh-hsin)*. As Johnston put it, "In making himself available to arguments, man transcends the horizons of his own perceptions, emotions, and instincts. . . . Knowledge and morality are possible only to the open-minded person who has transcended the horizons of immediate experience by taking the risks implicit in argument."[35]

II. THE PROBLEM OF MORAL REASONING

The problem of reasoning in Confucian ethics is basically a problem of philosophical reconstruction aiming at an ideal, plausible explication of the nature of Confucian discourse as a form of reasoned discourse engaged in for the exposition and defense of moral claims or normative proposals. Independently of our interest in Confucian rhetoric, there are at least two underlying motivations for this theoretical inquiry in moral philosophy. An examination of the various uses of *li** in Hsün Tzu or Wang Yang-ming, for example, may profit by regarding *li** as functionally equivalent to reason. Given the predominant ethical concern of the Confucianists, it is plausible to maintain that their principal uses of *li** in normative contexts pertain to the reasoned justification

---

33. Oliver, *Communication and Culture*, 271.
34. Arthur C. Danto, *The Transfiguration of the Commonplace* (Cambridge: Harvard University Press, 1981), 203–8.
35. Johnston and Natanson, *Philosophy, Rhetoric, and Argumentation*, 3.

of any value claim that is proffered in ethical argumentation.[36] A conceptual analysis of the notion of *i* also discloses a principal use that pertains to "reasoned or correct judgment on what is right and appropriate."[37] These notions of *li** (reason) and *i* (reasoned judgment) suggest that an inquiry into the problem of moral reasoning is a proper concern for Confucian moral philosophers. At the outset, I shall assume that the notion of morality is applicable to Confucian ethics, when this notion is broadly construed as embracing the concern with character and conduct in the light of *tao*, the Confucian ideal of the good human life as a whole. Also, this ideal of *tao* is explicable in terms of the basic, interdependent, aretaic notions: *jen, li* (ritual rules), and *i*.[38] Given these assumptions, I shall characterize the problem of moral reasoning as a problem of assessing reasons proffered in support of Confucian moral judgments. In what follows, I shall offer some observations on this problem by way of commenting on two different approaches.

Deductivism

Since reasoning may be properly characterized as an inferential activity, the problem of moral reasoning may be viewed as a problem of determining the validity of moral arguments. Differently put, the problem is essentially one of formal analysis and evaluation of Confucian reasoning in accordance with the canons of deductive logic. I shall call this approach 'deductivism.' The task here, more especially, lies in the reconstruction of Confucian reasoning, namely, appropriate arguments, and a subsequent determination of whether these arguments are proper substitution instances of valid argument forms. Recently, it has been claimed that in Confucian discourses, e.g., the *Analects* and *Mencius*, certain arguments do possess the forms of *modus ponens* and *modus tollens*.[39] While this claim seems uncontroversial, it is difficult to see how it throws light on the distinction between good and poor reasons. The notion of deductive validity does not enable us to distinguish acceptable from unacceptable premises.

Consider this famous argument on the importance of the right use of terms *(cheng-ming)* in the *Analects*:

36. For a detailed exposition and defense of this thesis, see *Ethical Argumentation*, 20–30; and *The Unity of Knowledge and Action*, 30–50.
37. See my "Hsün Tzu and the Unity of Virtues,"
38. See my "The Problem of Conceptual Unity in Hsün Tzu and Li Kou's Solution."
39. Hsueh-li Cheng, "Reasoning in Confucian Ethics." Presented at the International Symposium on Confucianism and the Modern World, Taipei, Taiwan, November 12–17, 1987. Cf. M. D. Resnik, "Logic and Methodology in the Writings of Mencius," *International Philosophical Quarterly* 7, no. 2 (1968): 212–30.

If terms are not correctly used, what is said will not sound reasonable; when what is said does not sound reasonable, undertaking will not culminate in success; when undertaking does not culminate in success, then *li* (ritual propriety) and music will not flourish. When *li* and music do not flourish, punishments will not fit the crimes; when punishments do not fit the crimes, the common people will not know where to put hand and foot."[40]

By making explicit the conclusion ("If terms are not correctly used, the common people will not know where to put hand and foot") and reformulation of the argument in propositional logic, we have a valid chain argument. But what we want to know is why these premises are considered acceptable? For example, the nature of the connection between the antecedent and the consequent in the first premise. While the argument, when formally reconstructed, is logically impeccable, the deductivist provides us no guide to the assessment of the acceptability of the premises.

There are additional grounds for doubting the plausibility of the deductivist approach. In the first place, Confucian reasoning, in general, is highly inexplicit in its use of plausible presumptions, i.e., appeal to shared knowledge, belief, or experience, as well as to the established or operative standards of argumentative competence.[41] Making explicit and intelligible the relevant plausible presumptions is an extremely difficult task. Consider the widespread use of what may be called "historical appeal," i.e., the ethical use of the distinction between the past *(ku)* and the present *(chin)*, of historical characters, situations, and events. The argumentative value of such an appeal does not seem to depend on conformity to rules of inference. Instead of regarding it as a form of argument, it is more illuminating to view it as a reasoned instrument performing a variety of legitimate functions in different contexts of discourse, e.g., pedagogical, rhetorical, explanatory, and justificatory functions. This thesis appears to be well supported by a study of Hsün Tzu's recurrent use of the historical appeal.[42] Deductivism offers us no guide to the study of the Confucian use of plausible presumptions. Since plausible presumptions, when articulated as premises of arguments, function as *prima facie* rather than conclusive reasons, they are essentially defeasible. It is not obvious that deductivism can help us in formulating the proper criteria of defeasibility for plausible presumptions. Moreover, it is doubtful whether such an effort is consistent with

40. This is Lau's translation with minor emendation. See D. C. Lau, *Confucius: The Analects* (Baltimore: Penguin Books, 1979), 13.3.

41. The term "plausible presumption" comes from Rescher. For further discussion, see *Ethical Argumentation*, chap. 1; and Nicholas Rescher, *Dialectics* (Albany: SUNY Press, 1977), 38. Cf. Perelman and Albrecht-Tyteca, *The New Rhetoric*, 70–74.

42. See my "Ethical Uses of the Past in Early Confucianism: The Case of Hsün Tzu."

the Confucian notion of *i* as reasoned judgment in a concrete situation of moral perplexity.

Another reason for rejecting deductivism rests on a plausible, though arguable, claim that one prominent type of reasoning in Confucian ethics, like a common form of legal reasoning, is case-by-case reasoning. This distinctive, non-formal, type of reasoning was first noted by I. A. Richards in his *Mencius on the Mind,* and can be shown to be a correct characterization of the Confucian use of argument from example, reminiscent of Aristotle's rhetorical induction.[43] The principal ground for this ascription lies in the Confucian distinction between *ching* and *ch'üan,* between normal and exigent situations.[44] For reasoning in normal situations, a deductivist characterization is quite in order. For example, if a situation is considered normal *(ching),* it can be viewed unproblematically as an instance of the application of an appropriate ritual rule *(li).* But in an exigent situation, what is required is an exercise of *ch'üan* (discretion) in accord with reasoned judgment *(i).* The reasoning here may, in part, be characterized as case-by-case reasoning rather than a deductive subsumption of all moral situations as instances of application of established rules or principles.[45] Reasoning in exigent situations is underdetermined by application of ritual rules, although in normal situations these ritual rules may function as premises of deductive arguments. The problem of Confucian reasoning, in this light, is more a problem of articulating the Confucian conception of reasoned discourse rather than a problem of logical analysis and evaluation.

Schematic Representation of Coordinative Reasoning

Nevertheless, the deductivist approach, in its insistence on the need for formal characterization, is valuable in calling our attention to the importance of schematic representation of reasoning in non-normal or exigent situations. For such a representation, while abstract, provides an illuminating way of clarifying the nature of such situations. Let us, by reflecting on an example, distinguish two different though complementary points of view in an exigent situation. Consider Shun's decision to marry the Emperor's two daughters without first informing his parents.[46] Suppose we regard his decision as based on a reasoned judg-

43. I. A. Richards, *Mencius on the Mind* (London: Kegan Paul, 1932), 55f.
44. For an elaboration of this distinction and its significance for moral philosophy, see my *Dimensions of Moral Creativity,* chaps. 4 and 5.
45. More accurately, case-by-case reasoning or argument from example is a characterization of the prospective significance of ethical justification as a form of analogical projection. For detailed discussion, see *Ethical Argumentation,* 51–101, esp. 95–101.
46. This case was reported and briefly discussed in *Mencius,* 5A:2 and more exten-

ment. The *li* (ritual rule) in question requires Shun to inform his parents first before marriage.[47] For him to go against this established rule, he must *think* that his situation is exigent rather than normal. But what makes this situation exigent is its unprecedented character. Of course, Shun wants to do the right thing, yet the only guide he has is his sense of rightness or *liang-chih*, his ability to distinguish right from wrong actions. Wang Yang-ming comments:

> As for Shun's marrying without first telling his parents, was there someone before him who did the same thing and served as an example for him, which he could find out by looking into certain records and asking certain people, after which he did as he did? Or did he search into his *liang-chih* in an instant of thought and weigh all factors as to what was proper, after which he could not help doing what he did?[48]

For Shun, there are no previous cases of paradigmatic agents' decisions to guide his decision, nor is there any existing rule, say a priority rule or principle that determines a right decision over conflicting claims of filiality and marital relations. All he can do is to rely on his *liang-chih*, his sense of what is right and good, weigh a variety of factors *(ch'üan)*, and arrive at a judgment on relevant factors. We may note also that just as there are no rules of inference, there are no rules of relevance. Suppose Shun arrives at the following relevant considerations: (1) the Emperor's wish, (2) the primacy of husband-wife over parents-and-son relationship,[49] (3) desire to marry someone with respectable social standing with the promise of acquiring political power and authority, and (4) desire to contribute to the promotion of a *jen*-state. All these factors, for Shun, have weight as reasons supporting his judgment. To

---

sively treated by Wang Yang-ming in *Ch'üan-hsi lu.* See W. T. Chan, *Instructions for Practical Living and Other Neo-Confucian Writings by Wang Yang-ming* (New York: Columbia University Press, 1963), sec. 139, 107–10. My hypothetical reconstruction of Shun's reasoning is largely based on Wang Yang-ming's remarks. For discussion of two other exigent cases in *Mencius:* the cases of drowning sister-in-law and killing of a sovereign, see my *Dimensions of Moral Creativity,* 72–76. Cf. D. C. Lau, trans., *Mencius* (Baltimore: Penguin Books, 1970), Appendix 5.

47. *Book of Odes,* 101, cited in *Mencius,* 5A:2.

48. Chan, *Instructions,* 109–10. I have retained *liang-chih* instead of Chan's translation "innate knowledge of the good." For present purposes, the sense of *liang-chih* may be construed along the line of Butler's notion of conscience. See Joseph Butler, *Five Sermons* (Indianapolis: Bobbs-Merrill, 1950), Sermon II. For a detailed analysis of the notion of *liang-chih,* see Essay 9.

49. This is Mencius's point. To the question "Why did Shun marry without telling his parents?" Mencius answers: "Because he would not have been allowed to marry if he had told them. A man and a woman living together is the most important of human relationships. If he had told his parents, he would have had to put aside the most important of human relationships and this would result in bitterness against his parents. That is why he did not tell them." D. C. Lau, *Mencius,* 5A:2.

depict his reasoning, *retrospectively,* we may construct a diagram showing how different lines, representing considerations of presumably equal weight, are coordinated and converge upon a single conclusion. We have here a sort of *coordinative* reasoning. We may say with Wisdom that here "the process of argument is not a *chain* of demonstrative reasoning. It is presenting and representing those features of the case which severally *cooperate* in favor of the conclusion, in favor of saying what the reasoner wishes said, in favor of calling the situation by the name by which he wishes to call it. The reasons are like the legs of a chair, not the links of a chain."[50] We find the same sort of coordinative reasoning in Hsün Tzu where he justifies his thesis on the necessity of regulative functions of ritual rules *(li).* When such factors as scarcity of resources to satisfy everyone's needs and desires, partiality or limited benevolence, limited foresight, and vulnerability are invoked together, they provide a sufficient warrant for accepting his thesis; yet each factor, viewed independently, is quite weak in supporting his thesis.[51]

For present purposes, we can thus regard reasoning in an exigent situation, as in Shun's case, *retrospectively,* as a coordinative form of reasoning. If we suppose that another person is in a similar situation and uses Shun's case as a paradigm for judgment, we can then say that its *prospective* significance can be represented as a form of case-by-case reasoning.[52] In short, reasoning in an exigent situation may be characterized as either coordinative or case-by-case from a retrospective or prospective point of view. Such diagrammatic representation, in my view, does help us to appreciate the non-deductive character of some types of reasoning.[53] Of course, there remains the question of assessing reasons in support of ethical judgment.

50. John Wisdom, *Philosophy and Psychoanalysis* (Oxford: Basil Blackwell, 1957), 156. For further discussion, see *Ethical Argumentation,* 92–95. An alternative term for coordinative reasoning is "linked reasoning." See Thomas, *Practical Reasoning in Natural Language,* 58–60.
51. See my "The Concept of *Li* in Confucian Moral Theory." For more detailed, complementary analysis of Hsün Tzu's arguments on human nature, see my "The Quasi-Empirical Aspect of Hsün Tzu's Philosophy of Human Nature," *Philosophy East and West* 28, no. 1 (1978): 3–19.
52. See *Ethical Argumentation,* 95–101.
53. A schematic approach is also useful in providing a starting point in mapping out the validity of different sorts of appeal in Confucian argumentation. By employing a broader notion of validity, somewhat corresponding to Dewey's notion of warranted assertability, we can represent different sorts of Confucian appeals in discursive vindication (see Essay 1). See John Dewey, *Logic: Theory of Inquiry* (New York; Henry Holt, 1938). This notion of validity, for example, allows us to speak of "degrees of validity" or "degrees of strength" of different reasons in support of conclusions, as explicated in Thomas, *Practical Reasoning in Natural Language,* 122–36.

III. THE *CHÜN-TZU* AS A COUNSELOR TO THE RULER

Before turning to the element of *pathos* in Confucian argumentation
and to Professor North's comparative remarks on Confucius and Aristotle, let me first supplement her discussion of the role of a Confucianist as a counselor to the ruler. Again, I base my discussion on that
of *Hsün-Tzu*, especially the essays on the ways of ruler and ministers
(chün-tao p'ien and *ch'en-tao p'ien).* At the outset, let me note that in classical Confucianism, there is an important distinction between a sage
(sheng-jen) and an ethically superior man or paradigmatic individual
(chün-tzu), a distinction presupposed in Part I of this paper. While this
distinction, perhaps, has no import in dealing with Neo-Confucian literature, it is implicit in Confucius's remark that he could not hope ever
to meet a sage *(sheng-jen),* but only *chün-tzu (Analects,* 7:26). It is plausible to conjecture that for Confucius, the ideal of sagehood is an abstract ideal of a perfect moral character or personality rather than a
practical objective of the moral life. Thus in his teachings he more often
made use of the notion of *chün-tzu* than he did of sagehood.

In Hsün Tzu, the distinction between *sheng-jen* and *chün-tzu* is explicit, though at time he seems to collapse it.[54] Consider the following:

> In the discourse of a *sheng-jen* (sage) there is no prior deliberation or planning.
> His utterances are fitting, refined, and in complete accord with his insight into
> the interconnection of different kinds of things *(lei).* Whether staying on one
> point or moving to another, he can respond to all changing circumstances. In
> the discourse of a scholar or *chün-tzu,* there is prior deliberation and planning.
> In any occasion, his utterances are worthy to be listened to, refined and yet in
> accord with facts *(fei-hsiang,* L89).[55]

In order to appreciate the role of a Confucian *(ju)* as a ruler's counselor, it is better to focus on *chün-tzu* than on *sheng-jen.* It is indeed a
common faith of classical and Neo-Confucianists that all humans are
innately capable of attaining sagehood. As Hsün Tzu reminds his readers, everyone is capable of becoming a sage, for he has the ability to
learn and discern the rationales of *jen, i,* and other standards of conduct, and put them into practice. So long as each of us applies himself
to study in seeking *tao* with singlemindedness and resolute will, examines things carefully and thoughtfully, persists in these efforts over
a long period of time, and accumulates good acts without cessation,
"we can achieve a godlike insight *(shen-ming)* into all things and form a

54. See Watson, *Hsün Tzu: Basic Writings,* 19n. For evidence not cited by Watson, see
ju-hsiao p'ieo. For further discussion, see *Ethical Argumentation,* 61–65.
55. For briefer passages, see *fei shih-erh tzu,* L102; *cheng-ming,* L525, D292, W149;
and *ta-lüeh,* L635.

triad with Heaven and Earth" (*hsing-o*, L554, W167*, D313). But in reality, sagehood is not actually possible *(neng)* for everyone because of lack of will to engage in the pursuit (ibid.). And we may add, it is doubtful that humans, no matter how intelligent, can have the sage's insight to respond to all changing circumstances of human life without the need of engaging in informed deliberation *(chih-lü)*. Perplexities over right and wrong conduct cannot be resolved without deliberation *(chün-tao*, L284).

Even for a *chün-tzu*, there are difficulties to be overcome in persuasion *(shui-nan)*. Generally, one cannot accomplish one's goals by being direct or straightforward, for there is a risk not only in avoiding factual errors and platitudes, but also the possibility of injuring the listeners' sense of self-respect. The appeal to historical events of the distant past, for example, unless carefully substantiated by evidence, is bound to be unreliable. The appeal to events near the present, unless their relevance or significance is demonstrated, risks in pronouncing platitudes. A *chün-tzu* will thus adapt himself to the time and circumstances, express his view fully after attending to all sides, and will not injure others' sense of self-respect. As a paradigmatic individual, he regulates his conduct by the standards of *jen, li,* and *i,* and guides others accordingly *(fei-hsiang,* L86).

Suppose a *chün-tzu* assumes the position of the minister; there are additional difficulties involved in relation to the ruler. As a person of integrity, he will follow *tao* rather than comply with his ruler's arbitrary wishes *(ts'ung-tao pu ts'ung-chün)*.[56] How he conducts himself depends on the kind of ruler he serves. Naturally, he should prove himself worthy of trust and gain the ruler's confidence, assuming that the ruler is a sage or enlightened ruler *(ming-chün)*. That is, an exemplar of virtue, who, apart from self-cultivation, loves his peoples, and enlists only the worthy for service. In this case, the *chün-tzu's* position is relatively easy. So long as the ruler's concern for *tao* is successfully expressed in policies, laws, and carried out in promoting order, there is only listening and obedience but no remonstration. "This is the way," Hsün Tzu notes, "to serve the sage-king: be respectful, reverent and modest, swift in carrying out orders and not daring to make decisions nor give or receive things for the sake of self-interest, and consider obedience as one's will" *(ch'en-tao,* L294). To be in such a fortunate position, of course, involves understanding the significance of laws and policies, not merely a mastery of their complexities. Unlike a muddle-headed ruler *(an-chün)*, who aims merely at acquiring power without regard to *tao*

56. *ch'en-tao*, L292; *tzu-tao*, L651.

and people's welfare, the enlightened ruler is a model to his people. In Hsün Tzu's words, "the enlightened ruler is like a sundial, and the people are like the shadows, when the sundial is set properly, the shadows will reflect accordingly" (*chün-tao*, L270). For a *chün-tzu*, serving an enlightened ruler is both a pleasure and a privilege, for in such a ruler he sees a marvelous exemplification of the actuating import of *tao* in human life.

Realistically, however, a *chün-tzu* is more likely to serve under a less than enlightened ruler. While Hsün Tzu, like Confucius and Mencius, believed in the Golden Age in the time of the sage kings, Yao, Shun, and more especially Yü and T'ang, he would be quite content with seeing a *pa* (hegemonist) ruling the world, for a *pa* at least relies upon laws and cares for his people (*ch'iang-kuo*, L342).[57]

If a *pa* is an average ruler (*chung-chün*), a *chün-tzu* may engage in remonstration but not flattery. The *chün-tzu* will be loyal and trustworthy, but refrain from self-depreciation; he will remonstrate and try to gain acceptance of his advice, but refrain from flattery; he will be firm and courageous in upholding his views with the sole intention of expressing what is correct and upright but will not allow his mind to be moved by extraneous considerations (*ch'en-tao*, L294–295). The most difficult situation is when the *chün-tzu* is compelled to serve a cruel ruler (*pao-chün*) in the time of disorder. While he will be extremely cautious in preserving his life, he will maintain his integrity. He will refrain from overt remonstration and rectification of the ruler's misconduct, but will attempt to transform the cruel ruler in a gentle and agreeable manner, with the hope that his words will gain the ruler's inner assent. For Hsün Tzu, a cruel ruler is like an untamed horse to be domesticated, or like an infant to be nourished. The process will be slow and requires utmost care and patience. The *chün-tzu* will "adapt himself to different situations in a flexible and circuitous fashion in the course of transforming the cruel ruler's temperament" (*ch'en-tao*, L295).

Pathos

The foregoing indicates Hsün Tzu's attitude in persuading a particular audience. In general, any means of persuasion that does not violate the standards of *jen*, *li*, and *i* will be endorsed. Were the participants in argumentation all actuated by these concerns, discourse would be facile in transforming disagreement into agreement. If, for analytical purposes, we distinguish the speaker from his or her audience and concentrate on the idea of a persuasive speaker, and further

57. For more extensive discussion, see *wang-chih p'ien*.

assume that the speaker is a *chün-tzu,* we can explore the appropriate emotions of the audience to be aroused in speech. The topic of emotions in Confucian ethics is an unexplored territory. My brief remarks here center on the divergent conceptions of Hsün Tzu and Mencius. This divergence reflects contrasting views of human nature.

As Professor North points out, Mencius's aim in persuading the king is to show him how he could "gallop on to goodness" and to demonstrate this by appealing to the king's original nature. For Mencius, all humans possess four beginnings or *hsin* (heart/mind). "The heart of compassion is the germ of benevolence *(jen);* the heart of shame, of dutifulness *(i);* the heart of courtesy and modesty, of the observance of rites *(li);* the heart of right and wrong, of wisdom."[58] Notably, the speaker's aim is to guide the listener by awakening his innately good nature, to encourage its development, for the virtues of *jen, li, i,* and wisdom are the flowering of the four beginnings. It is unclear in Mencius what other sentiments are relevant objects of persuasion. Hsün Tzu, on the contrary, believes that human nature is originally bad, in the sense that it presents problems for regulation, particularly, by *li* (ritual rules). Moods such as joy, sorrow, emotions such as love, hate, anger, and envy; and bodily feelings such as pleasure and pain, hunger, thirst, and so forth, comprise the basic human motivational structure. In themselves, these feelings *(ch'ing)* are morally neutral. But coupled with man's natural self-seeking propensity to satisfy the desires aroused by these emotions, expressions of these feelings are liable to conflict, especially in light of the scarcity of goods to satisfy them. Given this view, all feelings and desires are materials for moral transformation *(hua)* in accord with *jen, li,* and *i.* Persuading the listeners, in light of the speaker's *ethos,* amounts to transforming these desires into reflective desires, i.e., desires mediated by reason.[59] While they diverge in their conceptions of human nature, Mencius and Hsün Tzu both agree about the ultimate aim of persuasion. From the point of view of ethical theory, both are one in espousing the Confucian *tao,* though Mencius is more inclined to emphasize *jen* and *i* than *li* and *i.* This difference in emphasis does not constitute a difference in ethical intention. The role of *pathos* in Confucian rhetoric deserves exploration, as it has a key role to play in developing a Confucian moral psychology.

58. *Mencius,* 2A:6.
59. For further discussion, see my "The Concept of *Li* in Confucian Moral Theory;" "The Conceptual Aspect of Hsün Tzu's Philosophy of Human Nature" and "The Quasi-Empirical Aspect of Hsün Tzu's Philosophy of Human Nature," *Philosophy East and West* 27, nos. 4 and 28, no. 1 (1977, 1978).

CONCLUSION

This essay presents a sketch of the elements a Confucian theory of rhetoric. It is difficult to say how much it contributes to comparative East-West rhetorical studies. Along with Max Hamberger, Professor North has noted throughout her paper, some analogies and contrasts, particularly in comparing Confucius and Aristotle.[60] The theoretical significance of such efforts is difficult to assess, not because they are uninstructive, particularly for rectifying ethnocentrism, but because problems beset the inquirer when he or she focuses on the basic concepts of different ethical outlooks. *Jen*, for example, is functionally equivalent to benevolence. But Hamberger's comparison of *li* to *epeikeia* (reasonableness) is doubtful. In my view, the latter has some affinity to *i*, which is functionally equivalent to *phronesis*. *Chung*, often rendered as "the mean," does not exactly correspond to Aristotle's notion of the mean, nor is it unattainable by a *chün-tzu*. While *chung* does consist in "not being inclined to either side" (*Analects*, 6:27), it is better rendered as "centrality" or "equilibrium," as Legge has done, though not in his translation of the title *Chung Yung*. According to one interpretation based on Wang Yang-ming, the distinction between *chung* and *ho* (harmony) does not constitute a dichotomy. For *chung* may be viewed as an achieved state of mind, a result of the *ho* of emotions, and *ho* as an achieved state of mind is a result of the activation of the incipient tendency toward *chung*.[61] We may note with Hamberger, however, an interesting affinity between *chün-tzu* and Aristotle's *spoudaios*.[62] Functional equivalence of concepts is important in comparative inquiry, in exhibiting parallels of different conceptual schemes. Whether this sort of endeavor is helpful for constructing or developing a Confucian theory remains an open question. In my view, such an effort has value in pointing to the possibility of interaction of different conceptual schemes, thus providing an important resource for developing a rhetorical theory in Confucian moral philosophy.

60. See Max Hamberger, "Aristotle and Confucius: A Study in Comparative Philosophy," *Philosophy* 31 (1956); and "Aristotle and Confucius: A Comparison," *Journal of the History of Ideas* 20 (1959).
61. See Essay 2.
62. Cf. Hamberger, "Aristotle and Confucius: A Study in Comparative Philosophy," 355. See also *Dimensions of Moral Creativity*, 45–46.

Essay 11   A Confucian Perspective on Self-Deception

This essay is an inquiry into the possibility of a Confucian response to the problem of self-deception. A paucity of textual materials renders extensive reconstruction and interpretation necessary.[1] The following investigation is based mainly on my studies of Hsün Tzu's moral philosophy.[2] Section I treats the classical Confucian concern with self-deception in *Ta-hsüeh (The Great Learning)*. Section II deals with both the diagnosis of self-deception in the light of Hsün Tzu's conception of *pi* (obscuration) and the problems that arise in discussing the Confucian notion of the self.[3]

I

In *Ta-hsüeh* (adult education),[4] personal cultivation *(hsiu-shen)* is considered the foundation of peace and order both in the world and in family

1. This difficulty is compounded by lack of attention to the problem among Chinese and Western writers on Confucianism. To my knowledge, only one recent essay explicitly addresses the problem. See Chang Chung-hsing, "Tzu-ch'i chih t'i chi ch'i fang-chih," in *T'an tzu-ch'i ch'i-jen* (Taipei: Commercial Press, 1991).

2. Textual references to *Hsün Tzu* in this essay are the following: Li T'i-sheng, *Hsün Tzu chi-shih* (Taipei: Hsüeh-sheng, 1979), which is a careful and updated edition based on the standard one by Wang Hsien-ch'ien, *Hsün Tzu chi-chieh* (Taipei: World Publishing Co., 1961). Citations from Li's edition are indicated by the title of the essay followed by page number. Translations adopted from existing works will be indicated in appropriate places.

3. The parentheticals for transcriptions of Chinese characters are not translations but convenient indicators of possible meanings and of Chinese characters. Analytical explication of some characters such as *ch'i, ch'eng, pi,* and *huo* provide my constructive interpretation independently of the initial use of convenient indicators.

4. According to Chu Hsi, in antiquity there were two kinds of education or learning: the learning for adults *(ta-jen chih hsüeh)*, and the learning for the young or children *(hsiao-tzu chih hsüeh)*. "Learning for children consisted in the chores of cleaning and sweeping, in the formalities of polite conversation and good manners, and in the refinement of ritual, music, archery, charioteering, calligraphy, and mathematics. Learning for adults consisted in the way of probing principle *[ch'iung-li]*, of establishing harmony in the household, or governing the state well, and of bringing tranquility to the empire."

life. Along with the investigation of things *(ko-wu)*, extension of knowledge *(chih-chih)*, and rectification of the mind or heart *(cheng-hsin)*, *ch'eng-yi* is said to be an essential step or component of personal cultivation. The so-called "three principal items" *(san-kang)* provide the objective of abiding in the highest good or excellence *(chih-shan)* by manifesting clear character or virtue *(ming ming-te)* and loving the people *(ch'in-min)*.[5] The concern with self-deception is explicit in Chapter 6, a gloss on what it means to make one's thought sincere *(ch'eng ch'i yi)*. Before attending to this text, something must be said about the notions of *ch'eng* and *yi*.

The Notion of Ch'eng

At the first occurrence of *ch'eng* in *Ta-hsüeh*, Chu Hsi says, without further explanation, that *ch'eng* means *shih*.[6] A longer gloss on *ch'eng* in *Chung Yung (The Doctrine of the Mean)* is more helpful.[7] According to Chu Hsi, *ch'eng* means *chen-shih wu-wang*. Roughly, *ch'eng* means "truthfulness *[chen]*, genuineness *[shih]*, and freedom from falsity *[wu-wang]*."[8] I suggest that we regard *chen, shih,* and *wu-wang* as characteristics of *ch'eng* construed as an ideal, ethical condition of personhood. If a person possesses *ch'eng*, such characteristics would be expected to be present in his thought, belief, speech, and action. In Wang Yang-ming's

---

What this work treats is the learning for adults; hence it is named *Ta-hsüeh*." Translated by Daniel K. Gardner in *Chu Hsi and the Ta-hsüeh: Neo-Confucian Reflection on the Confucian Canon* (Cambridge: Harvard University Press, 1985), 51. For a different interpretation of *ta-hsüeh* as *t'ai-hsüeh* or education for the ruler, see Chao Tse-hou, *Ta-hsüeh yen-chiu* (Taipei: Chung-hua, 1972), 119–20. Chao's interpretation, however, seems to contradict the statement in the text: "From the Son of Heaven, down to the common people, all must regard cultivation of the personal life *[hsiu-shen]* as the root or foundation." See Wing-tsit Chan, trans., *A Source Book in Chinese Philosophy* (Princeton: Princeton University Press, 1963), 87. It must be noted that *Ta-hsüeh* is a subject of historical controversy. Aside from issues pertaining to textual arrangement, there have been disputes on the interpretation of key terms that occur throughout this short essay and original commentary. Gardner provides an informative account of the issues until Chu Hsi's times. A more extensive and updated discussion is given by Chao. A recent rearrangement is given in Yen Ling-feng, *Ta-hsüeh chang-chü hsin-pien* (Taipei: Pamir, 1984). See Gardner, *Chu Hsi and the Ta-hsüeh*, chap. 3; and Chao, *Ta-hsüeh*, chaps. 3–6.

5. Unless indicated otherwise, I adopt Chan's translation of *Ta-hsüeh* in his *Source Book*. The original text I use is Yang Liang-kang, *Ta-hsüeh chin-chu chin-i* (Taipei: Commercial Press, 1977).

6. Chu Hsi, *Ssu-shu chi-chu* (Hong Kong: T'ai-p'ing, 1980), 2.

7. I shall not follow Chu Hsi's elaboration in terms of the distinction between *t'ien-li* and *ssu-yü* or *jen-yü* (human desires). For a discussion of this distinction see Essay 9.

8. Chu Hsi, *Ssu-shu chi-chu*, 19. A different translation of *chen-shih wu-wang* is "Truth, reality, and freedom from error." See Wing-tsit Chan, trans., *Neo-Confucian Terms Explained (The Pei-hsi tzu-i)* (New York: Columbia University Press, 1985), 97. For Ch'en Ch'un's text, see *Pei-hsi hsien-sheng tzu-i hsiang-chiang* (Taipei: Kuang-wen, 1979), 117. Please read 'he,' 'his,' or 'him' as 'he or she,' 'his or hers,' and 'him or her.'

understanding of the term, such a person would embody the unity of knowledge and action *(chih-hsing ho-i)*.[9]

If we render *chen* as 'truthfulness,' we may say that a *ch'eng*-person *(ch'eng-che)* is one who is sincere in acknowledging his thoughts or beliefs to himself and to others. Presumed in this acknowledgment is a concern for the truth of the belief and for the explanation of factual claims and justification of normative ones. This presumption perhaps accounts for Hsün Tzu's recurrent emphasis on *li* (reason, principle) and *lei* (kinds, categories), and *fu-yen* (accord with evidence) as standards of argumentative discourse.[10] However, for the Confucian, *chen* is more than a desirable epistemic attitude or disposition, since the agent must also express this *chen*-concern with *kung* (respectfulness), *ching* (seriousness, reverence), and *chin* (caution, circumspection).[11] *Kung* is a virtue of *li* (ritual). At issue here is whether *chen* is expressed in a respectful manner. Often this respect takes the form of deference to the opinions and wishes of others, particularly the elders and more experienced persons in the community. *Ching* is seriousness in expressing one's convictions, especially those that affect the well-being of the family and the community. A related consideration is *chin* (caution, circumspection), since the expression of one's view must take account of the feelings of the audience. In the words of Hsün Tzu, "words of praise for another are warmer than clothing of linen and silk. The wound caused by words is deeper than that of spears and halberds."[12] Even more important is "to consider the long view of things and think of consequences."[13] In sum, *chen* as truthfulness is more than just a matter of sincere avowal of one's beliefs and concern for their truth; it is oriented toward the proper expres-

9. See my *The Unity of Knowledge and Action: A Study in Wang Yang-ming's Moral Psychology* (Honolulu: University Press of Hawaii, 1982), esp. chap. 1.

10. See my *Ethical Argumentation: A Study in Hsün Tzu's Moral Epistemology* (Honolulu: University of Hawaii Press, 1985), 26–36, 51–101.

11. The analysis below is suggested by a presumably common view of scholars in Ch'en Ch'un's times. Ch'en Ch'un rejects the view largely because it was supposed to describe the highest degree of *ch'eng* attainment in a sage. However, one would expect the characteristics of *chen*, *ching*, and *chin* to be present in different degrees of *ch'eng*-attainment among ordinary people as well as in the sage. See *Pei-hsi hsien-sheng tzu-i hsiang-chiang*, 117. Cf. Chan, *Neo-Confucian Terms Explained*, 97. Note that in his commentary of Mencius's expression of "the heart of *kung* and *ching*" (2A:6), Chu Hsi characterizes *ching* as inner and *kung* as outward manifestation of *ching* (*Ssu-shu chih chu*, 162). This comment does not seem to be a faithful rendering of Mencius's intent, but it does indicate Chu Hsi's own view. I am indebted to Kwong-loi Shun for calling my attention to this passage.

12. John Knoblock, *Xunzi: A Translation and Study of the Complete Works*, vol. I: Books 1–6 (Stanford: Stanford University Press, 1989), 186; *jung-ju p'ien*, 55.

13. Ibid., 195; *jung-ju p'ien*, 68.

sion of these beliefs in the context governed by *li* or rules of proper conduct.[14]

Shih can be rendered as 'genuineness' or 'reality' in the sense opposed to 'counterfeit.'[15] A genuine person, for example, is one who is devoid of any hypocrisy or pretense with respect to the expression of his thoughts or feelings.[16] In the case of ethical commitment, *shih* pertains to something concrete or substantial, that is, the committed person is one who is disposed to discharge his obligation in the appropriate situation. In the case of the commitment to the ideal of the good human life as a whole, say, to *tao* or *jen* (humanity) in the broad sense, such a commitment must not be halfhearted, though it does not preclude inquiry to dispel doubt in the course of the agent's endeavor to specify its concrete significance. The commitment to *tao* or *jen* calls for a creative clarifying of *jen*'s meaning in personal life. Chu Hsi's recurrent use of *shih-li*, commonly rendered as 'concrete principle,' displays a concern with the concrete significance of *tao*.[17] As an achievement word, however, *shih* stresses not only the genuineness of commitment, but also its actualization. Thus Tai Chen quite properly explains *ch'eng* in terms of *shih* in the sense of fulfillment.[18]

14. When *chen* is rendered as 'truthfulness,' but qualified in terms of *kung, ching,* and *chin,* a Confucian would find agreeable Martin's notion of truthfulness: "Truthfulness is caring about truth and manifesting that care in belief, reasoning, speech, conduct and relationships. It should be distinguished from knowing particular truths (truth-awareness) and stating truths (truth-telling); we can be truthful while unintentionally believing and uttering a falsehood." Mike W. Martin, "Honesty with Oneself," in Mary I. Bookover, ed., *Rules, Ritual, and Responsibility: Essays Dedicated to Herbert Fingarette* (La Salle: Open Court, 1991), 116.

15. For example, Bodde's translation of *chen* and *shih* as "truthfulness and genuineness" as used by Fung in his comment on Hsün Tzu's notion of *ch'eng*. See Fung Yu-lan, *A History of Chinese Philosophy,* Vol. I, trans. Derk Bodde (Princeton: Princeton University Press, 1952), 293; and Knoblock's translation of *ch'eng* as "truthfulness" in his *Xunzi,* I:177. See *pu-kou p'ien,* 47. For translation of *shih* as "reality," see Chan, *Neo-Confucian Terms Explained,* 97.

16. It is interesting to note here that a genuine person may also be called 'a true person,' but in Chinese the latter is more commonly used in translation of *chen-jen* as used by Chuang Tzu in his depiction of the Taoist sage. The Confucian counterpart is Hsün Tzu's characterization of *chün-tzu* as one who cherishes *ch'üan* (completeness) and *ts'ui* (purity). See Burton Watson, trans., *The Complete Works of Chuang Tzu* (New York: Columbia University Press, 1968), chap. 6; *ch'üan-hsüeh p'ien,* 19; Knoblock, *Xunzi,* I:142. For a different conception of genuineness as "being authentic and exerting effort in resolving personal problems," see Martin, "Honesty with Oneself," 116, 118–19.

17. For a discussion of Chu Hsi's uses of *li* (reason, principle) as contrasted with Wang Yang-ming's, see Essay 9, Section III. For a more general discussion, see my "Reason and Principle in Chinese Philosophy: An Interpretation of *Li*," in *Blackwell Companion to World Philosophy,* ed. Eliot Deutsch and Ron Bontekoe (Oxford: Blackwell, 1997).

18. See Ann-ping Chin and Mansfield Freeman, trans., *Tai Chen on Mencius: Explo-*

Finally, *wu-wang* can be rendered as 'freedom from falsity,' but the emphasis lies not so much in the abstention from making false statements, which may indicate a disregard for truth, as in the manner in which utterances are made. *Wang* is a characteristic of speech or action that is uttered or performed in a cunning or crafty fashion with the intention to mislead or deceive others; such deceit is not easily detectable especially by trustful persons. Perhaps for this reason, Ch'en Ch'un, Chu Hsi's eminent disciple, remarks that "the word *ch'eng* is closely similar in meaning to *chung* (loyalty, doing one's best) and *hsin* (trustworthiness, faithfulness), but *chung* must be distinguished from *ch'eng*."[19] *Wu-wang* is perhaps best rendered as 'freedom from deliberate and cunning deception.' And when we add that such an ascription to persons also involves *chen* and *shih*, we have a Confucian conception of *ch'eng* as an ideal ethical condition of personhood.[20]

The Notion of Yi

As Ch'en Ch'un observes, the basic sense of *yi* pertains to thinking and estimation or consideration *(ssu-liang)* with respect to feelings. Their expression requires the direction of the mind, the master *(hsin)*.[21] *Yi* can also be used concurrently to refer to will *[chih]*.

Take for example that some thing is encountered. The master inside that controls is the mind *[hsin]*. As it is activated to become joy or anger, that is feeling. That which is inside that can be activated is nature. To operate the mind and

---

rations in Words and Meaning (New Haven: Yale University Press, 1990), 159; Tai Chen, *Meng Tzu tzu-i* in *Tai Chen wen-chi* (Taipei: Ho-lo, 1975), 122.

19. "*Ch'eng tzu yü chung hsin tzu chi hsiang chin.*" See *Pei-hsi hsien-sheng tzu-i*, 116. Cf. Chan, *Neo-Confucian Terms Explained*, 97.

20. It is interesting to note that the whole expression *chen-shih wu-wang* has a modern Chinese use. One recent dictionary offers the following translation: "A really honest heart; genuinely honest without any guile." If our exposition of *chen*, *shih*, and *wu-wang* is assumed as the basis for elaboration, this entry could be used as a convenient summary of our discussion of *ch'eng* thus far. Adopting this entry, however, leaves entirely open the question how the notion of honesty or self-honesty is to be analyzed. Martin's analysis may be a useful beginning, though a Confucian would be most reluctant to embrace his emphasis on candor, autonomy, and self-disclosure without proper qualification in terms of *li* (ritual). I shall say something about the Confucian notion of autonomy in connection with *tzu*-locutions. See Martin, "Honesty With Oneself," 116–21; and *wang* entry in S. T. Lee (comp.), *A New Complete Chinese-English Dictionary* (Hong Kong: China Publishers, 1980), 317.

21. This recalls Hsün Tzu's view: "The mind *[hsin]* is the ruler of the body and the master of its godlike intelligence *[shen-ming]*." See Burton Watson, trans., *Hsün Tzu: Basic Writings* (New York: Columbia University Press, 1963), 129; *chieh-pi p'ien*, 488. For a discussion of *shen-ming*, see Knoblok, *Xunzi*, I:252–55; and Edward J. Machle, "The Mind and the 'Shen-ming' in *Xunzi*," *Journal of Chinese Philosophy* 19 (1992). For further discussion of Hsün Tzu's conception of mind *(hsin)*, see my *Ethical Argumentation*, 15–16, 30–37, 138–45.

to consider to whom the joy or anger is to be directd is *yi*. When the mind is directed to the person who is the object of joy or anger, it is will *[chih]*.²²

In another use, *yi* refers to intention *(i-ssu)*. As Ch'en Ch'un points out, "People often talk about intention *[i-ssu]*. *Ssu* is to think. Contemplation, consideration, etc., all belong to *yi*."²³ In sum, Ch'en Ch'un offers us a way of explaining *yi* in three possibly interconnected uses. In the basic sense, *yi* is thoughtful consideration of the proper expression of feelings, involving an appraisive judgment which furnishes the object of will, and it is often accompanied by the intention to carry it out in actual performance.²⁴

Before turning to a discussion of *ch'eng-yi* and *tzu-ch'i* (self-deception) something must be said about the connection of *ch'eng-yi* to the Confucian ideal of ethical excellence *(chih-shan)* which is the ultimate objective of *Ta-hsüeh*. A question naturally arises, what is its subject matter? The formal answer must involve such familiar notions as *jen* (humanity, benevolence), *i* (rightness, righteousness), and *li* (ritual, rules of proper conduct). But notably, these are generic notions. There is a need to draw attention to the concrete setting in which these notions function in the lives of committed persons. Tai Chen rightly points out that there are two complementary ways of speaking about *ch'eng* as an effort to realize the highest good: "Speaking plainly *(chih-yen chih)*, we mean human relationships, affairs and activities of everyday life. Speaking more accurately *(ching-yen chih)*, we mean *jen*, *li*, and *i*."²⁵ The former provide the concrete context, and the latter the objectives of our endeavor.

Ch'eng-yi *and* Tzu-ch'i *(Self-Deception)*

Presupposing our explication of *ch'eng* in terms of *chen, shih, wu-wang* (truthfulness, genuineness, and freedom from falsity), and *yi* in terms of *ssu-liang* (thought), let me adopt for convenience of reference, Legge's rendering of *ch'eng-i* as "sincerity of thought," and attend to the commentary in *Ta-hsüeh* enjoining avoidance of self-deception in

---

22. This is Chan's translation with retention of character *yi* and substitution of "will" for "purpose" for the character *chih*. See Chan, *Neo-Confucian Terms Explained*, 67–68; *Pei-hsi hsien-sheng tzu-i*, 66. It must be noted that *chih* can be used in the sense of memory. As noted in *Shuo-wen*, "*yi* means *chih*," i.e., what the mind knows or is familiar with *(shih)*. However, *chih* as will does involves memory, as it presupposes that the person is aware *(shih)* of the object of his will. See Tuan Yü-ts'ai, *Shuo-wen chieh-tzu chu* (Shanghai: Ku-chi, 1981), 513.

23. Chan, *Neo-Confucian Terms Explained*, 68; *Pei-hsi hsien-sheng tzu-i*, 67.

24. Apart from these three uses, *yi* is sometimes used to refer to motive or to desire in Wang Yang-ming. See my *The Unity of Knowledge and Action*, 21–26.

25. *Tai Chen wen-chi*, 122. Cf. Chin and Freeman, *Tai Chen on Mencius*, 159.

making one's thought sincere *(ch'eng ch'i yi)*. The analysis proceeds along the lines of Legge's division of chapter 6 into four sections.[26] The text runs:

Section 1. What is meant by 'making the thoughts sincere' *[ch'eng ch'i yi]*? One must not allow self-deception *[mu tzu-ch'i yeh]*, as when we detest a bad smell or as when we love a beautiful color. This is what is called *tzu-ch'ien*. Therefore, the superior man *[chün-tzu]* will always be watchful when alone.[27]

The difficulty of interpreting this section lies in the character *ch'ien* in the binomial *tzu-ch'ien*. According to Chu Hsi, *ch'ien* should be read in terms of *ch'ieh*, which means *tsu* (satisfaction or contentment). Thus *tzu-ch'ien* means 'self-satisfaction.'[28] This interpretation is puzzling, for what is the connection between detesting a bad smell or loving a beautiful color and self-deception? While the passage implicitly refers to avowal of aversion, preference, or desire, such an avowal hardly constitutes self-satisfaction. An alternative reading without the substitution of *ch'ien* is more plausible. In *Shuo-wen*, *ch'ien* means *ching* (respect).[29] Accordingly, the binomial *tzu-ch'ien* can be rendered as 'self-respect.' In this sense, avowal of one's preference, desire or aversion is a matter of self-respect. Whether such preference can be satisfied remains a separate issue. Of course, their realization may well lead to self-contentment or self-satisfaction *(tzu-tsu)*. The imperative "One must not allow self-deception," as Chao points out, appertains to *chen* (truthfulness) and *shih* (genuineness).[30] If a person really detests a bad smell, he will not pretend to himself or others to the contrary. Hence, the attitude of a self-respecting person is such that he will not deceive himself and others.

While Chu Hsi's substitution of *tzu-ch'ieh* for *tzu-ch'ien* is arbitrary, his explanation of *tzu-ch'i* (self-deception) is informative. The self-deceiver is "one who knows that he must do good and avoid evil, but what emanates from his mind contains something that is not yet genuine *[shih]*." Recall that a person concerned with *shih* is a genuine person devoid of any hypocrisy or pretense. Chu Hsi's explanation of *tzu-ch'i* thus suggests that the victim of self-deception may not be aware

26. James Legge, *The Chinese Classics* (Hong Kong: Hong Kong University Press, 1960), 1:366–67. Because of easy access, I adopt with modification Wing-tsit Chan's translation in *A Source Book in Chinese Philosophy*, 89–90. For the most part, my modification of Chan's translation is influenced by Legge.

27. Both Legge and Chan follow Chu Hsi. Gardner renders *tzu-ch'ien* properly as "self-respect," but this seems to be based on Chao's critique of Chu Hsi, as we shall note shortly. See Chu Hsi, *Ssu-shu chi-chu*, 6; Gardner, *Chu Hsi and the Ta-hsüeh*, 106.

28. My remarks below are based mainly on Chao, *Ta-hsüeh yen-chiu*, esp., 294–95.

29. Tuan Yü-ts'ai, *Shuo-wen chieh-tzu chu*, 94.

30. Chao, *Ta-hsüeh yen-chiu*, 194.

that he is in that state of mind. Says Chu Hsi, "The person who desires self-cultivation [tzu-hsiu] knows quite well that if he is to do good and avoid evil, he must exert effort in order to prevent self-deception."[31] Elsewhere Chu Hsi remarks that self-deception may be explained in this way: "A person knows well that he must realize excellence or goodness [shan-hao], that he must do good. Yet within his heart and mind (hsin) he thinks that there is no urgency in doing so. This is self-deception [tzu-ch'i], this is mere pretension, lacking genuine conviction [hsü-wei pu-shih]."[32]

In Chu Hsi's view the self-deceiver lacks genuine ethical conviction. He persuades himself, as it were, to believe that there is no urgency in doing good and avoiding evil and he persuades himself precisely in order to evade his responsibility. There is an element of purposiveness (yi) involved, but the self-deceiver need not be aware of his state of mind.[33] The lack of genuine conviction (pu-shih) is contrary to the requirement of ch'eng. As ch'eng involves chen (truthfulness), the self-deceiver may also disregard relevant truth or evidence. When he thinks that there is no urgency for ethical performance, it is this yi (thought) that misleads him. Of course, Chu Hsi is assuming that he is committed to doing good and avoiding evil. Chu Hsi's account of self-deception suggests that it is a product of lack of discernment or insensitivity to the relevant context of action. As we shall see later, there is likely to be a hidden, operative motive such as selfish desires (ssu-yü).[34]

Because of the possibility of self-deception, the chün-tzu, concerned with personal cultivation, "will always be watchful when he is alone." For it is solitude that affords ample opportunity to examine his thoughts and feelings. As Chu Hsi says, "when a man is alone [tu], he himself knows what others do not know. Hence he must be careful in examining

31. Chu Hsi, Ssu-shu chi-chu, 6. Cf. Gardner, Chu Hsi, 105n.

32. Chu Hsi goes on to say that such a state of mind may be compared to a physical object that is "coated with silver on the outside, but with iron inside." See Chu Tzu yü-lei, edited by Li Ching-te (Taipei: Wen-chin, 1986), vol. III, chap. 16, p. 328; Gardner, Chu Hsi, 105n.

33. These remarks are influenced by Herbert Fingarette, Self-Deception (London: Routledge and Kegan Paul, 1969), 28–29. We may note here that focus on purposiveness does not imply that the act of self-deception is intentional. For arguments on the subintentional as opposed to the intentional account of self-deception, see Mark Johnston, "Self-Deception and the Nature of Mind," in Brian P. McLauglin and Amélie Oksenberg Rorty, eds., Perspectives on Self-Deception (Berkeley: University of California Press, 1988), 63–91.

34. The self-deceiver may be said to be a self-misleader. As Johnston points out, "To be deceived is sometimes just to be misled without being intentionally misled or lied to. The self-deceiver is a self-misleader. As a result of his own activity he gets into a state in which he is misled at least at the level of conscious belief." Johnston, "Self-Deception and the Nature of Mind," 65.

his incipient tendencies *[chi].*"³⁵ Since human relationships, as noted earlier, furnish the context of action, they are the principal topic of examination. Recall Tseng Tzu's remark: "Everyday I examine myself on three counts. In what I have undertaken on another's behalf, have I failed to do my best? In my dealings with my friends have I failed to be trustworthy? Have I passed on to others anything that I have not tried out myself?"³⁶ Ideally the result of self-examination is freedom from self-reproach.³⁷ But this requires the person to engage in reflection detached from preoccupation with personal gain, especially when it is contrary to *i* (rightness). As Confucius reminds his pupils, the *chuntzu* considers *i* to be of the highest importance.³⁸ Moreover, "the right sort of self-examination . . . consists not in idle brooding over oneself but in examining the effects one produces. Only when these effects are good, and when one's influence on others is good, will the contemplation of one's own life bring the self-satisfaction of knowing oneself to be free of mistakes."³⁹

The aim of self-examination is self-knowledge. At a minimum, self-knowledge consists in acknowledging one's knowledge and ignorance.

35. Chu Hsi, *Ssu-shu chi-chu,* 6, my translation. In private communication dated September 6, 1994, Kwong-loi Shun points to an alternative reading of *tu-che.* The *che* in *tu-che* "functions to nominalize *tu* as a subject of discussion (rather than referring to the person who is *tu*), and so I would translate his [Chu Hsi's] commentary as something like this: '. . . As for *tu,* it is the location not known to others but known only to oneself. . . . For there is that which others are not able to know but which one alone knows, and that is why one needs to be cautious here so as to carefully examine oneself.' On this reading, what Chu takes *tu* to refer to is the innermost part of the heart/mind where the incipient tendencies arise and to which only oneself has immediate access, and this reading of Chu Hsi will lead to the translation of *chün-tzu pi shen ch'i tu yeh* as 'The superior man will always be watchful over the innermost part of the heart/mind (where the incipient tendencies arise),' unlike the Legge and Chan translation." Shun points out that he can't at the moment adjudicate between the two readings, though Chu Hsi sometimes also uses *tu* in the sense of "one's being alone" as in his commentary on the beginning of the section 2 to *Ta Hsüeh.* However, in either reading, my emphasis on self-examination of one's incipient tendencies remains central to the avoidance of self-deception.

36. D. C. Lau, trans., *The Analects of Confucius [Ln Yü]* (New York: Penguin Books, 1979), 1:4.

37. This point seems implicit in Confucius's saying: "If, on examining himself, a man finds nothing to reproach himself for, what worries or fear can he have?" (Lau, *The Analects,* 12:4).

38. My reading is based on the original text of *The Analects,* 17:23, 4:16. See Mao Tzu-shiu, *Lun Yü chin-chu chin-i* (Taipei: Commercial Press, 1977), 281, 54.

39. This citation is Wilhelm's incisive comment on hexagram no. 20 *(kuan)* in the *I Ching.* See the *I Ching or Book of Changes,* translated by Cary F. Baynes from the German version of Richard Wilhelm (New York: Pantheon Books, 1950), I:90–91. I owe this citation to Martin, who draws attention to the affinity with his own view that "insight comes only as we look outward to the full social context that gives meaning to both our inner states and outward behavior." See Mike W. Martin, *Self-Deception and Morality* (Lawrence: University Press of Kansas, 1986), 136, 159n.55.

This is perhaps the force of Confucius's saying: "To say you know when you know, and to say you do not when you do not, that is knowledge [chih]."[40] For Hsün Tzu, the cultivated Confucian (Ju) will be concerned with knowledge in this sense so that "within they do not delude themselves [u], and without they do not deceive others."[41] This means that they will be true to themselves (chen) and avow their knowledge or ignorance to themselves and to others.[42] Self-deception in this light may thus be characterized as a sort of "evasion of full self-acknowledgement of some truth or of what one would view as truth if one were to confront an issue squarely."[43] Self-deception and deception of others is a sort of concealment.[44] Such concealment is unlikely to be successful in "the eyes of others." As the commentary continues:

Sections 2–3. When the small man is alone and at leisure, there is no limit to which he does not go in his evil thoughts. Only when he sees a superior man [chün-tzu] does he then disguise himself, concealing his evil thoughts and displaying his goodness. But what is the use? For other people see him as if they see his lungs and livers. This is what is meant by the saying that what is true in a man's heart will be shown in outward appearance. Therefore the superior man must be watchful when he is alone. Tseng Tzu said, "What ten eyes are beholding and what ten hands are pointing to—isn't it frightening?"

The metaphor of sight is a familiar one in Western philosophy.[45] But as Fingarette justly points out, in the Analects, the emphasis is on shame

40. Analects, 12:17. Cf. Roger Ames, "Reflections on the Confucian Self," in Bookover, Rules, Rituals and Responsibility, 111.

41. Ju-hsiao p'ien, 149; Knoblock, Xunzi, II:80. An alternative to the first part of Knoblock's translation is "within they have no cause for self-reproach," since u literally means "to accuse falsely," thus the alternative translation of nei pu tzu-i u. In either case, self-deception or self-delusion is implied. See ju-hsiao p'ien, 151n.

42. Indeed, chih, apart from knowledge, is sometimes used in the sense of acknowledgment, especially in Wang Yang-ming's writings. For an examination of a related use of chih in the sense of realization in the Analects, see David L. Hall and Roger T. Ames, Thinking Through Confucius (Albany: State University of New York Press, 1987); for Wang Yang-ming, see my The Unity of Knowledge and Action, chap. 1.

43. Martin, Self-Deception and Morality, 13.

44. In Shuo-wen, ch'i (deception) means cha. To my knowledge the earliest definition of cha is ni-hsing (concealing conduct). See Tuan Yü-ts'ai, Shuo-wen chieh-tzu chu, 414; and hsiu-shen p'ien, 26; or Knoblock, Xunzi, I:153.

45. For some samples in Greek thought, see John King-Farlow and Richard Bosley, "Self-Formation and the Mean (Programmatic Remarks on Self-Deception)," in Mike W. Martin, ed., Self-Deception and Self-Understanding (Lawrence: University Press of Kansas, 1985), 199–202. The closing section of this essay contains an interesting dialogue between Aristotle and Confucius, but unfortunately, no specific textual reference is given. This presents a difficulty in locating their sources of interpretation, especially Lun Yü and Chung Yung (ibid., 215–19). We may note also the use of the sight metaphor in Butler and Kant. See "Upon Self-Deceit" in The Works of Joseph Butler, ed. Samuel Halifax (Oxford: Oxford University Press, 1850), 117, 124; Immanuel Kant, The Doctrine of Virtue, translated by Mary J. Gregor (New York: Harper Torchbooks, 1964), 92.

rather than guilt. Fingarette plausibly maintains that "there is developed in the *Analects* no notion of guilt and repentance as a moral response to one's wrongdoing."⁴⁶ But his thesis on the absence of a developed notion of choice in the *Analects* cannot be generalized to apply to both classical and Neo-Confucianism, for the notion *ch'üan* ("weighing of circumstances or alternatives") is explicit in Mencius and Hsün Tzu, as well as Chu Hsi.⁴⁷ Thus the classical Confucian concern with shame *(ch'ih, ju)* is not just a matter of disgrace, that is, the loss of honor in the "eyes of others." As Hsün Tzu insists, there is a distinction between intrinsic or just shame *(i-ju)* and circumstantial shame *(shih-ju)*, and between intrinsic honor *(i-jung)* and circumstantial honor *(shih-jung)*. A *chün-tzu* may have circumstantial shame, but not intrinsic shame, for the former is a matter of circumstance beyond one's power or control, while the latter has its source within oneself.⁴⁸ At any rate, self-deception is analogous to "self-presentation." The deception cannot succeed, "for other people will see him as if they see his lungs and livers" and "this is what is meant by saying that what is true *[ch'eng]* in a man's heart *[hsin]* will be shown in outward appearance." As we shall see later, concealing one's thought and conduct before oneself or others is an example of *pi* (obscuration, blindness).

The commentary continues:

Section 4. Wealth makes a house shining and virtue *[te]* makes a person shining. The mind is broad and the body at ease. Therefore, the *chün-tzu* always makes his thought or will sincere *[ch'eng ch'i yi]*.

The analogy of *te* (virtue) with wealth is instructive, for *te* is a sort of power or force. Thus a *chün-tzu* has the power or capacity to influence

46. Herbert Fingarette, *Confucius: The Secular as Sacred* (New York: Harper Torchbooks, 1972), 28ff.

47. See A. C. Graham, *Disputers of the Tao: Philosophical Argument in Ancient China* (LaSalle: Open Court, 1989), 27, 29, 252. For Mencius and Chu Hsi on *ch'üan* (weighing of circumstance), see my *Dimensions of Moral Creativity: Paradigms, Principles and Ideals* (University Park: Pennsylvania State University Press, 1978), 72–76; and Essay 12. For Hsün Tzu, see my "The Possibility of Ethical Knowledge: Reflections on a Theme in the *Hsün Tzu*," in Hans Lenk and Gregor Paul, eds., *Epistemological Questions in Ancient Chinese Philosophy* (Albany: State University of New York Press, 1993).

48. See *cheng-lun p'ien*, 410–11; or Homer H. Dubs, trans., *The Works of Hsüntze* (Taipei: Ch'eng-wen, 1966), 208–9. It is often said that modern Chinese are concerned with "face." But as Hu points out, there is a distinction between *mien-tzu* and *lien*. The former pertains to social standing and does not necessarily have moral implications. The latter implies satisfaction of the moral standards of the society. A person concerned with *lien* is one who possesses a sense of decency and regard for moral virtues. This distinction seems to reflect Hsün Tzu's distinction between intrinsic and circumstantial honor. See Hsien Chin Hu, "The Chinese Concepts of 'Face'," *American Anthropologist*, N.S., 46 (1944): 45–64. Cf. Ames, "Reflections on the Confucian Self," 111.

the course of human affairs. As Confucius once remarked, "Virtue *[te]* never stands alone. It is bound to have neighbors;" "The virtue of *chün-tzu* is like the wind. . . . Let the wind blow over the grass and it is sure to bend."[49] So also, no matter how a person conceals his wealth before others, it is likely evident to them. It is possible for a self-deceiver concerned with personal cultivation, and in the course of time preoccupied with earnest self-examination, to experience self-disclosure and accordingly to disavow self-deception.[50]

The preceding exposition of the commentary in *Ta-hsüeh*, provides, I hope, a coherent Confucian perspective on self-deception. Self-deception must be avoided because it undermines the task of personal cultivation *(hsiu-shen)*, in particular, the task of making one's thoughts sincere *(ch'eng-yi)*. Our discussion provides a picture of a person of ethical integrity or self-respect *(tzu-ch'ien)*, who engages in constant self-examination in order to attain *ch'eng*, involving *chen* (truthfulness), *shih* (genuineness), and *wu-wang* (freedom from falsity). However, self-examination cannot be carried out without some understanding of the potential sources of self-deception.

II

Diagnosis of Self-Deception

Given its primarily ethical orientation, the Confucian interest in self-deception lies in its use as an interpretive and diagnostic concept.[51] Chu Hsi's explanation of the binomial *tzu-ch'i* (self-deception), for example, is a textual interpretation.[52] Moreover, the interpretation is proffered in part as a diagnosis of failure to attain *ch'eng-yi*. For diagnosing the sources of self-deception I shall attend to Hsün Tzu's conception of *pi*.[53] Let me briefly note the background of Hsün Tzu's concern with *pi*.

49. Lau, *The Analects of Confucius*, 4:25; and 12:19.

50. Cf. Fingarette: "Self-deception is resolved when the disavowed engagement of the individual is avowed." Fingarette, *Self-Deception*, 110.

51. Cf. "the concept of self-deception is more interpretive and diagnostic than predictive." Robert Audi, "Self-Deception and Rationality," in Martin, ed., *Self-Deception and Self-Understanding*, 191. For a discussion of closely related use of 'self' as a diagnostic term, see Stephen Toulmin, "Self-Knowledge and Knowledge of the 'Self,'" in Theodore Mischel, ed., *The Self: Psychological and Philosophical Issues* (Oxford: Blackwell, 1977): 291–317.

52. For an instructive discussion of Chu Hsi's hermeneutical method, see Yü Ying-shih, "Morality and Knowledge in Chu Hsi's Philosophical System," in Wing-tsit Chan, ed., *Chu Hsi and Neo-Confucianism* (Honolulu: University of Hawaii Press, 1986), 228–54.

53. Below I confine my exposition to the relevance of *pi* and its attendant *huo*. For an extensive discussion of the diagnosis of erroneous ethical beliefs see my *Ethical Argumentation*, chap. 4.

For Hsün Tzu, *tao* is a holistic ideal of the good human life, comprising *li, i,* and *jen* as basic interdependent foci of ethical interest. The failure to comprehend the *tao* is a result of *pi*—a common human liability. Philosophers are not excepted. They err not so much because of mistaken doctrines, but because their doctrines represent only partial views of the whole. In his words, "some of what they advocate has a rational basis enough to deceive *[ch'i]* and mislead *[huo]* the masses."[54] Yang Liang's gloss on *pi* is this: "The man beset by *pi* is one who is unable to see through things clearly. His view is impeded by one corner as if there were things that hindered his vision."[55]

A *pi*, literally, is 'a screen, shelter, or cover.' *Pi* is Hsün Tzu's metaphor for an obscuration of the mind. In this condition the mind is obstructed in its proper functioning, e.g., thinking, remembering, imagining, and judging. In short, a *pi* is any sort of factor that obstructs the mind's cognitive task. When the mind is in the state of *pi*, reason is, so to speak, not operating properly. The opposite of *pi* is clarity of mind. Thus Hsün Tzu says, "If you guide it [the mind] with reason *[li]*, nourish it with clarity, and do not allow external objects to unbalance it, then it will be capable of determining right and wrong and of resolving doubts."[56] In this light, *pi* can also be rendered as 'blindness.' As Watson reminds us, Hsün Tzu's use of *pi* "denotes here [in *chieh-pi p'ien*] a clouding or darkening of the faculties or the understanding, and Hsün Tzu plays on the image of light and darkness throughout the chapter."[57]

Humans beset by *pi* may be said to be in the state of *huo* (delusion).[58]

54. Knoblock, *Xunzi*, I:233ff; *fei shih-erh tzu p'ien*, 94. Note, however, the distinction between 'rational' and 'reasonableness.' See my *The Unity of Knowledge and Action*, chap. 4. For the notion of partial grasp of a whole, see *t'ien-lun p'ien*, 381; *chieh-pi p'ien*, 472, 478; Watson, *Hsün Tzu*, 87–88, 121, 126.

55. Yang Liang, *Hsün Tzu, ssu-pu pi-yao* edition (Taipei: Chung-hua, 1976), chap. 15:1a. For similar use of *pi*, see *Analects*, 17:8.

56. Watson, *Hsün Tzu*, 131; *chieh-pi p'ien*, 490. These remarks on *pi* are based on *Ethical Argumentation*, 138–45.

57. Watson, *Hsün Tzu*, 121n. Thus Knoblock renders *chieh-pi p'ien* as "Dispelling Blindness" (Knoblock, *Xunzi*, II:111). I do not have on hand his translation in Volume III. Consistent with the concern with self-deception, a Confucian philosopher, I believe, can appreciate the view of self-deception as a form of "blindness to self." See David W. Hamlyn, "Self-Knowledge," in Mischel, ed., *The Self: Psychological and Philosophical Issues*, 179–80.

58. In *Shuo-wen, huo* means *luan* and *luan* means "not in order *(pu-chih yeh)*; when something is not in order, one then desires to put it into order." In other words, it is desirable to put into order what is in the state of disorder, chaos, or confusion. In the case of a mental state, we can properly construe *huo* as a state of delusion. Ascription of delusion, as Austin remarks, suggests that "something is really wrong, and what's more, wrong with the person who has them." See Tuan Yü-ts'ai, *Shuo-wen chieh-tzu chu*, 511, 740; J. L. Austin, *Sense and Sensibilia* (Oxford: Clarendon Press, 1962), 21–22.

For example, "A drunken man will try to leap a ditch a hundred paces wide as though it were a narrow gutter or stoop to go through a city gate as though it were a low doorway. This is because the wine has disordered his spirits."[59] In *huo* a person's mind is misled or misguided in his belief or judgment.[60] *Huo* is a condition in which the person is responsible for assenting to misleading guidance—a failure in the exercise of reasonable judgment in accord with his sense of *i* (rightness). A person in *huo* is a self-deceiver. The potential sources of *pi* may thus be construed as sources of self-deception.

According to *Hsün Tzu*, whenever we make distinctions among things, our minds are likely to be obscured *(pi)* by these distinctions. "This is a common affliction *[kung-huan]* of our ways of thinking."[61] For Hsün Tzu, all distinctions owe their origin to comparison and analogy of different kinds of things. They are made in accordance with our purposes, and thus are relative to the context of thought and discourse. Distinctions, while useful, are not dichotomies. In the case of *pi*, the person attends exclusively to the significance of one item without considering the significance of the other. Common people, as well as philosophers, are prone to exaggerate. For example, Mo Tzu is beset by *pi* in his exclusive attention to utility without recognizing the importance of culture *(wen)*; Chuang Tzu is beset by *pi* in his preoccupation with Heaven without recognizing the importance of human beings.[62] For Hsün Tzu, the common sources of *pi* are desire and aversion *(yü-wu)*, distance and nearness *(yüan-chin)*, breadth and shallowness of knowledge *(po-ch'ien)*, past and present *(ku-chin)*.[63] I shall discuss these sources of *pi* in terms of desires and aversions, or positive and negative desires proceeding on the assumption that in all cases of *pi*, there is present a desire as a motive.[64]

59. Watson, *Hsün Tzu*, 134; *chieh-pi p'ien*, 495. This is one of a few examples of perceptual delusions. For discussion of the role of wise and informed deliberation *(chih-lü)* with respect to both perceptual and ethical examples, see my "The Possibility of Ethical Knowledge," Part II.
60. For this use of *huo*, see also *Analects*, 12:10, 12:21, but note that there *huo* is part of the binomial *pien-huo* (misguided judgment). In the dialogue, it has no special connection with *li* (ritual) as Fingarette claims in his *Confucius: The Secular as Sacred*, 22–23.
61. *Chieh-pi p'ien*, 474, my translation. Cf. Watson, *Hsün Tzu*, 122; Dubs, *Hsüntze*, 260. Hereafter cited as Watson and Dubs.
62. For Hsün Tzu, only Confucius is free from *pi* as he embodied *jen* and wisdom, for his school alone has all-around understanding of *tao (chou-tao)*. See *chieh-pi p'ien*, 478, 481n. Cf. Dubs, *The Works of Hsüntze*, 265; Watson, *Hsün Tzu*, 126.
63. *Chieh-pi p'ien*, 474. Cf. Watson, 122; Dubs, 260.
64. This proceeding is in part justified in terms of Hsün Tzu's conception of human nature as a basic motivational structure consisting of feelings and desires. Desires are responses to feelings. For further discussion, see my "The Conceptual Aspect of Hsün Tzu's Philosophy of Human Nature," *Philosophy East and West* 27, no. 4 (1977): 373–89.

Since *pi* is contrary to reason *(li)*, it may be regarded as a state of irrational preoccupation with one side of a distinction at the expense of careful consideration of the other. Well aware of the distinction between desire and aversion, a person may pursue his current desire without attending to its possible unwanted consequences. That person's mind may be said to be in the state of *pi*. More generally, humans suffer because of their concern for acquisition of benefit and for the avoidance of harm. When they see something beneficial, they do not consider carefully whether it may lead to harmful consequences.[65] However, even if consequences are considered, the person may fail to attend to distant consequences *(yüan)* and simply focus upon near or immediate ones *(chin)*, well aware of the relevance of the distinction at issue. Conversely, a person may be preoccupied with distant consequences and not attend to immediate ones that may well bring disaster. Hsün Tzu cites examples of ancient rulers preoccupied with their concubines and ancient subjects preoccupied with the acquisition of power. Thus "their minds became deluded *[huo]* and their actions were thrown into confusion."[66] Similarly on matters of life and death, a person may be victim of *pi* because of his inordinate attention to one without regard to the other. So also as regards the present and past, and the breadth and shallowness of knowledge.

Hsün Tzu's discussion of *pi* does not provide us any systematic scheme for diagnosis of self-deception. However, it does suggest that our desires are the main motivating factors and that they cannot be reduced to just one factor such as selfish desires—a prominent view in Neo-Confucianism. Wang Yang-ming, for instance, thinks that selfish desires alone are the obscuring factor *(pi)* that accounts for moral failure, but the mind may be obscured *(pi)* in many ways.[67] We may expect that in the case of self-deception, such obscurations may be reflected in a variety of patterns such as willful ignorance, emotional detachment, pretentiousness, and rationalization.[68] Regarding the question of remedy, Hsün Tzu would recommend that the person concerned with self-cultivation be engaged in wise and informed deliberation *(chih-lü)*. In such deliberation, the person weighs all relevant considerations so as to arrive at a unified preference in the light of *tao*. This is a topic I examined elsewhere.[69]

65. See *pu-kou p'ien*, 53; Knoblock, *Xunzi*, I:180.
66. Translation based on Watson, 122 and Dubs, 260. See *chieh-pi p'ien*, 472.
67. See Conclusion of Essay 9.
68. See Martin, *Self-Deception and Morality*, 6–11.
69. See Part II of my "Possibility of Ethical Knowledge."

The Confucian Notion of the Self

Recently some scholars have proposed different conceptions of the self for Confucian ethics. I take these proposals as primarily constructive interpretations of an aspect of classics such as *The Analects (Lun Yü)* and *The Doctrine of the Mean (Chung Yung).*[70] Before expressing my critical appreciation of these efforts, I will consider the more general question whether there is a Confucian notion of the self in the classics.

Following Toulmin, we may distinguish three different uses of 'self' in English: (1) the use in everyday reflexive idioms as a prefix or postfix, i.e., 'self-' and '-self'; (2) the use in speculative psychology as "the name of a hypothetical entity, or intervening explanatory variable"; and (3) the diagnostic use in "clinical psychotherapy and comparable, nonmedical modes of psychological description."[71] Toulmin goes on to show how a careful extension of the reflexive use "provides grounding for, and in due course develops into, the fully-fledged terminology of the 'self,' as it figures in clinical theory, psychiatric diagnoses and/or psychoanalytic interpretation."[72]

Toulmin's threefold distinction of the uses of 'self' provides a useful approach to our question of the Confucian notion of the self. It is uncontroversial to note that one would search in vain for a theoretical use of 'self' in Confucian ethics. Earlier I suggested that the binomial *tzu-ch'i* (self-deception) is best construed as a diagnostic term. In light of Toulmin's essay, our question is perhaps best approached by examining reflexive binomials such as *tzu*-locutions, then exploring the possibility of the diagnostic use of some of these locutions, not as a means for developing a philosophical, psychological or clinical theory, but as a means of articulating an aspect of personal cultivation, especially in attaining the sincerity of thought *(ch'eng-yi)*. My remarks here, of course, amount to no more than a suggestion for inquiry.

In *Lun Yü*, for example, we find *tzu-hsing* (examine oneself), *tzu-sung* (reproach oneself), and *tzu-ju* (disgrace oneself).[73] In *Meng Tzu* we find

---

70. Herbert Fingarette, "The Problem of the Self in the *Analects*," *Philosophy East and West* 29, no. 2 (1979): 129–40; Roger T. Ames, "Reflections on the Confucian Self: A Response to Fingarette," in Bookover, ed., *Rules, Rituals and Responsibility*, 103–14; Tu Wei-ming, *Centrality and Commonality: An Essay on Chung Yung* (Honolulu: University Press of Hawaii, 1976); or the revised and expanded edition entitled *Centrality and Commonality: An Essay on Confucian Religiousness* (Albany: State University of New York Press, 1989). My remarks below refer to this revised edition. Note that in a couple of places I have also made use of a distinction between actual and ideal self and DeWitt H. Parker's distinction between matrix and focal self in discussing the Confucian notion of *tao*. See *The Unity of Knowledge and Action*, 57; and Essay 4.
71. Toulmin, "Self-Knowledge and Knowledge of the 'Self'," 291.
72. Ibid., 303f.
73. *Lun Yü*, 4:17, 5:27, 19:17, respectively. *Tzu-hsing* also occurs in Hsün Tzu's *hsiu-*

tzu-pao (do violence to oneself), *tzu-yang* (nourish oneself), and *tzu-te* (realize *[tao]* in oneself);[74] and in *Hsün Tzu,* apart from *tzu-hsing,* we find *tzu-ts'un* (preserve [goodness] in oneself), *tzu-chih* (know oneself).[75] In *Hsün Tzu,* one passage on mind *(hsin)* as "the ruler of the body" contains a series of six different *tzu*-locutions: *tzu-chin, tzu-shih, tzu-to, tzu-ch'ü, tzu-hsing,* and *tzu-chih,* roughly "the mind itself issues its own prohibitions and commands, makes its own decision and choices, initiates its own action and omission."[76] Except for Hsün Tzu's series of *tzu*-locutions in one passage, all the other *tzu*-locutions, even in Modern Chinese, are part of the language of practical, reflexive conduct. In Section I, we have drawn attention to *tzu-ch'i* (self-deception) and to the necessity of avoiding it in order to attain *tzu-ch'ien* (self-respect). Our earlier suggestion of *tzu-ch'i* as a diagnostic term perhaps can be applied to most of the other *tzu*-locutions with primary focus on *tzu-hsing* (self-examination) as the general context for constructive interpretation. The singular exception is *tzu-te,* but *tzu-te* (realize *[tao]* in oneself) for some Chinese thinkers, for example, Ch'en Pai-sha, has a special significance, influenced by Mencius and Ch'eng Hao. And quite apart from the use of *tzu-te,* Wang Yang-ming's insistence on *jen* or *tao* as a matter of *t'i-jen* (personal realization) reflects also these influences.[77]

As self-examination *(tzu-hsing)* is the keynote of the Confucian doctrine of personal cultivation *(hsiu-shen,* the other *tzu*-locutions may be construed as having primarily a diagnostic use; they call attention to the need of the learners of *tao* to preserve *(tzu-ts'un)* and nourish *(tzu-yang)* their ethical dispositions against the onset of wayward tendencies or proclivities that impede the pursuit of *tao,* in particular, those that do violence *(tzu-pao)* and bring disgrace to themselves *(tzu-ju).* Of especial importance in self-examination is a careful review of one's conduct in order to see whether one has done anything that merits self-reproach *(tzu-sung).* As Mencius says, "A *chün-tzu* differs from other men because he examines his heart *[hsin].* He examines his heart by means of *jen* and *li.*"[78] Suppose he is treated by someone in an outra-

---

shen p'ien, 23 and *wang-pa p'ien,* 251. In *Meng Tzu, tzu-fan* (to look within, to turn within and examine oneself) seems to be functionally equivalent to *tzu-hsing.* See *Meng Tzu,* 2A:2; 4B:28.

74. *Meng Tzu,* 4A:10, 3A:2, and 3A:4, 4B:14, respectively.

75. See *hsiu-shen p'ien,* 23; *jung-ju p'ien,* 59, respectively.

76. *Chieh-pi p'ien,* 488. The translation is based on Dubs, 269. For the problem of autonomy of mind in Hsün Tzu, see my *Ethical Argumentation,* 138–42.

77. See Paul Yung-ming Jiang, *The Search for Mind: Ch'en Pai-sha, Philosopher-Poet* (Singapore: Singapore University Press, 1980), esp. chap. 9. For Wang Yang-ming, see Tu Wei-ming, *Neo-Confucian Thought in Action: Wang Yang-ming's Youth* (1472–1529) (Berkeley: University of California Press, 1976), and Essay 9.

78. *Meng Tzu,* 4B:28. My translation here reads *ts'un* as *cha* (examine) in accordance

geous manner. He will turn around and examine himself *(tzu-fan)*, and say to himself "I must be lacking in *jen* and *li*, or how could such a thing happen to me?" When such a self-examination discloses that he has done nothing contrary to *jen* and *li*, and yet the outrageous treatment continues, he will say to himself "I must have failed to do my best for him."[79] Yet the possibility of others' reproach or the concern with one's "face" *(mien-tzu)* is also a proper subject of self-examination.[80] Ideally, intrinsic honor coincides with circumstantial honor (Section I).[81] In the end, if frequent self-examination is successful, one can then claim to have a modicum of self-knowledge *(tzu-chih)*. One hopes the process of self-examination in conjunction with the constant practice of *jen*, *li*, and *i* will culminate in personal attainment or realization of *tao (tzu-te)*.[82]

The foregoing suggestion on the possible connection between the reflexive and diagnostic uses of *tzu*-locutions is not an adequate response to the question of the Confucian notion of the self. For it is a legitimate question for a Confucian philosopher today whether he can find a use of 'self' other than as "a name of a hypothetical entity" in the construction of psychological or philosophical theory. Moreover, the suggestion does not seem to accommodate the insights into the use of 'self' in some writings of Tu Wei-ming, Fingarette, and Ames. This caveat, thus, is in order: My thesis is not intended as a solution to the philosophical problem of the self, say, as an alternative to the theses of an enduring self, no-self, and a constructed self.[83]

---

with Chiao Hsün's gloss. See Shih Tz'u-yün, *Meng Tzu chin-chu chin-i* (Taipei: Commercial Press, 1978), 233n.

79. *Meng Tzu*, 4B:28. The translation is based on D. C. Lau, trans., *Mencius* (Middlesex: Penguin Books, 1970), 134.

80. See n. 48 above.

81. For the Confucian, concern for one's name *(ming)* or reputation is always a reasonable concern except in the case of circumstantial shame *(shih-ju)*, i.e., when one is unjustly placed in the shameful situation. In this way, he may concur with Hume's insightful remark on the love of fame: "By our continual and earnest pursuit of a character, a name, a reputation in the world, we bring our own deportment and character frequently in review and consider how they appear in the eyes of those who approach and regard us. This constant habit of surveying ourselves, as it were, in reflection, keeps alive all the sentiments of right and wrong, and begets in noble natures a certain reverence for themselves as well as others, which is the surest guardian of every virtue." David Hume, *An Inquiry Concerning the Principles of Morals* (Indianapolis: Bobbs-Merrill, 1957), 96.

82. It is presumed that the learner of *tao*, pursuing sagehood, has at least some knowledge and understanding of ancient classics, say, the Four Books *(Lün Yü, Ta-hsüeh, Chung Yung,* and *Meng Tzu)*. Ideally the study of the classics aims at a comprehensive understanding of the concrete significance of *tao* as a thread that runs through the classics *(kuan-t'ung ching hsüeh)*. Having embodied the highest *ch'eng*, such a sage would "assist in the transforming and nourishing process of Heaven and Earth," thus forming "a trinity with Heaven and Earth." *Chung Yung*, sec. 22. Translation adapted from Chan, *A Source Book in Chinese Philosophy*, 108.

83. These are terms used by Kupperman. I think that with proper qualification, a

A Confucian today may proffer a nominal use of 'self' by adapting Hsün Tzu's distinction between generic *(kung-ming)* and specific terms *(pieh-ming).*[84] Suppose we regard 'self' as a generic term *(kung-ming).* Such a term has a proper use in formal, abstract, theoretical discourse. The use of 'self' as a generic term in the title of Fingarette's essay, "The Problem of the Self in the *Analects*" is quite intelligible. However, the question naturally arises, how is such a use to be rendered intelligible in expounding some passages in the *Analects (Lun Yü)?* This question can be handled by using specific terms such as those of *tzu*-locutions we have considered. Put differently, the generic term 'self' has its "cash value" in specific terms *(pieh-ming),* which function as possible specifications of the concrete significance of 'self' as a general term. To translate *tzu-hsing* in Tseng Tzu's remark cited earlier as "I examine my self," is a mistake,[85] for *tzu-hsing* is a binomial, reflexive idiom, as Fingarette later came to realize in his response to Ames's critique. This acknowledgment focuses on the use of the reflexive idiom in translating *tzu-hsing.*[86] Of course, specific terms *(pieh-ming),* such as *tzu-sung* (self-reproach), also may need further specification—for example, in answer to the question "what is the object or content of self-reproach?" in the context of practical discourse. We must note also that apart from *tzu*-locutions, such specific terms as *shen* (in one's own person) or *chi* as contrasted with *jen* (distinguishing oneself from others) can also function as specific terms for 'self' as a generic term.[87] The variability and degree of specification of 'self' as a generic term depend on the purpose and context of practical occasion.

Equipped with 'self' as a generic term, we can appreciate Tu Weiming's claim that in Confucian ethics the conception of the self is "a center of relationships." In his essay on *Chung Yung,* Tu declares: "Since a person in the Confucian tradition is always conceived of as a center

Confucian would find congenial the view of the constructed self favored by Kupperman, especially as he thinks that 'self' in this sense is virtually equivalent to 'character' emphasizing "matters of importance." See Joel Kupperman, *Character* (New York: Oxford University Press, 1991), chap. 1, esp. 44.

84. This distinction is used extensively in my *Ethical Argumentation* (see Index on terms), but elaborated in my "The Problem of Conceptual Unity in Hsün Tzu and Li Kou's Solution," *Philosophy East and West* 39, no. 2 (1989): 122–25.

85. See Fingarette, "The Problem of the Self in the *Analects*," 132.

86. It is puzzling that Fingarette focuses on the use of reflexive idioms in European languages, since reflexive idioms are quite familiar in colloquial English. See Fingarette, "Comment and Response," in Bookover, *Rules, Rituals and Responsibility,* 198–99.

87. Unless I am mistaken, these terms are not translatable as 'self,' though in translation, probably for economy, one is prone to use it. I notice this, for example, in Knoblok's excellent work, *Xunzi,* I, 136, 143, 154, 166. Cf. Fingarette, "The Problem of the Self in the *Analects*," 131–35. Note that my critical remarks of Fingarette's essay are not meant as a general evaluation of the insights and issues he raised.

of relationships, the more one penetrates into one's *inner self*, the more one will be capable of realizing the true nature of one's human relatedness." Alternatively, "as the Confucians argue, it is more difficult to imagine ourselves as isolable individuals than as centers of relationships constantly interacting with one another in a dynamic network of human relatedness."[88] As noted earlier (Section I), human relationships *(lun)* comprise the concrete setting for conduct in accord with *jen*, *li*, and *i*. Tu's metaphor of a dynamic network quite rightly points to the complex, indeterminate or changing character of the interconnection of varieties of role-playing in an individual human life. The individual concerned with self-cultivation *(hsiu-shen)* is, from his own standpoint, a center, the focal point around which interpersonal relationships revolve. The metaphor of center may be misleading in suggesting a self-centered or self-serving preoccupation, a potential source of *pi*. Moreover, Tu's use of "inner self" is best construed as a generic term subject to specification, for example, by the reflexive *tzu*-locutions, rather than as a name of an abstract entity—a reification of concrete reflexive *tzu*-locutions in practical Confucian discourse. But Tu seems to be aware of the possible misleading use of 'self' when he shifts to the term 'true self' as a convenient way of referring to "the Confucian *idea of the self* in terms such as self-cultivation *[hsiu-shen* or *hsiu-chi]*, in contrast to the idea of the 'private ego' in such terms as self-centeredness *[ssu]*."[89] But the retention of an idea of the self has force only if such an idea has implicit reference to reflexive *tzu*-locutions; otherwise the expression would be entirely free-standing without any concrete anchorage.

In his critique of Fingarette's essay on the self, Ames is implicitly committed to a process view of the self as contrasted with the substantive view; Ames's view is much reminiscent of Mead's thesis that "the self is not so much a substance as a process in which the conversation of gestures has been internalized within an organic form."[90] Indeed, Ames cites a passage from Mead on the relationship between the 'I' and the 'me' to elucidate of his thesis that "the conception of self in Confucius is dynamic as a complex of social roles." Ames points out

88. Tu Wei-ming, *Centrality and Commonality: An Essay on Religiousness*, 27, 95, my emphasis.

89. Ibid., 108, my emphasis. These remarks are from Tu's essay "On Confucian Religiousness" added to the second edition (1989) of his *Centrality and Commonality* (1976). Note the affinity of my use of "ideal and actual self" (*The Unity of Knowledge and Action*, 57), though my use has no special connection with the contrast of 'the self' with 'private ego.'

90. George H. Mead, *Mind, Self and Society* (Chicago: University of Chicago Press, 1934), 178.

that Fingarette fails to make the distinction between "autonomous individual and unique individual," that is, the distinction between individual as a member of a class of human beings and as "one-of-a-kind," like John Turner's *Seastorm*. Ames maintains that *jen*, "a unique person-specific goal can also be taken as a term denoting 'self.'" For Ames, "given that *jen* is always a unique and particular achievement, it can only refer to a self. . . . 'Self' as Confucius defines it is irreducibly interpersonal. It is not the case that *jen* refers to 'other' in contradistinction to 'self.'"[91] Before attending to Ames's insights, we must note again that, like Tu and Fingarette, Ames pays no attention to the crucial role of reflexive *tzu*-locutions in providing for his use of 'self' as a generic term. Also he gives no evidence for his claim that Confucius defines 'self' as "irreducibly interpersonal," though it is a plausible, interpretive claim acceptable to modern Confucians. However, the plausibility of this claim presupposes that, for the Confucian, the habitat of interpersonal relationships *(lun)* is a community with a traditions such as *li* (ritual) that renders intelligible any individual claim for being a distinct, unique individual. Ames rightly maintains that *jen* is a "unique and particular achievement," since *jen* is more an ideal theme, a standard of inspiration, than an ideal norm. The realization of *jen* will thus be manifested in an individual's style or manner of performance and/or style of life.[92] As an ideal theme, *jen* is a quasi-aesthetic vision that provides a point of orientation. It is expected that the achievement of *jen* as an ideal theme will be a polymorphous exemplification, especially in the lives of paradigmatic individuals.[93] As for Ames's insightful suggestion on the relevance of Mead to the Confucian notion of the self, I think it is a worthwhile project for further inquiry by anyone interested in comparative Chinese and Western ethics.[94]

The foregoing reflections on the ethical aspect of self-deception focus mainly on the Confucian conception of self-deception, its context and background, as well as the possibility of diagnosis and remedy. In

91. Ames, "Reflections on the Confucian Self," 105–8. Cf. my "Confucian Vision and the Human Community," *Journal of Chinese Philosophy* 11, no. 3 (1984): 226–38.
92. See my *Dimensions of Moral Creativity*, chaps. 7–8.
93. Ibid., 138–39.
94. These remarks are compatible with Ames's recent field-focus view of the self, and one can learn much from his incisive critique of four models of self: "the hollow man," "autonomous individuality," "the organic self," and "part of the whole self," though Ames would agree that the "autonomous individuality" model may well be one way to deal with Hsün Tzu's conception of the person's mind as autonomous in exercising the freedom of choice as indicated in the series of *tzu*-locutions (note 76 above). See Ames, "The Focus-Field Self in Classical Confucianism," in *Self as Person in Asian Theory and Practice*, ed. Roger Ames, Thomas P. Kasulis, and Wimal Dissanayake (Albany: State University of New York Press, 1994).

the Confucian perspective, avoidance of self-deception is required in personal cultivation or character formation, especially in the task of attaining sincerity of thought *(ch'eng-yi)*. Indispensable to the success of this task is constant engagement in self-examination, a process partially exemplified in the diagnostic use of reflexive *tzu*-locutions. Toward the end, a tentative thesis on the notion of the self is offered as a topic for further inquiry. In this sketch of the Confucian response to the problem of self-deception, no attempt has been made to respond to specific issues in current discussion. My aim has been solely to present some materials for comparative East-West dialogue.

Essay 12 The Confucian Tradition *(Tao-t'ung)*

Like other enduring ethical or religious traditions with long histories—for example, Buddhism or Christianity—the Confucian tradition, as embodied in the notion of *tao-t'ung* (the tradition of *tao*), is often the target of contemporary critique. Consider this familiar appraisal: The *Ju* (Confucian) tradition, is out of tune with our times. Like any cherished cultural artifact, it is best revered as a relic of the past. It is a museum piece best entrusted to the curator for exhibition in the proper season. Moreover, many adherents of the Confucian tradition are dogmatic. They are unwilling to accept reasonable proposals for change or modification of some components of the tradition.

Replying to this charge, a Confucian thinker or scholar might point out that, to a certain extent, the critique is reasonable. Throughout its long history, there has been a recurrent tendency of many adherents of the Confucian tradition to institute orthodoxy and/or uphold their perceived values of the tradition as the true values of the tradition, irrespective of the distinction between perceived and real values. A personal ascription of value to an object cannot be logically equated with the value inherent in the object. As we shall see later, in understanding tradition, one must attend to the distinction between the *noumenal* past and the *perceived* past, and the distinction between a living, robust and a dying, decaying tradition. In the succinct words of Jaroslav Pelikan, "Tradition is the living faith of the dead, traditionalism is the dead faith of the living."[1]

One basic task of a Confucian moral philosopher today is to explore the possibility of a plausible explication of Confucian ethics, particularly the notion of *tao-t'ung* or Confucian tradition. This is an abiding concern of Confucian thinkers throughout the history of Chinese philosophy. Such an exploration serves a twofold purpose: (1) a plausible presentation of a key aspect of Confucian ethics and (2) its critical de-

---

1. Jaroslav Pelikan, *The Vindication of Tradition* (New Haven: Yale University Press, 1984), 65.

velopment.[2] The inquiry is a task of philosophical reconstruction, or in Ronald Dworkin's term, constructive interpretation. It is a task of creative interpretation, "a matter of interaction between purpose and object."[3] The aim is to provide the best philosophical explanation and justification of Confucian ethical thought.

In this and the following lectures, I present a sketch of some fundamental considerations for the development of Confucian moral philosophy. I freely appropriate insights of classical and Sung-Ming Confucianism and Western moral philosophy. I do not try to expound these insights in adherence to the original texts. From a personal point of view, these lectures are a progress report of some aspects of my Confucian studies.

Until recent years moral traditions have not been an important topic for moral philosophy.[4] With few exceptions, attention was directed to the problem of moral justification, to the search for universal criteria for the assessment of moral beliefs or judgments regardless of their traditional provenance. Generally, philosophers aspire to formulate "the view from nowhere."[5] Since the publication of Alasdair MacIntyre's *After Virtue* (1981), there has been a revival of interest in the nature of living, ethical tradition (henceforth, tradition). The interest in tradition is particularly strong among moral philosophers concerned with the possibility of an ethics of virtue or character as an alternative to the ethics of principles, say, to deontological, utilitarian, and contractarian ethics.[6] We must observe here that in the three decades be-

2. See A. S. Cua, "Tasks of Confucian Ethics," *Journal of Chinese Philosophy* 6, no. 1 (1979): 55–67.

3. Ronald Dworkin, *Law's Empire* (Cambridge: Harvard University Press, 1986), 52.

4. The exceptions I have in mind are A. E. Murphy, *The Theory of Practical Reason* (La Salle: Open Court, 1965); A. I. Melden, *Rights and Right Conduct* (Oxford: Blackwell, 1959); Peter Winch, *Ethics and Action* (London: Routledge & Kegan Paul, 1972): D. Z. Phillips and H. O. Mounce, *Moral Practices* (London: Routledge & Kegan Paul, 1969); R. W. Beardsmore. *Moral Reasoning* (London: Routledge & Kegan Paul, 1969); Stuart Hampshire, *Morality and Conflict* (Cambridge: Harvard University Press, 1983); and Marvin Rader, *The Right to Hope: Crisis and Community* (Seattle: University of Washington Press, 1981. For a retrospective account of my own studies of the Confucian Tradition, see my "Reflections on Moral Theory and Understanding Moral Traditions," in Eliot Deutsch and Jerald James Larsen, eds., *Interpreting Across Cultures: New Essays in Comparative Philosophy* (Princeton: Princeton University Press, 1988).

5. Thomas Nagel, *The View from Nowhere* (New York: Oxford University Press, 1986).

6. For valuable survey and critical discussions of different versions of virtue ethics, see Gregory E. Pence, "Recent Works on Virtue," *American Philosophical Quarterly* 21 (1984); and Gregory Trianosky, "What Is Virtue Ethics All About?" *American Philosophical Quarterly* 27 (1990). For a valuable anthology with a good bibliography, see Robert B. Kruschwitz and Robert E. Roberts, eds., *The Virtues: Contemporary Essays in Moral Character* (Belmont: Wadsworth, 1987). Hampshire has stressed the historical dimension in his *Morality and Conflict,* but unlike MacIntyre, no actual historical investigation of the notion

fore 1981, some moral philosophers displayed similar concern with tradition, although terms other than "tradition" were used—for example, "forms of life," "ways of life," "moral practices," and "moral community."[7] John Rawls's conception of reflective equilibrium is also developed with an eye to tradition. Indeed, Rawls has been explicit about his tradition-oriented approach to moral theory: "What justifies a conception of justice is not its being true to an order antecedent to and given to us, but its congruence with our deeper understanding of ourselves and our aspirations, and our realization that, given our history and the traditions embedded in our public life, it is the most reasonable doctrine."[8]

As a serious subject of philosophical investigation, however, it is in MacIntyre's *After Virtue* that we find a central and distinctive focus on tradition. Particularly noteworthy is his insistence on the historical and argumentative aspects of moral traditions. A living tradition, according to MacIntyre, is a "historically extended, socially embodied argument, and an argument in part precisely about the goods which constitute that tradition."[9] This notion of tradition is later elaborated as a conception of rational inquiry, "a conception according to which the standards of rational justification themselves emerge from and are part of a history in which they are vindicated by the way in which they transcend the limitations of and provide remedies for the defects of their

---

of tradition is attempted. See especially MacIntyre, *Whose Justice? Which Rationality?* (Notre Dame: University of Notre Dame Press, 1989).

7. The wide currency of these terms probably comes from the focus on "forms of life" in L. Wittgenstein, *Philosophical Investigations* (New York: Macmillan, 1965). Winch, particularly, stresses the importance of understanding other forms of life or cultures. "What we may learn by studying other cultures are not merely possibilities and different ways of doing things, other techniques. More importantly, we may learn different possibilities of making sense of human life, different ideas about the possible importance that the carrying out of certain activities may take on for a man, trying to contemplate the sense of his life as a whole" (Winch, *Ethics and Action*, 41). It is interesting to note here that part 2 of this essay, where our citation occurs, is a response to MacIntyre's critique of his *The Idea of Social Science*. For the use of "moral practices," see Phillips and Mounce, *Moral Practices;* for the use of "moral community," see works of Melden and Murphy cited in n. 4 above. I have employed all these terms in *Dimensions of Moral Creativity* (University Park: Pennsylvania State University Press, 1978). Explanations of my use of "form of life," "way of life," or "moral practice" were given especially in chap. 1. For a discussion of the "conservative" aspects of Wittgenstein's later thought, see Anthony O'Hear, "Wittgenstein and the Transmission of Tradition," in *Wittgenstein Centenary Essays*, ed. A. Phillips Griffiths (Cambridge: Cambridge University Press, 1991).

8. John Rawls, "Kantian Constructivism in Moral Theory: The John Dewey Lectures, 1980," *Journal of Philosophy* 77, no. 9 (1980), 519. For his conception of moral theory as "a study of substantive moral conceptions and their relation to our moral sensibility," see Rawls, "The Independence of Moral Theory," *Proceedings and Addresses of the American Philosophical Association* (1974–75), 6–8.

9. MacIntyre, *After Virtue* (2d ed., 1984), 222. Hereafter this edition will be cited.

predecessors within the history of that same tradition."[10] As we shall see later, a similar understanding of tradition, more especially as a tradition of learning, is present in the works of Hsün Tzu and in Chu Hsi's (1130–1200) conception of *tao-t'ung* (tradition of the Way). *Tao-t'ung* may be construed as "reconstitution or repossession of *tao*"—a conception responsive to both internal and external challenges.[11]

In this lecture I offer some thought on this topic. Section I presents a general characterization of a living, ethical tradition. Special emphasis is given to the role of interpretation in the community of adherents. Section II builds on this discussion for explicating Chu Hsi's conception of *tao-t'ung*. Section III addresses a special problem in Chu Hsi's conception with respect to change and modification of the Confucian tradition. I maintain that this problem can in part be resolved by attending to the connection between *tao-t'ung* and *ch'üan* (weighing of circumstances). The concluding remarks briefly consider the role of argumentation in the evaluation of judgments based on the exercise of *ch'üan*. They suggest, as a project for further inquiry, the contrast between the Confucian cooperative model and the agonistic model of ethical argumentation.

I. THE CONCEPT OF TRADITION

For MacIntyre, moral philosophy and sociology are interdependent.[12] His account of the central role played by tradition in the "core concept" of the virtues illustrates part of this interdependence, that is, "that every moral philosophy has some particular sociology as its counterpart."[13] This suggests that a sociological study may throw some light on tradition. In a 1948 lecture, Karl Popper remarked: "A theory of tradition must be a sociological theory, because tradition is obviously a social phenomenon." Popper proposes a twofold task for such a theory: An account of (1) the emergence and persistence of traditions, and (2) "the function of tradition in social life."[14] What Popper says about the

10. MacIntyre, *Whose Justice? Which Rationality?* 7
11. See Tu Wei-ming, "Reconstituting the Confucian Tradition," in his *Humanity and Self-Cultivation: Essays in Confucian Thought* (Berkeley: Asian Humanities Press, 1979), chap. 9; William Theodore de Bary, *Neo-Confucian Orthodoxy and the Learning of the Mind-and-Heart* (New York: Columbia University Press, 1981), 9; and William Theodore de Bary, *The Liberal Tradition in China* (Hong Kong: Chinese University of Hong Kong Press, 1983), 15–16.
12. MacIntyre, *After Virtue*, 23, 116.
13. Ibid., 225.
14. Karl Popper, "Toward a Rational Theory of Tradition," reprinted in Karl Popper, *Conjectures and Refutations: The Growth of Scientific Knowledge* (London: Routledge & Kegan

second task is a useful reminder. A tradition of thought and conduct provides an anchorage for confidence in regularities and expectations.

The mere existence of these regularities is perhaps more important than their peculiar merits or demerits. They are needed as regularities, and therefore handed on as traditions, whether or not they are in other respects rational or necessary or good or beautiful or what you will. There is a need for tradition in social life.[15]

Edward Shils's *Tradition,* published in the same year (1981) as MacIntyre's *After Virtue,* is a pioneering, comprehensive sociological treatment of tradition.[16] Independently of the question of what constitutes an adequate sociological theory of tradition, moral philosophers can learn from Shils in explicating the concept of tradition. I am primarily interested in Shils's conceptual framework for his sociological study. It is this framework, with elaboration, that provides us a handle for dealing the Chu Hsi's *tao-t'ung* as an insightful expression of the idea of the Confucian tradition.

At the outset, let me observe that tradition is not a concept that can be profitably discussed as a matter of formal definition.[17] Tradition, to use Hilary Putnam's term, is a *cluster concept,* recalling Wittgenstein's

---

Paul, 1963), 123. With respect to the first task, Popper emphasized in particular the task of social theory in explaining "how the unintended consequences of our intentions and actions arise"; the second task is approached by "an analysis of particular tradition—the rational or scientific tradition—as an example" (ibid., 125).

15. Ibid., 130–31. We may note here that an adequate sociological theory of tradition seems indispensable to the history of ideas and the history of philosophy (both Western and non-Western). We do make use of the notion of tradition in distinguishing major themes and trends of philosophical thought in different historical periods, and arguably, the practice of modern philosophy in the West itself exemplifies an established social institution. See Avner Cohen and Marcedo Dascal, eds., *The Institution of Philosophy: A Discipline in Crisis?* (La Salle: Open Court, 1989).

16. Edward Shils, *Tradition* (Chicago: University of Chicago Press, 1981). It is interesting to observe that in two places Shils cites Popper's *Objective Knowledge: An Evolutionary Approach* (Oxford: Clarendon Press, 1972) rather than the article we cited from *Conjectures and Refutations.* Shils regard his *Tradition* as a pioneering work. In the Preface Shils remarks: "This book about tradition is evidence of the need of *Tradition.* If there had been other comprehensive books about tradition and traditions, this book would have been a better one. It would have given me a point of departure easier to start from, it would have made me aware of omissions and misapprehensions. But there is no such book. There are many books about particular traditions. . . . There is however no book about tradition which tries to see the common ground and elements of tradition and which analyzes what difference tradition makes in human life." On the back cover of the paperback edition, a reviewer (H. Leon Abrams, Jr.) concurs: "*Tradition* is the first comprehensive treatment of the subject that encompasses the totality of tradition in all its multifaceted variables and functions. . . . It is a landmark analytical and theoretical sociological study."

17. See *The Definition of Morality,* ed. G. Wallace and A. D. Walker (London: Methuen, 1970), 2.

metaphor of family resemblance or "the metaphor of a 'cluster,' the metaphor of a rope with many strands, no one of which runs the length of the rope." The meaning of a cluster concept, as the term suggests, lies in "a cluster of properties."

To abandon a large number of these properties, or what is tantamount to the same thing, to radically change the extension of the term 'man,' would be felt as an arbitrary change in its meaning. On the other hand, if most of the properties are present in any single case, then under suitable circumstances we should be inclined to say that what we had to deal with was a man.[18]

With this notion of a cluster concept in hand, allow me now to delineate Shils's characterization of tradition. Four properties or features are central to any conception or theory of tradition:

1. Tradition as *traditum* has a certain duration of existence.
2. Every tradition has custodians or exemplars.
3. Tradition is always an object of interpretation, thus subject to change or modification.
4. The way in which the stock of a tradition is possessed, for example, its texts, is selective, and typically a subject matter for specialized inquiries.[19]

Regarding (1), tradition as *traditum* is "anything which is transmitted or handed down from the past to the present," and this includes "material objects, beliefs about all sorts of things, images of persons and events, practices and institutions. It includes buildings, monuments, landscapes, sculpture, paintings, books, tools, machines."[20] The duration of the existence extends to at least three generations. While this criterion is vague, it does provide a way for distinguishing fashions from tradition.

With regard to (2), every tradition has its custodians or exemplars. Following Max Weber, Shils frequently stresses the force of charismatic

18. Hilary Putnam, *Mind, Language and Reality: Philosophical Papers* (Cambridge: Cambridge University Press, 1975), 2:52. See also the chapter on the role of "polythetic concepts" in social anthropology in Rodney Needham, *Against the Tranquility of Axioms* (Berkeley: University of California Press, 1983).

19. This is a list of the synchronic features of the cluster concept of tradition, based principally on Shils's Introduction to *Tradition* which he deployed in the first three chapters. The seven chapters that follow deal instructively with the diachronic features, the endogenous and exogenous changes and their patterns, rationalization and prospects of tradition. These chapters, however, mainly provide a sociological elaboration of the third feature in my list. Moreover, what is lacking is a conceptual typology of value change. See especially, Nicholas Rescher, *An Introduction of Value Theory* (Englewood Cliffs: Prentice Hall, 1969); and Stephen C. Pepper, *Sources of Values* (Berkeley: University of California Press, 1958).

20. Shils, *Tradition*, 12–13.

personalities, "charismatic episodes or an exemplary sequence of charismatic episodes" in the lives of the founders of world religions, e.g., Christianity and Islam.[21] For our purposes, custodians and exemplars may be more broadly construed as representative adherents or paradigmatic individuals.[22] In this connection, we can also appreciate MacIntyre's emphasis on what he calls "characters."

A character is an object of regard by the members of the culture generally or by some significant segment of them. He furnishes them with a cultural and moral ideal. Hence the demand is that in this type of case role and personality be fused. Social type and psychological type are required to coincide. The *character* morally legitimates a mode of social existence.[23]

Examples in our times are the Rich Aesthete, the Manager, and the Therapist. In focusing on the role of representative adherents in a *traditum*, we need to inquire into this difficult conceptual problem: Are terms such as charismatic persons, paradigmatic individuals, and characters functionally equivalent or do they pertain to different though related concepts? Assume that there is a connection between these concepts, how is the connection to be explicated? Furthermore, suppose we can unproblematically ascribe these labels to certain, particular adherents of a tradition, in what sense can these persons be deemed custodians? Or is custodianship a matter of ascription by fellow adherents? How seriously can we respect an ascribed or a self-proclaimed custodian without assessing his or her credentials? These are large questions I cannot pursue here.

It seems clear, however, that the concept of tradition cannot be properly explicated without some conception of exemplary embodiment in the lives of certain adherents. Arguably, Confucius's notion of *chün-tzu* expresses the idea of paradigmatic individuals as exemplary embodiments of the spirit and vitality of the tradition. In addition to functioning in moral education, they also serve as living exemplars of the transformative significance of the ideal of the tradition, thus invigorating the tradition. Even more important, for those committed to tra-

---

21. Ibid.

22. For the notion of paradigmatic individuals and its application to interpreting Confucius's ideal of *chün-tzu*, see my *Dimension of Moral Creativity*, chaps. 3–5. For *chün-tzu's* role in Confucian moral education, see Essay 8. Cf. Harold Alderman, "By Virtue of a Virtue," *Review of Metaphysics* 36 (1982): 127–53. For broadening Shils's notion of charismatic episodes, it may be useful to consider Needham's notion of exemplary or "paradigmatic scenes," those "which attribute order and meaning to human life." They "are in the main affective and iconic, and their impact is such as to convey a sense of deep and directive significance in the interpretation of human experience" (Needham 1985, 67).

23. MacIntyre, *After Virtue*, 29–30.

dition, paradigmatic individuals serve as points of orientation, as standards of inspiration.

With regard to (3), perhaps the most salient feature of a living tradition is that the things transmitted do not always retain their original character or significance. During transmission they undergo changes or modification. For example, the transmission of texts is mediated by interpretation. As Shils put it, "Constellations of symbols, clusters of images, are received and modified. They change in the process of transmission as interpretations are made of the tradition presented; they change also while they are in the possession of the recipients."[24] Shils reminds us of two different senses of the past: the *noumenal* and the *perceived*. The noumenal past is ineluctable, unchanging, and unfathomable. It comprises events, actions, works of art, literature and thought:

> This is the real past which has happened and left its residues behind. The residues are these hard facts of the human side of existence. Nothing can be done which will change these facts which are the scene of human action in the present. This is the noumenal past which historians attempt to discover and construct.
>
> There is another past. This is a much more plastic thing, more capable to being retrospectively reformed by human beings living in the present. It is the past recorded in memorial and in writing, formed from encounters with "the hard facts," not just from inescapable but also from sought for encounters.[25]

In the light of this distinction between noumenal and perceived past, we can now construe tradition as an embodiment of a perceived past rather than of a noumenal past. In this sense, tradition is always an object of interpretation. The concept of tradition may be said to be an *interpretive concept*.[26] Of course, we are here implicitly distinguishing tradition from traditionalism. Recall Pelikan's remark: "Tradition is the living faith of the dead, traditionalism is the dead faith of the living."[27] Much in the spirit of this distinction, we can appreciate MacIntyre's remark: "To be an adherent of a tradition is always to enact some further stage in the development of one's tradition."[28] So also can we appreciate Hans-Georg Gadamer's emphasis on the distinction between legitimate prejudices and all the countless others which always present a challenging task for "critical reason."[29]

24. Shils, *Tradition*, 13, also 77–78, 96–97.
25. Ibid., 195. Shils refers the use of this distinction to Henri Irenée Marrou, *De la connaissance historique* (Paris: Editions du Seuil, 1959), 37.
26. See Dworkin, *Law's Empire*, chap. 2.
27. Pelikan, *The Vindication of Tradition*, 65.
28. MacIntrye, *Whose Justice? Which Rationality?* 11.
29. Hans-Georg Gadamer, *Truth and Method* (New York: Seabury Press, 1975), 246.

As an interpretive concept, however, tradition is intelligible only if we suppose that the adherents constitute a *community* rather than a mere collection of individuals. To use an older term commonly used in the eighteenth century, we may say that the adherents of a tradition are actuated by *sensus communis*.[30] Reflecting on the complementary uses of the term by Giambattista Vico and Anthony Shaftesbury, we discover two aspects of *sensus communis*. The cognitive aspect stressed by Vico pertains to those shared unreflective judgments with "respect to human needs or utilities."[31] More broadly, the unreflective judgments embody shared basic beliefs or ideas about the noble and the good, the right and the fitting in the conduct of human affairs. The affective aspect of *sensus communis* is stressed by Shaftesbury. It is a "sense of public weal and of common interest; the love of the community or society, natural affection, humanity, or obligingness."[32] Adherents of a tradition may thus be described as sharers in "a common affection" informed by "a sense of partnership" in dealing with problems that affect them all. They are persons who care for one another as their lives are, so to speak, interwoven through well-being, fortune, and misfortune.

Thus, presupposed in any theory or conception of tradition is the presence of *sensus communis* among the adherents. Tradition as an interpretive concept implies that members of the community would acknowledge the possibility of conflicting judgments concerning the present significance of the tradition. Josiah Royce aptly characterizes the community as a *community of interpretation*. Obviously, a community consists of members who are distinct and separate individuals. At any given time, the individual interprets his experience as well as future anticipation, saying as it were to himself "that a past deed or future event

30. Gadamer gives a brief, critical survey of the notion of *sensus communis* in Vico, Roman and medieval antecedents, and in Vico's contemporaries such as Shaftesbury, Reid, and others. This is a large topic worthy of further study in moral philosophy. Though I am indebted to Gadamer, my remarks below on Vico and Shaftesbury differ from his. I place more stress on Shaftesbury than on Vico and regard them as proposing complementary points of view. Ibid., 19–29.

31. Giambattista Vico, *The New Science*, trans. Thomas Goddard Bergin and Max Fisch (Ithaca: Cornell University Press, 1988), 63. Reid's philosophy of common sense and Moore's "A Defence of Common Sense" may be regarded as an attempt to develop an epistemological theory of *sensus communis*. See Thomas Reid, *Essays on the Intellectual Powers of Man* (Cambridge: MIT Press, 1969), Essay VI, sec. 2; G. E. Moore, *Philosophical Papers* (London: George Allen & Unwin, 1959).

32. Anthony Shaftesbury, *Characteristics of Men, Manners, Opinions, Times*, ed. John M. Robertson (Indianapolis: Bobbs-Merrill, 1964), 1:72. For similar emphasis on this affective aspect, see Melden and Murphy cited in n. 4 above; and John Macmurray, *Persons in Relation* (London: Farber and Farber, 1961). For Confucian ethics, see my "Confucian Vision and the Human Community," *Journal of Chinese Philosophy* 11 (1984): 227–38.

belongs to my life." Especially in the ethical sense, personal identity at any moment is constituted by the individual's interpretation of its retrospective grounding as well as its prospective significance.

Actuated by *sensus communis*, adherents of a tradition are members of a community who have a common understanding of a shared history as constitutive of an aspect of personhood. This community is *a community of memory*. In Royce's words, it is "a community constituted by the fact that each of its members accepts as part of his own individual life and self the same past events that each of his fellow members accepts."[33]

More importantly, for its members, a community of memory is an object of personal affection, exemplified "in any group of persons who individually either remember or commemorate the same deed—each one finding, because of his personal affection or of reverence for the dead, that those whom he commemorates form for him a part of his own past experience."[34] We would expect that in such a community there will be an emphasis on the rites of commemoration, particularly of those paradigmatic individuals, the "saints and heroes," men and women who had made significant contributions, through devotion and personal sacrifice, to the maintenance or preservation of the community. In Confucian ethics, many rites or *li* have an ennobling function.[35]

Implicit in the community of memory is an *ideal of coherence*, a shared telos that makes sense of interpretation of both the individual and the common life. It is this ideal that provides a unity or unifying perspective for viewing the diversity of interpretations as interpretations of the same tradition. When the ideal is articulated in the form of a vision of the good human life as a whole and becomes the focus of a common venture among the members of the community, it acquires an actuating significance for present cooperative endeavor.

Informed by the prospective significance of the ideal, the community is also *a community of hope or expectation*. It is "a community constituted by the fact that each of its members accepts, as part of his own individual life and self, the same expected future events that each of his fellows accepts."[36] The perceived past of the tradition thus possesses a significance beyond its relevance to current problems and perplexi-

33. Josiah Royce, *Problem of Christianity* (Chicago: University of Chicago Press, 1969), 248.
34. Ibid.
35. See my "The Concept of *Li* in Confucian Moral Theory" in *Understanding the Chinese Thought: The Philosophical Roots*, ed. Robert E. Allinson (Hong Kong: Oxford University Press, 1988).
36. Royce, *Problem of Christianity*, 248.

ties. In both the community of memory and of hope, value judgments are undoubtedly involved. From the ideal, unifying perspective, these judgments are interpretive judgments about the significance of the tradition, though subject to critical discussion in the context of disagreement. It is also this ideal that provides practical understanding of *sensus communis* as a coherent set of basic beliefs, and thus the coherence and continuity of the tradition.

Because of the actuality of conflicting interpretations of the significance of tradition, intelligent and reasonable adherents of the tradition would engage in, to use Michael Oakeshott's felicitous term, "a pursuit of intimations." Oakeshott compares the enterprise of the pursuit of intimations to that of seamanship: "To keep afloat on an even keel; the sea is both friend and enemy; seamanship consists in using the resources of a traditional manner of behaviour in order to make a friend of every hostile occasion."[37]

A tradition of ethical thought and conduct inevitably faces the problem of coherence. Even if there is an implicit agreement in an ideal, unifying perspective, intelligent adherents of the tradition must make use of the tradition in order to confront external and internal challenges. The tradition is thus viewed as a reservoir of valuable resources. Practical wisdom is plausibly conceived, à la Chu Hsi, to be a depository of insights always available for appropriation to deal with present and future problems and perplexities of human life.[38] Perhaps this is also the point of Oakeshott's analogy between the pursuit of intimations and seamanship. As a beginner, the seaman is an apprentice learning the secrets of the trade. When mature, he shows his competence in handling unforeseeable and difficult situations of danger, displaying a sense of what is right or fitting. In Hsün Tzu's words, he would employ his sense of *i* (rightness) to vary his responses to changing circumstances.[39]

Let us turn briefly to (4), that is, tradition's stock and possession. For our purposes, we focus on texts. The possession of texts is highly selective. Selective judgment and decision determine the assignment of certain texts as having a canonical status, that is, as providing an authoritative point of reference for established standards of conduct. In different cultural, ethical traditions, these texts comprise a core of his-

37. Michael Oakeshott, *Rationalism in Politics and Other Essays* (Indianapolis: Liberty Press, 1991), 60.
38. See my "Hsün Tzu and the Unity of Virtues," *Journal of Chinese Philosophy* 14, no. 4 (1987): 381–400.
39. *Pu-kou p'ien.* Hereafter, citation to the works of *Hsün Tzu* indicated by title of the individual essays. Page reference is based on Li Ti-sheng, *Hsün Tzu chi-shih* (Taipei: Hsüeh-sheng, 1979).

torical scholarship, and the emergence of certain texts as authoritative may be a culmination of a process of disagreement and eventual acceptance.

In the Confucian tradition, the acknowledgment of the canonical status of the Four Books *(The Analects, Mencius, The Great Learning,* and *The Doctrine of the Mean)* is a result of Chu Hsi's scholarly efforts and represents his selective decision. Perhaps even more important, interpretation of these texts at a particular time and place also involves selective decision and judgment.[40] As Shils points out, "The process of tradition is always a process of selection. Parts of the traditional stock drift downward into obscurity so that they are known only to a few persons or conceivably to none at all."[41]

Pressure of present needs and exigent situations are probably among the crucial factors in the process of selection. In any case, one would expect the adherents of tradition to engage in argumentation to resolve their different or conflicting perceptions of their current predicament, as well as their aspirations.

II. THE TRADITION OF *TAO: TAO-T'UNG*

If our discussion of the concept of tradition is acceptable, we have a tentative way of explicating Chu Hsi's conception of *tao-t'ung* as a conception of tradition.[42] The explication, partly indebted to recent Chu Hsi scholarship,[43] is mainly intended as a proposal for reshaping

40. See my "Some Reflections on Methodology in Chinese Philosophy," *International Philosophical Quarterly* 11, no. 2 (1971): 236–48.

41. Shils, *Tradition,* 26.

42. The distinction between concept and conception I use throughout this lecture may be misleading, unless we introduce a qualification: a concept may well be a crystallized conception. Consider *tao:* were it to be viewed exclusively as a Confucian concept or as a generic term of Confucian discourse, it would be a crystallized conception of classical and Neo-Confucian thought. But for the Taoist, *tao* would represent an altogether different concept or crystallized conception of discourses such as those preeminently exemplified in Lao Tzu and Chuang Tzu. This suggests that we may properly speak of *tao* as representing two different concepts, each of which is a product of a crystallized conception. For further discussion, see Essay 8. For the distinction between concept and conception see, for example, John Rawls, *A Theory of Justice* (Cambridge: Harvard University Press, 1971), 5–9; Dworkin, *Law's Empire,* 71–72; Robin Attfield, "On Being Human," *Inquiry* 17 (1974), 175–76. A more extensive discussion is given in Roger Shiner, *Knowledge and Reality in Plato's* Philebus (Assum: Van Gorcum, 1974), chap. 1, which acknowledges the influence of C. I. Lewis's *Mind and the World Order* (New York: Dover, 1929), 67. I owe the last two references to Dr. Eugenio Benitez, University of Sidney.

43. Aside from Tu and de Bary cited in n. 11 above, see also Wing-tsit Chan, *Chu Hsi: New Studies* (Honolulu: University of Hawaii Press, 1989); and especially essays by Liu, Yü, Kao, and Takehiko in *Chu Hsi and Neo-Confucianism,* ed. Wing-tsit Chan (Honolulu: University of Hawaii Press, 1986).

tao-t'ung; it serves as a point of departure for the critical development of Confucian moral philosophy. In this task, I concur with J. G. A. Pocock's remark: "The concepts which we form from, and feed back into, tradition have a capacity to modify the content and character of the tradition conceptualized and even the extent to which it is conceived and regarded as a tradition."[44] In explicating *tao-t'ung,* I center attention on feature (3), that is, tradition as an interpretive concept. I assume that features (1) and (4) are present in any notion of a Confucian tradition, since it is not an issue for contention. At least in the Pre-Ch'in period, there was a *Ju* tradition. Hsün Tzu's critical discussion of three different grades of *Ju* (the great, refined, and vulgar *Ju*) suggests a persistent tradition with adherents varying in intelligence, degree of commitment, and ethical motivation.[45] The claim to a persistent *traditum,* for Mencius and Chu Hsi, is consistent with an acknowledgement of periods of interruption and discontinuity.[46] As de Bary points out, "Chu Hsi emphasized the discontinuities in the tradition almost more than the continuities, and underscored the contributions of inspired individuals who rediscovered or 'clarified' the Way in the new forms."[47] This emphasis on "inspired individuals" also recalls feature (2), the indispensable role of exemplary adherents who are custodians or paradigmatic individuals of the tradition, though as earlier indicated, there is a problem in labeling and justifying claims that ascribe custodianship.

As a conjecture, Chu Hsi's highly incredible claim of a line of succession in the Confucian tradition may be an expression of his concern with *preserving* the recognition of certain exemplary or paradigmatic individuals in the history of the tradition. Thus, Confucius (551–479 B.C.), and Mencius (371–298 B.C.?), Chou Tun-i (1017–1073), Ch'eng Hao (1032–1085), and Ch'eng I (1033–1107) figure in the line of the transmitters of the Confucian tradition.

As for feature (4), the selective possession of the stock of tradition, Chu Hsi's selective study of ancient texts, a life-long preoccupation,

44. J. G. A. Pocock, "Time, Institutions and Action: An Essay on Traditions and Their Understanding" in *Politics and Experience: Essays Presented to Michael Oakeshott,* ed. Preston King and B. C. Parehk (Cambridge: Cambridge University Press, 1968).
45. *Ju-hsiao* p'ien, Li, *Hsün Tzu.*
46. *Meng Tzu,* 7B:38.
47. de Bary, *Neo-Confucian Orthodoxy,* 99. Chu Hsi's concern with the Confucian tradition is analogous to Newman's attempt to defend a conception of Roman Catholicism. Quite apart from its relevance to the development of Confucian ethics, Newman's work is instructive for it provides an incisive way to elaborate feature (3) in our cluster concept of tradition. See John Henry Newman, *An Essay on the Development of Christian Doctrine* (Notre Dame: University of Notre Dame Press, 1989), esp. chap. 5. We may also note with MacIntyre that vital traditions "embody continuities of conflict" (*After Virtue,* 222).

shows his selective decision and concern with the recovery and revitalization of an ancient tradition. This is the point of Tu Wei-ming's remark that Chu Hsi's scholarly efforts "represent serious efforts to revitalize the tradition [which] involved creative adaptation as well as faithful interpretation."[48] Chu Hsi's recurrent emphasis on the importance of the method of book-learning (tu-shu fa) displays a concern, in de Bary's felicitous term, with repossession of tao.[49] The familiar status of the Four Books as basic sources of Confucianism is indebted to Chu Hsi's bold selective decision and singular achievement in the history of Chinese thought.

According to Wing-tsit Chan, Chu Hsi coined the term tao-t'ung. For assessing Chu Hsi's conception, Chan directs our attention to the distinction between Chu Hsi's philosophical interpretation and his arbitrary historical claim about a single line of succession.[50] The very idea of tao-t'ung as a doctrine of an orthodox line of transmission is probably Chu Hsi's fanciful speculation, a bit surprising in view of the pragmatic-scientific spirit displayed in his works.[51] One may even go further to observe with Liu Shu-hsien that "from a strictly historical perspective we may easily dismiss the story of the line of the transmission of orthodoxy as a big chunk of nonsense." For Liu "the crux of the matter actually lies in one's existential decision over one's ultimate commitment or philosophical faith." For Liu, the question lies in "the Confucian message" rather than in "the acceptance of a historical legend." "The Confucian message must be traced back to Confucius as the Christian message must be traced back to Jesus the Christ. It is through a study of the ideals Confucius embodied that we may hope to find the continuity between Neo-Confucianism and classical Confucianism." Liu goes on to provide an informative and plausible defense of his thesis that there are grounds for the Neo-Confucian claim that their

48. Tu Wei-ming, Humanity and Self-Cultivation, 134.

49. de Bary, Neo-Confucian Orthodoxy, 81. For Chu Hsi's conception of book-learning, see Yü Ying-shih, "Morality and Knowledge in Chu Hsi's Philosophical System" in Chu Hsi and Neo-Confucianism, 228–54. For a useful introduction and translation of relevant materials from Chu Tzu yü-lei, see Daniel K. Gardner, Chu Hsi: Learning to be a Sage (Berkeley: University of California Press, 1990).

50. According to Chan, the philosophical interpretation consists in Chu Hsi's citation of a passage from Book of History in describing the content of transmission from Yao to Shun. This passage runs: "The human mind (jen-hsin) is precarious. The moral mind is subtle. Have absolute refinement and singleness of mind." See Chan, Chu Hsi: New Studies, 321. As is well known, Book of History is later considered by most scholars to be a forgery.

51. See Hu Shih, "The Scientific Spirit and Method in Chinese Philosophy" in Philosophy and Culture: East and West, ed. Charles A. Moore (Honolulu: University of Hawaii Press, 1962): 199–222; and Wing-tsit Chan, "Hu Shih and Chu Hsi" in Chan, Chu Hsi: New Studies, 563–67.

understanding of the sagely mind or *ideals* are those "most clearly embodied in the person of Confucius."[52]

For present purposes, let me supplement Liu's contribution by focusing on a key and familiar aspect of Chu Hsi's conception of learning. In commenting on the expression "The perfection of knowledge depends on the investigation of things *[ko-wu]*" in the *Great Learning (Ta-hsüeh)*, Chu Hsi emphasizes the importance of *ch'iung-li*, i.e., the exhaustive investigation of principles or rationales for the existence of things. Chu Hsi writes:

> The first step in the education of the adult is to instruct the learner, in regard to all things in the world, to proceed from what knowledge he has of their principles *[li]*, and investigate further until he reaches the limit. After exerting himself in this way for a long time, he will one day achieve a *wide and far-reaching penetration [kuan-t'ung]*.[53]

For further elucidation of *kuan-t'ung* (wide and far-ranging penetration), it is instructive to recall briefly Hsün Tzu's use of *kuan* and *t'ung* and Chu Hsi's comment before attending to Chu Hsi's use of *kuan-t'ung* as a compound term. Chu Hsi's conception of *tao-t'ung* implicitly involves a conception of *kuan-t'ung chih hsüeh* (the learning of *kuan-t'ung*). His conception of *tao* in *tao-t'ung* provides a unifying perspective for understanding the coherence of the ideals in the sagely mind that Liu emphasized in his instructive paper.

In the *Hsün Tzu, kuan* and *t'ung* occur in one passage concerning the superior man's engrossment with completeness *(ch'üan)* and purity *(tsui):* "The superior man *[chün-tzu]* reads and recites texts in order to *kuan* through their meaning, reflects on them in order to achieve *t'ung*."[54] Chu Hsi endorses this remark of Hsün Tzu's as a very good explanation of the way of learning, and glosses *kuan* and *t'ung* as follows:

> The character *kuan* means *shu*, "to be intimately familiar with" as in "what we are accustomed to *[hsi-kuan]* becomes second nature to us." It also means *t'ung*,

52. Liu's discussion centers on two Neo-Confucian beliefs "that man's moral nature is good and that it is an endowment from Heaven." See Liu Shu-hsien, "The Problem of Orthodoxy in Chu Hsi's Philosophy" in *Chu Hsi and Neo-Confucianism*, 442–43.

53. This is Chan's translation in Wing-tsit Chan, *A Source Book in Chinese Philosophy* (Princeton: Princeton University Press, 1963), 89. See Chu Hsi, *Ssu Shu chi-chu* (Hong Kong: Tai-p'ing, 1980), 6. Unless otherwise indicated, all translations are my own.

54. *Ch'üan-hsüeh p'ien*, Li, *Hsün Tzu*, 19. For an extended discussion of Hsün Tzu's use of *kuan* and a defense of *tao-kuan* as an ideal unifying perspective, see my "The Possibility of Ethical Knowledge: Reflections on a Theme in the *Hsün Tzu*" in *Epistemological Issues in Classical Chinese Philosophy*, ed. Hans Lenk and Gregor Paul (Albany: State University of New York Press, 1993). For the interpretation of *tao* as an ideal of rational coherence, see my *Ethical Argumentation*, 17–18.

"to understand thoroughly." Only if we've read to the point of intimate familiarity are we able to understand thoroughly. And if we haven't read to the point of intimate familiarity, there is nothing we can possibly ponder.[55]

Following Yang Liang, *kuan* in the *Hsün Tzu* passage may be read as *kuan-chuan*, that is, "to penetrate."[56] However, in the light of the role of reflection *(ssu-so)* and the aim of *t'ung*, comprehensive or thorough understanding, we may also construe *kuan* in *kuan-chuan* in terms of its homophone *(*kuan-chuan)*, that is, "to piece together, interconnect, or interrelate." On this basis, Chu Hsi's frequent use of the binomial *kuan-t'ung* may be construed as a wide and far-reaching penetration. Significantly *kuan-t'ung* involves a comprehension of the interconnection of different items of learning. We may also note here that some recent commentators of the *Hsün Tzu*, in fact, use *kuan-t'ung* to explain *kuan* in our *Hsün Tzu* passage.[57]

Taking the two senses of *kuan*, we may simply render *kuan-t'ung* as "comprehensive understanding."[58] Chu Hsi's frequent use of *kuan-t'ung* in the recorded conversations on learning[59] suggests Hsün Tzu's influence, although Hsün Tzu's conception was commented on only in the one passage we have considered. For example, the emphasis on open mind *(hsü-hsin)* is reminiscent of Hsün-Tzu's use of *kung-hsin* (impartial mind) or freedom from preconception and Hsün Tzu's emphasis on the role of reflection in learning *(ssu-so)*. I recall one striking passage involving *kuan-t'ung:* "In general, after one has accumulated *(chih)* so many manifestations of *i-li* (moral norm, principle, or reason) with comprehensive understanding *(kuan-t'ung)*, one will naturally appreciate its efficacy [in conduct of life]."[60] This remark seems to reflect Hsün Tzu's distinctive conception of moral learning as accumulation *(chih)*, not only of knowledge, but also of excellence *(shan)* or of good deeds, say, based on *li* (ritual propriety) and *i* (sense of rightness).[61]

---

55. Gardner, *Chu Hsi: Learning to be a Sage*, 136 ("we're" emended as "we've"). See also *Chu Tzu yü-lei*, ed. Li Ching-te (Taipei: Cheng-chung, 1962), vol. 1, chap. 10, 8a-8b, 327–28. For another Chu Hsi's appreciative comment on Hsün Tzu, see *Chu Tzu yü-lei*, vol. 6, chap. 87, 19b-20a, pp. 3628–29.

56. Yang Liang, *Hsün Tzu* (Taipei: Chung-hua, 1976), chap. 1:6a.

57. See, for example, Ch'en Ta-ch'i, *Hsün Tzu hsüeh-shuo* (Taipei: Chung-hua wen-hua she, 1954), 78–79; Wang Chung-lin, *Hsin-i Hsün Tzu tou-pen* (Taipei: San Min, 1977), 62; Li, *Hsün Tzu*, 19–20n.

58. Note that Gardner often translates *kuan-t'ung* as "interconnect," sometimes simply as "comprehensive understanding." See Gardner, *Chu Hsi: Learning to be a Sage*, 100, 137, and 193.

59. *Chu Tzu yü-lei*, chap. 7–13.

60. Ibid. vol. 1, chap. 9, p. 309.

61. See *Hsing-o*; Li, *Hsün Tzu*, 550. For the notion of *chih* (accumulation), see esp. 1–21). I sometimes wonder whether the Neo-Confucian use of *i-li*, commonly rendered

However, Chu Hsi could have derived his idea directly from the famous and perplexing remark of Mencius on the flood-like *ch'i (hao-jan chih ch'i)*, where we find an emphasis on the accumulation of *i* (right actions).[62]

Regardless of the classical source of Chu Hsi's conception of moral learning; its ultimate objective is comprehensive understanding. The learning, *kuan-t'ung chih hsüeh*, is a form of integrated learning. I suggest, as a matter of constructive interpretation, that the *tao* in Chu Hsi's *tao-t'ung*, as the Hsün Tzu's *tao* in *tao-kuan*, be construed as the ideal unifying perspective or *telos* that provides the integration, the coherence of the *sensus communis* of the adherents of the Confucian tradition. *Tao-t'ung* as the tradition of *tao* may thus be construed as the Confucian tradition of coherent sagely understanding of *tao*, exemplified preeminently in the life of Confucius, which Liu justly regards as constitutive of "the Confucian message." The interpretation of the Confucian texts, from the personal point of view, is self-interpretation. In Chu Hsi's words, it is "an inner experience relevant to life." As Yü Yingshih has shown, for Chu Hsi, interpretation of the classics is a process that culminates in the stage in which the reader "can bring the text to life," that is, "what is interpreted is transformed into an organic part, so to speak, of the interpreter's spiritual life."[63] While interpretation must comply with objective rules of analysis, it ultimately involves the person as a whole and as a member of a community of interpretation. For the adherents of the Confucian tradition, the tradition is an object of affection and reverence, largely because the tradition is perceived as an embodiment of wisdom *(chih)*. As stated earlier, for Chu Hsi, tradition is a repository of insights available for personal and interpersonal appropriation, for coping with present problems and changing

---

as "moral principle" is more an emphasis on the interdependence of *i* (rightness) and *li* (principle/reason) rather than what is conveyed by the term "moral principle." For an attempt to sort out this term, along with *t'ien-li*, *tao-li*, and *t'iao-li*, see my *The Unity of Knowledge and Action: A Study in Wang Yang-ming's Moral Psychology* (Honolulu: University of Hawaii Press, 1982), 26–50. For an exposition of Hsün Tzu's conception of *chih* (accumulation), see Y. P. Mei, "Hsün Tzu's Theory of Education with an English Translation of the of the *Hsün Tzu*, Chapter I, An Exhortation to Learning," *Tsing Hua Journal of Chinese Studies* 2 (1961): 361–77.

62. *Meng Tzu*, 2A:2.

63. Yü gives a valuable discussion of a three-stage methodology in Chu Hsi's hermeneutics. "According to Chu Hsi, reading a text usually requires a person to undergo three stages. In the beginning he learns how to set his mind attentively on the text. In the second stage he penetrates into the text by following correct rules of textual analysis. Being bound by these rules, he can describe the text in its general outlines, but the description is lifeless. Only when he reaches the final stage can he bring the text to life." I here focus briefly on the final stage. (Yü, "Morality and Knowledge in Chu Hsi's Philosophical System," 238–39.)

circumstances.[64] *Tao-t'ung*, the tradition of *tao*, is thus a continuing object of interpretation, and of change and modification.

A notable corollary of the idea of *tao-t'ung*, often overlooked by the critics of the Confucian tradition, is the "conservative" character of the *tao*-perspective. In classical Confucianism, the tradition is represented by *li* (ritual propriety). For its adherents, the *li* is a set of social practices, e.g., customs, conventions, and acknowledged permissible forms of conduct. The *tao*-perspective is *conservative* in the sense that it is oriented toward a critical conservation of the values of a living ethical tradition, informed by the historical knowledge as a common culture embodied in the Confucian classics. Also, the perspective is conservative in that *tao*, specified in *li* (ritual propriety), conserves those natural feelings and dispositions that are deemed conducive to the acquisition and the promotion of the virtues *(te)*. Both these senses of "conservative" are present in the use of *fang* in the *Li Chi*. Confucius is said to compare *tao* to dikes *(fang)* for the sake of providing guidance in rectifying the deficiency of the customary standards of conduct followed by ordinary people. For this reason, "the superior person *[chün-tzu]* uses the *li* as a dike to conserve virtues *[fang-te]*, punishment as a dike against licentiousness, and prescriptions as a dike against evil desires." As James Legge comments, the character *fang* is used in this chapter both as a noun, meaning "a dike," and as a verb, "to serve as a dike." A dike has two uses: "to conserve what is inside it, preventing its flowing away, and to ward off what is without, barring its entrance and encroachment."[65]

III. TRANSFORMATION OF THE CONFUCIAN TRADITION

If the interpretation of classical Confucian texts is ultimately a matter of self-interpretation or self-transformation, its significance for dealing with changing circumstances in personal and social life remains a matter of individual judgment. The question about the relation of such a judgment to the judgment of one's fellows in the community of interpretation naturally arises. Even if such a relation can be shown in terms of their anchorage in *sensus communis,* there is a more general

64. See my "Hsün Tzu and the Unity of Virtues," 92–94; and Okada Takehito, "Chu Hsi and Wisdom as Hidden and Stored" in *Chu Hsi and Neo-Confucianism,* 197–211.

65. This translation follows the reading of Wang Meng-ou, *Li Chi chin-chu chin-i* (Taipei: Commercial Press, 1977), 2:671n. For an alternative reading, see James Legge, trans., *The Like or the Collection of Treatises on the Rules of Propriety and ceremonial Usages* (New Delhi: Matilal Barnarsidaas, 1966), 2:284. Legge's comment on *fang* appears at p. 284n.

and fundamental question concerning the possibility of change or modification of *tao-t'ung* as expressing the idea of the Confucian tradition.

From the conceptual point of view, a plausible answer lies in the explication of the Confucian framework, comprising three basic and interdependent notions, that is, *jen* (humanity), *li* (propriety), and *i* (rightness, righteousness). These basic notions represent the general specification of *tao* as a generic term which denominates a holistic vision of the good human life or unifying perspective in the Confucian community of interpretation.

Our approach employs Hsün Tzu's distinction between *kung-ming* and *pieh-ming*, rendered as generic and specific terms. A generic term is a formal, general, abstract term amenable to specific uses in either theoretical or practical contexts. These uses may be said to be specific terms in the sense that they specify the significance of a generic term adopted to a current purpose of discourse. Alternatively, we may say that there are various levels or degrees of abstraction or specification of the use of generic terms. Thus, a specific term in one context may function as a generic term in another context, depending on the current purpose of discourse.[66]

The conceptual framework consisting of *tao* as a generic term and *jen, li,* and *i* as specific terms may also be attributed to Chu Hsi, although important qualifications have to be noted. First, the framework is interpreted and elaborated by using the vocabulary of a Neo-Confucian moral metaphysics, e.g., *li-ch'i* (principle, reason/material force), *t'ai-chi*, (the Great Ultimate), and *t'ien-te chih hsin* (the Mind of Heaven and Earth). Second, Chu Hsi sometimes uses *jen* as both a generic and a specific term. For example, in "The Treatise on *Jen,*" *jen* is said to embrace the four moral qualities in the mind of man, that is, *jen* (humanity), *i* (righteousness), *li* (propriety), and *chih* (wisdom). *Jen* in the generic sense is said to be constitutive of *tao,* "which consists of the fact that the mind of Heaven and Earth to produce things is present in everything."[67] This remark suggests that *jen* as a generic term is functionally equivalent to *tao.* At any rate, with respect to *tao* as a generic term for the holistic ideal or unifying perspective, we may appeal to a couple of terse remarks in *Chu Tzu yu-lei:* (1) "*Tao* is a unifying term

66. See Ch'en Ta-ch'i, *Hsün Tzu hsüeh-shuo,* 125. For further discussion, see my "The Problem of Conceptual Unity in Hsün Tzu and Li Kou's Solution," *Philosophy East and West* 39 (1989): 121–25.

67. See Chan, *A Source Book in Chinese Philosophy,* 594; *Chu Tzu ta-ch'üan,* ed. Chu Tsai (Taipei: Chung-hua, 1970), vol. 8, ch. 67:20a. For other examples, see Ch'ien Mu, *Chu Tzu hsin hsüeh-an* (Taipei: San Min, 1982), 2:42–45.

[t'ung-ming], *li* [principle, reason] is [a term referring to its] detail items;" (2) *"Tao* is a holistic word *[tao tzu hung-ta]*, *li* is a word for details *[li tzu ching-mi]*."⁶⁸

These remarks suggest that *tao* is a holistic, generic term subject to specification of its significance using such specific terms as *jen, i, li,* and *chih* (wisdom). Note that *jen* can also be used as a generic term that embraces these four, and each in turn may need to be specified for its significance in a particular context of discourse. In addition, the specification must be governed by *li* (principle/reason), that is, a *reasoned* rather than a subjective, arbitrary specification. In this sense, the *li* refer to those detailed reasons that support one's claim to the adequacy of specification. Presumably the claim is based on an assessment of the merits of the particular situation at issue.⁶⁹

Our focus on conceptual framework brings out only the synchronic aspect of the tradition of *tao.* A fuller discussion of the possibility of transformation of the Confucian tradition must also attend to the diachronic aspect of *tao.* In Hsün Tzu's words, *"Tao* embodies constancy *[ch'ang]* and embraces all changes *[pien]*."⁷⁰ Perhaps, the same point may be made by using the Neo-Confucian language of *t'i-yung.* Recall Chu Hsi's saying: *"Tao* encompasses *t'i* [substance] and *yung* [function/ operation], one must speak of it in terms of the hidden *[yin]* and its extensive scope of operation *[fei]*."⁷¹ What is hidden (*yin*) may be said to be the latent or presupposed conceptual scheme, whose extensive scope of operation includes changing circumstances and human affairs.

However, Chu Hsi's contribution to our question on the possibility of transformation of the Confucian tradition of *tao* is better approached by attending to his discussion of the distinction and connection between *ching* and *ch'üan.* This distinction reflects a similar concern with *ch'ang* (the constant) and *pien* (the changing). Indeed, the latter is indispensable to elucidating the former. As Chu Hsi put it, *"Ching* pertains to the constant aspect of *tao [ching che tao chih ch'ang yeh]*, and *ch'üan* to the changing aspect of *tao [ch'üan che tao chih pien yeh]*."⁷²

68. *Chu Tzu yü-lei,* vol. 1, ch. 6:1a, 219.

69. This interpretation of Chu Hsi's uses of *li* pertains solely to its use as a normative notion, that is, as a standard that ought to be followed (*t'ang-jan chih che*). For his other uses, see Chan's (Ch'en Jung-chieh) entry on *li* in *Chung-kuo che-hsüeh tz'u-tien ta-ch'üan,* ed. Wei Cheng-t'ung (Taipei: Shui-niu, 1983), 479–86.

70. Watson, *Hsün Tzu: Basic Writings* (New York: Columbia University Press, 1963), 126.

71. *Chu Tzu yü-lei,* vol. 1, ch. 6:1a, 219. The distinction between *yin* (the hidden) and *fei* (the extensive scope of operation) echoes that of *Chung Yung,* sec. 12: "The Way of the superior man functions everywhere *[fei]* and yet is hidden *[yin]*;" Chan, *A Source Book in Chinese Philosophy,* 100.

72. *Chu Tzu yü-lei,* vol. 3, ch. 37, 1638.

Ching-ch'üan *Distinction*

We must now discuss at some length the *ching-ch'üan* distinction. The relevant meaning of *ching* is "an invariable rule or a standard of conduct; the constant or the recurring." (As we shall see, this meaning of *ching* poses no special problem for Chu Hsi.) The basic sense of *ch'üan* is "steel yard or balance," and as a verb, "to weigh, to estimate, or to consider." It is used not only in the sense of measuring the weight of a thing as on a balance or scale, but also in the metaphorical sense of "weighing the importance or unimportance of things or events."[73] A passage in *Meng Tzu* is clear on these uses:

It is by weighing [*ch'üan*] a thing that its weight [lightness or heaviness] can be known and by measuring it that its length can be ascertained. It is so with all things, but particularly so with the heart.[74]

More explicit is Ch'en Ch'un's (1159–1223) explanation:

[*Ch'üan*,] literally to weigh . . . , derives its meaning from a balance. A balance can weigh things, assess their weight, and obtain balance. That is why it is called *ch'üan*. To weigh means to change. In a balance there are dots to show the different degrees. To weigh is to move the scale left and right until, depending on the thing being weighed, the balance is on the level. This is similar to people applying [*ch'üan*] . . . to measure things in order to arrive at the Mean.[75]

In this sense, *ch'üan* pertains to a value judgment that aims at achieving the Mean or equilibrium of various competing considerations. Each of these considerations must be weighed, as on a balance. Significantly, for Chu Hsi and the Neo-Confucians, as well as for Hsün Tzu, the judgment must be based on *li* (principle, reason) or what we would call a principled or reasoned judgment. More briefly, as Tai Chen (1723–77) put it, *ch'üan* is "the means by which we determine what is important and what is unimportant."[76]

73. See Mathews, *Chinese-English Dictionary* (Cambridge: Harvard University Press, 1956), 235–36.
74. *Meng Tzu*, 1A:7; D. C. Lau, trans., *Mencius* (Baltimore: Penguin Books, 1970), 57.
75. For the purpose of later discussion, I have deliberately left out Chan's translation of *ch'üan* as "expediency" as indicated in the ellipses. See Ch'en Ch'un, *Neo-Confucian Terms Explained*, trans. Wing-tsit Chan (New York: Columbia University Press, 1986), 129.
76. It is interesting to observe here that Tai Chen continues his exposition of the *ching-ch'üan* distinction by employing the language of *ch'ang* (the constant) and *pien* (the changing). "Whenever the valuation that this is important and that is unimportant remains unchanged through the ages, this is meant by constancy [*ch'ang*]. . . . But when the important becomes unimportant or the unimportant becomes important, this is what is meant by change [*pien*]. In the case of change, unless a person applies his wisdom fully so that he is able to examine and analyze things accurately, he will not be able to understand it completely." Although Tai Chen goes on to criticize Cheng I and Chu Hsi, say,

When we consider the situation in which *ch'üan* is exercised, it is one in which *ching*, the normal or standard applications of basic Confucian notions, do not provide sufficient guidance. Earlier, Chan gave his rendering of the *ching-ch'üan* distinction as "the standard and the exceptional."[77] I elaborated this by the distinction between normal and exigent situations and applied the distinction to two problematic cases of regicide and of the drowning sister-in-law in the *Meng Tzu (Mencius)*. I argued for the significance of the distinction between normal and exigent situations for understanding the reconstitutive dimension of moral creativity.[78] This distinction accommodates some alternative renderings of *ch'üan*, for example, "weighing of occurring events," "peculiar exigency" (Legge), "weighing of circumstances" (Schwartz).[79]

Translation of *ch'üan* by "expediency" (as Chan gave in our passage from Ch'en Ch'un) would be misleading if it were to suggest the agent's concern for self-serving purpose rather than a concern for what is appropriate or proper under the circumstances. Expediency, in the first sense, seems to be contrary to the Confucian concern with *i* (rightness, righteousness). In the second sense, however, it is functionally equivalent to the other renderings. Lau's "moral discretion" is perhaps the best rendering of *ch'üan* in a perplexing passage in *The Analects*.

Reflection on the nature of moral discretion, along the lines of Mencius and Hsün Tzu, may provide us a systematic way of dealing with Chu Hsi's preoccupation with the *ching-ch'üan* distinction. In fact, as Wei Cheng-t'ung points out, Chu Hsi's concern was in part motivated by his students' repeated query on the notion of *ch'üan* in this passage.[80] This perplexing passage in *The Analects* runs:

---

on the dichotomy of *li* (reason/principle) and desire, surprisingly he shows no concern with their versions of the *ching-ch'üan* doctrine. The translation used here is from *Tai Chen on Mencius: Explorations in Words and Meaning*, trans. Ann-pin Chin and Mansfield Freeman (New Haven: Yale University Press, 1990), 163. For the original text, see Tai Chen, *Meng Tzu tzu-i shu-cheng* (Taipei: Ho-lu, 1975), 125. See also Hsiung Shih-li, *Tu-ching shih-yao* (Taipei: Kuang-wen, 1978), 31.

77. Chan, *A Source Book in Chinese Philosophy*, 26.

78. See my *Dimensions of Moral Creativity*, 76–78, 86–106.

79. All these renderings are suggested in one of the entries on *ch'üan* in Mathews' *Chinese-English Dictionary:* "(b) Exigency, circumstances. To act according to circumstances or expediency; opportunism; that which is irregular, and opposed to *ching*, that which is constant and normal—from this therefore comes the idea of temporary, etc." See also James Legge, trans., *The Chinese Classics* (Hong Kong Reprint from Oxford University Press, 1948), vol. 1: *The Works of Mencius*, 4A:17; and Benjamin Schwartz, *The World of Thought in Ancient China* (Cambridge: Harvard University Press, 1985), 386, 397.

80. Wei Cheng-t'ung, "Chu Hsi on the Standard *[Ching]* and the Expedient *[Ch'üan]*," trans. Roseanne E. Freece, in Chan, *Chu Hsi and Neo-Confucianism*, 255. In addition to this incisive essay, Wei also provides valuable source materials in his own entries on *ch'üan* in his *Chung Kuo che-hsüeh tz'u-tien* (Taipei: Talin, 1977), 803–05; and *Chung Kuo che-hsüeh tz'u-tien ta-ch'üan* (Taipei: Shui-niu, 1983), 848–51.

The Master said, "A man good enough as a partner in one's studies need not be good enough as a partner in the pursuit of the Way *[tao]*; a man good enough as a partner in the pursuit of the Way need not be good enough as a partner in a common stand; a man good enough as a partner in a common stand need not be good enough as a partner in the exercise of moral discretion *[ch'üan].*"[81]

The exercise of *ch'üan* is quite properly an exercise of discretion in the sense of the power of the individual to act according to his or her judgment in dealing with uncertain, exigent situations, or "hard cases." As contrasted with the "soft cases" or normal problems in human life, the hard cases are rule-indeterminate; thus, the established standards of conduct *(ching)* offer no clear guidance. Even if such standards are deemed appropriate, there may be a problem of application which calls for interpretive judgment and discretion. The problem cannot be resolved by mechanical or deductive procedures.

Most moral and legal traditions thus allow for the exercise of discretion, though such an exercise is always subject to constraints. In the Confucian context, the constraints comprise the *li*, the operative ritual rules or formal prescriptions of proper conduct. Arguably, Confucius has a recurrent interest in discretion as an indispensable means for coping with the hard cases of moral life. Recall his autobiographical remark: "I have no preconceptions about the permissible or impermissible"; and the student's description of his character: "There were four things the Master refused to have anything to do with: he refused to entertain conjectures or insist on certainty, he refused to be inflexible or to be egotistical."[82]

A study of Confucius's conception of *chün-tzu* or paradigmatic individuals also discloses his concern with the need of flexibility in conjunction with *jen* (humanity), *li* (ritual rules) and *i* (rightness).

In two different ways, the focus on *i* especially brings out the moral aspect of *ch'üan* or discretion. First, *i* is contrasted with personal gain or self-serving interest. Secondly, *i* focuses on doing the right thing as determined by a judgment of the relevance of moral rules to particular circumstances. More importantly, the exercise of *i* is required in dealing with changing, exigent situations of human life.[83] Hsün Tzu's emphasis on the use of *i* in varying one's response to changing circumstances *(yi i pien-ying)* echoes the same concern.[84] We would expect an adequate account of the *ching-ch'üan* distinction to give a pivotal role to *i*, since

81. *Lun Yü;* D.C. Lau, trans., *Confucius: The Analects* (New York: Penguin Books, 1979), 9:30.
82. Ibid., 18:8; 9:4.
83. See my *Dimensions of Moral Creativity,* chap. 4.
84. See my *Ethical Argumentation,* 23–24.

the exercise of *ch'üan* or discretion is fundamentally an exercise of *i*.[85] As we shall later see, one of Chu Hsi's insights lies in this emphasis.

The need for discretion in the interpretation of moral rules can in part be accounted for by the open texture of natural languages. That is, there is always a possibility of vagueness in the empirical and practical application of words in relation to the natural and the human world.[86] More fundamentally, the need for discretion arises out of two deficiencies of humanity. As H. L. A. Hart succinctly put it, "our relative ignorance of facts" and "indeterminacy of aim."[87] In formulating rules of conduct, presumably the ethical legislators rely on tradition and experience. They cannot always foresee the consequences of enforcement of rules nor anticipate without error our future situations, especially those that are exigent, demanding immediate attention and action. In these cases, discretion is necessary, given the human predicament. Thus, Aristotle considers that the subject matter of ethics cannot be treated with exactitude, and that "the truth" can only be indicated "with a rough and general sketch." There is a need to supplement legal justice by equity or reasonableness *(epieikeia)* as a corrective. Aristotle says:

> the reason is that all law is universal, but there are some things about which it is not possible to speak correctly in universal terms. . . . So in a situation in which the law speaks universally but the case at issue happens to fall outside the universal formula, it is correct to rectify the shortcoming.[88]

As is indicated by his preference for voluntary arbitration or mediation over adjudication in settling disputes within the community, and by his recurrent emphasis on the importance of being a *chün-tzu* (paradigmatic individual), Confucius would concur with Aristotle on the role of equity or reasonableness in human affairs. The preference for arbitration is evident in his remark in the *Analects:* "In hearing litigation, I am no different from any other men. But if you insist on a

85. Wei Cheng-t'ung, "Chu Hsi," 259–61.

86. H. L. A. Hart, *The Concept of Law* (Oxford: Oxford University Press, 1961), chap. 7, sec. 1. For the open texture of Confucian moral rules, see my *Dimensions of Moral Creativity,* 72–76, and generally, 83–86. For the idea of open texture, see F. Waismann, "Verifiability: in *Essays on Logic and Language* (First Series), ed. Antony Flew (Oxford: Basil Blackwell, 1952), 117–44.

87. Hart, *The Concept of Law,* 125.

88. Aristotle, *Nicomachean Ethics,* trans. Martin Ostwald (Indianapolis: Bobbs-Merrill, 1962), 1094b, 1137b. For a translation and discussion of *epieikeia* as reasonableness, see MacIntyre, *Whose Justice? Which Rationality?* 119–21. For the role of equity in American law, see Jerome Frank, *Law and the Modern Mind* (New York: Anchor Books, 1963), 149–58.

difference, it is, perhaps, that I try to get the parties not to resort to litigation in the first place."[89]

The exercise of *ch'üan*, moral discretion, is also necessary in the light of *tao* as a holistic ideal. This ideal of the good human life as a whole is more of a theme than a norm.[90] This ideal is a topic of communal discourse somewhat analogous to a theme in literary or musical composition, not only always recurring, in ever different ways, but even permeating the piece in its palpable absence, amenable to varying interpretations, calling for the diverse exercise of disciplined imagination. Discretion is essential especially in specifying practical objectives to be pursued in the hard cases of the moral life. It is this "indeterminacy of aims" in conjunction with human fallibility or "ignorance of facts" that renders such moral discretion *(ch'üan)* unavoidable.

Hence, if the Confucian agent is to cope with exigent, changing circumstances in the course of pursuing *tao,* he or she must be disposed to exercise *ch'üan.* This is perhaps the force of Chu Hsi's saying, "This substance of *tao* is vast and inexhaustible *[che tao-t'i hao-hao wu-ch'iung]*."[91] And Wang Yang-ming's remark: "*Tao* cannot be exhausted with finality *[tao wu chung-ch'iung]*."[92] I take this to mean that the concrete significance of *tao* cannot be specified with any claim to finality. Any attempt to do so is always governed by a sense of timeliness *(shih)* to attain the mean or equilibrium *(chung)*—that is, to aim at doing the right thing in accord with the agent's judgment of what a particular situation demands. Perhaps, this is the basis for Mencius's remark that Confucius was "the sage whose actions were timely."[93] As earlier indicated, the specification of the concrete significance of *tao* must be a reasoned or principled one. The exercise of *ch'üan* or moral discretion is thus constrained by the exercise of practical reason *(li).*

As in the study of the classics, so in the proper exercise of *ch'üan* or moral discretion, an open mind is required. While the objective is to

89. Lau, *The Analects of Confucius,* 12:13. For a Confucian conception reasonableness, see my *The Unity of Knowledge and Action,* 91–100; and more generally, my "Ideals and Values: A Study in Rescher's Moral Vision," in *Praxis and Reason: Studies in the Philosophy of Nicholas Rescher,* ed. Robert Almeder (Washington: University Press of America, 1982), 193–98.

90. For the distinction between ideal norms and ideal themes, see my *Dimensions of Moral Creativity,* chap. 8. For *Tao* as an ideal theme, see my *Ethical Argumentation,* 36–37.

91. *Chu Tzu yü-lei,* ch. 8:1a.

92. Compare with Chan's different interpretive translation: "The Way Is Infinite." See *Instructions for Practical Living and Other Neo-Confucian Writings by Wang Yang-ming,* trans. Wing-tsit Chan (New York: Columbia University Press, 1963), sec. 64, p. 46. For further discussion of Wang Yang-ming see my *The Unity of Knowledge and Action,* chap. 3; and Essay 9.

93. *Meng Tzu,* 5B:1; also 2A:2.

achieve timely equilibrium *(shih-chung)*, the Confucian tradition must not favor any one doctrine of interpretation, even if it happens to be a moderate position between extremes. As Mencius says:

> Holding on to the middle *[chung]* is closer to being right, but to do this without moral discretion *[chih chung wu-ch'üan]* is no different from holding to one extreme. The reason for disliking those who hold to one extreme is that they cripple the Way *[tao]*. One thing is singled out to the neglect of a hundred others.[94]

Moreover, Hsün Tzu would advise the Confucian agent to consider carefully all the salient features of the situation before pronouncing judgment on his current desires and aversions. In his words:

> When one sees something desirable, he must carefully consider *[lü]* whether or not it will lead to detestable consequences. When he sees something beneficial, he must carefully consider *[lü]* whether or not it will lead to harmful consequences. All these consequences must be weighed together *[chien-ch'üan]* in any mature plan before one determines which desire or aversion, choice or rejection, is to be preferred.[95]

The Concept of Ch'üan

The preceding discussion of the notion of *ch'üan* in the *ching-ch'üan* distinction provides a way to approach Chu Hsi's conception. I also assume that various renderings of *ch'üan* such as "weighing of circumstance," "exigency," "expediency," and "moral discretion" are helpful terms to use in a fuller explication of *ch'üan*. I have some doubt about "expediency," as it may suggest misleadingly that *ch'üan* may be used for self-serving purposes. I centered my attention on the expression "moral discretion," since the procedure designated by this term enables us to appreciate the plausibility and necessity of the *ching-ch'üan* distinction in any established or traditional morality. Before proceeding to Chu Hsi's distinctive contribution on the connection between *ching* and *ch'üan* let us summarize some of the salient features of the notion of *ch'üan* and briefly indicate some possible sources of support in *Chu Tzu yü-lei:*

1. As a metaphorical extension of the basic sense of a steel yard for measuring weight, *ch'üan* pertains to assessment of the importance of

---

94. This is Lau's translation except for substitution of "moral discretion" for "the proper measure." See D. C. Lau, trans., *Mencius* (Baltimore: Penguin Books, 1970. For a good discussion of Mencius's advice of "not holding to the one thing *(pu chih-i)*, see Ch'en Ta-ch'i, *Meng Tzu te ming-li ssu-hsiang chich'i pien-shuo shih-k'uang* (Taipei: Shang-wu, 1974), 24–39.
95. *Pu-kou p'ien.* See Li, *Hsün Tzu chi-shih*, 52. For further discussion on the nature of deliberation *(lü)*, see Essay 10. See also Ch'en Ta-ch'i, *Hsün Tzu hsüeh-shuo*, chap. 7.

moral considerations to a current matter of concern. Alternatively put, the exercise of *ch'üan* consists in a judgment of the comparative importance of competing options answering to a current problematic situation.

2. The situation is such that it presents a *hard case*, that is, a case falling outside the scope of operation of *ching*. Thus, normal standards of conduct provide insufficient guidance for the situation at hand.

3. *Ch'üan* is an exercise of moral discretion and must conform to the requirement of *i* (rightness, righteousness).

4. The judgment must accord with *li*, that is, be a principled or reasoned judgment.

5. The immediate objective of *ch'üan* is to attain timely equilibrium *(shih-chung)*, namely, to do the right thing *(i)* as appropriate to the demand of the current situation.

6. The ultimate objective of *ch'üan* is to further the realization of *tao* as the holistic ideal of the good human life. Moreover, the proper exercise of *ch'üan* presupposes that the agent has an open mind. As Mencius reminds the Confucian agent, he must not hold on to any one particular moral doctrine even if it represents a moderate position between extremes *(pu chih-i)*.

Features (1) and (3) are suggested by Chu Hsi's remark in response to his student's question whether or not *ch'üan* is the same as *i* (rightness, righteousness): "One must use *i* to exercise *ch'üan* before one can attain equilibrium *[chung]*. Compare *i* to a scale for measuring weight; *ch'üan* is the use of this scale to assess the importance of human affairs *[p'ing]*."[96]

Another response to a query of Cheng I's thesis that "*ching* is [nothing other than] *ch'üan [ching chi ch'üan yeh]* focuses on (5): "*Ch'üan* is timely equilibrium *[shih-chung]*. If [one does not aim at] equilibrium, one will exercise *ch'üan* in vacuo *[pu-chung che wu i-wei ch'üan yeh]*."[97] Feature (2) is quite explicit in this remark on the *ching-ch'üan* distinction: "*Ching* pertains to the normal practice of *tao* throughout the ages; *ch'üan* is employed in the situation where there is no alternative. *[Ch'üan]* must be exercised in accord with one's sense of rightness *[i]*."[98] Our earlier note on Chu Hsi's remark on *tao* as a holistic term *(t'ung-ming)* (Section B), and his recurrent use of such locutions as *tao-li* and *i-li* throughout the *Yü-lei* may be cited as evidence for features (4) and (5). However one interprets Chu Hsi's use of such terms, we may appeal to his remark that

96. *Chu Tzu yü-lei*, vol. 3, ch. 37, 1633.
97. Ibid., 1637.   98. Ibid., 1638.

ching is the normal practice of *tao-li* (moral norm or principle); the exercise of *ch'üan* is unavoidable *tao-li* in cases where such a practice fails [that is, *ch'üan* is the non-normal practice of *tao-li*.] *Ch'üan* is the *tao-li* for coping with changes [*t'ung-pien tao-li*]. When *ch'üan* attains equilibrium [*chung*], it does not differ from *ching*. All things considered, the exercise of *ch'üan* is admissible as a temporary measure, not as a method for dealing with normal situations of human life.[99]

Ching-ch'üan *Connection*

We must now discuss the *ching-ch'üan* connection. According to Wei Cheng-t'ung, Chu Hsi is especially concerned with reconciling Ch'eng I's view "that *ch'üan* is [nothing other than] *ching*" and the Han scholars' view that *ch'üan* is "that which is at variance with the standard [*ching*] but in accord with the Way [*tao*]."[100] The irony, of course, is that Ch'eng I proposed his view in opposition to that of the Han scholars. Wei's essay provides a valuable discussion of Chu Hsi's attempt and of some of the problems that arise out of Chu Hsi's application of his own view. In the light of our interest in the possibility of transformation, we focus primarily on Chu Hsi's insight into the *ching-ch'üan* connection and its bearing on the tradition of *tao (tao-t'ung)*. Chu Hsi is clear that Cheng I's seemingly reductionist thesis is unacceptable, for it collapses an important distinction. The fundamental issue is the *ching-ch'üan* connection. It is *tao* that provides the unifying connection. Says Chu Hsi: "*Ching* pertains to the constant aspect [*ch'ang*] of *tao*, *ch'üan* to the changing aspect [*pien*]. *Tao* is a unifying substance [*t'ung-t'i*] that permeates *ching* and *ch'üan*."[101] In the text we are given no further explanation, but when we turn to some other recorded remarks, we find three different interpretations. Below I cite the passages in which these interpretations are given, before proposing a reconstruction.

Passage (a): *Ching* is the *ch'üan* already determined *(ching shih yi-ting chih ch'üan)*. *Ch'üan* is *ching* prior to determination *(ch'üan shih wei-ting chih ching)*.[102]

Passage (b): *I* (rightness, righteousness) can be considered to embrace both *ching* and *ch'üan*. One should not use it only in regard to *ch'üan*. When *i* requires us to abide by *ching*, we should do so. When *i* requires us to use *ch'üan*, we should do so. This is what is meant by the saying *i* can embrace both *ching* and *ch'üan*.[103]

Passage (c): *Ching* is an outline, *ch'üan* pertains to the delicate twists

99. Ibid., 1639–40.
100. Wei Cheng-t'ung, "Chu Hsi," 255.
101. *Chu Tzu yü-lei*, vol. 3, ch. 37, 1638.
102. Ibid., 1639.   103. Ibid.

and turns [of human affairs]. For example, the ruler should be benevolent and the minister loyal, or the father should be compassionate and the son filial. These are normal, constant requirements of *tao (ching-ch'ang chih tao)*. How can they be disturbed? In their midst there must be something inexhaustible. Thus, it is necessary to exercise *ch'üan*. *Ch'üan* pertains to fine and delicate details. Unless one sees the *li* (principle, reason, rationale) in terms of its important sections and details, one cannot understand it *[ch'üan]*.[104]

Passage (a) may be used to elucidate Chu Hsi's general thesis: "*Tao* is the unifying substance *[t'ung-t'i]* that permeates *ching* and *ch'üan*." This passage suggests the connection present in their dynamic interplay. *Ching*, as comprising the normal standards of conduct, is a product of settled or determinate *ch'üan*. Presumably, the exercise of *ch'üan* in exigent situations may become accepted as constitutive of *ching* or conventional wisdom, perhaps in the sense of paradigms of applications for given standards. *Ch'üan*, on the other hand, may be regarded as *ching* prior to the determination of its significance in actual, particular situations. In other words, *ching*, the established standards of conduct, depend on *ch'üan*, in the sense that their application is undetermined prior to actual circumstances. When such a determination is made, *ch'üan* would become part of *ching*, given the assumption that the judgments are accepted by the Confucian community of interpretation. Concisely put, *ching* is the determinate *ch'üan* and *ch'üan* is the indeterminate *ching*. Of course, both represent the constant *(ch'ang)* and the changing *(pien)* aspects of tao.[105] If this interpretation is acceptable, the distinction between *ching* and *ch'üan* is a distinction explainable in terms of their dynamic, flexible connection. Any attempt to collapse or dichotomize the distinction must on this interpretation be rejected.

Passage (b) focuses on the central role of *i* (rightness, righteousness) in both *ching* and *ch'üan*. Our earlier account of the distinction in terms of the connection between *i* (rightness, righteousness) and *ch'üan* is misleading, since we have neglected the role of *i* in relation to *ching*. Thus this passage calls for an emendation of the earlier account. Judgment is necessary not only in exigent situations requiring the exercise of *ch'üan*, but also in normal situations where the intelligent agent of the tradition confronts the problem of interpretation and application. In both sorts of situation, the agent has the same moral objective, that is, to do the right thing. This is, perhaps, the point of Chu Hsi's saying

104. Ibid., 1642.   105. Ibid., 1638.

that *ch'üan* is unavoidably exercised in changing situations that fall out-side the scope of the regular practice of *tao-li* (moral norm, principle). However, "when *ch'üan* attains equilibrium [*chung*], it does not differ from *ching*,";[106] that is, they have achieved the same moral objective. As Passage (b) indicates, they are both governed by the exercise of *i* or one's sense of rightness. This passage thus renders explicit the respect in which *i* is presupposed in both normal and exigent situations. It also provides a way of understanding his general thesis that the "*tao* per-meates [*kuan*] *ching* and *ch'üan*." *I* constitutes the *kuan*, the thread that runs though *ching* and *ch'üan*.

Passage (c) advocates a different thesis that appears to be inconsis-tent with that of Passage (a). On the face of it, the connection between *ching* and *ch'üan* consists in the subordination of *ching* to *ch'üan*, in that *ching* requires the exercise of *ch'üan* in specifying the details that govern the application of the normal requirements of *tao*. On this reading, however, the exercise of *ch'üan* has no particular relation to exigent situations that fall outside the scope of application of *ching*, the normal standards of conduct. Rather, *ch'üan* is always relevant to determining the concrete significance of *ching* in those cases where the entrenched, established interpretations of standards of conduct do not provide proper guidance, or as Chu Hsi put it, in the unexhausted region of *ching*. While this is consistent with the notion of *ch'üan* as involving judgment of equity, Chu Hsi also maintains that the exercise of *ch'üan* centrally requires a comprehensive knowledge of all the *li*, the delicate details of all possible circumstances. This reflects Chu Hsi's view that only a sage could exercise *ch'üan*.[107] As Ch'en Ch'un, Chu Hsi's eminent disciple, put it, "Only a sage, who understands moral principles very clearly, can use it [*ch'üan*] without error."[108] If this is the case, ordinary intelligent adherents of the Confucian tradition are not entitled to ex-ercise *ch'üan*. This view is contrary to that in Passage (a) and to Men-cius's notion of *ch'üan*—a view Chu Hsi also accepts. The political implication of this view is no more acceptable to Confucians today than it was to Chu Hsi's critics. Consider Ch'en Ch'un's interpretation:

Ch'üan can be exercised only by people in a high position. Unless one under-stands moral principles [*i*, righteousness] clearly, one will be mistaken and will fail to see even when expediency should be applied. Although expediency [*ch'üan*] comes into play when the standard way fails to accomplish, it is not really opposed to the standard [*ching*]. When the standard has been exhausted, expediency must be used to remove the impasse.[109]

---

106. Ibid., 1639–40.   107. Ibid., 1634–38.
108. Ch'en Ch'un, *Neo-Confucian Terms Explained*, 130.
109. Ibid.

How can one be assured that such people have the requisite knowledge of *li* (principle, reason) in all possible human situations.[110] If they claim to have such knowledge, one would want to know their credentials or justification, and would also assess such credentials in argumentative discourse. Recall Mencius's rejection of the claim that rescuing a drowning sister-in-law violates the *li* that men and women are not to touch hands in giving or receiving anything. Mencius is emphatic that such a case calls for the exercise of *ch'üan* and has no special connection with people who occupy political positions. The exercise of *ch'üan* is recommended for quite ordinary persons encountering exigent situations. The liability to error in the exercise of *ch'üan* is a common human liability regardless of one's position in society or government. Becoming a sage with comprehensive knowledge is an ideal, but it can only sensibly be regarded as theoretically possible and not actually possible for human beings.[111] Recall Confucius's remark: "I have no hope of meeting a sage. I would be content to meet an ethically superior individual."[112]

Consider another reading of Passage (c), which may be consistent with Passage (a). Chu Hsi's thesis here may be construed as a conceptual thesis concerning the function of generic terms such as those that express the requirements of benevolence, loyalty, compassion, and filiality in Chu Hsi's example. As earlier noted, generic terms are subject to specification in terms of their concrete significance, that is, their relevance to occurrent situations. In the Confucian community of interpretation, there are always entrenched, established interpretations comprising *ching*, the normal or constant practice of *tao*. These interpretations are paradigms learned in the course of moral education. These paradigms are followed unquestioningly by ordinary members of the community. However, the paradigms cannot be said to exhaust completely the significance of *tao* in all possible worlds. Because of the lack of clear and determinate guidance in some situations in the moral life, ordinary agents committed to the ideal of *tao* may wonder about the right thing to do. Unavoidably, *ch'üan* is exercised in such cases. One's sense of rightness *(i)* remains no less involved. But *ch'üan* here is not something distinct from *i*, that is, *ch'üan* is functionally equivalent to *i* rather than being a notion contrasted with *ching*, as in our earlier discussion of the

110. For a critical response to the elitist pretension of Chu Hsi's followers, see John W. Haeger, "The Intellectual Context of Neo-Confucian Syncretism," *Journal of Asian Studies* 31 (1972): 507; cited in Donald J. Munro, *Images of Human Nature: A Sung Portrait* (Princeton"Princeton University Press, 1988, 19.

111. *Hsing-o p'ien*, Li, *Hsün Tzu*, 554.

112. *Analects*, 7:26.

ching-ch'üan distinction. Passage (c) also points to the ideal of comprehensive understanding in the study of the classics *(kuan-t'ung chih hsüeh)*, which involves a total understanding of the minute details in an unerring exercise of the reason *(li)*. On this reading, we do not need to revise our earlier reconstruction of the distinction and connection between *ching* and *ch'üan*. I suggest that we adopt this reading of Passage (c), since it furnishes a plausible, coherent interpretation of Chu Hsi's conception.

The foregoing reflections on the distinction and connection between *ching* and *ch'üan* afford us an answer to the question about the possibility of change or modification of the Confucian tradition of *tao*. Intelligent adherents of the Confucian tradition can deploy the skeptical challenge without fear of the corruption of the tradition. The dynamic interplay of *ching* and *ch'üan* in relation to constancy *(ch'ang)* and change *(pien)* shows that the distinction is not a fixed or absolute distinction. For as Tai Chen points out, what is deemed important or unimportant in our assessment will vary in different times and places.[113] Put differently, the substantive content of the tradition of *tao* cannot be considered settled without prejudging the merits of particular circumstances. The exercise of *ch'üan* in any situation requires a careful examination and analysis of all the relevant factors involved.[114] For a Confucian philosopher, further elaboration of the tradition of *tao* must consider the constructive interpretation of the basic conceptual framework, the critical development of tradition, and the possibility of reconciling competing interpretive judgments of the adherents of the tradition, especially those derived from the exercise of *ch'üan* or moral discretion. The urgent issue today is the adjudication of intercultural conflict. I suggest that what is needed is to develop the cooperative model of ethical argumentation and to explore how such a model can accommodate the agonistic, disputatious model dominating so much of Western moral philosophy.[115]

113. Chin and Freeman, trans., *Tai Chen on Mencius*, 162.
114. Ibid.
115. The cooperative model of ethical argumentation, according to some recent Greek scholars, is also implicit in Plato's *Protagoras* and Aristotle's *Eudemian Ethics*. See Martha Nussbaum and Amartya Sen, "Internal Criticism and Indian Rationalist Traditions" in *Relativism: Interpretation and Confrontation*, ed. Michael Krausz (Notre Dame: University of Notre Dame Press, 1989), 313; and Eugenio Benitez, "Argument, Rhetoric and Philosophic Method: Plato's *Protagoras*," *Philosophy and Rhetoric* 25, no. 3 (1992): 222–52. For Confucian argumentation, see my *Ethical Argumentation*, chap. 1; or "Hsün Tzu's Theory of Argumentation: A Reconstruction," *Review of Metaphysics* 36, no. 4 (1982): 867–94.

Essay 13

Basic Concepts of Confucian Ethics

The principal aim of this lecture is to present Confucian ethics as an ethics of virtue. The required task involves an explication of its conceptual framework. One major obstacle is the absence of definitions of important terms such as *jen, li,* and *i.* William Theodore de Bary justly remarks that "for the Chinese the idea is not so much to analyze and define concepts precisely as to expand them, to make them suggestive of the widest possible range of meaning."[1] Moreover, many key terms are, to borrow an expression from Phillip Wheelwright, plurisignations, capable of suggesting and stimulating different thoughts and interpretations.[2]

This pervasive feature of Confucian discourses may, from the point of view of contemporary moral philosophy, appear to be an anomaly, given the classical Confucian emphasis on the right use of terms *(cheng-meng).* A serious student of the works of Hsün Tzu, the classical Confucian generally considered the most rationalistic and systematic philosopher, will be frustrated in attempting to find definitions, in the sense of necessary and sufficient conditions, for the application of basic Confucian terms. This fact is particularly surprising in view of Hsün Tzu's recurrent employment of certain definitional locutions or quasi-definitional formulas for explaining his theses on human nature and the mind.[3] Hsün Tzu, like most major Confucians, has a pragmatic attitude toward the use of language. That is, the uses of terms that require explanation are those that are susceptible of misunderstanding in the context of a particular discourse. The Confucian explanation of

1. William Theodore de Bary, ed., *Self and Society in Ming Thought* (New York: Columbia University Press, 1970), v.
2. Phillip Wheelwright, *The Burning Fountain: A Study in the Language of Symbolism* (Indianapolis: Indiana University Press, 1968).
3. See my *Ethical Argumentation: A Study in Hsün Tzu's Moral Epistemology* (Honolulu: University of Hawaii Press, 1985), chap. 3.

the use of ethical terms is context-dependent, addressed to a particular rather than universal audience.[4]

Two different assumptions underlying this attitude toward language may account for the lack of Chinese interest in context-independent explanation of the use of ethical terms. First, there is an assumption of the primacy of practice implicit in the Confucian doctrine of the unity of knowledge and action.[5] Definition, in the sense of explanation, is a matter of practical rather than theoretical necessity. This assumption does not deprecate the importance of theoretical inquiry, but focuses instead on its relevance to the requirements of practice, particularly those that promote the unity and harmony among people in the community. Such requirements vary in time and place. In general, their concrete significance is affected by changing circumstances. A viable ethical theory is thus subject to pragmatic assessment in the light of changing circumstances. Consequently, ethical requirements cannot be stated in terms of absolute principles or rules. It is this assumption that renders plausible Donald Munro's claim: "The consideration important to the Chinese is the behavioral implications of belief or proposition in question. What effect does adherence to the belief have on people? What implications for social action can be drawn from the statement? . . . In Confucianism, there was no thought of 'knowing' that did not entail some consequence for action."[6]

Related to the primacy of practice is the assumption that reasoned discourse may legitimately appeal to what Nicholas Rescher calls "plausible presumptions," that is, to shared knowledge, belief, or experience, as well as to the established or operative standards of discourse.[7] For Confucian thinkers, most of these presumptions, while defeasible, represent the shared understanding of a common cultural heritage, a living ethical tradition. These presumptions are often suppressed and mainly form the background of practical discourse. Thus, Confucian reasoning and argumentation appear to be highly inexplicit. From the Aristotelian point of view, Confucian argumentation is "rhetorical," as it frequently involves enthymemes and arguments from examples.[8]

Given the assumptions of the primacy of practice and appeal to plau-

4. Chaim Perelman and Anna Olbrechts-Tyteca, *The New Rhetoric: A Treatise in Argumentation* (Notre Dame: University of Notre Dame Press, 1969), 31.

5. See my *The Unity of Knowledge and Action: A Study in Wang Yang-ming's Moral Psychology* (Honolulu: University Press of Hawaii, 1982).

6. Donald J. Munro, *The Concept of Man in Early China* (Stanford: Stanford University Press, 1969), 55–56.

7. Nicholas Rescher, *Dialectics* (Albany: State University of New York Press, 1977), 38.

8. George A. Kennedy, trans., *Aristotle on Rhetoric: A Theory of Civic Discourse* (New York: Oxford University Press, 1991), Book I.

sible presumptions, the task of explication of the conceptual frame-work of Confucian ethics is a task of philosophical reconstruction, a sort of experiment in conceptual hermeneutics. Such an exploration serves the purposes of reasonable explication and critical development of Confucian ethical thought.

I. AN ETHICS OF VIRTUE

While major Confucianists (e.g., Mencius and Hsün Tzu) differ in their conceptions of human nature in relation to conduct, most of them adopt Confucius's ideal of a well-ordered society based on good gov-ernment. Good government is responsive to the basic needs of the peo-ple, to issues of wise management of natural and human resources, and to a just distribution of burdens and benefits. In this vision of socio-political order, special emphasis is placed on harmonious human re-lationships *(lun)* in accord with *te,* virtues or standards of excellence. This vision is often called *tao,* a term appropriated by different classical schools of Chinese thought, for example, Taoism *(tao-chia)* and Legal-ism *(fa-chia).* In the *Lün Yu, tao* is sometimes used as a verb, meaning "to guide;" sometimes it is used as a concrete noun, meaning literally "road." In the latter sense, it can be rendered as "way." But in distinct Confucian ethical usage, as commonly acknowledged by commenta-tors, it is *tao* as an abstract noun that is meant, and more especially in the evaluative rather than descriptive sense, that is, as referring to the ethical ideal of a good human life as a whole.

Throughout its long history, Confucianism has stressed character formation or personal cultivation of virtues *(te).*[9] Thus it seems appro-priate to characterize Confucian ethics as an ethics of virtues. To avoid misunderstanding, two explanations are in order. First, the Confucian focus on the centrality of virtues assumes that *te* can be rendered as "virtue." Second, as we shall see later, this focus does not depreciate the importance of rule-governed conduct nor the principled interpre-tation of basic notions.

Sinologists differ in their interpretation of the Confucian use of *te.* Some maintain that *te* is functionally equivalent to "power," "force," or "potency," and in Confucian usage should be qualified as moral in con-trast to physical force. More commonly, *te* is rendered as "virtue" in the distinctively ethical sense, as pertaining to excellence of a character trait or disposition. Interestingly, these two construals of *te* are not incom-

9. For a classic statement see the "Great Learning" *(Ta-hsueh)* in Wing-sit Chan, *A Source Book in Chinese Philosophy* (Princeton: Princeton University Press, 1963).

patible in the light of some English uses of "virtue." We find the first sense in the sixth entry of "virtue" in *Webster's Third New International Dictionary:* "an active quality or power whether of physical or of moral nature: the capacity or power adequate to the production of a given effect"; and in the fifth entry: "a characteristic, quality, or trait known or felt to be excellent." Both these senses of "virtue" are present in the classical Chinese uses of *te*. Of course, there is, as in English, the value-neutral sense of *te* that leaves open the question whether personal traits or qualities merit ethical approval. This question is reflected in the distinction in Modern Chinese between *mei-te* and *o-te*. The former pertains to "beautiful" or "commendable" *te* and the latter to its contrary. *Mei-te* are those traits acquired through personal cultivation. *The Encyclopedic Dictionary of the Chinese Language* offers the following two entries for *te* in the ethical sense: (1) "That which is obtained in the *hsin* (mind/heart) as a result of personal cultivation," and (2) "The nature that is formed after successful personal cultivation." The first is suggested by an interpretation of its homophone, meaning "to get" or "to obtain," found in the *Li Chi*. Both these entries involve *mei-te*, commendable, acquired qualities of character, much in the sense of Hume's "personal merits."[10]

Also important is the sense of *te* as power or force, in view of the Confucian notion of *chün-tzu* (ethically superior or paradigmatic individual). The *chün-tzu* who exercises the virtues possesses the power of attraction or influence indicative of effective agency. Thus the *chün-tzu*, equipped with the various virtues *(te)*, has the power or capacity to influence the course of human affairs. This interpretation is suggested by two remarks of Confucius: "Virtue *[te]* never stands alone; it is bound to have neighbors," and "The virtue of the *chün-tzu* is like the wind; the virtue of the small man is like grass. Let the wind blow over the grass and it is sure to bend."[11] Even if the *chün-tzu's* power is limited, he has an indispensable educational role, not only in providing models for competence in *li* or rule following, but also in inculcating *jen*-attitude or ethical concern and reasonableness in rule application.[12] This educational role provides, at least, a partial account for Confucius's emphasis on the necessity of caution in speech and commitment prior to action in the light of his ideal of harmony of words and deeds, or in

10. David Hume, *An Inquiry Concerning the Principles of Morals* (Indianapolis: Bobbs-Merrill, 1957).
11. *Lun Yü,* 4:25 and 12:19. Translation adopted from D. C. Lau, trans., *Confucius: The Analects* (New York: Penguin Books, 1979). For a recent view of virtues as powers, see Philippa Foot, *Virtues and Vices* (Berkeley: University of California Press, 1979), 16–18.
12. See Essay 8.

the famous words of Wang Yang-ming, "the unity of knowledge and action."[13]

In sum, the Confucian notion of *te* can be properly rendered as a conception of ethical virtues that possesses a dual aspect: (1) an achieved condition of an ethically well-cultivated person, with commendable character traits in accord with the ideal of *tao;* and (2) a condition that is deemed to have a peculiar potency or power of efficacy in influencing the course of human life. The difficult problem is to present the Confucian *tao* and *te* as an ethics of virtue with a coherent conceptual scheme.

II. BASIC NOTIONS AND THE PROBLEM OF CONCEPTUAL UNITY

The *Lun Yü,* commonly considered the main and reliable source of Confucius's teachings, bequeaths to the Chinese a large and complex ethical vocabulary. This vocabulary contains a significant number of virtue *(te)* terms (henceforth, aretaic terms) that implicitly refer to the Confucian ideal of *tao.* Terms such as *jen, i,* and *li* occupy a central position both in the *Lun Yü* and throughout the history of Confucian discourse. Until recent times, few philosophical scholars of Confucianism attended to the conceptual explication and the unity of these basic notions, that is, their presumed interconnection or interdependence in the light of *tao* as an ideal, unifying perspective. While most Confucian terms for particular virtues can be rendered into English without the need of elaborate explanation (e.g., filiality, courage, dignity, fidelity, kindness, respectfulness), the apparently basic notions *(jen, li,* and *i)* are not amenable to the simple expedience of translation; they thus pose a problem for conceptual analysis and interpretation. Moreover, existing translations of these terms ineluctably embody the writer's interpretation, a sort of compendious statement of an implicit commentary, representing the writer's preunderstanding of the translated texts.

Likewise, an explication of basic Confucian notions involves philosophical commentary, a familiar feature in the development of the history of Chinese thought. However, the attempt is beset by a formidable difficulty, especially in the explication of the basic concepts of the Confucian framework. To my knowledge, the pioneering study of the conceptual aspect of Confucian ethics is Ch'en Ta-ch'i's *Kung Tzu hsüeh-*

13. See my *Dimensions of Moral Creativity: Paradigms, Principles, and Ideals* (University Park: Pennsylvania State University Press, 1978), chap. 4; and *The Unity of Knowledge and Action,* chap. 1.

shuo.[14] Ch'en reminds us that prior to interpreting the ideas of Confucius, it is essential to inquire into the conceptual status of some recurrent terms in the text. For determining the centrality or basic status of notions or concepts, Ch'en proposes four salient features. Basic concepts are (1) fundamental, (2) leading or guiding, (3) the most important, and (4) the most comprehensive.[15]

Fundamental Concepts

Feature (1) suggests the distinction between basic and derivative concepts. However, it is more plausible and accords better with Ch'en's discussion to construe his distinction as one between basic and dependent concepts. Given our characterization of Confucian ethics as an ethics of virtues, the conceptual distinction may be rephrased as a distinction between basic and dependent virtues. A concept may depend on another for its ethical significance without being a logical derivation. For instance, one cannot derive the concept of love from *jen*, yet the ethical significance of love depends on its connection with *jen*. This is perhaps the principal ground for Chu Hsi's famous contention that *jen* cannot be equated with love, for it is the rationale of love *(ai chih li)*.[16]

Leading or Guiding Concepts

Feature (2) recalls the purport of ethical terms as action guides and informs the Confucian agent that the enduring significance of ethical endeavors lies in *tao* or the ideal of the good human life as a whole, an ideal to be pursued and rendered concrete in particular circumstances.

Cardinal and Comprehensive Concepts

Feature (3) is the chief mark of basic ethical concepts as cardinal concepts. Feature (4) raises an issue in Confucian scholarship. It seems unproblematic if comprehensiveness is ascribed to *tao* or *jen* in the broad sense as signifying the holistic, ideal unifying perspective of Con-

14. Ch'en Ta-ch'i, *Kung Tzu hsüeh-shuo* (Taipei: Cheng-chung, 1976. The first edition appeared in 1964. Unaware of Ch'en's books, my earlier studies of Confucian ethics were much in the spirit of Chen's works, for example, "The Logic of Confucian Dialogues" in John K. Ryan, ed., *Studies in Philosophy and the History of Philosophy* (Washington: The Catholic University of America Press, 1969); and "Some Reflections on Methodology in Chinese Philosophy," *International Philosophical Quarterly* 11, no. 2 (1971): 236–48. Cf. Yeh Ching-kuei, *Kung Tzu te tao-te che-hsüeh* (Taipei: Cheng-chung, 1977); Herbert Fingarette, *Confucius: The Secular as Sacred* (New York: Harper Torchbooks, 1972); and David L. Hall and Roger Ames, *Thinking Through Confucius* (Albany: State University of New York Press, 1987).

15. Ch'en Ta-ch'i, *Kung Tzu hsüeh-shuo*, 98.

16. See Chan, *A Source Book in Chinese Philosophy*, 595. For more passages, see Ch'ien Mu, *Chu Tzu hsin hsüeh-an* (Taipei: San Min, 1982), vol. 2, 50–56.

fucian discourse. Again, consider Chu Hsi's thesis that *jen* (in the broad sense) embraces the four: *jen* (in the narrow sense), *i, li,* and wisdom. For an ethics of virtue, the fundamental distinction is the distinction between cardinal and dependent virtues. Accordingly, Ch'en proposes that in addition to *tao* and *te,* the Confucian scheme consists of *jen, li,* and *i* as the basic, cardinal concepts. This thesis is well supported by the recurrence of such concepts and their fundamental importance throughout the history of Confucianism.[17]

The foregoing remarks pertain to the identification of basic, cardinal concepts as contrasted with dependent concepts. A more formidable problem remains: How are these basic concepts related to one another? The following discussion presents a sketch of a philosophical reconstruction, which is essentially a conceptual experiment. The sketch offers a general characterization of Confucian ethics as a form of virtue ethics and provides a sample of how such basic notions as *li* and *i* can be shaped in response to questions deemed important for the development of a Confucian moral philosophy.

The Confucian ethical framework comprises the five basic concepts: *tao, te, jen, i,* and *li.* Perhaps, the best approach is to regard them initially, with a minimum of interpretation, as "focal notions," that is, terms that function as focal lenses for conveying distinct, though not unrelated centers of ethical concern.[18] As generic terms, focal notions are amenable to specification in particular contexts, by which they acquire specific or narrower senses. This distinction is an adaptation of Hsün Tzu's between generic *(kung-ming)* and specific terms *(pieh-ming).* However, in general, a term used as a specific term in one context may, in another context, be used as a generic term subject to further specification. In other words, the use of a term in either the generic or the specific sense is entirely relative to the speaker's purpose on a particular occasion, rather than to any theory concerning the intrinsic characters of terms or the essential attributes of things.

As earlier noted, *tao* is an evaluative term. Its focal point of interest lies in the Confucian vision of the good human life as a whole or the ideal of human excellence. Commonly rendered as "the way," *tao* is

---

17. Although various thinkers proffered different interpretations, these basic concepts remain the core of Confucian ethics until quite recent times. See, for example, Shen Tsing-sung, *Ch'üan-tung te tsai-sheng* (Taipei: Yeh-ch'iang, 1992). My earlier remarks on *tao* and *te* owe much to Ch'en Ta-ch'i's conceptual studies.

18. For more discussion on focal notions, see my *Dimensions of Moral Creativity,* chap. 2. For the basic Confucian concepts as focal notions, see my "The Problem of Conceptual Unity in Hsün Tzu and Li Kou's Solution," *Philosophy East and West* 39, no. 2 (1989): 115–34.

functionally equivalent to the ideal "way of life."[19] Unlike other basic terms, *tao* is most distinctive as an abstract, formal term in the highest generic sense, that is, subject to general specification by way of such virtue *(te)* words as *jen, li,* and *i.* Recall that *te* is an individual achievement through personal cultivation. When a person succeeds in realizing *tao,* he or she has attained such basic *te* as *jen, li,* and *i.* The specification of *te,* apart from *jen, li,* and *i,* can also be given by citation of any dependent virtue such as filiality, respectfulness, or fidelity. In this sense, *te* is an abstract noun like *tao,* but it depends on *tao* for its distinctive character. *Te* is thus functionally equivalent to ethical virtue. Thus, the opening remark of *Ta-hsüeh* ("Great Learning") points out that the way of great learning or adult, ethical education lies in the clear exemplification of the virtues *(ming ming-te).* With its emphasis on *tao* and *te,* Confucian ethics is properly characterized as an ethics of virtue, but more informatively as an ethics of *jen, li,* and *i,* relative to their concrete specification or particularization by terms of dependent virtues (e.g., filiality, respectfulness, integrity). As generic, focal terms: *jen, li,* and *i* are specific terms relative to *tao* as a generic term. Differently put, implicit in Ch'en's account is a distinction between basic, interdependent virtues *(jen, li,* and *i)* and dependent virtues (e.g., filiality, respectfulness). As indicated earlier, the latter are dependent in the sense that their ethical import depends on direct or indirect reference to one or more of the basic, interdependent virtues of *jen, li,* and *i,* respectively.

While *jen* has a long history of conceptual evolution and interpretation, as a focal notion it centers its ethical interest on the love and care for one's fellows, that is, an affectionate concern for the well-being of others—the one persistent idea in the Confucian tradition.[20] Thus *jen* has been felicitously rendered as "human-heartedness" or "humanity"—a concrete specification of the abstract ideal of *tao.* This core meaning of *jen* as fellow feeling is found in *Lun Yü.*[21] It is reported that Confucius once said to Tseng Tzu, "My *tao* has one thread that runs through it."[22] Tseng Tzu construed this *tao* to consist of *chung* and *shu,* an interpretation widely acknowledged as a method for pursuing *jen.* While the relation between *chung* and *shu* has divergent interpretations,

19. However, this ideal is more like a theme to be developed in the concrete setting of human life than a norm that contains specific precepts of conduct. See my *Dimensions of Moral Creativity,* chap. 8.

20. See Wing-tsit Chan, "The Evolution of the Concept *Jen," Philosophy East and West* 4, no. 4 (1955): 295–19; and Wing-tsit Chan, "Chinese and Western Interpretations of *Jen," Journal of Chinese Philosophy* 2, no. 2 (1975): 107–29.

21. *Lun Yü,* 12:22.

22. Ibid., 4:15.

chung may be rendered as "doing one's best,"[23] *shu* as "consideration" (of other people's feelings and desires).[24] In this light, Confucian ethics displays a concern for both self-regarding and other-regarding virtues.

However, the acquisition of these virtues presupposes a locus in which these particular, dependent virtues are exercised. Thus among dependent virtues, filiality and fraternity are considered primary, for the family is the natural home and the foundation for the extension of *jen*-affection. In Sung and Ming Confucianism (e.g., Ch'eng Hao, Wang Yang-ming), *tao* is sometimes used interchangeably with *jen*. In this manner, *jen* has attained the status of a supreme, all-embracing, ethical ideal of the well-being of every existent thing, human or non-human, animate or inanimate. Confucius's vision of a well-ordered human society is transformed into the vision of the universe as a moral community.[25] In this conception any thing that is an actual or potential object of human attention is considered an object of human concern. Exploitation of human and natural resources must be subject to evaluation in terms of *tao* as an all-embracing ethical ideal of existence. This ideal of *tao* makes no specific demands on ordinary humans. For the most part, conflict of values is left to individual determination, though the welfare of the parents is always the first consideration. Thus, the concrete significance of *tao* is open to the exercise of *i*, alternatively moral discretion *(ch'üan)*, or the agent's sense of rightness.

The exercise of *i* depends on ethical education based on *tao-t'ung* or the tradition of the community of interpretation. That is, reasoned interpretation of the educated members of the community informed by *sensus communis*, a sense of common interest, a regard for *tao* as the ideal unifying perspective. Disagreement or dispute on the pragmatic import of *tao* is expected, as members of the community of interpretation have their own conceptions of the human excellence *(shan)* and possibilities of fulfillment. The ethical solution of conflict of interpretation lies in transforming the disagreement into agreement in the light of *sensus communis*, not in a solution defined by agonistic debate, which presumes that there are impartial judges who can render their corporate decision by a majority vote. Unlike contemporary democratic polity, the majority rule cannot be reasonably accepted as a standard

23. Lau, *Confucius: the Analects,* Introduction, 16.
24. For a general discussion see Kwong-loi Shun, "Confucius," in Lawrence Becker and Charlotte Becker, eds., *Encyclopedia of Ethics* (New York: Garland, 1992), vol. 1. Cf. Herbert Fingarette, "Following the One Thread in the *Analects,*" *Journal of the American Academy of Religion: Thematic Issue: Studies in Classical Chinese Thought* 47, no. 3s: 373–406; and my "Confucian Vision and the Human Community," *Journal of Chinese Philosophy* 11, no. 3 (1984): 226–38.
25. See Essay 9, Part I.

for settling ethical disagreement. Sound ethical decision, contrary to the claim of a recent utilitarian, is not a matter of subjectivity and statistical evaluation.[26] For it is the ethical tradition that provides the background and guidelines to ethical conduct. Normative ethical theories have value because they provide different ways of assessing the significance of tradition. Like the basic concepts of Confucian ethics, they are focal notions for important centers of ethical concern, e.g., duty and interest (private or public), or in recent terminology, agent-relative and agent-neutral reasons for action.

The notion of *li* focuses on the ritual code. For this reason, it is commonly rendered as "rites," "ritual," "propriety," or "ceremonials." The ritual code is essentially a set of rules of proper conduct pertaining to the manner or style of performance.[27] As *i* is incompatible with exclusive regard for personal gain, the *li* set forth the rules of ethical responsibility. For Confucius and his followers, the *li* represent an enlightened tradition. As D. C. Lau put it:

The rites *(li)* were a body of rules governing action in every aspect of life and they were the repository of past insights into morality. It is, therefore, important that one should, unless there are strong reasons to the contrary, observe them. Though there is no guarantee that observance of the rites necessarily leads, in every case, to behaviour that is right, the chances are it will, in fact do so.[28]

Yet, the ethical significance of *li* is determined by the presence of the spirit of *jen*. As Confucius once said, "If a man has no *jen*, what has he to do with *li*?"[29]

Since the ritual code represents a customary practice, the early Confucians, particularly Hsün Tzu and writers of some chapters in the *Li Chi*, were concerned with providing a reasoned justification for compliance with *li* or traditional rules of proper conduct. Arthur Waley aptly remarks: "It was with the relation of ritual *[li]* as a whole to morality and not with the details of etiquette and precedence that the early Confucianists were chiefly concerned."[30] The same concern with reasoned justification is evident in Sung and Ming Confucianists (e.g., Chu Hsi and Wang Yang-ming), who maintain that the significance of *li* (ritual) lies in its rationale *(li chi li)*.[31]

26. Ching Lai Shiang, *A New Approach to Utilitarianism: A Unified Utilitarian Theory and Its Applications to Distributive Justice* (Dordrecht: Kluwer, 1991).
27. See my *Dimensions of Moral Creativity*, chap. 7.
28. Lau, *Confucius: the Analects*, Introduction, 20.
29. *Lun Yü*, 3:3.
30. Arthur Waley, trans., *The Analects of Confucius* (New York: Vintage Books, 1938), Introduction, 67.
31. See, for example, *Chu Tzu yu-lei*, ch. 84 and 86; and Wang Yang-ming, "Preface

The ethical significance of *i*, in part, is an attempt to provide a rationale for the acceptance of *li*. *I* focuses principally on what is right or fitting. The equation of *i* with its homophone meaning "appropriateness" is explicit in *Chung Yung*, Section 20, and generally accepted by Confucianists, e.g., Hsün Tzu, Li Kou, and Chu Hsi. However, what is right or fitting depends on reasoned judgment. As Hsün Tzu puts it: "The person concerned with *i* follows reason."[32] Thus, *i* may be construed as reasoned judgment concerning the right thing to do in particular exigencies. Recall Li Kou's plausible statement that *i* is "decisive judgment" that is appropriate to the situation at hand.[33] While both *jen* and *li* have been closely studied, *i* is largely neglected.[34] Below I offer a fuller explication for appreciating the ethical significance of *i* and its connection with *li*.

III. THE INTERDEPENDENCE OF *I* AND *LI*

For dealing with the problem of the distinction and relation between *i* and *li*, the following tentative scheme for analysis of *i* may be helpful. The scheme is a conceptual proposal for *i* as rightness independently of issues in textual scholarship.[35]

S_1 An action is *right* if
a. it conforms to the requirement of an established rule, or
b. it conforms to the agent's judgment of what is appropriate or fitting to the requirement of the situation-at-hand.

S_2 A person is *righteous* if he or she is conscientious in performing the right action as indicated in S_1.

S_3 A person's *judgment* concerning what is right (S_1) is correct (i.e., has a reasoned justification) if

---

to the Annotated Edition of the *Book of Rites*" in Julia Ching, *To Acquire Wisdom* (New York: Columbia University Press, 1976), 202–5.

32. Li Ti-sheng, *Hsün Tzu chi-shih* (Taipei: Hsüeh-sheng, 1979), *Ta-lüeh p'ien*, 605. Hereafter, reference to Li's edition of *Hsün Tzu* will also cite the title of the essay.

33. See the essay cited in n. 18 above.

34. To my knowledge, in English, the few exceptions are my "The Concept of Paradigmatic Individuals in the Ethics of Confucius," *Inquiry* 14 (1971): 41–55; and "Hsün Tzu and the Unity of Virtues," *Journal of Chinese Philosophy* 14, no. 4 (1987): 381–400; Chung-ying Cheng, "Yi as a Universal Principle of Specific Application," *Philosophy East and West* 22, no. 3 (1972); and Hall and Ames, *Thinking through Confucius*.

35. The discussion of this scheme is a revised version of my study of the uses of *i* in *Hsün Tzu* as reported in my "Hsün Tzu and the Unity of Virtues." The first part of that paper presents the general background in terms of the distinction between *chang* (the constant) and *pien* (the changing). See also Part C of Essay 12.

a. it can be shown to be a correct judgment of the relevance of an established rule to his action (S_{1a}), or

b. it can be shown to be consonant with other ethical values, which, in the situation, are considered to be relevant and not open to question (S_{1b}).

S_4 A person possesses *moral sense* if

a. he or she appreciates the distinction between right and wrong (moral distinction), or

b. he or she is actuated by a sense of duty as pertaining to what he ought or ought not to do in a particular situation which he confronts.

In a contemporary idiom, *i* as an ethical notion can be explicated as (S_1) a deontic, (S_2) an aretaic, (S_3) an epistemic, or (S_4) a psychological term. Thus *i* is a distinct plurisign adaptable to a range of meaning or significance in the various contexts of discourse.

With the foregoing scheme, along with the assumption that the *li* comprise a set of ritual rules, let us first take up the question of *li* and *i* as distinct notions. We may proceed by inquiring into the respect in which they differ. In other words, let us focus on each sense of *i* and see what can be plausibly said about *li* and *i* as distinct notions.

In general, both *li* and *i* have the same objective in ensuring the performance of right conduct. This is the strength of the functional equivalence thesis: *li* and *i* have the same regulative function, that is, the same purpose in indicating standards of conduct.[36] In our scheme, with respect to S_1, S_{1a} is functionally equivalent to *li*, since the *li* collectively represent the established rules for proper conduct. Plausibly, it is this thesis that explains Hsün Tzu's frequent association of *li* and laws *(fa)*, rules and regulations. But for him, the *li* collectively constitute the foundation for all rule-like requirements. According to S_{1a}, a right action is one that accords with an established rule, and unproblematically this rule may be said to be a part of *li*. But this leaves open to action in accord with S_{1b}, that is, to the case of right conduct that falls outside the scope of *li*. This is the merit of the delimitation thesis, that *i* in the sense of S_{1b} fixes the boundary or the scope of *li* in particular situations, which are deemed to be exigent rather than normal.[37] Hsün

36. Ch'en Ta-ch'i, *Hsün Tzu hsüeh-shuo* (Taipei: Chung-hua wen-hua she, 1954), 144. In the following discussion, I briefly deal with four different theses on the relation between *li* and *i*. Although these theses were originally proposed for resolving the problem of co-occurrence of *li* and *i* in the *Hsün Tzu*, they epitomize possible options for a general problem in interpreting Confucian ethics. See my "The Problem of Conceptual Unity."

37. Li, *Hsün Tzu, Ch'üan-hsüeh p'ien*, 10. For the delimitation thesis, see Wei Cheng-t'ung, *Hsün Tzu yü ku-tai che-hsüeh* (Taipei: Shang-wu, 1974), 7.

Tzu recognizes the real possibility of this sort of situation, as is evident in his remark: "Where there are established rules of conduct *[fa]*, comply with them. Where there are no such rules, act in the spirit of analogy *[lei]*."[38] Thus the *li* cannot deal with situations envisaged by S_{1b}. Our scheme suggests that *li* and *i* can be properly distinguished along the line indicated by the distinction between S_{1a} and S_{1b}. Alternatively, the distinction depicts a difference in the direction of focus. *Li* is rule-oriented and *i* situation-oriented. Thus even if an action is described as one that conforms to a rule of *li*, this description presupposes that the rule in question is relevant to the action in a particular situation. Now S_{1b} clearly points out that the action in a particular situation may be judged by the agent to be outside the operative scope of *li*. This judgment, of course, has to be justified as required by S_3. Thus both S_{1a} and S_{1b} imply S_3, which is the distinctive function of *i*. Let me briefly look at S_2.

S_2 is dependent on S_1 for explication, which in turn depends on S_3. The focus of S_2 is *i* as an aretaic term with reference to a virtue, desirable character trait, or virtuous disposition. Since Confucius, major Confucian thinkers contrast *i* with the concern for personal gain or profit. To act in the spirit of *i* is to display a conscientious regard for moral distinctions (S_4) in considering whether one should carry out one's self-serving projects. In this sense *i* is an aretaic term. *Li* can also be construed as an aretaic term referring to the virtue of rule responsibility or compliance, that is, to the ethically commendable disposition *(mei-te)* to conform to established requirements. *Li* is a first-order virtue; *i* as conscientiousness is a second-order virtue. As William Frankena points out, "Besides first order virtues such as these [e.g., honesty, fidelity, benevolence, and justice], there are certain other moral virtues that ought to be cultivated, which are in a way more abstract and general and may be called second-order virtues. Conscientiousness is such a virtue; it is not limited to a certain sector of the moral life, as gratitude and honesty are, but a virtue covering the whole of the moral life."[39] Of course, a Confucian will add that the ultimate significance of *i* lies in its connection with *tao* or *jen* as an ideal of extensive affection for all things in the world. Also, he or she will emphasize such dependent virtues as integrity, courage, circumspection, informed and wise deliberation—a common theme in both Confucian and Western ethical thought.

38. Li, *Hsün Tzu, Wang-chih p'ien*, 163; emended translation of Burton Watson, trans., *Hsün Tzu: Basic Writing* (New York: Columbia University Press, 1963), 34.
39. William Frankena, *Ethics*, 2d ed. (Englewood-Cliff: Prentice-Hall, 1973), 46.

In connection with S_3, it is important to note that i as a virtue implicitly presupposes impartiality *(kung)*.[40] *I* in the sense of S_2 implies the likely divergence and opposition between morality and personal advantage. When a conflict occurs, concern for i must take precedence. Although this contrast is sometimes present in *li*-performance, there the emphasis is on the importance of compliance with conventional standards of conduct. In the case of i, the emphasis is on detachment from the desire for personal gain as required by consideration of situational appropriateness. Again, Hsün Tzu is emphatic on this point: "A clear system of rules and regulations, weights and measure, exists for the sake of proper employment; they are not conventions to be blindly followed."[41] *Li* and i in S_2 are thus distinct notions, for compliance with *li* may be based on consideration of personal gain rather than on conscientious regard for established standards of conduct. It is also possible for a committed person to perform a conscientious action devoid of a reasoned judgment of appropriate action in a particular situation. Thus S_2 depends on the force of S_3.

Let us now turn to S_3, which lies at the heart of i as a distinct ethical notion. It is essentially the notion of reasoned or correct judgment or ruling.[42] In S_{3a}, i pertains to the judgment of the relevance of a rule to a particular situation; in S_{3b}, to the judgment that appeals to the relevance of other ethical notions. This sense of i is hardly detachable for *ch'üan*, the exercise of moral discretion.[43] Within Confucian ethics, such notions as *jen*, in the narrow sense of benevolence, may be deemed operative in particular cases. It cannot be denied that if *li* is broadly construed as a comprehensive ethical term in Confucian ethics, *jen* and i would be subsumed under *li*.[44] The plausibility of this interpretation of the *Lun Yü* presupposes that *li* is a set of ideal-embedded rules rather than a mere set of established rules. This means that this use of *li* entails its connection with *jen*. Also, *li* in the primary regulative sense depends on i for assessing the relevance of rules to particular cases. *I* in the distinctive sense of S_3, as a focus on reasoned judgment, is essentially an epistemic notion, thus involving explanation and justification of ethical judgments.[45]

Again, i in S_4 cannot be equated with *li* in the regulative sense. Moral

---

40. See my *Ethical Argumentation*, chap. 1.

41. Li, *Hsün Tzu, Chün-tao p'ien*, 286.

42. See my *Dimensions of Moral Creativity*, chaps. 4 & 5.

43. See Essay 12, 255–66.

44. Homer H. Dubs, *Hsüntze: The Moulder of Ancient Confucianism* (London: Arthur Probsthain, 1927), 66; and Fingarette, *Confucius: The Secular as Sacred*.

45. See my *Ethical Argumentation*, 51–86.

sense is essentially a cognitive appreciation of moral distinction (S_{4a}) and more especially a sense of duty (S_{4b}). It is this notion of i that renders plausible a basic aspect of Wang Yang-ming's Mencian conception of *liang-chih* as the native ability of humans to distinguish right from wrong conduct.[46] One can perform a *li*-action without appreciating its rationale. As a cognitive ability for appreciating ethical distinctions, i presupposes the capacity to form reasoned judgment (i in S_3) or to engage in informed deliberation *(chih-lü)*—a theme that pervades Hsün Tzu's concern with reasoned response to changing circumstances *(yi-i pien-ying)*. Our analytic scheme for the analysis of i in relation to *li* thus provides us a way for locating *li* and i as distinct ethical notions.

The preceding remarks, however, pertain to the distinction between *li* and i. While we acknowledge that in terms of S_{1a}, both *li* and i are functionally equivalent, it is also important to inquire into their connection. As specific terms for the elaboration of *tao* as a generic term, both *li* and i are partners in the same enterprise of morality. They are focal and complementary notions in Confucian ethics. Generally, within Confucian ethical thought, the distinction between notions is important only because some connection can be made out in appropriate contexts of discourse. Let us now go through the various senses of i and exhibit, if possible, their connection.

With respect to S_{1a}, we may construe the connection as the priority of *li* over i, for S_{1a} clearly implies such a thesis, that is, we need to appeal to our own judgment of the appropriate thing to do in a particular situation only when the *li*, as embodying the established rules, in some sense fail to guide us in resolving our current problem. In other words, this is the sort of situation in which a *li*-requirement is considered but, on reflection, the agent deems it inoperative or inapplicable to a case at hand. As Hsün Tzu points out, "Just as weights and measures are the standard for things, the *li* are the standard for rules and regulations. Weights and measures establish quantity; the *li* fix the different sorts of human relationship."[47] The *li*, always in the first instance, provide ethical considerations as reasons for action, though in a particular situation, they may not furnish sufficient guidance. In the sense of *li* as the first consideration, i is thus dependent on *li*.

However, in another sense i in S_3 is prior to *li*. For in S_{3a}, i in the sense of reasoned judgment on the relevance of rule to a particular case is presupposed by any application of *li*. For Hsün Tzu, just as there are no rules or laws that can establish their own efficacy without men

46. See my "Between Commitment and Realization," sec. III.
47. Li, *Hsün Tzu, Chih-shih p'ien*, 307.

to carry them out, so also there are no types *(lei)* of rules that contain their own rules for application.[48] Thus i in S_{3a} can claim a priority in determining the relevance of rules to particular cases. If the *li* are deemed applicable to particular cases, they must be judged to be the right sort of rule. In S_{3b}, this claim of priority of i over *li* is even more obvious, for *li* has to be declared irrelevant to exigent situations. This is the basis for our last remark at the end of Section II, that i may be construed as reasoned judgment concerning the right thing to do in particular exigencies. Thus, while the *li* always present a claim to attention in ethical thinking, it is i in S_3 that decisively establishes their relevance or irrelevance. The same sort of priority may be said of i in S_2 as a second-order virtue, for acting ethically requires not only rule following (S_{1a}), but also a disposition to do the right thing in a particular situation. Whether the disposition is properly directed depends on a judgment of appropriateness (S_{1b}), which, in turn, requires reasoned justification (S_3). Moreover, as we have earlier observed, acting from a virtuous disposition is quite different from mere rule responsibility, for it requires the willingness to forego one's personal interests for the sake of the requirement of righteousness. As Hsün Tzu puts it, "A superior man must be able to overcome his private desires in favor of impartiality *[kung]* and rightness *[I]*."[49]

When we turn to i in S_4, the appreciation of moral distinctions and sense of duty, we can again claim the priority of i over *li*. The former (S_{4a}) implies, in particular, that one possesses an enlightened understanding of the significance of *li*. In Hsün Tzu's words, "A superior man engages in extensive learning and daily examines himself, so that his understanding will be enlightened and his conduct be without fault."[50] This enlightened understanding essentially involves an appreciation of the rationale of *li* and related matters, i.e., its connection with other moral values (S_{3b}), principally *jen*. Indeed great insight into the living significance of *tao* and the interconnection of basic ethical notions depends on preserving the clarity of mind. This clarity of mind is a prerequisite to reflection and reasoned justification of ethical judgments and decisions in exigent situations. We may thus conclude that, with the exception of i in S_{1a}, which is functionally equivalent to *li*, in all other cases, i is prior to *li* in moral thought and action. This claim of priority of i over *li* is not an absolute claim. For if it were to be a claim to absolute priority, it might misleadingly suggest that *li* could be

48. Ibid., *Chün-tao p'ien*, 263.
49. Ibid., *Hsiu-shen p'ien*, 36.
50. Ibid., *Ch'üan-hsüeh p'ien*, 2; Watson, *Hsün Tzu*, 15 ("superior man" in lieu of "gentleman").

ignored when one judged that a particular rule is irrelevant to an exigent circumstance. After all, given the functional equivalence of *li* and *i* (S_{1a}) in some contexts, both have the same objective in governing conduct. This sense of *i* is exemplified in the expression *shih-i*, the ten duties of the classical five human relationships.[51] Given *i* in S_3, for instance, *li* may again become relevant in communicating our reasoned judgments to others as they affect their well-being. In so doing, the *li*, as rules of civility, need to be attended to, for they are an essential requirement for participation in traditional ethical life and argumentation.[52] Consequently, the question of priority regarding *li* and *i* cannot be answered in an absolute or abstract statement of priority. It is a contextual question to be answered in dealing with the normal and changing circumstances of human life. In this light, while *li* in *i* are distinct focal notions, in context they may be mutually dependent for their actuating import for moral conduct. In this way, we may regard *li* and *i* as partners in the same human enterprise.

In sum, we may state the interdependence of Confucian basic notions in this way. Given *tao* as the ideal of the good human life as a whole, *jen*, *li*, and *i*, the basic, interdependent Confucian virtues *(te)*, are constitutive rather than mere instrumental means to the fulfillment of *tao*. In other words, the realization of *tao* requires the co-satisfaction of the standards expressed in *jen*, *li*, and *i*. Since these focal notions pertain to different foci of ethical interest, we may also say that the realization of *tao* requires a coordination or harmonious interaction of three equally important centers of ethical interest and endeavor. The connection between these foci is one of interdependence rather than subordination. Thus, in the ideal case, *jen*, *li*, and *i* are mutually supportive and adherent to the same ideal of *tao*. When *tao* is in fact realized, *jen*, *li*, and *i* would be deemed constituents of this condition of achievement. On the other hand, when one attends to the prospect of *tao*-realization, *jen*, *li*, and *i* would be regarded as complementary foci and means to *tao* as an ultimate end. *Jen*, *li*, and *i* are complementary aspects of *tao*.

For readers of *Meng Tzu*, our presentation of the basic, interdependent concepts of virtues in Confucian ethics has a glaring omission, namely, *chih* (wisdom). This omission is deliberate, not because *chih* is not a cardinal virtue, but because the Confucian notion of wisdom is perhaps best understood as a storehouse of insights derived from past

51. Wang Meng-ou, *Li Chi hsin-chu hsin-i* (Taipei: Shang-wu, 1977), vol. 1, chap. 9, *Li Yun.*
52. See my *Ethical Argumentation,* 8–11.

ethical experiences, principally those not codifiable in terms of *li* as a set of formal rules of proper behavior. This conception of wisdom seems to be implicit in Chu Hsi's conception of wisdom as that which is " hidden and stored" *(chih-ts'ang)*. As Takehiko points out, this is one of the neglected and important themes in Chu Hsi scholarship.

Chu Hsi's idea of wisdom as hidden and stored is a comprehensive synthesis not only of ideas on it before the Ch'in period (221–206 B.C.) and those handed down through the Han and the T'ang periods, but also of the opinions of Northern Sung Confucian scholars in regard to wisdom. His 'wisdom,' which is based on realization through personal experience, should be differentiated from the literal and philological interpretations of the Han and T'ang scholars. By rejecting the Buddhist and the Taoist ideas of wisdom, Chu Hsi raised the traditional understanding of wisdom to a higher level.[53]

The emphasis on personal experience for acquiring wisdom recalls an important feature of Chu Hsi's conception of interpreting the classics. As Yü Ying-shih has shown, for Chu Hsi the interpretive process must culminate in a stage in which the reader can reanimate a text in such a manner that it becomes an integral part of the reader's life.[54] Below, I present a personal reading of Chu Hsi's conception of wisdom by pondering the parallels he draws between the four attributes of Heaven and Earth and the four seasons, and the latter with the four cardinal virtues, as stated in his classic essay entitled *Jen Shuo* or "A Treatise on *Jen*."

The moral qualities *[te]* of Heaven and Earth are four: origination *[yüan]*, flourish *[heng]*, advantage *[li]*, and firmness *[chen]*. And the principle of origination unites and controls them all. In their operation they constitute the course of the four seasons, and the vital force of Spring permeates them all. Therefore in the mind of man there are also four moral qualities—namely, *jen*, righteousness *[i]*, propriety *[li]*, and wisdom *[chih]*—and *jen* embraces them all.[55]

Consider the analogy of the four seasons and the four cardinal virtues. Were we to take Chu Hsi's passage as stating a correspondence thesis, from our perspective today, the analogy would be nothing but a fanciful speculation, a thesis with no empirical support. On the other hand, if we take the analogy, not as a thesis with factual grounding, but

53. Takehiko's paper provides a valuable account of the sources of Chu Hsi's conception. See Okada Takehiko, "Chu Hsi and Wisdom as Hidden and Stored" in Wing-tsit Chan, ed., *Chu Hsi and Neo-Confucianism* (Honolulu: University of Hawaii press, 1986), 200.

54. Yü Ying-shih, "Morality and Knowledge in Chu Hsi's Philosophical System," in Chan, *Chu Hsi and Neo-Confucianism*, 238–39.

55. Chan, *A Source Book in Chinese Philosophy*, 593–94. For original text, see *Chu Tzu Ta-ch'üan* (Taipei: Chung-hua, 1970), vol. 8, chap. 67:20.

as an expression of the symbolic significance of the seasonal analogy, it is suggestive of valuable insights concerning the nature of wisdom and the dynamic relation of the four cardinal virtues. This reading presupposes the analogy between the four attributes or virtues *(te)* of Heaven and Earth and the four seasons. Our symbolic interpretation is plausible, since Chu Hsi's attribution of the four attributes of Heaven and Earth are indebted to the commentary of the first and second hexagrams of the *I Ching*, which was an attempt to give a symbolic representation of the hexagrams *ch'ien* (Heaven) and *kun* (Earth). Derivatively, the four seasons are the symbolic representation of concrete significance of the abstract ideas of the four Confucian cardinal virtues. Notably, a symbolic representation of an abstract, general idea is a device for providing an example of concrete specification of the practical significance of the idea in actual human life. In this light, the seasonal analogy is insightful, expressing Chu Hsi's notion of wisdom and an elucidation of a possible relation of the four cardinal virtues.[56]

Recall Ch'eng I's metaphor "*jen* is seed." *Jen* conveys the requisite ethical motivation and creative vitality, the source or beginning of the ethical life dedicated to the realization of *tao*. The cultivation of *jen* requires a period for "planting" the seeds or ethical education, providing the *yüan* (origination) of the ethical life. Metaphorically, this is the Spring of ethical life. Again, recall Confucius's notion of *jen* as extensive love and Wang Yang-ming's vision of the universe as a moral community.[57] For ordinary intelligent people, without some concrete example of how this ideal may be realized, it will appear merely as a mere speculative idea. This is perhaps the basis for Mencius's doctrine of the four *hsin* (heart/mind), especially when the *hsin* of commiseration is conceived as the first beginning. For it is the inculcation of compassion that provides the material for developing the virtue of *jen*. Absent the sensitivity to the suffering of one's fellows, it is not possible to acquire the virtue of *jen*. Appreciating Mencius's doctrine of the four *hsin* as the seeds for the four cardinal virtues does not imply an acceptance of his thesis on the inherent goodness of human nature.[58] Ideally a *jen*-person will not confine his benevolence to his family, society, or state. He or she will enlarge the scope of affectionate concern for humanity whenever possible, and ultimately, for all things in the world.

The efforts to realize *jen* depends on *i* (S_3), the agent's reasoned judg-

---

56. See Essay 5.
57. See Essay 9.
58. Meng Tzu, 2A:6. For my view on the dispute between Hsün Tzu and Mencius on human nature, see my "The Quasi-Empirical Aspect of Hsün Tzu's Philosophy of Human Nature," *Philosophy East and West* 28, no. 1 (1978): 373–89.

ment of what one ought to do in a particular, uncertain situation. It is, so to speak, the "summer" of the ethical life, a time in which *jen* develops or flourishes *(heng)*. There are times in one's life where the intense preoccupation with self-interest renders the commitment to *jen* a side issue. Also, the concern with self-interest often conflicts with one's sense of rightness *(i)*. The cultivation of the ethical motivation for attainment of *jen* depends on the exercise of *i*. Given the interdependence of *jen* and *i*, the attainment of *jen* presupposes that the pursuit of *jen* pay due attention to particular circumstances. This, in turn, presupposes that the agent has sufficient self-discipline *(ke-chi)*, the ability to control his or her desires or passions. This is perhaps the force of Confucius's conception that self-mastery is a constitutive means for the realization of *jen*.[59] As Confucius reminds his pupils, the *chün-tzu* regards *i* as indispensable to the ethical life.[60] The "summer" is, so to speak, the maturation of the activity of *jen*, which entails the successful exercise of *i* in coping with changing, exigent circumstances of human life.

Autumn is, so to speak, a time of maturity, a season for gathering the crops and fruits of moral experiences, owing to the exercise of *i* or *ch'uan* (moral discretion) in exigent circumstances. For the most part, these experiences consist of unrelated particular judgments which need to be put in some systematic order, i.e., in the form of *li* or rules of proper conduct. The *li* represent a codification of the products of the exercise of *i*. Moreover, from the point of view of the tradition, the *li*, as we shall see shortly, have a supportive function, enabling individuals to satisfy their desires within the boundary of propriety. Since the *li* are a code of proper conduct, it is expected that the exercise of *i* will also be involved in the process of codification. For reasoned value judgment is required to decide what is to be rightly included in a coherent code. When such a code has been followed in a few generations, they acquire a *de jure* status and constitute the established tradition of proper behavior. In Rawls's term, the *li* are originally summary rules or generalization of ethical experiences, though in the course of time, because of general acceptance and/or blind conformity, they become practice rules.[61]

Instead of discarding the uncodifiable cases, they are to be preserved or stored, say, as a savings account in a bank. Selective, reasoned judgment is involved in the process. At the same time, the deposit re-

59. *Lun Yü*, 12:1.
60. Ibid., 17:23.
61. John Rawls, "Two Concepts of Rules," *Philosophical Review* 64 (1955).

quires attention as to its possible future use. In this light, wisdom is the ability to make use of the depository of moral insights derived from the exercise of *i*, those ethical experiences that cannot be codified in terms of *li*. It is important that the storehouse be located in a firm *(chen)* or rock solid place.

An ethical life devoted to the pursuit of *tao* requires vigilance even in times of tranquility. These are the occasions indispensable for contemplating the significance of the uncodified ethical experiences. Here is perhaps the import of Chu Hsi's analogy of wisdom *(chih)* and winter. Metaphorically, winter is the time for the acquisition of wisdom, for gathering the fruits of ethical experience, a time for contemplating the prospective import of the temporal upshot of moral experience. The practical efficacy in employing wisdom lies in the agent's ability to make intelligent use of the gathering *(shou-lien)* or depository of insights derived from the exercises of *jen*, *li*, and *i*, the basic interdependent virtues of the tradition. In this light, wisdom *(chih)* is a virtue of sagacity, a second-order virtue like *i*, which, as Chu Hsi has shown, is implicit in the intelligent exercise of moral discretion *(ch'üan)* in dealing with changing circumstances of human life.[62] A Confucian sage, the idealized perfect person possessing wisdom, without any thought or deliberation, would simply respond to things as they come. In the words of Hsün Tzu: "The sage considers himself as a measure *[tu]* or standard for appraising things. Hence, by means of his [knowledge of] of men in the present, he can judge those of the past. . . . By means of *tao* he can command a comprehensive view of all things." But for ordinary agents, the realistic hope is to become a *chün-tzu*, a paradigmatic individual who must engage in deliberation, especially in coping with changing circumstances.[63]

IV. THE CONCEPT OF LI

In this section, I center my attention on *li* as a generic term *open* to specification of its significance in response to certain critical questions concerning its subject matter, scope, and purposes and functions. The section that follows deals with the question of justification. The connection of *li*, *jen*, and *i* is assumed to be unproblematic.[64] The principal aim is to shape the notion of *li* into a distinctive ethical concept by sketching a set of coherent and plausible answers to certain critical

62. See Essay 12, sec. C.
63. See Li, *Hsün Tzu, fei-hsiang* p'ien, 82. For further discussion, see my *Ethical Argumentation*, 64–69.
64. See my "The Problem of Conceptual Unity in Hsün Tzu and Li Kou's Solution."

questions. No claim to final adequacy is intended, since any of these answers may be further challenged or contested. While a reasonable question may be said to presuppose the existence of a right answer, as Collingwood reminds us, a right answer is ". . . an answer which enables us to get ahead with the process of questioning and answering."[65] In this sense, *li* is an essentially contested concept.[66] For my task, I have drawn freely from the works of Hsün Tzu, supplemented by contributions of other Confucian thinkers. To my knowledge Hsün Tzu is sensitive to these critical questions, and offers us, perhaps, the best insights into the significance of *li* in Confucian ethics.

Scope and Evolution of Li

Because of its distinctive character and role in Confucian ethics as well as its pervasive influence in traditional China, the notion of *li* requires special attention. Implicit in the notion is the concept of rule-governed conduct. In the *Li Chi*, the subject matter ranges widely from formal prescriptions (henceforth, ritual rules) concerning mourning, sacrifices, marriage, and communal festivities to the more ordinary occasions relating to conduct toward ruler, superior, parent, elder, teacher, and guest. Because of its emphasis on the form or manner of behavior, *li* is often translated as "religious rites, ceremony, deportment, decorum, propriety, formality, politeness, courtesy, etiquette, good form, good behaviour, [or] good manner."[67]

The first critical question is the issue of change of ritual rules. One may wonder whether these rules are amenable to modification. A Confucian theorist would point out that adapting to changing circumstances may reasonably call for addition, subtraction, or modification of established rules. As one writer in *Li Chi* remarks: "Kings of the Three Dynasties did not copy the *li* of the preceding dynasty, because of differences in society."[68]

In order to elucidate this key feature of Confucian ethics, following the insight of Hu Shih, it is instructive to view the wide-ranging scope as exemplifying three different stages in the conceptual evolution of *li*.[69] The basic meaning of *li* lies in the idea of rule. The evolution of *li*

65. R. G. Collingwood, *An Autobiography* (Oxford: Oxford University Press, 1939), 17.

66. See W. G. Gallie, *Philosophy and Historical Understanding* (London: Chatto & Windus, 1964), chap. 4.

67. Homer H. Dubs, *Hsüntze: The Moulder of Ancient Confucianism* (London: Arthur Probsthain, 1927), 113n.

68. See Kao Ming, "Chu Hsi's Discipline of Propriety" in Chan, *Chu Hsi and Neo-Confucianism*, 322.

69. The following account is based on Hu Shih, *Chung-kuo che-hsüeh shih ta-kang* [1918] Part I (Taipei: Commercial Press, 1947), 134–43. My use of Hu Shih does not

pertains to its increasing extension. The earliest use, as far as scholars are able to ascertain, is confined to religious rites. The etymology of *li* suggests its connection with religious practices. The *Shuo-wen* notes that "*li* is compliance [with rules] for serving spirits and obtaining blessing."[70] In a subsequent stage, *li* becomes a comprehensive notion embracing all social practices and customs, comprising a set of action-guiding rules. In this sense, the scope of *li* is coextensive with that of tradition, that is, customs and usages deemed as a coherent set of precedents. For the Confucian, this is the domain of *wen* or culture. As the term suggests, *wen* characteristically focuses on grace or elegant form of behavior. As I have discussed elsewhere, the Confucian *li* has an aesthetic as well as moral and religious dimensions.[71] A writer of the *Li Chi* put it, a *li*-performance is not just an exhibition of an empty form, for the ethically superior person *(chün-tzu)* complies with *li* in order "to give proper and elegant expression to his feelings."[72] In this way, the *li* provide ample opportunity for individual agents to display personal sensitivities and style of performance.[73]

The third stage in the evolution of *li* is connected with the notion of *i* and reason. In this sense, any rule that is considered right and reasonable can be accepted as an exemplary rule of conduct. Rules can be constructed, revised, or even eradicated. For this reason, they are not exclusively determined by old customs and usages.[74] This conception is evident in a few places in the *Li Chi*. The *li* are said to be "the right ordering of affairs." "The *li* are [the prescriptions of] reason. . . . The superior man makes no movement without [a ground of] reason." One emphatic passage maintains that the *li* are "the embodied expression of what is right *[i]*. If an observance stand[s] the test of being judged by the standard of what is right, although it may not have been among the usages of the ancient kings, it may be adopted on the ground of its

---

presuppose an acceptance of his claim to being a historical account. As Kato points out, it is not plausible to regard the original meaning of *li* as pertaining exclusively to religious rites. "The religious rites go back to the oldest antiquity when they were not something different from [those of] everyday life." But Kato did not deny that the Confucians in the classics made a distinction between religious and moral rules as suggested by Hu Shih. Kato is more interested in the anthropological than the philosophical significance of *li*. Joken Kato, "The Meaning of Li," *Philosophical Studies of Japan* 4 (1963): 82. Note that for elaborating Hu Shih's doctrine of three stages, I make use of insights derived from my study of *Li Chi* and *Hsün Tzu*.

70. Tuan, Yü-tsai, *Shuo-wen chieh-tzu chu* (Shanghai: Shanghai ku-chi, 1981).

71. See my "Dimensions of *Li* (Propriety): Reflections on an Aspect of Hsün Tzu's Ethics," *Philosophy East and West* 29, no. 4 (1979): 373–94.

72. *Li Chi, Tseng Tzu wen;* James Legge, trans., *The Liki or Collection of Treatises on the Rules of Propriety and Ceremonial Usages* (New Delhi: Motilal Barnarsidaas, 1966), 1:331.

73. See my *Dimensions of Moral Creativity*, chap. 7.

74. Hu Shih, *Chung-kuo che-hsüeh shih ta-kang*, 137–38.

being right."[75] It is quite evident that the *Li Chi*, like the *Hsün Tzu*, was concerned with the problem of rational justification. If we regard *li* as a tradition of ritual propriety, then for the Confucian, its authoritative character depends on rational acceptance.

Accordingly, the issue of modification of *li* or ritual rules is a practical rather than a merely theoretical issue. The governing consideration is the exercise of *i* or the sense of appropriateness to the time and place of a particular society. More generally, one must use *i* to cope with changing circumstances *(yi-i pien-ying)*.[76] As indicated in the last section, the traditional ritual code is essentially a codification of ethical experiences based on *jen* and *i*. Its relevance to the present, particularly in exigent situations, is a matter of reasoned judgment. Wherefore, the *li* are subject to revision or even elimination. Notably, as Chu Hsi points out, we must reject rules that are unreasonably burdensome and superfluous, and retain rules that are practicable and essential to the maintenance of the social order.[77] A respect for a living tradition is quite different from the attitude of the traditionalist. Because of this decisive difference, from the internal point of view, a respect for tradition entails an openness to critical examination of the tradition. This examination is "made obligatory, not only by the inner dynamic of the tradition itself, but by outsiders who have raised questions about the unexamined assumptions of the tradition."[78]

Similar consideration applies to the query whether the *li* are absolute or relative to particular circumstances. In normal situations within a community, the *li* may be said to be absolute, in that they pose no serious moral perplexity; they have no exceptions. But in dealing with exigent situations or with the customary practices of other communities, one's sense of appropriateness *(i)* must determine proper conduct. As is said in the *Li Chi*, "In (observing) the rules of propriety *(li)*, what is right (for the time and in the circumstances) should be followed. In discharging a mission (to another state), its customs are to be observed."[79] Of course, an ethically cultivated person *(chün-tzu)*, informed by the spirit of *jen* and *i*, while exercising his art of accommodation *(chien-shu)* will not sacrifice his integrity *(te-ts'ao)*. He cannot be subverted either by his natural desire for personal gain or by the power of an established authority or the masses.[80] (More importantly, in any

75. *Li Chi, Chung-ni yen-chü & Li Yün;* Legge, 2:275; 1:390.
76. See Li, *Hsün Tzu, Pu-kou p'ien* and *Chih-shih p'ien.*
77. Kao Ming, "Chu Hsi's Discipline of Propriety," 324.
78. Pelikan, *The Vindication of Tradition* (New Haven: Yale University Press, 1984), 65, 72.
79. *Chü Li;* Legge, *Liki,* 1:62–63.
80. Li, *Hsün Tzu, Ch'üan-hsüeh p'ien,* 19.

situation which he deems exigent, whether within or outside his own community, the commonly presumed relevance of a rule of *li* has to be declared irrelevant, inspite of its reasonable claim to be "absolute" as a first consideration in ethical reflection. An exigent situation calls for the exercise of moral discretion *(ch'üan).* The issue here has nothing to do with building an exception to the rule but with making an exception to the rule. The rule retains its absolute character, but judged as irrelevant to the exigent situation. When the judgment is challenged, a reasonable Confucian agent will engage in argumentation.[81]

In ordinary life, the enforcement of the *li* of human relationships, for example, require unquestioning compliance. In exigent situations, refusal to follow the *li* may well be necessary. In the case of an ethically responsible minister, whenever the ruler has departed from the *tao*, it is quite proper for the minister to follow *tao* rather than the ruler. So also, while filial piety enjoins obedience, there are situations where disobedience is morally justified. When, for example, one's compliance with parental wishes will bring them disgrace rather than honor; when one will endanger the lives of the parents rather than bring them peace; and when the parents' wishes are such as to compel one to behave like a dumb creature rather than a man of moral cultivation. In all these cases, one must follow *i* or one's sense of what is right.[82]

For Wittgenstein, rules do not determine the application of rules. "A rule stands there like a sign-post." "The sign-post is in order—if, under normal circumstances, it fulfills its purpose."[83] Much in the same spirit, Hsün Tzu reminds his readers: "Just as there are no laws that can stand by themselves [without men who carry them out], there are no classes *[lei]* that can by themselves be applied."[84] I take this to mean that class terms and rules do not contain their own rules of application. The application of rules depends on the purpose and context of discourse. More importantly, Hsün Tzu explicitly cautions us: "A clear system of rules and regulations, weights and measure, exist for the sake of proper employment; they are not conventions to be blindly followed."[85] In general, rules must be diligently enforced. In exigent circumstances where they are deemed inapplicable, one must exercise one's sense of rightness *(i).* This concern with reasoned justification of the application of *li* is particularly evident with the occasional tendency

81. See my *Dimensions of Moral Creativity,* 72–104.
82. Li, *Hsün Tzu, Tzu-tao P'ien,* 651.
83. Ludwig Wittgenstein, *Philosophical Investigations* (New York: Macmillan, 1969), secs. 84, 87.
84. Li, *Hsün Tzu, Chün-tao p'ien,* 263.
85. Ibid., 286.

of early Confucians to associate *li* with its homophone, meaning "principle," "reason," or "rationale." As Hsün Tzu put it, the rationale of *li* is profound, it is not a subject for the exercise of logical acumen, say, the collapse of "the distinction between hardness and whiteness," or of "the distinction between sameness and difference"—the favorite topics of the "logicians" who specialize in discursive paradoxes.[86] Hsün Tzu was critical, for example, of Hui Shih's thesis that "Heaven is as low as the earth; mountains and marshes are on the same level."[87] "Hui Shih's mind was excessively preoccupied with verbal expressions *(ts'u)* without regard to actualities."[88]

Three Functions of Li

However, any reasoned attempt to revise or replace *li* presupposes an understanding of their purposes or functions. It is this understanding that distinguishes the Confucian scholar from a pedant, who may have a mastery of rules without understanding their rationales. Again, I rely mainly on Hsün Tzu for elucidation, since some of his essays present the most articulate concern and defense of *li* as an embodiment of a living, ethical tradition.

The *li,* as a set of formal prescriptions for proper behavior, have a threefold function: delimiting, supportive, and ennobling. The *delimiting function* is primary, in that the *li* are fundamentally directed to the prevention of human conflict. They comprise a set of constraints that delineate the boundaries for the pursuit of individual needs, desires, and interests. The *li* purport to set forth rules of proceeding in an orderly fashion, ultimately to promote the unity and harmony of human association in a state ruled by a sage king imbued with the spirit of *jen* and *i.* This orderliness consists of social distinctions or divisions in various kinds of human relationships *(lun),* namely, the distinctions between ruler and minister, father and son, the eminent and the humble, the elder and the younger, the rich and the poor, and the important and unimportant members of society. In Section V, we shall elaborate this important aspect of Confucian ethics.

In abstraction from the connection with *jen* and *i,* the delimiting function of *li* may be compared to that of negative moral rules or criminal law. Like rules against killing, stealing, or lying, the *li* impose constraints on conduct. They create, so to speak, paths of obstruction, thereby blocking certain moves of agents in the pursuit of their desires

---

86. Ibid., 428.
87. Chan, *A Source Book in Chinese Philosophy,* 233.
88. Li, *Hsün Tzu, Chieh-pi p'ien,* 478.

or interests. They, in effect, stipulate the conditions of the eligibility or permissibility of actions. They do not prejudge the substantive character or value of individual pursuit. Agents acquire information on the limiting conditions of action, but no positive guidance as to how his or her desires may be properly satisfied. Put differently, the *li* tell agents what goals *not* to pursue, but not how to go about pursuing their goals within the prescribed limits of action.

Apart from the delimiting function, the *li* have also a *supportive function;* that is, they provide conditions or opportunities for satisfaction of a person's desires within the prescribed limits of action. Instead of suppressing desires, the *li* provide acceptable channels or outlets for their fulfillment. In contemporary idiom, the *li* have a sublimating function. The supportive function of *li* acknowledges the integrity of our natural desires. So long as they are pursued within the bounds of propriety, we accept them for what they are, regardless of whether these desires are reasonable or unreasonable, wise or foolish, good or bad. The main supportive function of *li* is the redirection of the course of individual self-seeking activities, not the suppression of the motivating desires. Just as the delimiting function of *li* may be compared with that of criminal law, their supportive function may be compared with that of procedural law, which contains rules that enable us to carry out our desires (e.g., the law of wills or of contracts). Instead of suppressing these desires, the *li* offer an outlet for our search for their satisfaction. What distinguishes an ethically superior person *(chün-tzu)* from a petty one *(hsiao-jen)* lies not in the love of honor and the hate of shame, or in the love of what is beneficial and the hate of what is injurious, but in the contrary ways in which they pursue their self-serving aims.[89]

The focus on the *ennobling function* of *li* is a distinctive feature of Confucian ethics and traditional Chinese culture. The keynote of the ennobling function is "cultural refinement" *(wen)*, the education and nourishment *(yang)* of emotions or their transformation in accord with the spirit of *jen* and *i*. The characteristic concern with the form of proper behavior is still present. However, the form stressed is not just a matter of fitting into a structure of social or political organization, nor a matter of methodic procedure that facilitates the satisfaction of the agent's desires and wishes. Rather, it involves the elegant form *(wen)* of pursuing the satisfaction of desires. In other words, the ennobling function of *li* is primarily concerned with the development of beautiful or commendable virtues *(mei-te)*, or excellence *(shan)*, which is essentially the outcome of transformed human desires. In this sense, the *li*

89. Ibid., *Jung-ju p'ien*, 60.

represent "the acme of *tao* and *te* (virtue)."[90] Perhaps this is the basis for the preference of "noble person" as a translation for *chün-tzu*, because implicit in the notion of *chün-tzu* is the idea of nobility in the sense of exemplary achievement of ethical excellence, ethically superior person or paradigmatic individual of a moral tradition.

The "beauty" (*mei*) of the expression of an ethical character lies in the balance of emotion and form. What is deemed admirable in the virtuous conduct of a *chün-tzu* is the harmonious blending of elegant form and emotions. As indicated earlier, a *li*-performance has an aesthetic dimension. In two different and related ways, a *li*-performance may be said to be an object of delight. Of course, this view presupposes that the audience of a discourse of *li* enjoys the beauty of forms in any of its varieties, whether they are a product of nature or human design. In the first place, the elegant human form is something that gratifies our senses. The form can be contemplated with delight quite apart from the expressed emotional quality. In the second place, when we attend to the emotion or emotional quality expressed by a human action, which we perceive as a sign of an ethical virtue or character, our mind is delighted and exalted—presuming, of course, that we are also agents interested in the promotion of ethical virtues in general. Doing justice to the ennobling function of *li* requires a complex characterization and evaluation, quite beyond the scope of this lecture. The general idea is aptly stated by Thomé H. Fang: *li* is "cultural refinement, boding forth either in the prudence of conduct, or the balance of emotion, or the rationality of knowledge, or the intelligent working of order. Especially, it is blended with the excellent spirit of fine arts such as poetry and music. In short, what is called *Li* in Chinese is a standard of measurement for the general cultural values, according to which we can enjoy the beauties of life in the rational order of political societies."[91]

Being prescriptions of reason, it is justly said that the idea of rational rule "connects all shades of meaning of *li*."[92] Of course, given the importance of the exercise of moral discretion (*ch'üan*) in accord with the agent's sense of rightness (*i*), the main concern is with reasonableness rather than rationality in the sense of logical deduction or derivation of the significant functions of *li* from prior principles of conduct. In the next essay we will deal with the question of the status of principles in Confucian ethics.[93]

Each of the three functions of *li* admits of further elaboration in

90. Ibid., *Ch'üan-hsüeh p'ien*, 10.
91. Thomé H. Fang, *The Chinese View of Life* (Taipei: Linking, 1980), 169.
92. Kato, "The Meaning of *Li*," 82.
93. See Essay 14.

response to queries concerning its relevance to substantive issues of human conduct. The importance of *i*, in the sense of reasoned judgment on what is right and appropriate, suggests that concrete issues cannot be settled in advance of a careful consideration of actual circumstances of human life. The more difficult issue pertains to the justification of the three-fold function of *li*, the subject of the next section.

V. JUSTIFICATION OF *LI*

At the outset, let us observe that the three-fold function of *li* provides a basis for distinguishing two different kinds of rules of proper conduct. Following John Searle, we may say that the rules that perform the delimiting and supportive functions are regulative rules, in that they "regulate antecedently existing forms of behavior."[94] The rules that perform the ennobling function, on the other hand, are constitutive rules, in that "they do not merely regulate, but create or define new forms of behavior."[95] Given this distinction, the justification of the Confucian conception of *li* calls for two sorts of consideration. The justification for the necessity of regulative rules, on the whole, seems unproblematic, as it involves plausible presumptions. The justification for the necessity of constitutive rules, however, is extremely difficult. My discussion will be largely confined to raising some questions that are worthy of further exploration.

Human Predicament[96]

To make apparent the necessity of regulative rules, I shall make use of some of Hsün Tzu's insights on the problematic character of human

94. As an example of regulative rules, Searle cites the "rules of polite table behavior." For a Confucian, however, rules of etiquette are constitutive rather than regulative rules in Searle's sense. Rules of etiquette are part of the *li* of civility that perform the ennobling function. Serving guests at the table, for example, is quite distinct from placing food at the table. Negative moral rules or precepts, e.g., against lying, cheating, and killing, are better examples of regulative rules. Unlike rules of chess (Searle's example of constitutive rules), these precepts do not define the nature of the antecedent forms of behavior (John Searle, "How to Derive 'Ought' from 'Is'," *Philosophical Review* 73 (1964). Reprinted in W. D. Hudson, ed., *The Is/Ought Question* (London: Macmillan, 1969), 131. For a distinction in the same terminology, but used for a different purpose, see J. D. Mabbott, *An Introduction to Ethics* (London: Hutcheson University Library, 1966), 43–45.
95. Ibid.
96. The following set of observations on the human predicament in the absence of regulative rules is fairly familiar in the history of Western moral philosophy, for example, Protagoras, Hobbes, Hume, Hart, Rawls, and Warnock. However, this set of observations has been used for establishing quite different theses. Hsün Tzu's view, briefly expounded below, is closer to Hume and Hart. Also, it must be noted that this set of observations may be recast in terms of arguments from thought experiment, given a reconstruction

nature. Reflection on the motivational aspects of human nature *(hsing)* discloses a self-seeking propensity to satisfy desires. If this propensity is conjoined with the observed scarcity of resources to satisfy everyone's desires, it is plausible to maintain that, in the absence of regulation, conflict or contention, social disorder, and eventually poverty will result. As Hsün Tzu succinctly put it, "People have desires and aversions for the same things. Their desires are many, while things are few. This scarcity will inevitably lead to contention."[97]

The natural tendency to seek satisfaction of desires, however, need not be construed as selfish, as excluding any concern for other people's feelings and desires. Rather, it is a tendency to be partial *(pien)*, to favor things and persons of one's own relation and affection.[98] This natural partiality is in some way "bad" *(o)*, for without regulation, it is liable to produce discord and strife, which are undesirable from the point of view of good social order. Were humans intrinsically good, that is, "upright, reasonable, and orderly," Hsün Tzu asks, "what need would there be for sage-kings and *li?*"[99] Imagine the situation in which all regulative rules were removed, the respect for *li* and *i* gone, along with laws and punishment: how would the people in the world deal with one another? It is reasonable to think that, in this situation, "the strong would injure the weak and rob them, and many would do violence to the few and shout them down. The whole world would be in violence

---

of the conceptual aspect of Hsün Tzu's theory of human nature. For a survey and critical discussion, see J. L. Mackie, *Ethics: Inventing Right and Wrong* (Middlesex: Penguin Books, 1977), chap. 5. For Hsün Tzu's view, see my "The Conceptual Aspect of Hsün Tzu's Philosophy of Human Nature," *Philosophy East and West* 27, no. 4 (1977): 373–89; and "The Quasi-Empirical Aspect of Hsün Tzu's Philosophy of Human Nature," *Philosophy East and West* 28, no. 1 (1978): 1–19. For a comparative critique, see Essay 6. For an incisive exposition of Hsün Tzu's view, see D. C. Lau, "Theories of Human Nature in Mencius and Shyuntzyy," *Bulletin of Oriental and African Studies* 15 (1953).

97. Li, *Hsün Tzu, Fu-kuo p'ien*, 195. Emended translation of Homer H. Dubs, trans., *The Works of Hsüntze* (Taipei: Cheng-wen, 1966), 152.

98. "Yao asked Shun, 'What are man's passions like?' Shun replied, 'Man's passions are very unlovely things indeed! What need is there to ask any further? Once a man acquires a wife and children, he no longer treats his parents as a filial son should. Once he succeeds in satisfying his cravings and desires, he neglects his duty to friends. Once he has won a high position and a good stipend, he ceases to serve his sovereign with a loyal heart" (ibid., *Hsing-o p'ien*, 555; Watson, *Hsün Tzu*, 168). Recall Hume's similar, but more perspicuous observation on the confined generosity of man: "Now it appears, that in the original frame of our mind, our strongest attention is confined to ourselves; our next is extended to our relations and acquaintance; and 'tis only the weakest which reaches to strangers and indifferent persons. This partiality, then, and unequal affection, must not only have an influence on our behaviour and conduct in society, but even on our ideas of vice and virtue." David Hume, *A Treatise of Human Nature* (Oxford: Clarendon Press, 1951), Book 3, Part 2, Section 2.

99. I., *Hsing-o p'ien*, 547; Watson, *Hsün Tzu*, 162.

and disorder."[100] Without regulative rules, in particular the *li* that perform the delimiting function, social disorder or chaos would likely result.

Apart from the prevention of human conflict, the regulative *li* with the delimiting function, in focusing upon the division of labor or distinction of occupations, promotes social existence. "Humans cannot live without society or social organization *[chun]*."[101] Given the scarcity of resources to satisfy all of their wants, there is a special need of cooperation. "For the fruits of the hundred crafts contribute to the sustenance of one man whose capacities cannot be directed toward all the crafts and who cannot attend to all tasks, with the result that if he cut himself off from society, he would find himself in an impossible situation."[102]

Similar consideration justifies the acceptance of the *li* that perform the supportive function. In providing the appropriate outlet for the satisfaction of desires within the prescribed limits of action, these regulative rules may be viewed as a guiding norm for weighing desires and aversions, and thus averting the individual agents from untoward and unwanted consequences. For humans are partial *(pien)*, not only in the sense of being biased toward their objects of affection, but also in the sense of limited foresight. According to Hsün Tzu, humans generally suffer because of this sort of partiality. When they encounter an object of desire, they tend to pursue it without considering its possible harmful consequences. This is an affliction that besets us all—"the harm that ensues from partiality *[pien]*."[103]

The foregoing considerations offer a defense of the necessity of regulative rules, invoking some familiar plausible presumptions concerning the human predicament. Taken together, they may be viewed as an informal, coordinative argument, in that each standing alone is quite weak to support the thesis. Each factor (scarcity of resources, partially or limited benevolence and foresight, and vulnerability), independently, does not provide sufficient warrant for the thesis of the necessity of regulative rules.[104] Moreover, each factor is also open to further query. The scarcity factor, for example, may give rise to a further question of diagnosis. On this question, Hsün Tzu thought that the situa-

100. Ibid., My translation.
101. Ibid., *Fu-kuo p'ien,* 202.
102. Ibid., 196. This translation is Lau's. I have not, however, followed his manner of exposition. The original context of the passage deals with the problem of scarcity of natural resources for the satisfaction of human needs and wants. See Lau, "Theories of Human Nature in Mencius and Shyuntzyy," 552.
103. Li, *Hsün Tzu, Pu-kou p'ien,* 208.
104. See my *Ethical Argumentation,* 91–95.

tion of scarcity in his own time (third century BC) was brought about by a failure in managing natural resources. He believed that if there were men in authority who possessed skill in managing available resources, there would be more than sufficient goods, if not surplus, to satisfy human needs and desires.[105] So long as there are *li* that perform both the delimiting and the supportive functions, and effective, uniform compliance, human desires and goods can be attended to and satisfied without strife or danger of social disorder.[106]

Regulative rules are essential to remedy the ills that befall all humans. Whether they are sufficient to resolve this predicament remains an important question to explore. At any rate, the *li* of regulation are an antidote to the plight that afflicts common humanity. The *li* are an artifice *(wei)* "to enable people to reap the benefit of living in society while avoiding the accompanying evils."[107] This insight of Hsün Tzu, however, must be dissociated from his problematic claim that it is the sage-kings or the sages who established the *li* in accord with their sense of rightness *(i)*. This historical claim is highly implausible, for, apart from the difficulty of identification and authentication, there is a lack of evidence. However, there are passages in his works that suggest a different view, that is, that the sages are ideal persons who embody *jen*, *li*, and *i*.[108] At any rate, the historical claim makes no contribution to the problem of justification of *li* as a set of regulative rules.

Human Excellence

When we turn to constitutive rules or the *li* that perform the ennobling function, we are concerned not merely with regulation of conduct, but more fundamentally with the realization of *tao*, the Confucian vision of human excellence [Section II]. In this vision, the good human life as a whole comprises *jen*, *i*, and *li*. The special role of *li* lies in their being the constitutive, rather than instrumental, means to the attainment of *jen* and *i*, for ultimately the good life is also an elegant and beautiful form of life.

For several reasons, the justification of *li* as a set of constitutive rules, for a Confucian moral theorist, is an onerous task. As noted in Section II, while agreeing to the general thesis that *jen*, *i*, and *li* are basic, interdependent notions, the Confuciansts hold different views on their relation to one another. Also, the notion of *jen* has a divergence of in-

---

105. Li, *Hsün Tzu, Fu-kuo p'ien*, 208
106. Ibid., *Li-lun p'ien*, 417.
107. Lau, "Theories of Human Nature in Mencius and Shyuntzyy," 556.
108. See my *Ethical Argumentation*, 61–65; and "Ethical Uses of History in Early Confucianism: The Case of Hsün Tzu," *Philosophy East and West* 35, no. 2 (1985): 133–56.

terpretation throughout the history of Chinese philosophy and in contemporary Chinese and Western scholarship.[109] More generally, there is the question of vindicating the adoption of the Confucian vision, even granting that a coherent characterization is possible and sufficiently significant to command attention in moral philosophy.[110]

In stressing the beauty of elegant form *(mei)* in the expression of feelings and transformation of desires, justifying the ennobling function of *li* today is an arduous task. Aside from the difficulty of rendering intelligible the notion of beauty *(mei)* in ethical discourse, it seems a heroic undertaking to incorporate this notion in an ethical theory that has any promise of attracting serious attention from contemporary moral philosophers. For the ennobling function of *li* points to the significance of an aesthetic dimension of ethical experience.[111] In this conception, an ethically good character transformed by *li*, imbued with the concern for *jen* and *i,* will express his concern in a graceful and joyful manner, displaying a harmony of inward feelings and attitudes with outward expression and circumstances. For a philosopher who has a critical appreciation of the Greek notion of *kalos kagathos* (wherein grace, rhythm, and harmony are the hallmarks of moral character) or the propriety of the language of "the beauty of virtue and the deformity of vice" (as was prevalent in the major writings of the eighteenth-century British Moralists), the problem may not appear insurmountable. Recall also that Kant, in spite of his unqualified insistence on the autonomy of ethical theory or "pure moral philosophy," acknowledges the notion of beauty as "the symbol of morality."[112]

A Confucian theorist will acknowledge the distinction between form and content of ethical conduct. The real difficulty lies in articulating their connection, more especially in establishing the connection between ritual rules and moral rules as standardly understood in moral philosophy. A general line of response is to invoke the notion of functional equivalence. It may be said, for example, that since ritual rules are the prescriptions of reason, any so-called moral, or for that matter legal, rules that perform the same function as ritual rules can be properly considered parts of *li.* In this view, acceptable moral rules will be seen as ideally embedded rules informed by a concern for *jen* and *i.* Perhaps, what is at issue is the relation between substantive and pro-

109. See n. 20 above.
110. See my *The Unity of Knowledge and Action,* chap. 4.
111. See my "Dimensions of *Li* (Propriety)."
112. I. Kant, *Critique of Judgment,* trans. J. H. Bernard (New York: Hafner, 1951). For a rare defense of the notion of moral beauty, see Guy Sircello, *A New Theory of Beauty* (Princeton: Princeton University Press, 1975), 81–97.

cedural rules of conduct, much akin to the issue between substantive
and procedural due process theories in American constitutional law.[113]
It may be worthwhile for a Confucian theorist to pursue this affinity
in dealing with the problem of form and content in Confucian ethics.
But this general line of response is not very helpful, for conceding the
distinction between ritual and morality carries the burden of showing
their connection. In the next section I shall make some suggestions on
this topic.

VI. RITUAL AND MORALITY

In the two previous sections [IV and V], I have endeavored to present the Confucian *li* as a distinctive, yet complex, ethical concept by
sketching some answers to queries concerning its scope, functions, and
justification. These answers, amenable to further elaboration and questions, are best construed in the spirit of critical self-understanding of
Confucian ethics. Some of them, especially the ones on justifying the
ennobling function of *li*, represent no more than intimations for the
sake of further inquiry into the role of *li* in constructing a Confucian
moral philosophy. From a point of view external to Confucian ethics,
there is one major difficulty in appraising the significance of *li* for
moral philosophy: the utility of *li* in understanding contemporary
moral discourse is open to doubt. No major metaethical theory, for example, makes use of any notion that is functionally equivalent to *li* in
its stress on ritual form of character or conduct.[114] Moreover, in the

113. See, for example, John Hart Ely, *Democracy and Distrust* (Cambridge: Harvard
University Press, 1980) and Michael J. Perry, *The Constitution, the Courts, and Human Rights*
(New Haven: Yale University Press, 1982).

114. There are some rare exceptions to the standard lines of metaethics. I have in
mind some remarks of Austin, MacDonald, and Hampshire. Austin, for example, once
claimed that ethics cannot be adequately studied without paying attention to "conventional or ritual acts." MacDonald, perhaps inspired by Austin's notion of performatives,
maintains that when philosophers attend to the analogy between moral judgments and
"performatory and ritual speech," they can derive some insights into "the impersonal,
authoritative, and practical features unaccounted for or distorted in other analyses." She
suggests that closer study may disclose more than just an analogy, for "moral judgments
are . . . , as it were, impersonal verdicts of a common moral ritual." Among contemporary
philosophers, Hampshire is singular in drawing attention to the importance of the connection between ritual and morality. I shall cite some of his suggestions shortly. See J. L.
Austin, *How to Do Things with Words* (Cambridge: Harvard University Press, 1962) , 19–
20; Margaret MacDonald, "Ethics and the Ceremonial Use of Language," in Max Black,
ed., *Philosophical Analysis: A Collection of Essays* (Ithaca: Cornell University Press, 1950),
227–29; and Stuart Hampshire, *Morality and Conflict* (Cambridge: Harvard University
Press, 1983), 227–29. For a couple of samples of this rare concern in recent years, see
Judith Martin and Gunther S. Stent, "Etiquette" in Becker and Becker, ed., *Encyclopedia*

analysis of moral issues today, a notion like *li* seems entirely out of place. If a Confucian theorist is to respond to this external challenge, he must at least make clear the desired connection between ritual and morality. In this section, I shall suggest a possible approach to this complex and difficult challenge.

Except as an uninteresting stipulation, a Confucian theorist cannot maintain the thesis of a necessary connection between ritual and morality. What is wanted is a thesis on non-contingent connection, much in the sense in which intention is non-contingently related to action. Though not every intention need be followed by relevant action, "the concept of intention could hardly have arisen unless intentions were usually followed by the relevant action."[115] Similarly, we may say that the concept of morality is non-contingently related to ritual, in that it is ritual, as comprising customs, conventions, or formal rules of proper conduct, that provides the starting point of individual morality. Even if we distinguish customary or positive from reflective or critical morality, the distinction is relative rather than absolute. For as Dewey points out, "Some degree of reflective thought must have entered occasionally into systems which in the main were founded on social wont and use, while in contemporary morals, even when the need of critical judgment is most recognized, there is an immense amount of conduct that is merely accommodated to social usage."[116] Recall also that tradition is quintessentially a critical, interpretive concept.[117] The *li*-tradition, as we have indicated in Section IV, is thus subject to reasonable critique and transformation.

Even if a member of a society develops an autonomous and rational set of moral beliefs and attitudes, the possibility of successfully communicating his standards or rules of conduct depends on deploying a conventional or ritual language. One need not espouse the extreme thesis that moral values are "the ceremonial treatment of a wide variety of natural facts and situations."[118] It is a plausible presumption that compliance with a common ritual language, say, something like the *li* that perform the delimiting and supportive functions, is more than just a matter of personal convenience. For it is doubtful that intelligible communication of personal moral beliefs and feelings, however well-founded and reasonable a response to others' moral beliefs and feel-

of Ethics; and Mark Kingwell, "Is It Rational to Be Polite?" *Journal of Philosophy* 90, no. 8 (1993).

115. A. R. Lacey, *A Dictionary of Philosophy* (New York: Charles Scribner's Sons, 1976).
116. John Dewey, *The Theory of the Moral Life* (New York: Holt, 1966), 3.
117. See Essay 12.
118. MacDonald, "Ethics and the Ceremonial Use of Language," 228.

ings, is possible without a commitment to the value of an established set of conventions. As Hampshire reminds us, "If a person disclaimed any commitment to any set of conventions, he would lack the normal means of conveying his feelings, and of responding to the feelings of others through shared discrimination and evaluations."[119] Recalling also the importance of the *li* that perform the ennobling function, in the extensive concern for the well-being of one's fellows (*jen*) informed by the reasoned exercise of the sense of what is right and appropriate (*i*), we may quite properly say with Hampshire that "customs and rituals that govern, in different societies, the relations between the sexes, marriage, property rights, family relationships, and the celebration of the dead, are primary moral customs; they always disclose the peculiar kind of respect for human life, and occasions for disrespect, which a particular people or society recognizes, and therefore their more fundamental moral beliefs and attitudes."[120] As noted in Section IV, these rituals and customs are subject to critical modification or diminishing significance, especially in developing nations such as China and India, owing to modern industrialization. But even in today's modern societies, there appears a large overlapping between "the claims of good manners and moral claims."[121] For the Confucian, so long as some customs and manners survive in modern industrial societies, something like the *li* that perform the ennobling function will be present, embodying a diversity of forms for the pursuit of *tao* or common humanity (*jen*). In the words of Wang Yang-ming, "the practical significance of *tao* cannot be exhausted with any claim to finality."[122]

119. Hampshire, *Morality and Conflict*, 97.
120. Max Gluckman, *Essays on the Ritual of Social Relations* (Manchester: Manchester University Press, 1962), 25–26.
121. Hampshire, *Morality and Conflict*, 102–3.
122. Wing-tsit Chan, trans., *Instructions on Practical Living and Other Neo-Confucian Writings by Wang Yang-ming* (New York: Columbia University Press, 1963), sec. 64.

Essay 14   Principles as Preconditions of Adjudication

I. THE ROLE OF PRINCIPLES IN CONFUCIAN ETHICS

Modern moral philosophy presents both metaethical and normative challenges to Confucian ethics. The metaethical challenge may be met by a reconstruction of a coherent conceptual scheme, with the ideal of *tao* (the Way) as a unifying perspective for viewing the interdependence of basic aretaic notions (notions of virtue), i.e., *jen* (benevolence), *li* (propriety), and *i* (rightness).[1] Given this scheme, one may proceed to deal with questions concerning ethical language and justification via a conception of argumentation as a cooperative enterprise aimed at a reasoned solution to a problem of common interest among concerned and responsible members of a moral community. Recently, based on *Hsün Tzu,* I offered a profile of Confucian argumentation, consisting of a characterization of desirable qualities of participants, standards of competence, phases of discourse, diagnosis of erroneous beliefs, as well as uses of definition in overcoming difficulties in communication.[2]

According to that account, justification is a phase of discourse, a reasoned response to a challenge to the acceptability of one's thesis. This response is chiefly anchored in ethical knowledge, that is, in the participant's understanding of an ethical tradition's significance for coping with novel or exigent circumstances. Since there are no formulas or rules for resolving these hard cases, the task of justification in the final analysis lies in the unification of the participant's understanding of the actuating force of his ethical knowledge with judgment arrived at through a critical and informed deliberation upon matters at hand. Thus judgment is essentially the product of the reasoned exercise of one's sense of rightness in response to changing circumstances *(yi-i pien-ying),* and not derived from the application of so-called principles

---

1. See Essay 13.
2. See A. S. Cua, *Ethical Argumentation: A Study in Hsün Tzu's Moral Epistemology* (Honolulu: University of Hawaii Press, 1985).

of conduct.[3] While there is indirect guidance provided by knowledge of accepted applications of *li* (ritual rules) and other aretaic notions, it is the special function of *i* (sense of rightness) to interpret and judge their relevance or irrelevance in a concrete and ethically perplexing setting.[4]

This conception of justification does not appeal to the notion of principle that possesses the status of objective validity and universal applicability, an appeal that is deemed requisite by most contemporary ethical thinkers (e.g., Kantian, utilitarian, and contractarian). Nevertheless, it seems proper to me that when principles are construed somewhat along the line of Kant's notion of maxims or "subjective principles of volition," i.e., as personal rules of conduct, they can play an important role in ethical deliberation and/or justification—indeed, even for the conception of justification sketched in the preceding paragraph. These personal rules of conduct may be called "preceptive principles" or "first-personal precepts." As Aiken points out, their authoritative status is "contingent entirely upon the conscientious submission of the persons who adopt them."[5] More importantly, for a reflective Confucian agent, the adoption of such principles involves a reasoned assessment of his purposes, preferences, and desires in relation to the ideal of *tao*, the vision of the good human life. The *Lun Yü (Analects)* provides an ample source for the adoption and development of personal rules of conduct. Most of the recorded conversations of Confucius and his students may be viewed as counsels to doing one's best *(chung)* in the pursuit of *tao*. For example, one may recall his stress on respectfulness, courtesy, trustworthiness, kindness, generosity, and concern for and consideration of the well-being, feelings, and desires of one's fellows. These remarks are more than mere counsels of prudence in the Kantian sense, but are notably intended as pointers to the constitutive means for the realization of *tao*.

Preceptive principles, though dependent on personal acceptance,

3. This is one reason for my preference for "reason" or "rationale" rather than "principle" for capturing the epistemic significance of *li* in the works of Hsün Tzu and Wang Yang-ming. See *Ethical Argumentation*, 20–24; *The Unity of Knowledge and Action: A Study in Wang Yang-ming's moral Psychology* (Honolulu: University of Hawaii Press, 1982), 28–30. For more discussion, see my "Reason and Principle in Chinese Philisophy: An Interpretation of *Li*," in *Blackwell Companion to World Philosophy*, ed. Eliot Deutsch and Ron Bontekoe (Oxford: Blackwell, 1997).

4. The foregoing merely highlights certain aspects of the complex activity of justification. For detailed discussion, see *Ethical Argumentation*, 51–101.

5. Henry David Aiken, "On the Concept of a Moral Principle," in *The Isenberg Memorial Lecture Series, 1965–1966* (East Lansing: Michigan State University Press, 1969), 114; I. Kant, *Foundations of the Metaphysics of Morals* (Indianapolis: Bobbs-Merrill, 1959), 16–17; and Julius Kovesi, *Moral Notions* (London: Routledge & Kegan Paul, 1969), 93.

may serve to articulate the significance of the agent's commitment to *tao* in his or her own life. When habitually adhered to, they may even be considered a counterpart of the *li* (ritual rules) of the ethical tradition. In other words, these personal principles are rules of self-discipline and quite in accord with the spirit of Confucius's teaching that to attain *jen,* the person must possess the ability to overcome or restrain those seemingly ungovernable passions that obstruct compliance with *li* (*Lun Yü,* 12:1). Possessing such personal disciplinary principles entitles the person to commendation. For the Confucian, self-mastery *(k'e-chi)* is a precondition to the attainment of *jen.* But, as Mencius points out, there are many paths to *jen.* If one attends to the difference in personal capacity and circumstance, it is unreasonable to expect all agents, particularly the paradigmatic individuals *(chün-tzu),* to behave in the same way (*Meng Tzu,* 6B:6).[6]

As personal rules of conduct, principles can also play a valuable role in representing a committed agent's interpretation of the *preceptive* import of particular aretaic notions. Confucius's use of such notions as trustworthiness *(hsin)* and respectfulness *(ching)* are open to individual interpretation regarding their practical import. Since *tao* is the unifying perspective, these principles, as the outcome of the exercise of reason *(li),* may properly be construed as ethical principles, as suggested by Wang Yang-ming's notion of *tao-li.* In the light of *tao,* these principles are ideal-embedded, oriented toward the actualization of *tao* in human life. Again, they make no claim to universal validity or to prescription of absolute or fixed rules of conduct. In elucidating Mencius's saying that "holding the mean without allowing for special circumstances is like holding onto one particular thing," Wang Yang-ming remarks that "the mean is nothing but the change. It changes according to the time. How can one hold it fast? One must have a sense of timing in determining what is the appropriate thing to do. It is difficult to fix a pattern or action in advance."[7]

Of course, when the agent is acknowledged as a paradigmatic individual by his fellows in the community, his principles can have a projective significance for others. But whether his preceptive interpretation of aretaic notions deserves attention from other agents remains an open question. An agent may publicly advocate his principles, but this

6. For the notion of paradigmatic individuals and its application to *chün-tzu,* see my *Dimensions of Moral Creativity: Paradigms, Principles, and Ideals* (University Park: Pennsylvania State University Press, 1978), chap. 5.

7. See Wing-tsit Chan, trans., *Instructions for Practical Living and Other Neo-Confucian Essays by Wang Yang-ming* (New York: Columbia University Press, 1963), sec. 52 (with minor emendation). For further discussion, see *The Unity of Knowledge and Action,* 35–45.

advocacy is subject to critical consideration and acceptance by others. They cannot be proffered as self-certifying, authoritative pronouncements.

In an argumentative context, personal, ideal-embedded principles may also be an articulation of the participant's understanding of the inherited core of common ethical knowledge, that is, the knowledge of those operative standards of conduct plausibly presumed to be a matter of conventional wisdom. Since such a presumption is defeasible, each participant carries a burden of reasonable persuasion in advocating his principles as "the" correct or sound interpretation of what is deemed implicit in common ethical knowledge. It is to be expected that in a particular situation, there may be an absence of agreement or even disagreement among competent participants in their different or incompatible understandings of the import of ethical knowledge. Given that argumentation is undertaken cooperatively to resolve a problem of common interest, the absence of agreement should provide an occasion for transforming it into one of agreement. In the larger view of the ennobling function of *li* (ritual rules), i.e., the promotion of the virtues of nobility and goodness,[8] a Confucian would endorse Collingwood's view that "being civilized means living, so far as possible, dialectically, that is, in constant endeavour to convert every occasion of non-agreement into an occasion of agreement."[9]

In the case of disagreement, a concerned and responsible participant would adhere to the cooperative spirit in investigating alternatives congenial to the pursuit of a common enterprise, rather than hold tenaciously to his own view. For his view may be the product of obscuration of mind *(pi)*, rather than an impartial exercise of reason *(li)*.[10] While disagreement may not be transformed into agreement, personal principles, when sincerely espoused in argumentation, are not without value, for they can function as critical instruments for the transformation of the ethical tradition. They provide a range of possible options for interpreting the living significance of tradition in dealing with present problematic situations. As one eminent historian of the Christian tradition puts it, "Ultimately . . . , tradition will be vindicated for us, for each of us as an individual and for us as communities, by how it manages to accord with our deepest intuitions and highest aspirations," which are themselves "imbedded in the tradition."[11] A living

8. See Essay 13, Section IV.
9. R. G. Collingwood, *The New Leviathan: or Man, Society, Civilization and Barbarism* (Oxford: Clarendon Press, 1985), 326.
10. See *Ethical Argumentation*, 138–59.
11. Jaroslav Pelikan, *The Vindication of Tradition* (New Haven: Yale University Press,

tradition is enriched by its historical past, interpreted by members of the community as having a present significance.

Seen in this way, Confucian argumentation may properly be considered an exemplification of a Roycean community of interpretation, an ongoing dialectical process that has no terminus.[12] While the goal is to seek agreement, the claim to the interpersonal significance of personal principles is essentially contestable by fellow agents. The exercise of *li* (reason) has no single voice that commands allegiance of all agents. The search for a monolithic account of the use of reason appears to be a delusion *(huo),* a condition to be rectified by cultivating the clarity of mind *(ming)* to dispel the varieties of obscurations, those factors that obstruct the mind's cognitive task. I suggest, then, that in argumentation, the claim to interpersonal significance of personal principles is best construed as a claim to an experiment in moral change, as an attempt to endow ethical knowledge with renewed significance. Were such a claim to be accepted by all the participants and become a basis of teaching, personal principles would acquire a *de jure* status, and become part of the content of an established tradition. In this manner, personal principles may be transmuted into impersonal principles. But they remain subject to further critical interpretation of their significance as future issues of human conduct are dealt with.[13]

The preceding observations on the role and status of principles as personal rules of conduct presuppose a critical appreciation of the internal point of view of Confucian ethics as an ethics of virtue that stresses the value of principles in contributing to the cultivation of the virtues of self-discipline and cooperation. Notably, it is an ethics that is preoccupied with cultural renaissance or the continuing vitality of a cultural tradition, but makes no claim to certainty nor universality in interpretation. As set forth in Chang Tsai's powerful essay entitled "Western Inscription" *(Hsi-ming),* the vision of *tao,* or *jen* in the broad sense, is indeed universal, in that it expresses an ideal of human care and concern for the well-being of all existent things, an ideal of the unity and harmony of humans and all things in the world. Implied in this vision is not a norm to be spelled out in a set of universal principles of conduct, but something more like a *theme* that admits of diverse interpretations of its concrete significance. Crucially, the realization of the ideal theme depends on the agents' serious regard for an operative

1984), 60. See also, Alastair MacIntyre, *After Virtue* (Notre Dame: University of Notre Dame Press, 1981), chap. 14.

12. See Josiah Royce, *The Problem of Christianity,* Vol. II (Chicago: Henry Regnery Co., 1968), esp. Lectures IX and X.

13. See *Ethical Argumentation* and *Hsün Tzu, chieh-pi p'ien.*

ethical tradition.[14] Moreover, in this *tao*-oriented conceptual scheme, the application of aretaic notions and their correlative principles is essentially culture-bound.

For a philosopher who does not share this orientation and is impressed with ethical objectivism, doubts may be raised on the plausibility of Confucian ethics as a universal ethics. Although its vision is universal in the sense that it encompasses all things in the universe, its focus on the continuing significance of a living tradition smacks of provincialism or relativism. Also, the implicit conception of practical reason as an exercise of *i* (sense of rightness) in dealing with exigent and changing circumstances suggests that some ethical judgments are ad hoc judgments. It may be questioned whether such judgments are rationally defensible without an appeal to principles that have the status of moral truths, truths independent of human thought and interest. A Confucianist may rejoin by pointing out that such a critique is proffered from an external point of view of an observer. It is not denied that an observer can have an insight into the merits and defects of Confucian ethics, but such an insight must be based on an appreciation of what it means to take the internal point of view of Confucian ethics, rather than on a deduction from an abstract doctrine such as objectivism, which is itself a product of a philosophical tradition, and thus can hardly be said to be representative of consensus among moral philosophers.[15] Arguably, by imaginative anticipation of the evaluative purpose of the use of a Confucian concept, an observer can have insight into its use without endorsing it. But in so doing, "he cannot quite stand outside the evaluative interest of the community he is observing and pick up the concept simply as a device for dividing up in a rather strange way certain neutral features of the world."[16]

Nor can an observer understand practical reason in Confucian ethics without appreciating the internal point of view of those operative standards of argumentative competence and the guidelines provided by language and culture. More generally, it is plausible to maintain that

14. For the distinction between ideal norm and ideal theme, see *Dimensions of Moral Creativity*, chap. 8. See also the distinction between teleology A and teleology B in Dorothy Emmet, *The Moral Prism* (London: Macmillan, 1979), chap. 1.

15. Perhaps, more strongly, a Confuciainst can rejoin that the external critique presupposes an internal point of view of a different philosophical tradition. Consequently, it can claim to be no more privileged than the internal point of view of the Confucianist. For the distinction between internal and external points of views, see H. L. A. Hart, *The Concept of Law* (Oxford: Clarendon Press, 1961), 86, 244. For an elaboration of the relation between these two point of view of a moral practice or tradition, see my *Dimensions of Moral Creativity*, chap. 6, secs. A and B.

16. Bernard Williams, *Ethics and the Limits of Philosophy* (Cambridge: Harvard University Press, 1985), 141–42.

there is a "social practice of reason" that comprises such activities as deliberating, explaining, justifying, reasoning, and choosing. Associated with this practice is a set of general guidelines provided by tradition and culture. The aim of these activities and guidelines is to enable the members of the community "to achieve better solutions to their problems than would be possible without the help of these publicly available guidelines."[17] Any claim to the acceptability of a thesis may be challenged and assessed in terms of its being a good or adequate solution to a problem at hand, with due regard to the operative standards of argumentative competence. The appeal to moral truths does not shed much light on this use of practical reason.

In sum, a just critique of Confucian ethics presupposes an appreciation of its internal point of view. This does not mean that the external point of view is irrelevant or unworthy of attention from sincere and critical adherents of Confucian ethics. Indeed, for a reflective Confucian agent, the shift from the internal to the external point of view is indispensable, if he is interested in improving or reforming current practices. His position here is analogous to that of a reviewer of a court's decisions, who asks external, critical questions, not merely for the sake of obtaining an accurate description of an operative legal system, but for the purpose of advancing proposals for the change of legal rules and rulings.[18] Perhaps it is in this context that the challenge of ethical objectivism, quite apart from the issue of philosophical plausibility, is valuable, as a reasonable demand for a statement of principles that have the status of objectivity independently of personal commitment to an ethical tradition. A rationale for changing a current practice has a greater persuasive force when it employs the language of objective principles. When seriously entertained in Confucian discourse, these principles, unlike the conventional *li* or rules of proper behavior, are emphatic, i.e., they present claims to priority of attention in resolving a problem of common concern among participants in ethical argumentation.[19]

Of course, these principles have to compete with those of others that have a similar claim to objectivity, and thus cannot be considered self-evident. In this way, the language of objective principles performs a

---

17. Kurt Baier, "Rationality, Reason, and the Good," in David Copp and David Zimmerman, eds., *Morality, Reason and Truth* (Totawa: Rowman & Allanheld, 1985), 200.

18. In an earlier work, the importance of this shift for understanding creative agency was discussed in general terms apart from Confucian ethics. See *Dimensions of Moral Creativity*, chap. 6.

19. Cf. Ronald Dworkin, *Taking Rights Seriously* (Cambridge: Harvard University Press, 1978), 26; and *Law's Empire* (Cambridge: Harvard University Press, 1986), 81.

valuable service to understanding individual efforts at modification or qualification of the substantive content of an existing Confucian practice. Like those personal principles that acquire interpersonal significance, these objective principles, when accepted, may become a part of the Confucian tradition—again, subject to critical interpretation of their import in exigent situations. For a contemporary Confucian philosopher, the major challenge of normative ethics is the problem of objective principles.[20] This is the problem of incorporating objective principles within Confucian ethics as an ethics of virtue.

II. THE PROBLEM OF INCORPORATING OBJECTIVE PRINCIPLES

For pursuing this problem, some remarks must be made about the concept of objective principle and the absence of this concept in Confucian ethics. I assume that an objective principle is a basis for evaluation, invested with a privileged status or authority, quite apart from personal endorsement.[21] This suggests that the concept is a context-variable concept. Different spheres of human activity, whether thought or action, will have distinct objective principles relative to the purpose of the enterprise. In an ethical context, one primary employment of an objective principle, in contrast to that of personal precepts, aims at a conclusive determination or settlement of disputes that arise out of human conflict. While any determination may be a subject of further dispute, the invocation of objective principles, say, of moral obligation or of rights, serves as a purportedly impartial means for dispute-resolution. Underlying this use of principles is a legalistic model of ethical discourse. In this model, ethical disputes are to be *adjudicated* by principles that play the role of an impartial judge, deciding the right or wrong of the conduct of contending parties.[22]

The lack of Confucian concern with objective principles may in part be explained by its attitude toward legal adjudication. Recall Confu-

20. See my "Reflections on Moral Theory and Understanding Moral Traditions," in Eliot Deutsch and Gerald Larson, eds., *Interpreting across Boundaries: New Essays in Comparative Philosophy* (Princeton: Princeton University Press, 1988); and "Tasks of Confucian Ethics," *Journal of Chinese Philosophy* 6, no. 1 (1979).

21. Cf. Aiken, "The Concept of a Moral Principle," 107. Note that in adopting Aiken's notion of principle, I do not embrace his controversial thesis that all moral principles are first-personal precepts (ibid., 122–23).

22. For an explicit avowal of the legal model in defense of universal prescriptivism, see Bernard Mayo, *The Philosophy of Right and Wrong* (London: Routledge & Kegan Paul, 1986), chap. V. Cf. R. M. Hare, *Freedom and Reason* (Oxford: Clarendon Press, 1963); and *Moral Thinking* (Oxford: Clarendon Press, 1981).

cius's saying, "In hearing litigation, I am no different from any other man. But if you insist on a difference, it is, perhaps, that I try to get the parties not to resort to litigation in the first place."[23] A person genuinely committed to *jen* is one who finds repose in abiding by *jen,* one who cultivates virtuous dispositions, not for self-glorification, but for bringing peace and security to his fellows.[24] Implicit in this attitude toward human conflict is a model of personal relationship wherein disputes are seen to be a subject of voluntary *arbitration* or mediation, rather than adjudication, within a moral community.[25] At issue in arbitration is an impartial resolution of disputes oriented toward the reconciliation of the contending parties in the light of the concern for harmonious human intercourse. The arbitrator, chosen by the parties in dispute, is concerned with repairing the rupture of human relationship *(lun)* rather than with deciding the rights or wrongs of the parties. The task of an arbitrator is not only to interpret the meaning of a current practice,[26] but also to shape the expectations of the contending parties along the line of mutual concern, to get them to appreciate one another as interacting members in a community. An appeal to objective principles, just as an exaggerated emphasis on *li* (ritual rules) as mere formal prescriptions, is likely to alienate people from one another, instead of encouraging them to maintain or develop personal relationships.[27] For a Confucian philosopher, the translation of "ethics" as *lun-li hsüeh* is quite apt, for it conveys the Confucian conception of ethics as an inquiry into the *li* (rationales) of human relations, leaving entirely open the question whether the *li* are to be construed as objective or personal principles.

23. *Lun Yü,* 12:13; D. C. Lau's translation in *Confucius: The Analects* (New York: Penguin Books, 1979).

24. Ibid., 4:2 & 14:42. For an insightful discussion of this Confucian theme, see Ch'en Ta-ch'i, *P'ing-fan te tao-te kuan* (Taipei: Chung-hua, 1976).

25. For further discussion, see my "Confucian Vision and the Human Community," *Journal of Chinese Philosophy* 11, no. 3 (1984).

26. Lon Fuller, *The Morality of Law* (New Haven: Yale University Press, 1969), 228.

27. In this connection, we can appreciate the lack of concern in traditional China with the Western conception of human rights. As Hsu points out: "In the Chinese philosophy, the interpretation of law is based upon human feelings and situations not upon absolute standards. Disputants do not turn to lawyers who argue a client's case in abstract terms joined with appeals to legal precedent. Instead, they look to middleman or peacemaker. . . . The Chinese middleman does not uphold one party against another or insist that one is completely right and the other wholly wrong. His mission is to smooth ruffled feelings by having each disputant sacrifice a little, whether the sacrifice involves principles or not." See Francis L. K. Hsu, *Americans and Chinese: Reflections on Two Cultures and Their People* (Garden City: Doubleday Natural History Press, 1970), 361. For this danger in exaggerating the importance of *li* (ritual rules) and the possibility of accommodating the notion of human rights in Confucian ethics, see my "*Li* and Moral Justification: A Study in the Li Chi," *Philosophy East and West* 23, no. 1 (1983).

Closely tied to the Confucian attitude toward human conflict is its focus on the exercise of *i* in particular circumstances rather than on compliance with rules or principles. For Confucius, a well-cultivated person *(chün-tzu),* "in dealing with affairs of the world, does not form any preconceived opinions. He simply acts in accord with *i.*" Confucius said of himself, "I have no preconceptions about the permissible and the impermissible."[28] This attitude of neutrality is essential to appreciating the nature of a concrete situation prior to judgment and decision. In the context of arbitration, it is especially important for the arbitrator to preserve his independent sense of *i.* An appeal to objective principles may distract the arbitrator from a careful examination of the merits of a particular case and thus may lead to a failure in rendering an equitable decision. If objective principles were acknowledged in Confucian ethics, there would be a danger of "the tyranny of principles" over the exercise of *i.* Even in a case where general rules are deemed relevant, we would expect an arbitrator to be reasonable and sensitive to the demands of the parties before applying these rules to a case at hand.[29]

The above preliminaries serve as a basis for construing the problem of incorporating objective principles into Confucian ethics as an ethics of virtue. The problem of objective principles is to be viewed against the background of the concern with adjudication rather than arbitration of human conflict. The difficulty is to develop a thesis that is compatible with the emphasis on the exercise of *i* and with the spirit of the Confucian doctrine of the unity of knowledge and action.

As a matter of abstract theory, there are at least four different options: (1) subordination, (2) double-language, (3) coordination, and (4) complementarity.[30]

For a Confucian theorist, the subordination thesis, i.e., subsuming

28. *Lun Yü,* 18:8; Lau, *The Analects of Confucius.* For the notion of *chün-tzu,* see *Dimensions of Moral Creativity,* chap. 5.

29. For an insightful discussion of the importance of equity in law, ethics, and public administration, see Stephen Toulmin, "The Tyranny of Principles," in Norman Bowie, ed., *Making Ethical Decisions* (New York: McGraw-Hill, 1985); and Jerome Frank, *Law and the Modern Mind* (New York: Anchor Books, 1963), 168–69.

30. For suggestions of these options in contemporary moral philosophy, see (1) Harold Alderman, "By Virtue of a Virtue," *Review of Metaphysics* 36 (1982); Edmund L. Pincoffs, *Quandaries and Virtues* (Lawrence: University Press of Kansas, 1986), 105–6, 145–46; (2) G. Warnock, *The Object of Morality* (London: Methuen, 1971), 86–88; (3) H. A. Prichard, "Does Moral Philosophy Rest on a Mistake," *Mind* 21 (1912); and Robert B. Louton, "On Some Vices of Virtue Ethics," *American Philosophical Quarterly* 21, no. 3 (1984). We may note that our problem of the connection between principles and virtues does not occupy the center of attention of most recent works on virtue ethics: see for example, the lack of this concern in the instructive survey by Gregory E. Pence, "Recent Work on Virtues," *American Philosophical Quarterly* 21, no. 4 (1984).

objective principles under aretaic standards, is not an appealing option. For it is unclear how such a subsumption can be explicated without collapsing the distinction between arbitration and adjudication. A Confucianist is likely to approve the latter process only when arbitration has failed to achieve the desired result. Quite properly, aretaic notions have an essential role in arbitration as a reminder of the importance of maintaining personal relationship. But when the disputing parties cannot agree to the arbitrator's recommendation, they have recourse to adjudication in order to obtain an authoritative decision that settles the conflict. In this context objective principles can play a crucial role quite independently of the characters of the parties. Moreover, embracing the subordination thesis would amount to a dogmatic rejection of the independent role of objective principles in the justification of those moral rules which cannot plausibly be reduced to aretaic standards. On the contrary, it is arguable that the interpretation of the content or concrete significance of some aretaic notions in part depends on an acknowledgement of relevant moral rules and their justification. Consider Mencius's remark: "It is contrary to benevolence *(jen)* to kill one innocent man."[31] This suggests that *jen* cannot be properly understood without paying heed to the moral injunction against killing the innocent, an injunction that has force and justification independently of the concern for cultivating *jen*-disposition.[32] Of course, *jen* is open to non-preceptive interpretation, e.g., kindness *(hui)* and generosity *(k'uan)*, but such interpretation can hardly be said to be consistent with the reasoned exercise of *i* (sense of rightness) if it ignores the injunction against killing the innocent, against cruelty, or against ruthlessness.[33]

The double-language thesis maintains that the notions of virtue and objective principle are alternative expressions of the same ethical concern. But this thesis pays no serious attention to the distinction between the concern for human relationships *(lun)* and the concern for impersonal human intercourse. As in the case of subordination thesis, it fails to recognize the divergence of purpose in arbitration and adjudication.

31. *Mencius,* 7A:33; D. C. Lau's translation, *Mencius* (Baltimore: Penguin Books, 1970), 189. For the same theme in *Hsün Tzu,* see *Ju-hsiao p'ien.*
32. More generally, as Gewirth points out, "when the criterion for a quality's being a virtue does not include the requirement that the virtue reflect or conform to moral rules, there is no assurance that the alleged virtue will be morally right or valid" (Alan Gewirth, "Rights and Virtues," *Review of Metaphysics* 38 [June 1985]: 752). Of course, a Confucian theorist cannot endorse Gewirth's Kantianism. For the priority of moral rules in the pursuit of ideals, see *Dimensions of Moral Creativity,* 116–17, 135–36.
33. See *Mencius,* 4A:3, 4A:8, and 7B:1. For the role of *i* in understanding the ethical significance of particular aretaic notions, see the insightful discussion in Ch'en Ta-ch'i, *Kung Tzu hsüeh-shuo* (Taipei: Cheng-chung, 1964).

Also, as earlier noted, adopting this thesis may lead to "the tyranny of principles" over the exercise of i in doing justice to the merits of the claims of parties in dispute. It is difficult to see how an appeal to aretaic standards can help toward the resolution of human conflict that constitutes the subject matter of adjudication.[34]

In stressing the irreducibility of the concepts of virtue and objective principles and their equal importance in ethical inquiry, the coordination thesis is an attractive option. For these concepts are, so to speak, partners in the same enterprise of conflict-resolution. However, for a Confucian theorist, this cannot be taken to imply an exclusiveness of independent unrelated concerns, which hardly comports with the notion of *tao* as a unifying perspective of ethical discourse or as a vision of things in the universe as forming a moral community *(t'ien-jen ho-i)*. Perhaps even more important, the suggestion of a conceptual dichotomy forecloses the inquiry into the possibility of establishing a connection between virtues and objective principles. As earlier remarked (Section I), there is a likely historical scenario according to which personal principles, representing preceptive interpretaion of aretaic notions, become transmuted into impersonal principles through communal acceptance. These principles may contribute to the promotion of the virtues of cooperation, and may also be rationally justifiable from an external point of view. If this possibility obtains, impersonal principles in an established ethical tradition may properly be regarded as objective principles that are intimately connected with the cooperative virtues. Likewise, the virtues of self-control can also contribute to the performance of duties deemed justifiable by objective principles. The conceptual dichotomy inherent in the coordination thesis implies an a priori injunction against the pursuit of the reasonable question concerning the relation between virtues and objective principles.

For a Confucian theorist, the complementarity thesis is the best option to explore, and, to some extent, may be elucidated by pondering a hint in *Hsün Tzu*. I have in mind this passage: "*Tao* embodies con-

---

34. Perhaps the double language thesis is a misleading, compendious statement of two other, not necessarily connected, theses: correspondence and logical equivalence, and both seem to be suggested in Warnock's *The Object of Morality*. The correspondence thesis would hold that "for every virtue of character there is a corresponding principle of duty." To the principle of beneficence, for example, there is a corresponding virtue of benevolence. The equivalence thesis, on the other hand, would hold that any statement of virtue is logically derivable from a statement of principle, and conversely. For the reasons stated in the text both the correspondence and equivalence theses, as in the double language thesis, are not viable options for a Confucianist. Cf. Tom L. Beauchamp, *Philosophical Ethics* (New York: McGraw Hill, 1982), 163–66.

stancy *(chang)* and embraces all changes."[35] The notions of virtue and objective principle may be viewed as complementary ways of interpreting the concrete significance of *tao*. The former expresses a steadfast concern with the promotion of virtue in arbitration, the latter with adjudication, with those problematic cases that cannot be handled by arbitration. Nevertheless, the ultimate aim of both arbitration and adjudication, in the light of *tao*, is the same. It is to inculcate an attitude of mutual care and concern among conflicting parties as members of a community. While objective principles have their proper function in adjudication, they subserve the same end as that of arbitration in promoting a constant concern for *jen* in human intercourse. From the Confucian point of view, the acknowledgment of the propriety of adjudication, in the event of failure in arbitration, does not entail the irrelevance of the primacy of concern of *jen*. Rather, adjudication is considered to be a complement of arbitration. Likewise, the failure of adjudication is deemed consistent with a renewed effort at finding further objective principles that have the promise of securing agreement or at urging the conflicting parties to transcend their private stations for the sake of harmony implicit in the ideal of *tao*. Also, in the case of successful adjudication, a Confucian would remind the parties that the agreeable settlement of an issue at stake may well be an occasion for developing personal relationship within a moral community. Of course, we have no assurance that acceptable objective principles are forthcoming, nor that, when these are found, they will always promote *jen*-realization.

Nonetheless, the complementarity thesis is worthy of further investigation. As compared with other options, the thesis provides a viable avenue for incorporating objective principles in Confucian ethics. The thesis, unlike that of subordination, calls for no subsumption of objective principles, for these principles are accorded a status independent of aretaic standards. Nor does it abolish the distinction between the two concepts as in the case of double language thesis. And unlike the coordination thesis, there is no suggestion of two exclusive and unrelated goals of ethical inquiry. The complementarity thesis is, so to speak, a *yin-yang* thesis. In arbitration, aretaic notions play the role of *yang*, and objective principles the subdued role of *yin;* the reverse is true in adjudication. The primacy of either depends on the nature of the human conflict at issue. And it is the reasoned exercise of *i* that determines the appropriateness of the desirable process in conflict-resolution. Since the *yin* contains a seed for the generation of *yang*, and conversely, the

35. *Hsün Tzu, Chieh-pi p'ien.*

dominance of either virtue or objective principle is not a question to be determined in advance of confrontation with particular circumstances. In the words of Wang Yang-ming, "the significance of *tao* cannot be exhausted with finality."[36]

III. PRINCIPLES AS PRECONDITIONS OF ADJUDICATION

Suppose we adopt the complementarity thesis, how can we develop this? What more can be said about the nature and status of objective principles? How do we formulate these principles in a manner that is coherent with the Confucian conception of ethical argumentation as a cooperative enterprise aimed at securing agreement among participants, and yet at the same time avoid the pitfalls of the subordination and double-language theses? In what follows, I offer a clarification and suggest a direction for further inquiry, rather than point to conclusive solutions to these vexing questions.

As a first step, let us note the consequence of accepting the complementarity thesis. It is entirely unproblematic to incorporate objective principles for the purpose of adjudication within Confucian thought and practice, quite independently of critical challenges from an external point of view based on a different ethical tradition. These principles express the *principium*, the fundamental status of core ethical beliefs, which are implicit in the use of basic concepts in the Confucian tradition or community of interpretation. While the significance of these principles is open to further interpretation, at a given time, these principles provide an impartial method for settling disputes within Confucian argumentation. It is this sort of principle that Hsün Tzu appeals to in proposing his classification of *ju* or Confucians. Hsün Tzu urges his readers to distinguish common people from three sorts of *ju*: the vulgar or conventional *(su-ju)*, the refined *(ya-ju)*, and the great or sagely Confucians *(ta-ju)*. Common people neither seek nor respect scholarship. Devoid of any sense of justice and rightness *(cheng-yi)*, they regard wealth and profit as the ultimate end of human life. In attire and deportment, the conventional Confucians are no different from common people. They are, however, men of pretension, i.e., they uncritically adopt erroneous doctrines, they have no real comprehension of the classics and the rationales for exalting *li* and *i*. With only a sketchy understanding of the words of former kings, they would invoke "former kings" to deceive the stupid and seek a living. The refined Confucians, on the other hand, are men of integrity who honor the *li* and

36. Chan, *Instructions*, sec. 64.

i and the classics; yet they do not possess sufficient intelligence and experience to comprehend the coherence of their rationales. As men of integrity, they would candidly avow their knowledge and ignorance, free from self-deception and desire to deceive others. For this reason they honor the worthy and fear the law without remiss or pride. The great or sagely Confucians are those who have the knowledge of the unity of *li* and *i*, i.e., their interdependence and prospective significance. Thus, they can deal with the present by means of knowledge of the past. On matters pertaining to *jen* and *i*, they render discriminating judgements without error, as if "distinguishing white from black."[37]

We can now broaden the context in which these principles function, independently of the issue of plausibility of Confucian ethics. I suggest that we regard this broader context as the context of conflict between peoples belonging to different cultural, ethical traditions. In this way, objective principles may be conceived as preconditions for intercultural ethical discourse, wherein a resolution of conflicting ideals of the good life or substantive normative proposals may be sought. Differently put, these principles are *transcultural principles* serving as ground rules in impartial adjudication. The basic function of these principles, in fact, corresponds to the delimiting function of Confucian *li* as a system of formal prescriptions of proper conduct. They serve the purpose of defining the boundaries of proper behavior, without prejudging the value of the content of different ethical traditions or ways of life. They are like the negative precepts of the Decalogue, providing limiting conditions or constraints upon human action. But unlike these precepts, they imply no value judgment on the desirability of the conduct of contending parties.[38]

At issue in intercultural ethical conflict is not the convergence of substantive values (and thus the irrelevance of any appeal to culturally specific aretaic standards) but rather the problem of accommodating diversity of goods, the problem of striking a balance between the claim to justice or fairness in adjudication and the claim to the integrity of contrastive ways of life.[39] While our approach presupposes the existence of cultural diversity, it does not deny that there is a common hu-

---

37. This discussion of the three types of Confucian is a partial interpretive reading of a long passage in *ju-hsiao p'ien*. For further discussion of the great or sagely Confucian as distinct from the superior men, see my *Ethical Argumentation*, 67–78. For an anticipation, recall *Analects*, 6:13: "The Master said to Tzu-hsia, 'Be a noble *ju*, not a petty *ju*'."
38. See Essay 13, sec. D.
39. Cf. Charles Taylor, "The Diversity of Goods," and Stuart Hampshire, "Morality and Convention," in Amartya Sen & Bernard Williams, eds., *Utilitarianism and Beyond* (London: Cambridge University Press, 1982).

man nature; nor does it embrace the view that distinctive cultural ways of life are incommensurable.[40] On the contrary, a Confucian theorist can accept the idea of a common human nature in the sense that all humans possess the same natural capacities, e.g., those capacities that underlie feeding, locomotion, and mating; but notably these capacities are developed "and *exercised* in specific cultural contexts and forms."[41] Even more important, from the ethical point of view, our basic motivational structure, comprising native feelings and desires, as Hsün Tzu points out, constitutes the "raw materials" for transformation *(hua)*, much like the potter's clay or the carpenter's wood in making vessels or utensils.[42] These elements of common human nature are historically shaped and reshaped by different cultures in different ways; and in themselves, they can hardly serve as impartial determinants for conflict-resolution in intercultural intercourse. This does not mean that different ethical, cultural traditions are incommensurable. Appreciation of cultural diversity is consistent with the acknowledgement of transcultural principles of adjudication.[43]

The deeper Confucian task is to specify these principles in a way that is consistent with the Confucian conception of ethical argumentation as a cooperative venture. The more general and difficult philosophical problem is the ancient Greek problem of nature versus convention. In the language of Aristotle, our problem pertains to the specification of the idea of universal political justice, of what, in contrast to convention, is "just by nature," viz., having "the same force everywhere and does not depend on what we regard or do not regard

40. Cf. Renford Bambrough, "The Scope of Reason: An Epistle to the Persians," in S. C. Brown, ed., *Objectivity and Cultural Divergence* (Cambridge: Cambridge University Press, 1984) and Ruth Benedict, *Patterns of Culture* (Boston: Houghton Mifflin, 1934), esp. 22, 223, and 278.

41. See Ted Benton, "Biological Ideas and Their Cultural Uses," 122.

42. For further discussion, see Essay 6.

43. More likely a Confucian theorist may consider the issue of commensurability as a purely speculative question, and focus, instead, on actual differences between particular ways of life, and explore areas of common interest as a basis for developing the ground rules for resolving intercultural conflicts. This inquiry is consistent with accepting Benedict's view, apart from her incommensurability thesis, that cultural diversity is a diversity of configurations. In understanding a culture, she urges us "to imagine a great arc on which are arranged possible interests provided either by the human age-cycle or by the environment or by man's various activities. . . . Its identity as a culture depends upon the selection of some segments of this arc. Every human society everywhere has made such selection in its cultural institutions. Each from the point of view of another ignores fundamentals and exploits irrelevancies." See Benedict, *Patterns of Culture*, 24. See also her paper entitled "Configurations of Culture in North America," in Margaret Mead, *Ruth Benedict* (New York: Columbia University Press, 1974). Cf. Alasdair MacIntyre, *Whose Justice? Which Rationality?* (Notre Dame: University of Notre Press, 1988).

as just."[44] Without joining in the issue over the adequacy of some version of the Natural Law Theory, I think we can appropriate this notion of political justice in the present context. Natural Law Theory can be taken as embodying the idea that any system of positive law or morality is subject to an external critique, i.e., a critique of its limitations, limitations which are, in some sense, reasonable to accept regardless of the culturally specific demands of different ways of life.[45] In this light, the problem of specifying transcultural principles is a problem of seeking consensus among reasonable peoples with their distinctive and cherished ways of life.[46]

IV. FIVE PRINCIPLES OF INTERCULTURAL ADJUDICATION

Preliminary to a provisional statement of principles as preconditions of intercultural adjudication in ethical argumentation, let me set forth certain assumptions. These assumptions comprise my philosophical, Neo-Confucian reading of the significance of *tao* regarding reasoned discourse on intercultural ethical conflict.[47] I take it that the *tao* is a proper subject for ethical discourse. In the words of Wang Yang-ming, "The Way *(tao)* is public and belongs to the whole world, and the doc-

44. Aristotle, *Nicomachean Ethics*, trans. Martin Ostwald (Indianapolis: Bobbs-Merrill, 1962), 1134b.

45. Cf. Paul Forrier and Chaim Perelman, "Law, Natural and Natural Rights," *Dictionary of the History of Ideas*, vol. III (New York: Charles Scribner's Sons, 1973), esp. 23–26.

46. In terms of normative ethics, the Confucian task, though not designed to yield a general doctrine, may be seen as a contractarian rather than utilitarian problem. As Scanlon has shown, any account of moral wrongness must appeal to some notion of reasonableness in the sense that excludes "rejections that would be unreasonable given the aim of finding principles which could be the basis of informed, unforced general agreement." Similar theme is found in Rawls's emphasis on exploring "overlapping consensus" in seeking a conception of justice that will provide "a reasonable way of shaping into one coherent view the deeper bases of agreement embedded in the public culture of a constitutional regime and acceptable to its most firmly held considered convictions." This notion of reasonableness and focus on overlapping consensus is congenial to the Confucian notion of reasonableness. See my *Unity of Knowledge and Action;* T. M. Scanlon, "Contractarianism and Utilitarianism," in Sen and Williams, *Utilitarianism and Beyond,* 111; and Rawls, "Justice and Fairness: Political and not Metaphysical," *Philosophy and Public Affairs* 14, no. 3 (1985), 229.

47. I leave open the question of the plausibility of MacIntyre's conception of "rationality of traditions," thus freeing myself from his preoccupation with the relativist and perspectivist challenges. I am more concerned with exploring the significance of his suggestion that, though conflict between alternative traditions may take the form of rivalry, "it can also happen that two traditions, hitherto independent and even antagonistic, can come to recognize certain possibilities of fundamental agreement and reconstitute themselves as a single, more complex debate." (MacIntyre, *Whose Justice? Which Rationality?* 12). However, my stress is on prior agreement on the preconditions of discourse in the light of the non-agonistic conception of Confucian ethical argumentation.

trine is also public and belongs to the whole world. They are not the private properties of Master Chu (Hsi) or even Confucius."[48] My reading of *tao*, indeed indebted to Wang Yang-ming, is thus open to critical evaluation by fellow Confucian moral philosophers.

The Confucian *tao* is an overarching vision of the good human life, an ideal theme of excellence, a holistic, unifying perspective for harmonizing diverse and conflicting elements of moral experience. While it is fundamentally homocentric, the vision has a comprehensive scope, encompassing all existent entities. A commitment to the realization of *tao*, or alternatively *jen* in the broad sense, involves an acknowledgement and concern for the integrity or intrinsic value of every existent thing. What is envisaged in *tao* may be characterized as an ideal of the universe as a moral community.[49] Metaphorically, *tao* is the vision of "the genuinely ethical symphony"[50] or "congeniality of excellences."[51]

In light of *tao*, the desirable interplay among humans, and between humans and other things, is one of concord *(ho)*. In actuality, such a state of affairs is a rare occurrence. There is an antinomic character to all values.[52] Absent a doctrine of hierarchy of values, a reflective, sincere *(ch'eng)* Confucian would regard value conflict, especially among humans, to be a matter of regret, yet also an invitation to employ persistently one's abilities and resources in order to bring about a state of harmonious coexistence or equilibrium *(chung)*.[53] Dealing with the problem of conflict requires *kan-ying* (influence and response), an

48. These assumptions are my response to what I take to be a common aspiration of Chinese thinkers today for creative synthesis of Chinese and Western cultures. See, for example, the recurrent theme in the journal *Che-hsüeh yü wen-hua* (Universitas); the *Proceedings of the First World Conference in Chinese Philosophy* (Taipei, August 19–25, 1984) published in the Bulletin of the Chinese Philosophical Association, vol. 3 (1985), 763 pages; and the 1987 *Proceedings of the International Symposium on Confucianism and the Modern World*, which contained 1827 pages. Samples of earlier studies may be found in Arne Naess and Alastair Hannay, eds., *Invitation to Chinese Philosophy* (Oslo: Universitetsforlaget, 1972). The synoptic statement below is derived from a series of studies inspired by Wang Yang-ming. (See, for example, my *The Unity of Knowledge and Action;* "Practical Causation and Confucian Ethics," *Philosophy East and West* 25, no. 1 (1975); "Ideals and Values: A Study in Rescher's Moral Vision," in Robert Almeder, ed., *Praxis and Reason: Studies in the Philosophy of Nicholas Rescher* (Washington: University Press of America, 1982); and Essays 2 and 9.

49. See Essay 9.

50. See Williams James, *Essays on Faith and Morals* (New York: Longmans, Green and Co., 1949), 212.

51. This notion, according to Norton, is said to be implicit in Plato's *Lysis*. See David Norton, *Personal Destinies* (Princeton: Princeton University Press, 1982), 306–7; 362–63. For my use with qualification in connection with Rescher's moral vision, see "Ideals and Values," 181–84 and n. 26.

52. Nicolai Hartmann, *Ethics* (London: George Allen & Unwin, 1932), 2:76.

53. This reading of *chung* and *ho* in *The Doctrine of the Mean (Chung Yung)* is indebted to Wang Yang-ming. See Essay 2.

imaginative model or schema for mediating the ideal *tao* and the actual world. The vertical aspect of *kan-ying,* so to speak, consists in practical causation with respect to nature. In this manner, natural events are viewed as actual and potential factors that affect human life, but subject to human control with due cognizance of its limitations. Differently put, events are challenges to action. The point of commitment to *tao* is in part to alter natural circumstances and states of affairs for the furtherance of the good human life. The task posed by the horizontal aspect of *kan-ying* pertains to conflict in human intercourse. It is as formidable as the vertical task, perhaps even more complex, in that humans are actuated by a wide cultural diversity of conceptions of value. It calls for the exercise of the art of accommodation *(chien-shu),*[54] involving coordination of diversity of goods or ideals implicit in various ways of life.[55]

A recognition of the varieties of cultures as coherent ways of life is compatible with what Hampshire calls "the no-shopping principle," for "one cannot pick and choose bits of one picture to put besides bits of another; the coherence of the pictures comes from their distinct histories."[56] For a Confucian, such an appreciation of cultural diversity is a prelude to an endeavor to explore the areas of common interest as candidates for arbitration in cases of conflict or radical disagreement. Moreover, since *tao* is the telos of ethical argumentation, the disputed questions of value, rooted in different ethical traditions, admit of reasonable solution, on the presumption that the participants have a shared interest in resolving common problems. When such a presumption is defeated, arbitration will probably not secure the desired outcome of agreement. Failure in arbitration thus calls for adjudication. I assume that the theoretical Confucian task here lies in reshaping some of its key notions for the purpose of developing a set of transcultural principles of adjudication. These principles could be formulated by reflecting upon Hsün Tzu's conception of the style of performance, those desirable qualities of participants of Confucian argumentation, e.g.,

---

54. See *Hsün Tzu, Fei-hsiang p'ien.*

55. As Rescher put it: "Each ideal can—and should—be pursued and cultivated in consonance with the realization of other values. The pluralism of ideals, the fact that each must be taken in context, means that in the pursuit of our ideals we must moderate them to one another." See Nicholas Rescher, *Unpopular Essays on Technological Progress* (Pittsburgh: University of Pittsburgh Press, 1980), 59. And more recently, Rescher, *Ethical Idealism* (Berkeley: University of California Press, 1987), 76–78. For further discussion, see "Ideals and Values," 185–90.

56. Stuart Hampshire, *Morality and Conflict* (Cambridge: Harvard University Press, 1983), 148. See also Ruth Benedict, *Patterns of Culture,* and "Configuration of Culture in North America.

humaneness *(jen-hsin)* and fairmindedness or impartiality *(kung-hsin)*, and *li*.[57]

By reflecting on the style of performance, it is possible to find a guide to dealing with the problem of formulating transcultural principles. According to Hsün Tzu, it is expected that a scholar or a superior person would manifest three qualities in discourse: (1) "a humane mind" *(jen-hsin)*, (2) "a receptive mind" *(hsüeh-hsin)*, and (3) "an impartial mind" *(kung-hsin)*.[58] Typically, a humane *(jen)* person has an active and affectionate concern for others, but, more importantly, he respects others regardless of whether they are worthy or unworthy of personal association. A desirable participant is also one who is "receptive" or openminded in displaying a willingness to listen to other's normative claims and impartial or fairminded in his judgment or decision, who seeks to achieve consensus rather than to attain personal gain or glory. Moreover, the participants must also observe at least some *li* or rules of civility.

These characteristics of desirable participants suggest that a Confucian theorist can expand and deepen such notions such as *jen* (humaneness), *hsüeh* (receptivity), and *kung* (impartiality or fairness) in formulating certain transcultural principles consistent with its conception of argumentation.

Given the above assumptions, with no claim to completeness, I propose the following principles as a point of departure for further inquiry:[59]

P1   non-prescriptivity
P2   mutuality
P3   procedural justice
P4   rectification
P5   reconsideration.

Before proceeding to discuss these principles, let me say something more about their status in adjudication. These transcultural principles are to be viewed as heuristic or leading principles of inquiry into the possibility of achieving consensus of substantive norms.[60] As ground

---

57. See my *Ethical Argumentation*, chap. 1.

58. Ibid.

59. My discussion of these principles is intended as no more than another sketch in a progress report toward the development of a Confucian moral philosophy.

60. With Rawls, I suppose that "one of the aims of moral philosophy is to look for possible bases of agreement where none seem to exist. It must attempt to extend the range of consensus and to frame more discriminating moral conceptions for our consideration." However, given the radical disagreement rooted in tradition-oriented perspectives, the prior task is to look for those principles, à la Scanlon, that cannot be

rules for intercultural discourse, they are, so to speak, protocols of ethical diplomacy. Their functions reflect, in part, the basic sense of *li* as a set of formal prescriptions for proper behavior. These principles focus primarily on the delimiting and supportive functions of *li*, i.e., conditions that acknowledge the necessity of constraints that define the limits of proper conduct and conditions that facilitate the satisfaction of tradition-oriented value claims.[61]

P1. Principle of Non-Prescriptivity

The principle of non-prescriptivity may also be called the principle of integrity. It is a principle of respect for the integrity of ethical traditions. More generally, from the *tao*-perspective, it is the principle of respect for the diversity of goods, for various experiments of living in distinct cultural forms of life. In particular, the principle captures an aspect of humaneness *(jen-hsin)*. Mencius is emphatic on this theme of integrity exemplified in different, worthy ways of pursuing *jen* in the light of personal situations.[62] This principle is valuation-neutral regarding the substantive content of different ethical traditions. Acceptance of this principle, however, does not preclude the adherents of different traditions from learning from one another. While traditions that survived the crucial test of their long history deserve respect, it is a Confucian tenet that healthy interaction of modern cultures of the East and West will eventually lead to the "higher form of creative synthesis which will emerge as a new culture of the future with both the East and the West as its necessary ingredients."[63] As Winch reminds us, "the concept of *learning from* which is involved in the study of other cultures is closely linked with the concept of *wisdom*. We are confronted not just with different techniques, but with new possibilities of good and evil, in relation to which men may come to terms with life."[64]

Accepting this principle as a precondition for discourse on issues of substantive cultural norms is also compatible with Williams's view of

---

reasonably rejected, given "the aim of finding principles which could be the basis of informed, unforced general agreement." The proposed transcultural principles may be construed in the sense of Scanlon's principles but they are not intended to be contractarian normative principles. See John Rawls, *A Theory of Justice* (Cambridge: Harvard University Press, 1971), 582; John Rawls, "Justice and Fairness: Political and not Metaphysical;" Scanlon, "Contractarianism and Utilitarianism."

61. See Essay 13, sec. IV.

62. While this principle recalls Kant's Principle of Humanity, it is not a formula of the Categorical Imperative, and thus pretends to no status of being an apodictic and universal principle of conduct. For Mencius, see *Mencius*, esp. 5A:7; 6B:6; and 6A:10.

63. Thomé H. Fang, *Creativity in Man and Nature* (Taipei: Linking, 1980), 141.

64. Peter Winch, *Ethics and Action* (London: Routledge and Kegan Paul, 1972), 42. See also MacIntyre, *Whose Justice? Which Rationality?* 394–95.

"relativism at a distance"; an encounter with an alien tradition, from each culture-oriented point of view, may be merely a matter of notional rather than real confrontation. But as Williams says, "Today all confrontations between cultures must be real confrontations." Unlike Williams, however, a Confucian would cast doubt on his thesis that "reflection might destroy knowledge, because thick ethical concepts might be driven from use by reflection, while the more abstract general ethical thoughts that would probably take their place would not satisfy the conditions of propositional knowledge."[65] Consider Williams's examples of "thick" ethical concepts such as treachery, promise, brutality, courage, lie, and gratitude. These concepts seem "to express a union of fact and value" as contrasted with "thin" concepts as good, right, and ought. A Confucian would view this distinction as a distinction between levels of abstraction. Given his or her faith in the creative synthesis of the cultures of the East and West, the "thick" culturally operative concepts are in principle subject to conceptual transformation via analogical projection of the significance of *jen, li,* and *i*. Thus, in spite of their usual locus of ethical significance, these concepts may be shaped into "thin" general notions, subject to specification of their concrete significance in different cultural habitat. Moreover, for the Confucian, the basic issue concerns the possibility of reasoned agreement to conflict resolution in the light of acknowledged preconditions of discourse and not the adoption of some version of moral realism. This does not mean that conflicting value claims cannot be assessed in terms of their truth dimension. Rather, such an assessment depends on a context of discourse consisting of a particular rather than a universal audience. As Austin once remarked, "In real life, as opposed to the simple situations envisaged in logical theory, one cannot always answer in a simple manner whether it [a statement] is true or false."[66]

P2. Mutuality

Confucius did not claim to be a man of *jen*, for commitment to *jen*, as it involves persistent effort in extending benevolence, is a heavy burden. However, the practice of *jen* "depends on oneself alone and not on

65. Bernard Williams, *Ethics and the Limits of Philosophy* (Cambridge: Harvard University Press, 1985), 129, 140, and 169.

66. J. L. Austin, *How To Do Things with Words* (Cambridge: Harvard University Press, 1962), 142. For the distinction between universal and particular audience, see Ch. Perelman and Anna Olbrechts-Tyteca, *The New Rhetoric: A Treatise on Argumentation* (Notre Dame: University of Notre Dame Press, 1969), 87; and my "Some Aspects of Ethical Argumentation: A Reply to Daniel Dahlstrom and John Marshall," *Journal of Chinese Philosophy* 14, no. 4 (1987): 509–12.

others."[67] On one occasion, responding to the question whether there is a single word that can serve as a guide to one's whole life, Confucius said, "It is perhaps the word '*shu.*' Do not impose on others what you yourself do not desire *(yü).*"[68] As a method for the practice of *jen, shu* calls for "the ability to take as an analogy what is near at hand," i.e., using "oneself as a measure"[69] The notion of *shu,* reminiscent of the Golden Rule, includes two elements: desire *(yü)* and the use of analogy. The desire in question pertains to second-order, reflective, rather than to first-order, occurrent desire, that is, desire as mediated by reason or reflection.[70] And this reflection is conducted with due regard to *jen,* the concern for the well-being of another. The element of analogy may be viewed as an imaginative projection of one's concern for *jen* in taking into account other peoples' desires and interest.[71] As Fingarette put it, analogy or comparison is "an act of creative imagination." "The spirit of such teaching as *shu* and the Golden Rule is obviously to call upon us to take the other person's situation into account in some central way."[72]

67. *Lun Yü,* 7:34; 8:7, 12:1; 15:21.

68. Ibid., 15:24. See also 5:11; 6:20; 12:2; and 4:15. *Chung* (doing one's best) and *shu* are said by Tseng Tzu to characterize the thread of Confucius's *tao* (ibid., 4:15). I here focus only on *shu* with Lau's reminder that "*chung* is the doing of one's best and it is through *chung* that one puts into effect what one had found out by the method of *shu*" (Lau, *Confucius: The Analects,* 16). I take it that *chung* here may be construed as an expression of one's sincere commitment to *jen.* For further discussion, see my "Confucian Vision and the Human Community." For fuller alternative readings of relevant passages, see Herbert Fingarette, "Following the 'One Thread' of the Analects," *Journal of the American Academy of Religion* XLVII, no. 35 (1979); and David L. Hall and Roger T. Ames, *Thinking Through Confucius* (Albany: State University of New York Press, 1987), 283–304.

69. Lau, *Confucius: The Analects,* 15.

70. See Harry Frankfurt, "Freedom of the Will and the Concept of a Person," *Journal of Philosophy* 68, no. 1 (1971): 10. This distinction is implicit in Hsün Tzu: "A single desire which one receives from nature *(tien)* is regulated and directed by the mind in many different ways. Consequently, it may be difficult to identify and distinguish it in terms of its original appearance. . . . If the guidance of the mind is in accord with reason, although desires are many, what harm will this be to good government." [This translation is a revision of Burton Watson, trans., *Hsun Tzu: Basic Writings* (New York: Columbia University Press, 1963), 151.] See my "Dimensions of Li (Propriety): Reflections on An Aspect of Hsün Tzu's Ethics," *Philosophy East and West* 29, no. 4 (1979): 380–81. For a similar interpretation, see Liang Ch'i-hsiung, *Hsün Tzu chien-shi* (Taipei: Shang-wu, 1978), 323.

71. For a detailed discussion of analogical projection, see *Ethical Argumentation,* esp. 78–86.

72. Fingaratte, "Following the 'One Thread' in the *Analects,*" 383. It may be noted that the negative formulation of *shu* or the Golden Rule, i.e., "What I do not desire, I ought not to impose on others" (*Lun Yü,* 12:12, 15:23), is more important than the more positive version, especially in the context of intercultural conflict. The negative version counsels modesty and humility, or a presumption of arrogance of ethical, cultural superiority. For further discussion, see Robert E. Allinson, "The Confucian Golden Rule:

Reflection on the significance of the notion of *shu* for intercultural discourse suggests what I call the principle of mutuality or consideration, a collateral principle of integrity, which enjoins the parties in dispute to exercise sympathetic imagination in appreciating the integrity of an alien, conflicting tradition and to endeavor, whenever opportunity arises, to transform disagreement into an occasion for exploring the possibility of convergence of values. One's desire to impose one's own norms must thus be mediated by reflection that attends to the other's similar desire. Analogical projection of the extensive significance of one's cultural norms is not discouraged, but it must be moderated by due consideration for the other's own conception of their locus of operation. Given the real possibility of "relativism at a distance," the principle of mutuality remains a procedural rather than a substantive requirement. Of course, in the light of *tao*, the aim of attaining congenial coexistence within the limits of *li* also calls for supporting or facilitating the realization of the ideals of other ways of life. Coupled with this concern, the principle of mutuality would enjoin sustaining the vitality of different ways of life, seen by their adherents to be worthy of continuing preservation.

P3. Procedural Justice

The argumentative role of *li* as a set of formal prescriptions for proper behavior and fairmindedness or impartiality *(kung-hsin)* may be construed as a requirement of consistency or the principle of procedural justice. Consistency is not just a matter of compliance with formal requirements of deductive logic, for "these formal requirements tell us nothing about what in particular is to count as consistency, just as the rules of the propositional calculus limit, but do not themselves determine what are to be proper values of p, q, etc."[73] The principle of procedural justice, in Rawls's term, is that of pure procedural, as distinct from perfect or imperfect procedural justice. Unlike the former, no substantive criterion of justice is presupposed for insuring just outcome; and unlike the latter, there is no guarantee that any given substantive criterion will yield the desired outcome. "Pure procedural justice obtains when there is no independent criterion for the right result: instead there is a correct or fair procedure such that the outcome

---

A Negative Formulation," *Journal of Chinese Philosophy* 12, no. 3 (1985); and my "Reasonable Persons and the Good: Reflections on an Aspect of Weiss' Ethical Thought" in Lewis Hahn, ed., *Philosophy of Paul Weiss*, Library of Living Philosophers (Chicago and LaSalle: Open Court, 1996).

73. Winch, *Ethics and Action*, 34.

is likewise correct or fair, whatever it is, provided that the procedure has been properly followed."[74]

The principle of procedural justice embodies a concern for the establishment of three different and related sorts of procedures as preconditions for adjudication: (1) procedures that maintain the argumentative process as an orderly proceeding for the presentation of competing value claims; (2) even more important, procedures that ensure equal participation of the disputing parties in an open forum; (3) procedures that pertain to the impartial enforcement of any agreed solution to the problem of common concern. The first sort of procedure reflects the concern of *li* in its basic focus on form, manner, and order of conduct; the second and the third that of fairmindedness *(kung-hsin).* For further exploration, a Confucian theorist may appropriate some insights from process theory of judicial review without taking a position on its adequacy as an explanatory cum justificatory theory of American constitutional law. The stress on the procedural side of due process, on the preservation of structure rather than "identification and preservation of specific substantive values" is a dominant theme in the Constitution of the United States and some of the Amendments.[75] The due process and equal protection clauses of the Fourteenth Amendment, for example, as a matter of minimum interpretation, seem to address the guarantee of fair procedures, say, for airing grievances of the citizenry against unjustified treatment by its government. This dominant theme suggests the primacy of procedural justice over agreement on substantive norms for settlement of disputes. More generally, when competing substantive value claims have implicit reference to a divergence of tradition-oriented ideals, it is plausible to maintain that the hope for peaceful resolution depends on an acknowledgement of some procedural rules as a precondition for negotiation and for consideration of the possibility of mutual accommodation.[76]

74. Rawls, *A Theory of Justice,* 85–86.

75. This appropriation of Ely's insight is consistent with an appreciation of Dworkin's moral theory of judicial review, in particular, that the due process and equal protection clauses of the Fourteenth Amendment are best viewed as embodying "abstract intention" rather than "concrete intention," i.e., as enacting the "concepts of justice and equality" rather than particular conceptions of justice. It must also be noted that in light of *tao,* the right sort of procedures to be spelled out may well involve competing substantive value judgments to be resolved within argumentation. Again, like the question of truth, the question here is a matter of context of discourse consisting of particular rather than universal audience. See John Hart Ely, *Democracy and Distrust* (Cambridge: Harvard University Press, 1980), 92; and Ronald Dworkin, *A Matter of Principle* (Cambridge: Harvard University Press, 1986), 49. For Dworkin's emphasis on procedural due process, see *Law's Empire,* 166–67, passim.

76. For the priority of moral rules over the pursuit of ideals, see my *Dimensions of Moral Creativity,* esp. 135–39.

P4 and P5. Principles of Rectification and Reconsideration

Coupled with *tao* or *jen* as an overarching ideal of extensive concern for the integrity and well-being of every existent thing, the principle of procedural justice must be supplemented by the principle of rectification or restoration of the values lost in conflict resolution. Accommodating coherently the diversity of competing goods and ideals, with due regard to fairmindedness *(kung-hsin)*, inevitably involves the loss or sacrifice of values. The problem of *kan-ying* or coordinating the satisfaction of the demands of varieties of ethical excellence is, so to speak, a design problem "akin to that of landscape gardening or interior decoration."[77] In this setting, we are concerned with the meshing of elements in a life arrangement. The possibility of obtaining the desired solution depends on recognizing the constraints imposed by limited natural resources as well as those of human nature and culture. Factors such as partiality or limited benevolence, foresight, and vulnerability, as well as those of the cultural traditions, need to be taken into account in an overall design of life.[78] Cognizance of these constraints points to the need of making comparative judgment of importance.[79] But this judgment must not be based on so-called "presumption of equal respect or worth" of cultures cherished by different ethnic groups in a multicultural society like America or Canada. For the presumption of equal worth of all cultures in American pluralism implicitly smacks of cultural arrogance. Like the "presumption of innocence" in American law, in practice, the accused is already held on bail or imprisoned. The idea of presumption of equal worth of all cultures seems to imply, from the point of view of the speaker, that the other culture in question is bizarre, though he or she must reserve judgment pending further study. While this sort of attitude seems to display a liberal's generous response to "the politics of recognition," for many members of the minority cultural groups, it is a demeaning response to the "politics of difference." What is wanted is an *acknowledgment* of one's cultural integrity without prejudgment, not "a presumption of equal worth."[80]

---

77. Rescher, *Unpopular Essays on Technological Progress*, 60.
78. Hsün Tzu, like Hume, Hart, Warnock, and Rawls, regards these factors in human nature and scarcity of resources as the principal causes of human conflict. I take it that these same factors are equally germane to conflict resolution, for they act as constraints on the articulation of feasible objectives—a theme that pervades Rescher's various writings on values. For further discussion, see my "Quasi-Empirical Aspect of Hsün Tzu's Philosophy of Human Nature," *Philosophy East and West* 28, no. 1 (1978); and "Ideals and Values."
79. See *Mencius*, 7A:46. Also, 6A:10 and 6A:14.
80. Charles Taylor, "The Politics of Recognition" in Amy Gutman, ed. *Multicul-*

At any rate, for the Confucian, the principle of non-prescriptivity enjoins respect for the integrity of every cultural tradition, not a presumption of equal worth. However, the need for comparative judgment of importance concerning issues of intercultural conflict gives rise to a difficult question: What sort of measure is required for rectifying the loss or degradation of cultural values in adjudication. In the light of *tao,* the loss of value in such a judgment is always a matter of regret. More important, that experience of regret has a prospective significance in that it calls also for an active concern for restoration of the value lost or its functional equivalent.[81]

In addition to the principle of rectification, we may also propose a principle of reconsideration, that is, that any substantive ethical agreement reached in argumentation is subject to reasonable reconsideration in the light of changing local, cultural circumstances as well as their relevance to future issues of value conflict.[82]

In this essay, I hope that I have succeeded in showing that principles can be incorporated into Confucian ethics without leading to internal incoherence. Other Confucian thinkers will propose quite different directions for further inquiry in the light of their interpretations of the spirit of Confucian ethics. Nevertheless, on the basis of the considerations presented here, the complementarity thesis appears to be a viable option in the development of Confucian moral philosophy. Moreover, the thesis has also practical import for the issue of intercultural conflict today. The thesis suggests that failure in adjudication via objective principles should not be regarded as a deadlock, an insoluble problematic situation that inevitably calls for the use of might. Rather, the situation is best viewed as an occasion for renewed effort in arbitration, in seeking possibilities of reconciliation. Given the Confucian emphasis on *jen,* concern for coexistence and harmony of diverse ways of life, and the reasoned exercise of *i* in coping with changing circumstances, there can be no absolute or fixed determination of the priority of either adjudication or arbitration. In the end, which approach is the most effective in intercultural discourse depends on the situation at

---

turalism and "The Politics of Recognition" (Princeton: Princeton University Press, 1992), 62f.

81. See *The Unity of Knowledge and Action,* 37–42. For similar concern with rectification in Weiss's metaphysics, see my "Reasonable Persons and the Good: Reflections on an Aspect of Weiss' Ethical Thought," in Lewis Hahn, ed., *Philosophy of Paul Weiss,* Library of Living Philosophers (Chicago and LaSalle: Open Court, 1996), 340–41.

82. For the Confucian notion of reasonableness, see *The Unity of Knowledge and Action,* 94–100. For affinity to Rescher's notion, see "Ideals and Values," 193–98.

hand. Nevertheless, by reshaping some of the key concepts of Confucian ethics, along with certain assumptions, it is possible to propose a set of transcultural principles, preconditions or ground rules for intercultural adjudication. Admittedly, what is presented is a sketch of principles that requires further development.

Bibliography

Aiken, Henry David. "On the Concept of a Moral Principle." In *The Isenberg Memorial Lecture Series, 1965–1966*. East Lansing: Michigan State University Press, 1969.

Alderman, Harold. "By Virtue of a Virtue." *Review of Metaphysics* 36 (1982): 127–53.

Allinson, Robert E. "The Confucian Golden Rule: A Negative Formulation." *Journal of Chinese Philosophy* 12, no. 3 (1985): 305–15.

———, ed. *Understanding the Chinese Mind: The Philosophical Roots*. Hong Kong: Oxford University Press, 1988.

Ames, Roger. "Reflections on the Confucian Self." In *Rules, Rituals and Responsibility*, edited by Mary I. Bookover. La Salle: Open Court, 1991.

———. "The Focus-Field Self in Classical Confucianism." In *Self as Person in Asian Theory and Practice*, edited by Roger Ames, Thomas P. Kasulis, and Wimal Dissanayake. Albany: State University of New York Press, 1994.

Anscombe, G. E. "Modern Moral Philosophy." In *The Definition of Morality*, edited by G. Wallace and A. D. Walker. London: Methuen, 1970.

Attfield, Robin. "On Being Human." *Inquiry* 17 (1974): 175–92.

Aristotle, *Nicomachean Ethics*. Translated by Martin Ostwald. Indianapolis: Bobbs-Merrill, 1962.

———. *Rhetorica*. In *The Works of Aristotle*, edited by W. D. Ross. Oxford: Oxford University Press, 1955.

Aschenbrenner, Karl. *Concepts of Value: Foundations of Value Theory*. Dordrecht-Holland: Reidel, 1971.

Audi, Robert. "Self-Deception and Rationality." In *Self-Deception and Self-Understanding*, edited by Mike Martin. Lawrence: University Press of Kansas, 1986.

Austin, J. L. *Sense and Sensibilia*. Oxford: Clarendon Press, 1962.

———. *How to Do Things with Words*. Cambridge: Harvard University Press, 1962.

———. *Philosophical Papers*, 2d ed. New York: Oxford University Press, 1970.

Baier, Kurt. *The Moral Point of View*. Ithaca: Cornell University Press, 1958.

———. "Rationality, Reason, and the Good." In *Morality, Reason and Truth*, ed. David Copp and David Zimmerman. Totowa: Rowman & Allanheld, 1985.

Bambrough, Renford. "Essay on Man." In *Nature and Conduct*, edited by R. S. Peters. New York: St. Martin's Press, 1975.

———. "The Scope of Reason: An Epistle to the Persians." In *Objectivity and Cultural Divergence*, edited by S. C. Brown. Cambridge: Cambridge University Press, 1984.

Baylis, C. A. "Grading, Values, and Choice." *Mind* 67, no. 268 (1958): 485–501.

Beardsmore, R. W. *Moral Reasoning*. London: Routledge & Kegan Paul, 1969.
Beauchamp, Tom L. *Philosophical Ethics*. New York: McGraw Hill, 1982.
Benedict, Ruth. *Patterns of Culture*. Boston: Houghton Mifflin, 1934.
———. "Configurations of Culture in North America." In *Ruth Benedict*. Edited by Margaret Mead. New York: Columbia University Press, 1974.
Benitez, Eugenio. "Argument, Rhetoric and Philosophic Method: Plato's *Protagoras*." *Philosophy and Rhetoric* 25, no. 3 (1993): 222–52.
Bentham, Jeremy. *An Introduction to the Principles of Morals and Legislation*. New York: Hafner Publishing Company, 1948.
Benton, Ted. "Biological Ideas and Their Cultural Uses." In *Objectivity and Cultural Divergence*, edited by S. C. Brown. Cambridge: Cambridge University Press, 1984.
Berkeley, George. *A Treatise concerning the Principles of Human Knowledge*. In vol. 2 of *The Works of George Berkeley*, edited by A. A. Luce and T. E. Jessop. London: Thomas Nelson & Sons, 1953.
———. "Passive Obedience." In vol. 4 of *The Works of George Berkeley*, edited by A. A. Luce and T. E. Jessop. London: Thomas Nelson & Sons, 1953.
Blanshard, Brand. "Wisdom." In *Encyclopedia of Philosophy*, edited by Paul Edwards. New York: Macmillan, 1967.
Bosley, Richard, and John King-Farlow. "Self-Formation and the Mean (Programmatic Remarks on Self-Deception)." In *Self-Deception and Self-Understanding*, edited by Mike W. Martin. Lawrence: University Press of Kansas, 1985.
Brentano, Franz. *The Origin of Our Knowledge of Right and Wrong*. London: Routledge & Kegan Paul, 1969.
Burch, Robert W. "Are There Moral Experts?" *The Monist* 58, no. 4 (1974): 646–58.
Butler, Joseph. *Fifteen Sermons Preached at Rolls Chapel*. London: G. Bell and Sons, 1953.
———. "Upon Self-Deceit." In *The Works of Joseph Butler*, edited by Samuel Halifax. Oxford: Oxford University Press, 1850.
Chan, Wing-tsit. "The Evolution of Confucian Concept *Jen*." *Philosophy East and West* 4 (1955): 295–319.
———. "Chinese Theory and Practice." In *Philosophy and Culture: East and West*, edited by Charles A. Moore. Honolulu: University of Hawaii Press, 1962.
———, trans. *A Source Book in Chinese Philosophy*. Princeton: Princeton University Press, 1963.
———. *The Way of Lao Tzu*. Indianapolis: Bobbs-Merrill, 1963.
———. "The Evolution of the Neo-Confucian Concept *Li* as Principle." *Tsing Hua Journal of Chinese Studies*, NS IV, no. 2 (1964): 123–49.
———. "Neo-Confucianism: New Ideas in Old Terminology." *Philosophy East and West* 17, nos. 1–4 (1967): 15–35.
———. "Chinese and Western Interpretations of *Jen*." *Journal of Chinese Philosophy* 2, no. 2 (1975): 107–29.
———. (Ch'en Jung-chieh). *Ch'uan-hsi lu hsiang-chu chi-p'ing*. Taipei: Hsüeh-sheng, 1983.
———. "*Li*." In *Chung-kuo che-hsüeh tz'u-tien ta-ch'üan*, edited by Wei Cheng-t'ung. Taipei: Shui-niu, 1983.
———, trans. *Neo-Confucian Terms Explained (The Pei-hsi tzu-i)*. New York: Columbia University Press, 1985.

————, ed. *Chu Hsi and Neo-Confucianism*. Honolulu: University of Hawaii Press, 1986.

————. *Chu Hsi: New Studies*. Honolulu: University of Hawaii Press, 1989.

Chang, Carsun. *Wang Yang-ming: Idealist Philosopher of Sixteenth Century China*. Jamaica, N.Y.: St. John's University Press, 1962.

Chang, Chung-hsing. "Tzu-ch'i chih t'i chi ch'i fang-chih." In *T'an tzu-ch'i ch'i-jen*. Taipei: Commercial Press, 1991.

Chao, Seng. "Nirvana is Nameless" (translated by Chang Chung-yuan), *Journal of Chinese Philosophy* 1, nos. 3/4 (1974): 247–74.

Chao, Tse-ho. *Ta-hsüeh yen-chiu*. Taipei: Chung-hua, 1972.

Ch'en, Ch'un. *Pei-hsi hsien-sheng tzu-i hsiang-chiang*. Taipei: Kuang-wen, 1979.

Ch'en, Ku-ying. *Lao Tzu chin-chu chin-i*. Taipei: Commercial Press, 1970.

Ch'en, Ta-ch'i. *Hsün Tzu hsüeh-shuo*. Taipei: Chung-hua wen-hua she, 1954.

————. *Meng Tzu te ming-li ssu-hsiang chi ch'i pien-shuo shih-k'uang*. Taipei: Shang-wu, 1974.

————. *P'ing-fan te tao-te kuan*. Taipei: Chung-hua, 1976.

————. *Kung Tzu hsüeh-shuo*. Taipei: Cheng-chung, 1977.

Cheng, Chung-ying. "Rectifying Names *(cheng-ming)* in Classical Confucianism." *East Asian Occasional Papers*, I, edited by H. J. Lamley. University of Hawaii Asian Studies Program (1969): 82–96.

————. "*Yi* as a Universal Principle of Specific Application in Confucian Morality." *Philosophy East and West* 22 (1972): 269–80.

————. "Chinese Philosophy: A Characterization." In *Invitation to Chinese Philosophy*, edited by Arne Naess and Alastair Hannay. Oslo: Universitetsforlaget, 1972.

————. "Toward Constructing a Dialectics of Harmonization: Harmony and Conflict in Chinese Philosophy." *Journal of Chinese Philosophy* 4, no. 3, (1977): 209–45.

Cheng, Hsueh-li. "Reasoning in Confucian Ethics." Presented at the International Symposium on Confucianism and the Modern World, Taipei, Taiwan, November 12–17, 1987.

Cheng, Yi-li. *A New English-Chinese Dictionary*. Hong Kong: Kwang Tai, 1966.

Ch'ien, Mu. *Lun Yü hsin-chieh*. Taipei: Sheng-wu, 1965.

————. *Chu Tzu hsin hsüeh-an*. 5 vols. Taipei: San-min, 1982.

Chin, Ann-ping, and Mansfield Freeman. Translators. *Tai Chen on Mencius: Explorations in Words and Meaning*. New Haven: Yale University Press, 1990.

Ching, Julia. *To Acquire Wisdom: The Way of Wang Yang-ming*. New York: Columbia University Press, 1976.

Chu, Hsi. *Chu Tzu yü-lei*. 8 vols. Taipei: Cheng-chung, 1962.

————. *Chu Tzu ta-ch'üan*. Taipei: Chung-hua, 1970.

————. *Ssu-shu chi-chu*. Hong Kong: T'ai-p'ing, 1980.

Chu, Hsi, and Lü Tsu-ch'ien, eds. *Reflections on Things at Hand: The Neo-Confucian Anthology*. Translated by W. T. Chan. New York and London: Columbia University Press, 1967.

Cohen, Avner, and Marcedo Dascal, eds. *The Institution of Philosophy: A Discipline in Crisis?* La Salle: Open Court, 1989.

Chuang Tzu. *The Complete Works of Chuang Tzu*. Translated by Burton Watson. New York: Columbia University Press, 1968.

Chung-wen ta ts'u-tien (The Encyclopedic Dictionary of the Chinese Language). 10 vols. Taipei: San-min, 1976.

Clarke, Stanley G., and Evan Simpson, eds. *Anti-Theory in Ethics and Moral Conservatism.* New York: State University of New York Press, 1989.

Collingwood, R. G. *The Principles of Art.* Oxford: The Clarendon Press, 1938.

———. *An Autobiography.* Oxford: Oxford University Press, 1964.

———. *The New Leviathan: or Man, Society, Civilization and Barbarism.* Oxford: Clarendon Press, 1985.

Creel, Herrlee G. *What Is Taoism? and Other Studies in Chinese Cultural History.* Chicago: University of Chicago Press, 1970.

Cua, A. S. *Reason and Virtue: A Study in the Ethics of Richard Price.* Athens: Ohio University Press, 1966.

———. "Morality and Paradigmatic Individuals." *American Philosophical Quarterly* 6, no. 4 (1969): 324–29.

———. "Logic of Confucian Dialogues." In *Studies in Philosophy and the History of Philosophy,* vol. 4, edited by J. K. Ryan. Washington, D.C.: The Catholic University of America Press, 1969.

———. "Problem of Moral Actuation." *Man and World* 3, nos. 3 and 4 (1970): 338–50.

———. "Some Reflections on Methodology in Chinese Philosophy." *International Philosophical Quarterly* 11, no. 2 (1971): 236–48.

———. "Reflections on the Structure of Confucian Ethics." *Philosophy East and West* 21, no. 2 (1971): 125–40.

———. "The Concept of Paradigmatic Individuals in the Ethics of Confucius." *Inquiry* 14 (1971): 41–55.

———. "Relevance of Moral Rules and Creative Agency." *New Scholasticism* 47, no. 1 (1973): 1–20.

———. "Practical Causation and Confucian Ethics." *Philosophy East and West* 25, no. 1 (1975): 1–10.

———. "Uses of Dialogue and Moral Understanding." *Journal of Chinese Philosophy* 2 (1975): 131–48.

———. "On the Quality of Human Life." *Systems Thinking and the Quality of Life.* Proceedings of the Annual North American Meetings, Society for General Systems Research (1975): 64–67.

———. "The Conceptual Aspect of Hsün Tzu's Philosophy of Human Nature." *Philosophy East and West* 27, no. 4 (1977): 373–89.

———. "The Quasi-Empirical Aspect of Hsün Tzu's Philosophy of Human Nature." *Philosophy East and West* 28, no. 1 (1978): 1–19.

———. *Dimensions of Moral Creativity: Paradigms, Principles, and Ideals.* University Park: Pennsylvania State University Press, 1978.

———. "Dimensions of Li (Propriety): Reflections on an Aspect of Hsün Tzu's Ethics." *Philosophy East and West* 29, no. 4 (1979): 373–94.

———. "Tasks of Confucian Ethics." *Journal of Chinese Philosophy* 6, no. 1 (1979): 55–67.

———. "Ideal Themes, Justification, and Moral Understanding." *Journal of Chinese Philosophy* 7, no. 1 (1980): 55–65.

———. *The Unity of Knowledge and Action: A Study in Wang Yang-ming's Moral Psychology.* Honolulu: University Press of Hawaii, 1982.

———. "Ideals and Value: A Study in Rescher's Moral Vision." In *Praxis and Reason: Studies in the Philosophy of Nicholas Rescher,* edited by Robert Almeder. Washington: University Press of America, 1982.

————. "Basic Metaphors and the Emergence of Root Metaphors," *Journal of Mind and Behavior* 3 (1982): 251–58.

————. "*Li* and Moral Justification: A Study in the *Li Chi.*" *Philosophy East and West* 33, no. 1 (1983): 1–16.

————. "Confucian Vision and the Human Community." *Journal of Chinese Philosophy* 11, no. 3 (1984): 227–38.

————. *Ethical Argumenetation: A Study in Hsün Tzu's Moral Epistemology.* Honolulu: University of Hawaii Press, 1985.

————. "The Ethical Uses of the Past in Early Confucianism: The Case of Hsün Tzu." *Philosophy East and West* 35, no. 2 (1985): 133–56.

————. "The Structure of Social Complexes." *Review of Metaphysics* 41, no. 2 (1987): 335–53.

————. "Some Aspects of Ethical Argumentation: A Reply to Daniel Dahlstrom and John Marshall." *Journal of Chinese Philosophy* 14, no. 4 (1987): 501–16.

————. "Reflections on Moral Theory and Understanding Moral Traditions." In *Interpreting across Cultures: New Essays in Comparative Philosophy,* edited by Gerald James Larson and Eliot Deutsch. Princeton: Princeton University Press, 1988.

————. "The Problem of Conceptual Unity in Hsün Tzu and Li Kou's Solution." *Philosophy East and West* 39, no. 2 (1989): 115–34.

————. "The Possibility of Ethical Knowledge: Reflections on a Theme in the *Hsün Tzu.*" In *Epistemological Issues in Classical Chinese Philosophy,* edited by Hans Lenk and Gregor Paul. Albany: State University of New York Press, 1993.

————. "Reasonable Persons and the Good: Reflections on an Aspect of Weiss' Ethical Thought." In *Philosophy of Paul Weiss,* Library of Living Philosophers, edited by Lewis Hahn. LaSalle: Open Court, 1995.

————. "Reason and Principle in Chinese Philosophy: An Interpretation of *Li.*" In *Blackwell Companion to World Philosophy,* edited by Eliot Deutsch and Ron Bontekoe. Oxford: Blackwell, 1997.

Dahlstrom, Daniel. "*Tao* and Ethical Argumentation." *Journal of Chinese Philosophy* 14, no. 4 (1987): 475–85.

Danto, Arthur. *Morality and Mysticism: Oriental Thought and Moral Philosophy.* New York: Basic Books, 1972

————. *Analytical Philosophy of Action.* Cambridge: Cambridge University Press, 1973.

————. "Language and the Tao: Some Reflections on Ineffability." *Journal of Chinese Philosophy* 1, no. 1 (1973): 45–56.

————. *The Transfiguration of the Commonplace.* Cambridge: Harvard University Press, 1981.

de Bary, William Theodore, ed. *Self and Society in Ming Thought.* New York: Columbia University Press, 1970.

————. *Neo-Confucian Orthodoxy and the Learning of the Mind-and-Heart.* New York: Columbia University Press, 1981.

————. *The Liberal Tradition in China.* Hong Kong: Chinese University of Hong Kong Press, 1983.

Dewey, John. *Human Nature and Conduct.* New York: Modern Library, 1930.

————. *Logic: Theory of Inquiry.* New York; Henry Holt, 1938.

————. *Reconstruction in Philosophy.* Boston: Beacon Press, 1957.

————. *Theory of the Moral Life.* New York: Holt, Rinehart and Winston, 1960.

Deutsch, Eliot. *On Truth: An Ontological Theory*. Honolulu: University of Hawaii Press, 1979.

———, and Ron Bontekoe, eds. *Blackwell Companion to World Philosophy*. Oxford: Blackwell, 1997.

Dietrichson, Paul. "Kant's Criteria of Universalizability." In *Kant: Foundations of the Metaphysics of Morals: Text and Critical Essays*, edited by Robert Paul Wolff. Indianapolis: Bobbs-Merrill, 1969.

Dilman, Iliam, and D. Z. Phillips. *Sense and Delusion*. London: Routledge & Kegan Paul, 1971.

Donagan, Alan. *The Later Philosophy of R. G. Collingwood*. Oxford: Clarendon Press, 1962.

Downie, R. S., and Elizabeth Telfer. *Respect for Persons*. London: George Allen & Unwin, 1969.

Dubs, Homer H. *Hsüntze: The Moulder of Ancient Confucianism*. London: Arthur Probsthain, 1927.

———, trans. *The Works of Hsüntze*. Taipei: Ch'eng-wen, 1966.

Dworkin, Ronald. *Law's Empire*. Cambridge: Harvard University Press, 1986.

———. *Taking Rights Seriously*. Cambridge: Harvard University Press, 1978.

———. *A Matter of Principle*. Cambridge: Harvard University Press, 1986.

Ely, John Hart. *Democracy and Distrust*. Cambridge: Harvard University Press, 1980.

Emmet, Dorothy. *The Moral Prism*. London: Macmillan Press, 1979.

Erh Ch'eng ch'üan-shu. In *Ssu-pu pei-yao*. Taipei: Chung-hwa, 1976.

Fang, Thomé H. "The World and the Individual in Chinese Metaphysics." In *The Chinese Mind*, edited by Charles A. Moore. Honolulu: East-West Center Press, 1967.

———. *The Chinese View of Life*. Taipei: Linking, 1980.

———. *Creativity in Man and Nature*. Taipei: Linking, 1980.

Fingarette, Herbert. *Self-Deception*. London: Routledge & Kegan Paul, 1969.

———. *Confucius: The Secular as Sacred*. New York: Harper and Row, 1972.

———. "The Problem of the Self in the *Analects*." *Philosophy East and West* 29, no. 2 (1979): 129–40.

———. "Following the One Thread in the *Analects*," *Journal of the American Academy of Religion: Thematic Issue: Studies in Classical Chinese Thought* 47, no. 3s (1979): 373–406.

Fogelin, Robert J. *Evidence and Meaning*. London: Routledge & Kegan Paul, 1967.

———. *Understanding Arguments: An Introduction to Informal Logic*. New York: Harcourt Brace Jovanovich, 1978.

Foot, Philippa. *Virtues and Vices*. Berkeley: University of California Press, 1979.

Forke, Alfred, trans. *Lun Heng, Part I: Philosophical Essays of Wang Chung*. New York: Paragon Book Gallery, 1962.

Forrier, Paul, and Chaim Perelman. "Law, Natural and Natural Rights." In *Dictionary of the History of Ideas*, vol. III, edited by Philip P. Wiener. New York: Charles Scribner's Sons, 1973.

Frank, Jerome. *Law and the Modern Mind*. New York: Anchor Books, 1963.

Frankena, William K. *Ethics*. 2d ed. Englewood Cliffs: Prentice Hall, 1973.

———. *Thinking about Morality*. Ann Arbor: Univ. of Michigan Press, 1980.

Frankfurt, Harry. "Freedom of the Will and the Concept of a Person." *Journal of Philosophy* 68, no. 1 (1971): 5–20.

Fuller, Lon. *The Morality of Law.* New Haven: Yale University Press, 1969.

Fung, Yu-lan. *History of Chinese Philosophy.* 2 vols. Translated by Derk Bodde. Princeton: Princeton University Press, 1953.

———. *The Spirit of Chinese Philosophy.* London: Routledge & Kegan Paul, 1962.

———. *Chuang Tzu: A New Selected Translation with an Exposition of the Philosophy of Kuo Hsiang.* New York: Paragon Book Reprint, 1964.

Gadamer, Hans-Georg. *Truth and Method.* New York: Seabury Press, 1975.

Gallie, W. B. "Essentially Contested Concepts." *Proceedings of the Aristotelian Society* 56 (1956): 197–99.

———. *Philosophy and Historical Understanding.* London: Chatto and Windus, 1964.

Gardner, Daniel K. *Chu Hsi and the Ta-hsüeh: Neo-Confucian Reflection on the Confucian Canon.* Cambridge: Harvard University Press, 1985.

———, trans. *Chu Hsi: Learning to Be a Sage.* Berkeley: University of California Press, 1990.

Gasking, D. A. T. "Mr. Williams on the A Priori." *Analysis* 6 (1939): 69–78.

Gewirth, Alan. "Rights and Virtues." *Review of Metaphysics* 38 (1985): 739–62.

Gluckman, Max. *Essays on the Ritual of Social Relations.* Manchester: Manchester University Press, 1962.

Graham, A. C. *Two Chinese Philosophers: Ch'eng Ming-Tao and Ch'eng Yi-ch'uan.* London: Lund Humphries, 1958.

———, trans. *Lieh Tzu.* London: John Murray, 1960.

———. *Disputers of the Tao: Philosophical Argument in Ancient China.* LaSalle: Open Court, 1989.

Grimaldi, William M. A. *Studies in the Philosophy of Aristotle's Rhetoric.* Wiesbaden: Franz Steiner Verlag, 1972.

Grote, J. A. *Treatise on Moral Ideals.* Cambridge: Deighton, Bell & Co., 1876.

Haeger, John W. "The Intellectual Context of Neo-Confucian Syncretism." *Journal of Asian Studies* 31 (1972): 499–513.

Hall, David L., and Roger T. Ames. *Thinking through Confucius.* Albany: State University of New York Press, 1987.

Hamberger, Max. "Aristotle and Confucius: A Study in Comparative Philosophy." *Philosophy* 31 (1956): 324–57.

———. "Aristotle and Confucius: A Comparison." *Journal of the History of Ideas* 20 (1959): 236–49.

Hamlyn, David W. "Self-Knowledge." In *The Self: Psychological and Philosophical Issues,* edited by Theodore Mischel. Oxford: Blackwell, 1977.

Hampshire, Stuart. *Freedom of Mind.* Princeton: Princeton Univ. Press, 1971.

———. *Two Theories of Morality.* Oxford: Oxford University Press, 1977.

———. "Morality and Convention." In *Utilitarianism and Beyond,* edited by Amartya Sen and Bernard Williams. London: Cambridge University Press, 1982.

———. *Morality and Conflict.* Cambridge: Harvard University Press, 1983.

Hare, R. M. *Freedom and Reason.* Oxford: Clarendon Press, 1963.

———. *Moral Thinking.* Oxford: Clarendon Press, 1981.

Hart, H. L. A. *The Concept of Law.* Oxford: Clarendon Press, 1961.

———. *Law, Liberty, and Morality.* Stanford: Stanford University Press, 1963.

Hartmann, Nicolai. *Ethics,* vol. II. London: George Allen & Unwin, 1932.

Hendricks, Robert. "Hsi Kang and Argumentation in the Wei." *Journal of Chinese Philosophy* 8, no. 2 (1981): 169–224.

Hesse, Herman. *Narcissus and Goldmund.* Translated by Ursula Molinaro. New York: Bantam Books, 1971.

———. *My Belief: Essay on Life and Art.* Translated by Denver Lindley. New York: Farrar, Straus and Giroux, 1974.

Hobbes, Thomas. *Leviathan.* Oxford: Clarendon Press, 1952.

Hsu, Francis L. K. *Americans and Chinese: Reflections on Two Cultures and Their People.* Garden City: Doubleday Natural History Press, 1970.

Hsu, Sung-peng. "Two Kinds of Changes in Lao Tzu's Thought." *Journal of Chinese Philosophy* 4, no. 4 (1977): 329–55.

Hu, Hsien Chin. "The Chinese Concepts of 'Face'." *American Anthropologist,* N.S., 46 (1944): 45–64.

Hu, Shih. *Chung-kuo che-hsüeh shih ta-kang, Part I.* Taipei: Commercial Press, 1947.

———. "The Scientific Spirit and Method in Chinese Philosophy." In *Philosophy and Culture: East and West,* edited by Charles A. Moore. Honolulu: University of Hawaii Press, 1962.

Hudson, Hoyt. "The Field of Rhetoric." In *Philosophy, Rhetoric and Argumentation,* edited by Maurice Natanson and Henry W. Johnston. University Park: Pennsylvania State University Press, 1965.

Hudson, W. D., ed. *The Is/Ought Question.* London: Macmillan, 1969.

Hume, David. *A Treatise of Human Nature.* Oxford: Clarendon Press, 1951.

———. *An Inquiry Concerning the Principles of Morals.* Indianapolis: The Library of Liberal Arts, 1957.

———. *Essays: Morals, Political and Literary.* Oxford: Oxford University Press, 1963.

Hyman, A., and J. J. Walsh, eds. *Philosophy in the Middle Ages.* Indianapolis: Hackett Publishing Co., 1973.

James, William. *Essays on Faith and Morals.* New York: Longmans, Green & Co., 1949.

———. *Essays in Radical Empiricism* and *A Pluralistic Universe.* New York: E. P. Dutton, 1971.

Jiang, Paul Yung-ming. *The Search for Mind: Ch'en Pai-sha, Philosopher-Poet.* Singapore: Singapore University Press, 1980.

Johnston, Mark. "Self-Deception and the Nature of Mind." In *Perspectives on Self-Deception,* edited by Brian P. McLauglin and Amélie Oksenberg Rorty. Berkeley: University of California Press, 1988.

Johnston, Henry, and Maurice Natanson, eds. *Philosophy, Rhetoric, and Argumentation.* University Park: Pennsylvania State University Press, 1965.

Kant, Immanuel. *Foundations of the Metaphysics of Morals.* Translated by Lewis White Beck. Indianapolis: Bobbs-Merrill, 1959.

———. *Critique of Judgment.* Translated by J. H. Bernard. New York: Hafner, 1951.

———. *The Doctrine of Virtue.* Translated by Mary J. Gregor. New York: Harper Torchbooks, 1964.

Kao, Ming. "Chu Hsi's Discipline of Propriety." In *Chu Hsi and Neo-Confucianism,* edited by W. T.Chan. Honolulu: University of Hawaii Press, 1986.

Kato, Joken. "The Meaning of Li." *Philosophical Studies of Japan,* vol. 4 (1963).

Kennedy, George A., trans. *Aristotle on Rhetoric: A Theory of Civic Discourse.* New York: Oxford University Press, 1991.

Kierkegaard, Søren. *Concluding Unscientific Postscript.* Translated by David F. Swensen and Walter Lowrie. Princeton: Princeton University Press, 1941.

———. *The Journals of Kierkegaard*. Translated by Alexander Dru. Princeton: Princeton University Press, 1941.

———. *Either/Or*, vol. II. Translated by David F. Swensen and Lillian Marvin Swensen. New York: Anchor Books, 1959.

Kingwell, Mark. "Is It Rational to Be Polite?" *Journal of Philosophy* 90, no. 8 (1993): 307–404.

Knoblock, John. *Xunzi: A Translation and Study of the Complete Works*. Vol. I, pp. 182–95. Stanford: Stanford University Press, 1988.

Körner, Stephen. *What Is Philosophy?* Baltimore: Penguin Books, 1969.

Kovesi, J. *Moral Notions*. London: Routledge & Kegan Paul, 1967.

Kruschwitz, Robert B., and Robert E. Roberts, eds. *The Virtues: Contemporary Essays in Moral Character*. Belmont: Wadsworth, 1987.

Kupperman, Joel. *Character*. New York: Oxford University Press, 1991.

Lacey, A. R. *A Dictionary of Philosophy*. New York: Charles Scribner's Sons, 1976.

Larsen, Jerald James, and Eliot Deutsch, eds. *Interpreting across Cultures: New Essays in Comparative Philosophy*. Princeton: Princeton University Press, 1988.

Lau, D. C. "Theories of Human Nature in Mencius and Shyuntzyy." *Bulletin of Oriental and African Studies* 15 (1953): 541–65.

———, trans. *Leo Tzu: Tao Te Ching*. Baltimore: Penguin Books, 1963.

———, trans. *Mencius*. London: Penguin Books, 1970.

———, trans. *Confucius:The Analects*. Baltimore: Penguin Press, 1978.

Lee, S. T., comp. *A New Complete Chinese-English Dictionary*. Hong Kong: China Publishers, 1980.

Legge, James, trans. *Chinese Classics*, vol. I. Oxford: Clarendon Press, 1893.

———, trans. *The Li Ki or Collection of Treatises on the Rules of Propriety or Ceremonial Usages*. In The Sacred Books of the East Series, edited by Max Müller. Delhi: Moltilal Barnasidass, 1966.

———, trans. *Texts of Taoism*. New York: The Julian Press, 1959.

Lewis, C. I. *Mind and the World Order*. New York: Dover, 1929.

———. *An Analysis of Knowledge and Valuation*. La Salle: Open Court, 1946.

Lewis, H. D., ed. *Contemporary British Philosophy*, 3d ser. London: George Allen & Unwin, 1956.

Li, Ti-sheng. *Hsün Tzu chi-shih*. Taipei: Hsüeh-sheng, 1979.

Liang, Ch'i-hsiung. *Hsün Tzu chien-shi*. Taipei: Shang-wu, 1978.

Lin, Yutang. *Wisdom of Confucius*. New York: The Modern Library, 1938.

Liu, Shu-hsien. "The Problem of Orthodoxy in Chu Hsi's Philosophy." In *Chu Hsi and Neo-Confucianism*, edited by W. T. Chan. Honolulu: University of Hawaii Press, 1986.

Louton, Robert B. "On Some Vices of Virtue Ethics." *American Philosophical Quarterly* 21, no. 3 (1984): 227–36.

Lucas, J. R. "The Philosophy of Reasonable Man." *Philosophical Quarterly* 13, no. 51 (1963): 97–106.

Mabbott, J. D. *An Introduction to Ethics*. London: Hutcheson University Library, 1966.

Macbeath, A. *Experiments in Living*. London: Macmillan & Co., 1952.

MacDonald, Margaret. "Ethics and the Ceremonial Use of Language." In *Philosophical Analysis: A Collection of Essays*, edited by Max Black. Ithaca: Cornell University Press, 1950.

MacIntyre, Alasdair. *After Virtue*. Notre Dame: University of Notre Dame Press, 1984.

————. *Whose Justice? Which Rationality?* Notre Dame: University of Notre Dame Press, 1989.

Machle, Edward J. "The Mind and the *Shen-ming* in the *Xunzi.*" *Journal of Chinese Philosophy* 19 (1992): 361–86.

Macmurray, John. *Persons in Relation.* London: Farber & Farber, 1961.

Mackie, J. L. *Ethics: Inventing Right and Wrong.* Baltimore: Penguin Books, 1977.

Mao, Tzu-shiu. *Lun Yü chin-chu chin-i.* Taipei: Commercial Press, 1977.

Martin, Judith, and Gunther S. Stent. "Etiquette." In *Encyclopedia of Ethics,* edited by Lawrence Becker and Charlotte Becker. New York: Garland, 1992.

Martin, Mike W. *Self-Deception and Morality.* Lawrence: University Press of Kansas, 1986.

————. "Honesty with Oneself." In *Rules, Ritual, and Responsibility: Essays Dedicated to Herbert Fingarette,* edited by Mary I. Bookover. La Salle: Open Court, 1991.

Mathews' Chinese-English Dictionary. Cambridge: Harvard University Press, 1956.

Mayo, Bernard. *The Philosophy of Right and Wrong.* London: Routledge & Kegan Paul, 1986.

Mead, George H. *Mind, Self and Society.* Chicago: University of Chicago Press, 1934.

Mei, Y. P. "Hsün Tzu's Theory of Education with an English Translation of the *Hsün Tzu,* Chapter I, An Exhortation to Learning." *Tsing Hua Journal of Chinese Studies* 2 (1961): 361–77.

Melden, A. L. *Rights and Right Conduct.* Oxford: Blackwell, 1958.

Midgely, Mary. *Beast and Man: The Roots of Human Nature.* Ithaca, New York: Cornell University Press, 1978.

Mitchell, John J., ed. *Human Nature: Theories, Conjectures, and Descriptions.* Metuchen: Scarecrow Press, 1972.

Moore, Charles A., ed. *The Chinese Mind.* Honolulu: East-West Center Press, 1967.

Moore, G. E. *Principia Ethica.* Cambridge: Cambridge University Press, 1951.

————. *Some Main Problems of Philosophy.* London: George Allen & Unwin, 1953.

————. *Philosophical Papers.* London: George Allen & Unwin, 1959.

Mou Tsung-san. *T'sung Lu Hsiang-shan tao Liu Chi-shan.* Taipei: Hsüeh-sheng, 1979.

Mullan, Hugh. "Horney's Contribution to a Rational Approach to Morals." *American Journal of Psychoanalysis* 48, no. 2 (1988): 127–37.

Munitz, Milton K. *The Mystery of Existence: An Essay in Philosophical Cosmology.* New York: Appleton-Century-Crofts, 1965.

————. "The Concept of the World." In *Language, Belief, and Metaphysics,* edited by Milton K. Munitz and Howard Kiefer. Albany: State University of New York Press, 1970.

Munro, Donald J. *The Concept of Man in Ancient China.* Stanford: Stanford University Press, 1969.

————. *Images of Human Nature: A Sung Portrait.* Princeton: Princeton University Press, 1988.

Murphy, Arthur E. *The Theory of Practical Reason.* La Salle: Open Court, 1965.

Naess, Arne, and Alastair Hannay, eds. *Invitation to Chinese Philosophy.* Oslo: Universitetsforlaget, 1972.

Nagel, Thomas. *The View from Nowhere.* New York: Oxford University Press, 1986.

Needham, Joseph. *Science and Civilization in China.* Vol. 2: *History of Scientific Thought.* Cambridge: Cambridge University Press, 1962.
Needham, Rodney. *Against the Tranquility of Axioms.* Berkeley: University of California Press, 1983.
Neurath, Otto. *Empiricism and Sociology.* Edited by Marie Neurath and Robert S. Cohen. Dordrecht-Holland: D. Reidel, 1973.
Newman, John Henry. *An Essay on the Development of Christian Doctrine.* Notre Dame: University of Notre Dame Press, 1989.
Nivison, David S. "Two Roots or One?" *Proceedings and Addresses of the American Philosophical Association* 53, no. 6 (1980): 739–61.
North, Helen. "Ethical Values in Classic Eastern Texts." Presented at the conference on Rhetoric: East and West, East-West Center, Honolulu, Hawaii, June 12–18, 1988.
Norton, David. *Personal Destinies.* Princeton: Princeton University Press, 1982
Nussbaum, Martha, and Amartya Sen. "Internal Criticism and Indian Rationalist Traditions." In *Relativism: Interpretation and Confrontation,* edited by Michael Krausz. Notre Dame: University of Notre Dame Press, 1989.
Oakeshott, Michael. *Rationalism in Politics and Other Essays.* Indianapolis: Liberty Press, 1991.
O'Hear, Anthony. "Wittgenstein and the Transmission of Tradition." In *Wittgenstein Centenary Essays,* edited by A. Phillips Griffiths. Cambridge: Cambridge University Press, 1991.
Okabe, Roichi. "Can the East Meet the West Rhetorically? An Overview of Rhetorical Divergence and Convergence from the Eastern Perspectives." Presented at the conference on Rhetoric: East and West, East-West Center, Honolulu, Hawaii, June 12–18, 1988.
Oliver, Robert T. *Communication and Culture in Ancient India and China.* Syracuse: Syracuse University Press, 1971.
Parker, Dewitt H. *The Philosophy of Value.* Ann Arbor: University of Michigan Press, 1958.
Pelikan, Jaroslav. *The Vindication of Tradition.* New Haven: Yale University Press, 1981.
Pence, Gregory E. "Recent Works on Virtue." *American Philosophical Quarterly* 21 (1984): 281–96.
Pepper, Stephen C. *World Hypothesis.* Berkeley: University of California Press, 1948.
———. *Sources of Value.* Berkeley: University of California Press, 1958.
Perelman, Chaim. *The New Rhetoric and the Humanities.* Dordrecht: D. Reidel, 1979.
———. *The Realm of Rhetoric.* Notre Dame: University of Notre Dame Press, 1982.
Perelman, Chaim, and Anna Olbrechts-Tyteca. *The New Rhetoric: A Treatise on Argumentation.* Notre Dame: University of Notre Dame Press, 1969.
Perry, Michael J. *The Constitution, the Courts, and Human Rights.* New Haven: Yale University Press, 1982.
Perry, Ralph Barton. *General Theory of Value.* Cambridge: Harvard University Press, 1950.
Phillips, D. Z., and H. O. Mounce. *Moral Practices.* London: Routledge & Kegan Paul, 1969.
Pincoffs, Edmund L. *Quandaries and Virtues.* Lawrence: University Press of Kansas, Press, 1986.

Pocock, J. G. A. "Time, Institutions and Action: An Essay on Traditions and Their Understanding." In *Politics and Experience: Essays Presented to Michael Oakeshott,* edited by Preston King and B. C. Parekh. Cambridge: Cambridge University Press, 1968.

Popper, Karl. *Conjectures and Refutation: The Growth of Scientific Knowledge.* London: Rouledge & Kegan Paul, 1963.

———. *Objective Knowledge: An Evolutionary Approach.* Oxford: Clarendon Press, 1972.

Peters, R. S, ed. *Nature and Conduct.* New York: St. Martin's Press, 1975.

Price, Richard. *A Review of the Principal Questions in Morals.* Oxford: Clarendon Press, 1948.

Prichard, H. A. "Does Moral Philosophy Rest on a Mistake." *Mind* 21 (1912): 21–37.

Putnam, Hilary. *Mind, Language and Reality: Philosophical Papers,* vol. 2. Cambridge: Cambridge University Press, 1975.

Rader, Marvin. *The Right to Hope: Crisis and Community.* Seattle: University of Washington Press, 1981.

Raphael, D. D, ed. *British Moralists: 1650–1800.* 2 vols. Oxford: Clarendon Press, 1969.

Rawls, John. "Two Concepts of Rules." *Philosophical Review* 64 (1955): 3–32.

———. *A Theory of Justice.* Cambridge: Harvard University Press, 1971.

———. "The Independence of Moral Theory." *Proceedings and Addresses of the American Philosophical Association* (1974–75): 5–22.

———. "Kantian Constructivism in Moral Theory: The John Dewey Lectures, 1980." *Journal of Philosophy* 77, no. 9 (1980): 515–72.

———. "Justice and Fairness: Political and Not Metaphysical." *Philosophy and Public Affairs* 14, no. 3 (1985): 223–51.

Reid, Thomas. *Essays on the Intellectual Powers of Man.* Cambridge: MIT Press, 1969.

Rescher, Nicholas. *An Introduction of Value Theory.* Englewood Cliffs: Prentice Hall, 1969.

———. *Primacy of Practice.* Oxford: Blackwell, 1973.

———. *Conceptual Idealism.* Oxford: Basil Blackwell, 1973.

———. *Dialectics.* Albany: State University of New York Press, 1977.

———. *Unpopular Essays on Technological Progress.* Pittsburgh: University of Pittsburgh Press, 1980.

———. *Ethical Idealism.* Berkeley: University of California Press, 1987.

Resnik, M. D. "Logic and Methodology in the Writings of Mencius." *International Philosophical Quarterly* 7, no. 2 (1968): 212–30.

Rhees, Rush. *Without Answers.* London: Routledge & Kegan Paul, 1969.

Richards, I. A. *Mencius on the Mind.* London: Kegan Paul, Trench, Trubner, & Ltd, 1932.

Rist, John M., ed. *The Stoics.* Berkeley: University of California Press, 1978.

Rorty, Richard. *Philosophy and the Mirror of Nature.* Princeton, New Jersey: Princeton University Press, 1979.

———. "Pragmatism, Relativism, and Irrationslism." *Proceedings and Addresses of the American Philosophical Association* 53, no. 6 (1980): 719–38.

Rousseau, J. J. *The Social Contract and Discourses.* New York: E. P. Dutton, 1950.

Royce, Josiah. *Problem of Christianity.* Chicago: University of Chicago Press, 1969.

Russell, Bertrand. *Problems of Philosophy.* Oxford: Oxford University Press, 1950.
Ryle, Gilbert. "On Forgetting the Difference Between Right and Wrong." In *Essays in Moral Philosophy,* edited by A. I. Melden. Seattle: University of Washington Press, 1958.
Scanlon, T. M. "Contractarianism and Utilitarianism." In *Utilitarianism and Beyond,* edited by Amartya Sen and Bernard Williams. Cambridge: Cambridge University Press, 1982.
Schwartz, Benjamin. *The World of Thought in Ancient China.* Cambridge: Harvard University Press, 1985
Searle, John. *Speech Acts: An Essay in the Philosophy of Language.* Cambridge: Cambridge University Press, 1969.
Sellars, Wilfred, and John Hospers, eds. *Readings in Ethical Theory.* New York: Appleton-Century Crofts, 1970.
Shaftesbury, Anthony. *Characteristics of Men, Manners, Opinions, Times.* Edited by J. M. Robertson. Indianapolis: Bobbs-Merrill, 1964.
Shen, Vincent Tsing-*sung. Ch'üan-tung te tsai-sheng.* Taipei: Yeh-ch'iang, 1992.
Shiang, Ching Lai. *A New Approach to Utilitarianism: A Unified Utilitarian Theory and Its Applications to Distributive Justice.* Dordrecht: Kluwer, 1991.
Shils, Edward. *Tradition.* Chicago: University of Chicago Press, 1981.
Shiner, Roger. *Knowledge and Reality in Plato's* Philebus. Assum, Netherlands: Van Gorcum, 1974.
Shun, Kwong-loi. "Confucius." In vol. 1 of *Encyclopedia of Ethics,* edited by Lawrence and Charlotte Becker. New York: Garland, 1992.
Sidgwick, Henry. *Methods of Ethics.* 7th ed. London: Macmillan, 1972.
Sircello, Guy. *A New Theory of Beauty.* Princeton: Princeton University Press, 1975.
Strawson, P. F. "Freedom and Resentment." *Proceedings of British Academy* 48 (1962): 187–221.
Tai, Chen. *Meng Tzu tzu-i.* In *Tai Chen wen-chi.* Taipei: Ho-lo, 1975.
Takehiko, Okada. "Chu Hsi and Wisdom as Hidden and Stored." In *Chu Hsi and Neo-Confucianism,* edited by Wing-tsit Chan. Honolulu: University of Hawaii Press, 1986.
T'ang, Chün-i. "The Individual and the World in Chinese Methodology." In *The Chinese Mind,* edited by Charles E. Moore. Honolulu: East-West Center Press, 1967.
———. *Chung-Kuo che-hsüeh yüan-lun, tao-lun p'ien.* Taipei: Hsüeh-sheng, 1978.
Tatarkiewicz, Wladyslaw. *History of Aesthetics,* vol. I. Edited by J. Harrell. The Hague: Mouton and Warsaw: Polish Scientific Publications, 1970.
Taylor, Charles. "Interpretation and the Sciences of Man." *Review of Metaphysics* 25, no. 1 (1971): 3–51.
———. "The Diversity of Goods." In *Utilitarianism and Beyond,* edited by Amartya Sen and Bernard Williams. London: Cambridge University Press, 1982.
———. "The Politics of Recognition." In *Multiculturalism and "The Politics of Recognition": An Essay by Charles Taylor.* Edited by Amy Gutman. Princeton: Princeton University Press, 1992.
Taylor, Paul. *Normative Discourse.* Englewood Cliffs: Prentice-Hall, 1961.
Thomas, Stephen Nalor. *Reasoning in Natural Language.* 3d ed. Englewood Cliffs: Prentice-Hall, 1986.
Toulmin, Stephen. *The Uses of Argument.* Cambridge: Cambridge University Press, 1958.

————. "Self-Knowledge and Knowledge of the 'Self.'" In *The Self: Psychological and Philosophical Issues*, edited by Theodore Mischel. Oxford: Blackwell, 1977.

————. "The Tyranny of Principles." In *Making Ethical Decision*, edited by Norman Bowie. New York: McGraw-Hill, 1985.

Toulmin, Stephen, Richard Rieke, and Alan Janik. *An Introduction to Reasoning.* New York: Macmillan, 1979.

Trianosky, Gregory. "What Is Virtue Ethics All About? Recent Work on the Virtues." *American Philosophical Quarterly* 27, no. 4 (1990): 335–44.

Tu, Wei-ming. *Neo-Confucian Thought in Action: Wang Yang-ming's Youth (1472–1509).* Berkeley: University of California Press, 1976.

————. *Humanity and Self-Cultivation: Essays in Confucian Thought.* Berkeley: Asian Humanities Press, 1979.

————. *Confucian Thought: Selfhood as Creative Transformation.* Albany: State University of New York Press, 1985.

————. *Centrality and Commonality: An Essay on Confucian Religiousness.* Albany: State University of New York Press, 1989.

Tuan, Yü-ts'ai. *Shuo-wen chieh-tzu chu.* Shanghai: 1981.

Turbayne, C. M. *The Myth of Metaphor.* New Haven: Yale University Press, 1962.

Vico, Giambattista. *The New Science.* Translated by Thomas Goddard Bergin and Max Fisch. Ithaca: Cornell University Press, 1988.

von Wright, Henrik. *Explanation and Understanding.* Ithaca: Cornell University Press, 1971.

Waismann, F. "How I See Philosophy." In *Contemporary British Philosophy.* 3d ser. Edited by H. D. Lewis. London: George Allen & Unwin, 1956.

————. "Verifiability." In *Essays on Logic and Language.* 1st ser. Edited by Antony Flew. Oxford: Basil Blackwell, 1952.

Waley, Arthur, trans. *The Analects of Confucius.* New York: Vintage Books, 1938.

Walker, Janet. "Herman Hesse and Asian Literature." Presented at the Seventh Annual Meeting of the Mid-Atlantic Region of the Association for Asian Studies, at George Washington University, Washington, D.C., October 28–29, 1978.

Wallace, G., and A. D. Walker, eds. *The Definition of Morality.* London: Methuen, 1970.

Wang, Hsien-ch'ien. *Hsün Tzu chi-chieh.* Taipei: World Publishing Co., 1961.

Wang, Meng-ou. *Li Chi chin-chu chin-i.* Taipei: Commercial Press, 1977.

Wang, Yang-ming. *Instructions for Practical Living and Other Neo-Confucian Writings.* Translated and edited by Wing-tsit Chan. New York: Columbia University Press, 1963.

————. *Yang-ming ch'üan-shu.* In *Ssu-pu pei-yao.* Taipei: Chung Hwa, 1970.

Warnock, G. *The Object of Morality.* London: Methuen, 1971.

Watson, Burton, trans. *Hsün Tzu: Basic Works.* New York: Columbia University Press, 1963.

Wei, Cheng-t'ung. *Hsün Tzu yü ku-tai che-hsüeh.* Taipei: Shang-wu, 1974.

————, ed. *Chung-kuo che-hsüeh t'su-tien ta-ch'üan.* Taipei: Shui-neu, 1983.

————. "Chu Hsi on the Standard *[Ching]* and the Expedient *[Ch'üan].*" In *Chu Hsi and Neo-Confucianism*, edited by W. T. Chan. Honolulu: University of Hawaii Press, 1986.

Weil, Simone. *The Need for Roots.* New York: Harper and Row, 1971.

Wellman, Carl. *Challenge and Response: Justification in Ethics.* Carbondale: Southern Illinois University Press, 1971.

Wheelwright, Phillip. *The Burning Fountain: A Study in the Language of Symbolism.* Indianapolis: Indiana University Press, 1968.

White, Alan. *Philosophy of Mind.* New York: Random House, 1967.

Wiggens, David. "Deliberation and Practical Reason." *Proceedings of the Aristotelian Society* (1975–1976): 29–51.

Williams, Bernard. *Morality: An Introduction.* New York: Harper Torchbooks, 1972.

———. *Ethics and the Limits of Philosophy.* Cambridge: Harvard University Press, 1985.

Winch, Peter. *The Idea of Social Science.* London: Routledge & Kegan Paul, 1958.

———. *Ethics and Action.* London: Routledge & Kegan Paul, 1972.

Winterowd, W. Ross. *Rhetoric: A Synthesis.* New York: Holt, Rinehart and Winston, 1968.

Wisdom, John. *Philosophy and Psychoanalysis.* Oxford: Basil Blackwell, 1957.

Wittgenstein, Ludwig. *Philosophical Investigations.* Translated by G. E. M. Anscombe. New York: Macmillan, 1969.

———. *Zettel.* Translated by G. E. M. Anscombe and G. H. von Wright. Oxford: Basil Blackwell, 1967

Wong, David. *Moral Relativity.* Berkeley: University of California Press, 1984.

Yang, Liang. *Hsün Tzu.* In *Ssu-pu pi-yao* edition. Taipei: Chung-hua, 1976.

Yang, Liang-kan. *Ta-hsüeh chin-chu chin-i.* Taipei: Commercial Press, 1977.

Yeh, Ching-kuei. *Kung Tzu te tao-te che-hsüeh.* Taipei: Cheng-chung, 1977.

Yen, Ling-feng. *Ta-hsüeh chang-chü hsin-pien.* Taipei: Pamir, 1984.

Yü, Ying-shih. "Morality and Knowledge in Chu Hsi's Philosophical System." In *Chu Hsi and Neo-Confucianism,* edited by Wing-tsit Chan. Honolulu: University of Hawaii Press, 1986.

Index of Names

348   *Index of Names*

Ely, J., 300n113, 327n75

Fang, T., 21n6, 294, 323n63
Fingarette, H., 68n14, 220n33, 222–23, 224n50, 230, 231–32, 325
Fogelin, R. J., 34n31
Forke, A., 101n2
Forrier, P., 319n45
Frank, J., 258n88, 312n29
Frankfort, H., 325n70
Frankena, W., 51n50, 116n40, 279
Fuller, L., 311n26
Fung, Y., 38, 45n29

Gadamer, H., 242
Gallie, W., 110n28, 198
Gardner, D., 213n4, 250n58
Gasking, D., 13n33
Gewirth, A., 313n32
Gluckman, M., 302n121
Graham, A., 46n34, 49n39, 66n12, 122n12, 130, 164, 169n46, 170
Gregory, I., 107n19
Grote, J., 3n8

Hall, D., 148n43, 222n42, 277n34
Hamlyn, D., 225n57
Hampshire, S., 137n55, 236n6, 300n114, 302, 317n39, 321
Han Fei Tzu, 195
Hare, R., 3n8, 310n22
Hart, H., 103n9, 112n30, 141n9, 195n13, 258, 295n96, 308n15, 328n78
Hartmann, N., 320n52
Henke, F., 158n9
Hendricks, R., 193n6
Hesse, H., 81, 82, 83n11, 85n13, 86
Hobbes, T., 95, 295n96
Hsi, Kang, 193n6
Hsu, F., 311n27
Hsu, Sung-peng, 94n22
Hsün Tzu, 102, 103, 108, 110, 112, 119, 138n1, 144, 146, 148, 149, 155, 170, 172, 181n93, 189–90, 194–96, 199–200, 202, 206, 210–11, 213, 215, 216n16, 222, 223, 224–27, 229, 245, 247, 249–50, 254, 255, 256, 257, 260, 267, 269, 276, 277, 280–300, 303, 314, 316, 322, 325n70, 328n78
Hu, Hsien Chin, 223n48
Hu, Shih, 248n51; 283
Hudson, H., 197n18
Hudson, W., 295n94
Hui, Shih, 292
Hume, D., 102, 106, 112, 115, 152, 270, 295n96, 328n78

Hutcheson, F., 182

James, W., 30, 38n3, 51n50, 54, 62, 73n22, 188, 320n50
Jesus, 149n47
Jiang, P., 229n77
Johnston, H., 202
Johnston, M., 220n33–34

Kant, I., 82, 150n51, 222n45, 299, 304, 323n62
Kao Tzu, 9
Kato, J., 288n69, 294n92
Kierkegaard, S., 31, 122, 157, 158
King-Farlow, J., 222n45
Kingwell, M., 300n114
Kluckholn, C., 104n11
Knoblock, J., 215n12, 222n41, 225n57
Körner, S., 83n10
Kovesi, 14, 27n12, 35n32, 134
Ku, Hung-ming, 21n5
Kung, Chih-jen, 149ff
Kuo, Hsiang, 46
Kupperman, J., 229n83

Lacey, A., 301n115
Lapidge, M., 164n33
Lao Tzu, 61, 62, 65n8, 66, 73, 83n11, 80–99, 93, 95
Larson, G., 194n11
Lau, D. C., 38n7, 94n22, 149n45, 164n33, 256, 276, 295n96, 325n68
Legge, J., 219, 252
Lewis, C., 76n30, 137
Li, Kou, 277
Li, Ti-sheng, 138n1, 195n12, 250n57
Lieh Tzu, 46, 62
Linton, R., 104n11
Liu, Shu-hsien, 248–49, 251
Locke, D., 128n31
Louton, R., 312n30
Lu, Ch'eng, 164
Lucas, J., 4n11

Mabbott, J., 295n94
MacBeath, G., 104
MacCormick, N., 194n9
MacDonald, M., 300n114
MacIntyre, A., 236–38, 241, 242, 247n47, 258n88, 319n47
Mackie, J., 107, 295n96
Macmurray, J., 243n32
Martin, J., 300n114
Martin, M., 216n14, 217n20, 222n43
Matson, W., 133
Mayo, B., 310n22

Index of Subjects

rectification, 328
re-enactment, 154–55
reflective desirability, 74
relativism, 104–5
reputation, 230n81; *see also* face
respect for established practices, 144; *see also* moral rules, moral tradition
respect for persons, 144–45, 200, 209, 215
respectfulness *(kung)*, 215
resolution, 158
responsional characterizations, 34
rhetoric, concept and conceptions of, 197
rhetorical theory, 197
right action, rightness, 115–16, 144; *see also i*, moral distinctions, moral notions
rights, human, 311
ritual and morality, 300–302
root metaphor, 25–26
roots, need for, 56–57, 164–65
rulers, 208–10
rules of conduct, personal, 31, 304–10
rulings, in exigent situations 5–6, 13, 15–16; projective character of, 6, 17–18; semantic, 13n33; paradigmatic and universalizable, 16; defeasible, 16

sage , 15, 26, 38, 46, 47, 47n36, 48, 49n38, 50–51, 80, 82, 94, 119–37, 177, 186–88, 190–91, 264, 298; character of the, 126–31; contrasted with *chün-tzu*, 32–34, 208–9, 287; foreknowledge of the, 32n24; learning to become a, 156–91, 230; mind of the, 33
sanctions, 150
sensus communis, 243–45, 251, 252, 275
self, 29, 38, 90–91; uses of the term, 228; Confucian notion of the, 228–34; focal/matrix, 60–61; and action, 178, 178n79; ideal and actual, 90–91, 178
self-consciousness, 180n86
self-cultivation, 121, 131, 138, 146, 213–14, 232
self-deception, 32, 219–24; diagnosis of, 224–27
self-discipline, 286, 305
self-examination, 70, 75, 138, 220–22, 228–30
self-interest, 102, 144,-45, 150, 171, 209, 286
self-interpretation, 111, 117, 251
self-knowledge/self-understanding, 97–99, 113, 115, 117, 146, 221–22; *see also* understanding

self-presentation, 223
self-realization, *see* personal realization
self-reliance, 167–68
self-reproach, 221, 228, 229–30, 231
self-respect, 200, 209, 219, 229; *see also* respect for others
self-satisfaction, 219
self-transformation, 45, 72n19, 73, 95–99, 122–23
self-understanding, 97–99
selfishness, selfish desires, 103, 128, 169, 171–72, 174, 180–81, 182, 189, 201, 220, 221, 227, 232, 292; *see also* self-interest
seriousness *(ching)*, 121, 125, 143, 215
shame, and honor, 147–48, 222–23, 230n81
sheng (sage), *see* sage
shih (affair, event), 27, 159
shih (genuineness, reality), 216
shu (reciprocity, consideration, mutuality), 145, 325–26
sight metaphor, 222
sincerity, 29–30, 67; *see also ch'eng*
situations, normal and exigent/abnormal, 5–6, 8, 17–18, 64, 67, 119, 133, 185–87, 205–6, 256, 290–91; *see also ching-ch'üan*
solitude, 220–21
speech, *see* words
standards of inspiration, 30; *see also* ideal theme
styles of performance, 199–202
substance and function, 28

tai-chi (the Great Ultimate), 88n14
tao (way), 11n30, 12, 19, 26, 27, 29, 32, 33, 37, 45, 49, 59–99 (Essays 4 and 5), 121, 199, 298, 304, 305, 313, 314–15, 319–20, 326; a crystallized conception, 196; a generic term, 253–54; a unifying perspective, 251–52, 320; and creative agency or creativity, 69–72, 87–89, 125; an ideal theme, 54, 59–65, 69, 81, 121, 177–78, 259; and *ch'uan* (moral discretion), 259; as *jen*, 62, 76, 121, 121n9, 123; 132, 135–37, 177, 253, 216, 307, 320; inexhaustible significance of, 259; makeshift descriptions of, 93–99; symbolic representation of, 82; subject to public discussion, 183, 319–21; the concept of, 269, 274
tao-attitude, 51, 51n48–49, 53–54
tao-experience, 37–40, 82
tao-t'ung (Confucian tradition), 235–67